THE
LYLE
OFFICIAL
ANTIQUES
REVIEW 1983

All prices quoted in this book are obtained from a variety of auctions in various countries during the twelve months prior to publication and are converted to dollars at the rate of exchange prevalent at the time of sale.

DRAWINGS BY
PETER KNOX
PETER TENCH
DENISE FREEMAN

THE
LYLE
OFFICIAL
ANTIQUES
REVIEW 1983

COMPILED BY MARGOT RUTHERFORD
EDITED by ANTHONY CURTIS

The publishers wish to express their sincere thanks
to the following for their kind help and assistance
in the production of this volume:

JANICE MONCRIEFF
NICOLA PARK
KAREN KILGOUR
JENNIFER KNOX
MAY MUTCH
CHRISTINE O'BRIEN
JOSEPHINE McLAREN
TANYA FAIRBAIRN
MARION McKILLOP
ELAINE HARLAND

The Library of Congress Cataloged This Serial as Follows:

The Lyle official antiques review.

Galashiels, Scot.₎
v. Illus. 23 cm. annual.
Began with 1971/72 issue. Cf. new serial titles.

1. Art objects—Collectors and collecting—Catalogs.
NK1133.L9   745.1   74-640592
MARC-S

ISBN 0-698-11190-7 hardcover
ISBN 0-698-11204-0 flexible binding
Printed in the United States of America
Distributed in the United States by Coward, McCann & Geoghegan,
200 Madison Avenue, New York, N.Y. 10016

INTRODUCTION

This year over 100,000 Antique Dealers and Collectors will make full and profitable use of their Lyle Official Antiques Review. They know that only in this one volume will they find the widest possible variety of goods — illustrated, described and given a current market value to enable them to BUY RIGHT AND SELL RIGHT throughout the year of issue.

They know, too, that by building a collection of these immensely valuable volumes year by year, they will equip themselves with an unparalleled reference library of facts, figures and illustrations which, properly used, cannot fail to help them keep one step ahead of the market.

In its thirteen years of publication, Lyle's has gone from strength to strength and has become without doubt the pre-eminent book of reference for the antique trade throughout the world. Each of its fact filled pages are packed with precisely the kind of profitable information the professional Dealer needs — including descriptions, illustrations and values of thousands and thousands of individual items carefully selected to give a representative picture of the current market in antiques and collectables — and remember all values are prices actually paid, based on accurate sales records in the twelve months prior to publication from the best established and most highly respected auction houses in America and Europe.

This is THE book for the Professional Antiques Dealer. 'The Lyle Book' — we've even heard it called 'The Dealer's Bible'.

Compiled and published afresh each year, the Lyle Official Antiques Review is the most comprehensive up-to-date antiques price guide available. THIS COULD BE YOUR WISEST INVESTMENT OF THE YEAR!

ANTHONY CURTIS

CONTENTS

Acknowledgements

Abbots, *The Hill, Wickham Market, Suffolk*
Ader Picard Tajan, *12 Rue Favart, 75002, Paris*
Aldridge's, *130-132 Walcot Street, Bath, Avon*
Allen & May, *18 Bridge Street, Andover*
Anderson & Garland, *Anderson House, Market Street, Newcastle*
Gilbert Baitson, *194 Anlaby Road, Hull, Yorks.*
Richard Baker & Thomson, *9 Hamilton Street, Birkenhead, Merseyside*
T. Bannister & Co., *7 Calbourne, Haywards Heath, W. Sussex*
Barber's, *Town Mill, Bagshot Road, Chobham, Surrey*
Biddle & Webb, *Ladywood, Middleway, Birmingham*
Boardman's, *Station Road Corner, Haverhill, Suffolk*
Bonhams, *Montpelier Galleries, Montpelier Street, London*
Bonsor Penningtons, *82 Eden Street, Kingston-on-Thames*
Richard A. Bourne, *P.O. Box 141, Hyannis Port, Mass.*
Brogden & Co., *38 & 39 Silver Street, Lincoln*
Wm. H. Brown, *31 St. Peter's Hill, Grantham, Lincs.*
Bruton, Knowles & Co., *Albion Chambers, 55 Barton Street, Gloucester*
Buckell & Ballard, *49 Parsons Street, Banbury, Oxfordshire*
Burrows & Day, *39/41 Bank Street, Ashford, Kent*
Burtenshaw Walker, *66 High Street, Lewes, Suffolk*
Butler & Hatch Waterman, *86 High Street, Hythe, Kent*
Butterfield & Butterfield, *1244 Sutter Street, San Francisco*
Button, Menhenitt & Mutton, *Belmont Auction Rooms, Wadebridge*
Capes, Dunn & Co., *The Auction Galleries, 38 Charles Street, Manchester*
Michael Capo Antiques Ltd., *831 Broadway, New York, 10003*
Chancellor's, *31 High Street, Ascot, Berks.*
H. C. Chapman & Son, *The Auction Mart, North Street, Scarborough*
C. B. Charles Galleries, *825 Woodward Avenue, Pontiac, Michigan*
Christie's, *8 King Street, St. James's, London*
Christie's East, *219 East 67th Street, New York, NY 10021*
Christie's & Edmiston's, *164-166 Bath Street, Glasgow*
Christie's Geneva, *8 Place de la Taconnerie, 1204 Geneva*
Christie's, *502 Park Avenue, New York, NY 10022*
Christie's S. Kensington, *85 Old Brompton Road, London*
Christie's Zurich, *Steinwiesplatz, 8032, Zurich*
Clarke Gammon, *45 High Street, Guildford, Surrey*
Clements, *Box 747, Forney, Texas 75126*

Coles, Knapp & Kennedy, *Georgian Rooms, Ross-on-Wye*
Cooper Hirst, *Goldway House, Parkway, Chelmsford*
Crystals Auctions, *Athol Street, Douglas, I.O.M.*
Dacre, Son & Hartley, *1-5 The Grove, Ilkley, Yorks.*
Dee & Atkinson, *The Exchange, Driffield, Yorks.*
Dickinson, Davy & Markham, *10 Wrawby Street, Brigg, S. Humberside*
Wm. Doyle Galleries Inc., *175 East 87th Street, New York*
Drewatt, Watson & Barton, *Donnington Priory, Newbury, Berks.*
Hy. Duke & Son, *40 South Street, Dorchester, Dorset*
Du Mouchelle Art Galleries, *409 East Jefferson Avenue, Detroit*
John Edelmann Galleries, *123 East 77th Street, New York, NY 10021*
Edwards, Bigwood & Bewlay, *The Old School, Tiddington, Stratford-on-Avon*
Robert C. Eldred, *Route 6a, Box 796a, East Dennis, Mass.*
Elliott & Green, *40 High Street, Lymington, Hants.*
Farrant & Wightman, *2/3 Newport Street, Old Town, Swindon*
John Francis, Thomas Jones & Sons, *King Street, Carmarthen*
Frank H. Fellows & Sons, *Bedford House, 88 Hagley Road, Birmingham*
John D. Fleming & Co., *Melton House, High Street, Dulverton*
Fletcher Galleries, *2119 Westheimer, Houston, Texas*
Fox & Sons, *5 & 7 Salisbury Street, Fordingbridge, Hants.*
Galerie Moderne, *Rue Caroly 31, 1040 Brussels*
Garrett's, *1800 Irving Boulevard, Dallas, Texas 75207*
Garrod Turner, *50 St. Nicholas Street, Ipswich, Suffolk*
Garth's Auctions, *2690 Stratford Road, Delaware, Ohio*
Geering & Colyer, *Highgate, Hawkhurst, Kent*
Andrew Grant, *59-60 Foregate Street, Worcester*
Graves, Son & Pilcher, *38 Holland Road, Hove, Sussex*
Gribble, Booth & Taylor, *West Street, Axminster, Devon*
Arthur G. Griffiths & Sons, *57 Foregate Street, Worcester*
Rowland Gorringe, *15 North Street, Lewes, Sussex*
Hall Wateridge & Owen, *Welsh Bridge, Shrewsbury*
James Harrison, *35 West End, Hebden Bridge, W. Yorks.*
Heathcote Ball & Co., *47 New Walk, Leicester*
John Hogbin & Son, *53 High Street, Tenterden, Kent*
Honiton Galleries, *High Street, Honiton, Devon*
Edgar Horn, *47 Cornfield Road, Eastbourne, Sussex*
Jackson-Stops & Staff, *Fine Art Dept., 14 Curzon Street, London W1*
G. A. Key, *Market Place, Aylesham*

Lacy Scott & Sons, *3 Hatter Street, Bury St. Edmunds*
Lalonde Bros. & Parham, *Station Road, Weston-Super-Mare*
W. H. Lane & Son, *Morrab Road, Penzance, Cornwall*
Langlois, *10 Waterloo Street, Jersey, C.I.*
Laurin, Guilloux, Buffetaud, Tailleur, *Paris, France*
Lawrence Fine Art, *South Street, Crewkerne*
James & Lister Lea, *11 Newhall Street, Birmingham*
Locke & England, *Walton House, 11 The Parade, Leamington Spa*
Love's, *St. John's Place, Perth*
Mallams, *24 St. Michael's Street, Oxford*
May, Whetter & Grose, *Cornubia Hall, Par, Cornwall*
John Milne, *9-11 North Silver Street, Aberdeen*
Milwaukee Galleries, *4747 West Bradley Road, Milwaukee*
Moore, Allen & Innocent, *33 Castle Street, Cirencester*
Morphets, *4-6 Albert Street, Harrogate, Yorks.*
Morris, Marshall & Poole, *2 Short Bridge Street, Newtown, Powys.*
Mortons Auction Exchange, *643 Magazine Street, New Orleans*
Alfred Mossop & Co., *Kelsick Road, Ambleside, Cumbria*
McCartney, Morris & Barker, *Corve Street, Ludlow, Salop*
Neales, *192 Mansfield Road, Nottingham*
D. M. Nesbit & Co., *7 Clarendon Road, Southsea, Hants.*
Northampton Auction Galleries, *33-39 Sheep Street, Northampton*
Olivers, *23-24 Market Hill, Sudbury, Suffolk*
Osmond, Tricks, *Regent Street Auction Rooms, Clifton, Bristol*
Outhwaite & Litherland, *Kingsway Galleries, Fontenoy Street, Liverpool*
J. R. Parkinson, Son & Hamer, *14 Bolton Street, Bury, Lancs.*
Parsons, Welch & Cowell, *129 High Street, Sevenoaks, Kent*
Pattison Partners & Scott, *Ryton*
Pearsons, *Walcote Chambers, High Street, Winchester*
Phillips, *7 Blenheim Street, New Bond Street, London*
Phillips, *867 Madison Avenue, New York, NY 10021*
Phillips & Brooks, *39 Park End Street, Oxford*
Phillips & Jolly's, *The Auction Rooms, Old King Street, Bath*
John H. Raby & Son, *St. Mary's Road, Bradford*
Samuel Rains & Son, *Trinity House, 114 Northenden Road, Sale, Manchester*
Renton & Renton, *16 Albert Street, Harrogate, Yorks.*
Riddetts, *Richmond Hill, The Square, Bournemouth*
Russell, Baldwin & Bright, *Ryelands Road, Leominster*

Sandoe, Luce Panes, *Chipping Manor Salerooms, Wotton-under-Edge*
Schrader Galleries, *211, 3rd St. South, St. Petersburg, Florida*
M. Philip H. Scott, *East View, Bedale, Yorks.*
Shouler & Son, *43 Nottingham Street, Melton Mowbray*
Robert W. Skinner Inc., *Bolton Gallery, Mass.*
Smith-Woolley & Perry, *43 Castle Hill Avenue, Folkestone*
Sotheby's, *34-35 New Bond Street, London*
Sotheby's, *980 Madison Avenue, New York*
Sotheby Bearne, *Rainbow, Torquay, Devon*
Sotheby's Belgravia, *19 Motcomb Street, London*
Sotheby Beresford Adams, *Booth Mansion, Chester*
Sotheby's Chester, *Watergate Street, Chester*
Sotheby, King & Chasemore, *Station Road, Pulborough*
Spear & Sons, *The Hill, Wickham Market, Suffolk*
H. Spencer & Sons Ltd., *20 The Square, Retford, Notts.*
Stalker & Boos, *280 N. Woodward Avenue, Birmingham, Michigan*
Stride & Son, *Southdown House, St. John's Street, Chichester*
David Symonds, *High Street, Crediton, Devon*
Taylor, Lane & Creber, *Western Auction Rooms, Plymouth*
Laurence & Martin Taylor, *63 High Street, Honiton, Devon*
Louis Taylor & Sons, *Percy Street, Hanley, Stoke-on-Trent*
Terry Antiques, *175 Junction Road, London N19*
Theriault, *P.O. Box 151, Annapolis, Maryland, 21404*
Trosby, *Tower Place Suite 200, 3340 Peach Tree Road, NE Atlanta*
Turner, Rudge & Turner, *29 High Street, East Grinstead*
V. & V's., *The Memorial Hall, Shiplake-on-Thames*
Vernon's, *1 Westgate, Chichester*
Vidler & Co., *Auction Offices, Cinque Ports St., Rye, Sussex*
Warren & Wignall, *113 Towngate, Leyland, Lancs.*
Way, Riddett & Co., *Town Hall Chambers, Lind Street, Ryde, I.O.W.*
J. M. Welch & Son, *The Old Town Hall, Great Dunmow, Essex*
Whitehead's, *111-113 Elm Grove, Southsea, Hants.*
Whitton & Laing, *32 Okehampton Street, Exeter*
Richard Withington, *Hillsboro, New Hampshire 03244*
Woolley & Wallis, *The Castle Auction Mart, Salisbury*
Eldon E. Worrall & Co., *15 Seel Street, Liverpool*
Wyatt & Son with Whiteheads, *59 East Street, Chichester, Sussex*

ANTIQUES
REVIEW 1983

Americans are savvy collectors who have spent the last decade educating themselves about antiques before venturing into the salerooms, shops and flea markets. This is the strong picture that emerges after speaking with auctioneers and dealers throughout the country. It's true that we are in the throes of a troubled economy, but the difference between these hard times and the recession of 1974 is that Americans today are still a strong buying force, whereas they virtually disappeared from the market nine years ago. It's easy to see that they've learned a valuable lesson by witnessing the meteoric rise of antique prices just three short years after the 1974 scare. And it will happen again! Lyle predicts that 1983 will see a definite upswing and 1984 will experience a boomtime. And smart collectors have systematically equipped themselves with the knowledge necessary to reap huge benefits when that boomtime hits. Books about antiques proliferate and trade magazine circulation figures are way up, lending credence to the assumption that every year thousands more understand the investment potential of antiques, as well as the sheer enjoyment of owning something unique that complements a particular lifestyle.

America, always a nation with an independent spirit, has recently experienced a surge of confidence in buying on all levels. It has been proven that 'keeping up with the Jonses' doesn't always mean keeping up with quality. Perhaps the economy has dictated the need to choose carefully and purchase wisely with an eye towards durability. Younger buyers, when furnishing a home, see that new furniture is constructed poorly and depreciates the minute it leaves the store, while an antique will last and consistently increase in value. Charles Hudgins, a dealer in Minnesota, echoes that thought and adds, 'today the crate is more substantial than the furniture inside.'

Older, more experienced buyers, are holding onto what they have and adding quality pieces to enhance their collections both for aesthetic reasons and importance for future sales. Professional women, a growing segment of the population eager to insure themselves against possible money problems, have begun to invest heavily in jewelry and silver, items that can be used and enjoyed while appreciating.

Whoever the buyer and whatever the purchase, there is a definite pattern: A confident, well-educated public is showing strength in buying the best items up for sale sure that these may well prove to be the soundest investment opportunities available today.

And the major recipients of this buying

fervor continues to be the top auction houses in New York City. They are, after all, the beneficiaries of major estates and collections and can therefore claim the highest sale prices (i.e. the highest profits). Even though there have been fewer large estates available recently and major collectors tend to hold on in times like these, incredible record sales have been reported by all four houses (Sotheby Parke-Bernet, Christies, Phillips and William Doyle) and there is no sense of the impending doom that the economy might suggest is right around the corner.

Sotheby Parke-Bernet has had to pull in its belt perhaps more than the others by virtue of the fact that it is the largest, has the most locations and employs the most people. A particular financial thorn has been the lease, construction and decoration of sales facilities, and the ensuing interest payments. It would have been hard to predict the extent of the current crises while they were riding the crest of a wave 18 months ago. It has become necessary to consolidate showrooms and offices in New York and London, streamline staff worldwide and cut costs on catalogues for certain auctions – all temporary measures, it is hoped, until the state of the economy improves. Even so, the company is holding its own with the best lots. According to Hugh Hildesley, Senior Vice President of Sotheby's, 'If the quality is there the market is fully alive,' and he has seen increasing interest with no-holds-barred bidding on important American furniture and paintings. American furniture has appreciated considerably because there is less of it and is harder to find than the greater volume of European furniture on the market. Strong evidence of the desire for fine and rare American pieces is seen in the

Spencer Gay Family Queen Anne carved and inlaid walnut and maple flat top highboy, North Shore, Mass., 1720-40, sold with a companion lowboy. (Sotheby's) $190,000

Late 19th century molded and gilded copper statue of Liberty Weathervane from the J. L. Mott Iron Works, New York. (Sotheby's) $75,000

'Marsh Hawk' by Andrew Wyeth. (Sotheby's) $420,000

results of the Joseph Hirshhorn sale wherein a Spencer Gay Family Queen Anne carved and inlaid walnut and maple highboy and companion lowboy were sold for $190,000. In another sale, an Andrew Wyeth painting 'Marsh Hawk' realized $420,000 and set a record. Folk art continues to gain. Items have sold well at all price levels but the most striking example was a Statue of Liberty Weathervane from the Thomas G. Rizzo collection which realized $75,000.

Christies has faired better this year because its growth has been more contained with expansion financed out-of-pocket to a large extent. There was no extraordinary staff build-up in brighter days so no significant staff paring has occurred. This is also due in part to added income from a lucrative graphics business. Brian Cole, President of Christies, has also seen a decline in the

Early 18th century Queen Anne black japanned bureau bookcase, 39in. wide x 95in. high. (Christie's) $860,000

An upholstered sycamore and chrome folding armchair by Eileen Gray,
designed in 1926. (Christie's)   *$16,000*

number of collections available, but consistently sees the finest goods selling exceptionally well. Particularly strong is good English furniture from the 18th and early 19th centuries, and good French pieces 'with names'. The highest price paid in North America for furniture, and a record for English furniture, was $860,000 for a very fine Queen Anne Black Japanned Bureau Bookcase, early 18th century.

Art Nouveau and Art Deco continue to sell well but have reached stability after the incredible price jumps of the past 4 years. One sale saw an upholstered Sycamore and chrome folding armchair by Eileen Gray, 1926, make $16,000, while a fine double overlay and carved glass vase by Emile Galle estimated at

$6,500 fetched $18,000. Christies has seen an increasing number of top lots go to 'anonymous' bidders — perhaps a sign that private buyers plan and can afford to hold on to these pieces for a long time for investment purposes.

The credit for Phillips ability to achieve good sales now is due in large part to the appointment of President Russell Burke. According to Cintra Huber, Vice President of Marketing and Public Relations, Mr Burke has eschewed specialty sales in favor of a return to the traditional. Phillips has, in the past, been associated with the promotion of unique specialty items as collectibles. In times of recession, however, newer collectibles such as posters and photography do not fair well. The more tradi-

A fine double-overlay and carved glass vase by Emile Galle, for 1889 Exposition, 3¼in. high. (Christie's) **$18,000**

tional items seem to represent security for the long run. In this vein, Phillips reports that they have seen most interest in 18th century English furniture, American and English silver, and 19th century American paintings. In an April 16th sale a pair of important George IV candelabra by Philip Rundell, London 1820, realized $60,000. Antique jewelry sales continue an impressive, steady growth, so much so that the jewelry department holds frequent seminars on investment potential. Phillips also maintains that it is able to withstand the economic pressures felt by the other big houses because it owns the Madison Avenue property which houses all New York salerooms and offices.

Helen Kippax, Director of Public Relations for William Doyle Galleries, says that even though the market resembles a roller coaster now, sales in quality American, English and French furniture

An important pair of George IV silver gilt candelabra, London, 1820, by Philip Rundell. (Phillips) **$60,000**

are a major strength; an example being a pair of George III Satinwood card tables which fetched $10,000. Decoys have emerged as a particularly important collectible and this year a Lesser Yellowlegs, William Bowman, sold for a record $23,000. Antique jewelry continues strong here, especially Art Deco pieces of outstanding craftsmanship.

Auction sales of china and porcelain, silver in quantity, and Art Nouveau and Art Deco glass have levelled off. Middle market (i.e. middle quality and reproductions) items are totally dead at the moment. It is the concensus in New York that collectors are buying only the top quality in every category and can do so because they have spent the time and energy to investigate and prepare.

Americans no longer need to feel intimidated by Europeans with centuries of antique knowledge; they are now and forever more a major force in the saleroom.

Dealers are finding the same to be true in every state of the Union. It used to be that there was a buyer for everything, no matter what the condition, but that is no longer the case. Even Sunday browsers know what to look for and buy with an eye towards quality. Many dealers who opened their doors a couple of years ago to make a quick killing have had to close up shop because they've seen the antique fever tempered. The same number of people (and more) are buying but they won't be sold a bill of goods by anyone on

One of a pair of George III satinwood card tables, height 28½in., width approx. 35½in. (Wm. Doyle Galleries, Inc.)   *$10,000*

any item. These times are positive for the antique market — and especially the buyer — in that the amateurs will be weeded out leaving a good solid core of professional dealers who develop long-standing, honest relationships with their clients. This is true on every level from the most sophisticated down to the crossroads store which has been in existence since your grandmothers time. Recently, after hearing so much about the bubble bursting, Albert Sack of Israel Sack, New York, sent question-aires to fellow members of the National Antique and Art Dealers Association to get their opinions about the market. All of the dealers who responded concurred that business has increased and they've seen a whole new group of buyers eager to pay for top quality goods. Whether the specialty was fine furniture or Oriental Art, the theme was optimism. Many felt the new clients were confident, experienced and highly discriminating. More than one dealer suggested the clients had become disillusioned with auction house policies and, in particular, paying the premiums required. 'The auction houses have been caught by their own hype,' which can only benefit the best dealers.

These feelings of optimism are substantiated nationwide. Dealers Lyle spoke with, who have existed for many years in places as diverse as St. Paul, Houston, Santa Barbara, Chicago and Raleigh, all agree that the best dealers will unquestionably survive and continue to do well indefinitely. They've all been through it before, have learned to adjust their profit margins, and know that relationships nurtured today will bring incredible gains in soon-to-come rosier days. Little, however, complain about big drops in business. As a matter of fact, it's difficult to keep quality items in stock. One dealer in fine Victorian furniture from Americus, Texas, said that on a recent trip to Buffalo — usually one of the cities most affected by hard times — 'the only thing I didn't find was the recession. They were literally buying things off the truck.' It can be said that sales are steady in every part of the country and increasing greatly in most urban centers. Perhaps the recent rash of articles pointing to the flaws in many money saving schemes have given people food for thought. A year ago, when rumors of the demise of the Social Security System were rife, Americans panicked and ran scared to the first money market scheme that presented itself. Now there seems to be a turnaround and more positive feelings which translate into healthy respect in antiques for investment.

Good investments today are fine porcelain (early French, English and Oriental) which has seen an amazing drop in the last year; silver, which was badly bungled during the Hunt Brothers fiasco, and is at its lowest point in recent memory; oriental rugs, extremely disappointing today but surely of tremendous value; and good quality American, English and French furniture of every period.

Americana is the collecting craze which has swept the country. There is definitely a re-enforced nationalistic pride; a feeling that we have finally come of age as a culture. There is also the realization that America, being relatively young, will always have fewer antiques available and therefore they will increase in value considerably faster than the majority of like items from abroad. This is especially true of very fine Shaker furniture, the best pieces of Colonial glass, and American Indian jewelry, clothing, basketry and pottery.

Folk Art is finally considered a true art form and one which glories a special talent indigenous to these shores. Prices have literally zoomed in the last two years, but good bargains can still be found in every region. It's easier to find examples of good folk art at country auctions, and at garage sales in the most rural areas. Younger collectors favor Folk Art because it is, for the most part, still relatively inexpensive while being unique. Quilts are the fastest selling item and are displayed as art on walls from Boston to San Francisco.

The passion for everything Deco and Nouveau has been subdued and only the very best furniture, lamps and silver reach astronomical heights in the salerooms and shops. Sothebys say that Art Deco and Art Nouveau has levelled off to where it should be. Collectors had created a false market by hiking prices way beyond expectations and 'it had to quiet down.' Jewelry continues to do well at every sale because the design, and quality of craftsmanship blend perfectly with almost every big city lifestyle. Most Tiffany objects are considered to be the definition of the word classic. And Galle glass is still enjoying an avid specialist public.

Besides a love of the Art Deco and Art Nouveau periods, New Yorkers share a true appreciation for very fine English furniture. Middle quality English furniture is practically unsaleable here as they would rather have the best pieces or concentrate on other collectibles. There is a growing admiration for the elegant simplicity of Shaker furniture and accoutrements as it complements a recent strong movement of the big city residents to lead less complicated lives. Likewise, paintings, sculpture and prints by American artists have gained a

stronghold. The Oriental antiques market has ebbed with only very unique pieces selling well. Recently, at William Doyle, a Ming Dynasty Cachepot made $13,000, way above the estimate. Antique jewelry is at a premium in New York where, for safety reasons, women would rather wear these pieces than flashy jewels which might present dangerous situations. Diamonds and other precious gems are way down except for unique offerings such as the 41.94 carat Emperor Maximilian Diamond estimated at $200,000-$300,000, and which sold for $760,000 at Christie's.

Further up the Eastern Seaboard Robert Skinner reports a very strong interest in Art Deco and Art Nouveau and in important American furniture, but a waning feeling for English period furniture. He finds there are less foreign dealers in his salerooms and 'competition on things a collector wants or a dealer feels he can move advantageously is keen.' New England has always felt a special fondness for Early American collectibles in every category and, on the whole, rarely strays from the fold. There are small enclaves of Victorian enthusiasts and they communicate regularly with dealers in the South who are consigned the biggest and best estates. This is probably the most prolific region in the United States in terms of available antique outlets. Many New Yorkers and New Jerseyites make regular trips to browse for bargains.

Victorian furniture will always have a home in the South. Collectors from Atlanta, New Orleans and Houston enter into fierce competitions for the very best pieces of Victoriana. The Old World opulence meshes perfectly with the grandeur of the Southern lifestyle. And sentimentality plays a big part in sales. Recently a five-piece Victorian bedroom suite that once belonged to Dorothy Dix, famous Southern authoress and Advice to the Lovelorn Columnist fetched $4,250, almost twice the estimate. There is a recent trend towards furnishing offices in this period rather than buying modern. Dealers here report their clients say it lends substance to the businesses. David Goldberg of Mortons in New Orleans also sees a continuing interest in good English furniture in the Queen Anne and Regency styles, as well as fine examples of American Empire 1810-1860. Elsewhere, in the Carolinas, Tennessee and Alabama, painted furniture, basketry and dolls are the hot collectibles.

The Midwest is the second largest area for the sale of Victoriana — and every-thing finds a home there. Victorian jewelry, silver and clothing can be found in many Midwestern cities. Americana and Art Deco do not do well because there is no understanding of or interest in those periods. Art Nouveau glass, however, does sell well as accent pieces. There is a sudden rash of requests for copper lustre and majolica. Early Staffordshire sells well as Midwesterners feel American pottery has been too much in demand lately, and therefore too expensive. The exception to popular Victorian taste is the City of Chicago where residents still favor French and English furniture, French porcelain and Georgian silver. Art Deco clocks remain highly desired items while the rest of the Deco and Nouveau market has stabi-lized. Donrose Antiques recommends investing in Meissen and Sevre at the moment. Prices are reasonable but sure

Five-piece Victorian bedroom suite that once belonged to Dorothy Dix, famous Southern authoress and Writer of a newspaper column with Advice for the Love-lorn. (Morton's, New Orleans)   *$4,250*

to go through the roof in the near future.

New Mexico, Arizona and Colorado residents have a strong sense of local history and tend to preserve the flavor of the Southwest by buying only those pieces created there and handed down through generations. Mission furniture and pieces that reflect early Spanish influence are prime collectibles, as are Indian jewelry and clothing. The lifestyle tends to be simple and most homes strive to keep the theme going throughout. Adobe-type houses boast valuable American Indian rugs and doll collections. Certain pocket areas like Colorado Springs, which has a large military population, cater to a taste for Orientalia. Military personnel and tourists (mostly doctors and security analysts) are the best clients for Oriental bronzes and Cloisonne. Ivory netsukes also do well but the preponderance of fakes in recent years has made people wary, and cautious when buying.

California has always been the last state to feel any adverse effects in the economy. According to John Gallo, Executive Vice President of Butterfields in San Francisco, the state is booming in comparison with the rest of the country, due in large part to the presence of the technological industries headquartered there. Items that have sold particularly well this year were English and American paintings, with a strong preference for Western artists, good pre-1850 American furniture, antique and Art Deco jewelry, and good Spanish furniture brought here when the state was settled. A 17th century Spanish desk estimated at $7,500 was sold at Butterfields for $27,000. San Francisco also likes to collect Victorian and Georgian silver, good Art Nouveau and Deco pieces in every category, and 18th century porcelain. Southern California tastes tend to be incredibly eclectic. Almost anything goes but dealers say they do very well with Victorian and Edwardian furniture which arrive in big shipments from England. Los Angeles is the place where you can find dealers offering 'miles of antiques and miles of bargains' — you just have to know what you're looking for.

And this is the common thread which holds American collectors all over the country. People are not afraid to spend, they simply want to get the best for their money. In order to do this they are reading everything they can get their hands on relating to specific collectibles; they have formed discussion and seminar groups to find people with similar interests to promote understanding; they are planning vacations to coincide with country auction circuits; and they are constantly reassessing their own collections in an effort to trade-up and make the wisest investments. Dealers and auctioneers have reported a marked increase in new buyers of all ages who buy items like English and French furniture which previously were bought and shipped back to those countries by foreign dealers. Americans are able to take advantage of the fact that those dealers, concerned about the economic situation in their own countries, opt to forgo tremendous shipping costs.

This is probably the best time in recent history to buy, if you buy intelligently. There are incredible bargains to be had — the stuff for future millionaires. So educate yourself and enjoy the treasure hunt, secure in the knowledge that good antiques will always be valuable.

ELLEN KAPLAN

ALABASTER

Alabaster jar of Necho II, barrel-shaped with twin handles, 13¼in. high, circa 610-595 B.C. (Christie's)$7,275

Mid 17th century alabaster statue of the Virgin and Child, 68.5cm. high. (Christie's)$8,450

Early 15th century Nottingham alabaster relief of the Adoration of the Kings, 16¾in. high. (Sotheby's) $14,000

19th century Italian alabaster and marble statue of Beatrice, inscribed P. Bazzanti Firenze, 69.5cm. high.(Christie's)$580

15th century Nottingham alabaster panel of The Trinity, 46cm. high. (Christie's)$9,715

Gilt bronze and alabaster figure entitled 'Nature unveiling herself', circa 1893, 42in. high. (Wm. Doyle Galleries Inc.) $12,000

Early 17th century English kneeling alabaster figure, 20in. high. (Sotheby's) $1,245

15th century Nottingham alabaster plaque carved in high relief with the head of St. John the Baptist, 8 x 5in. (Sotheby's) $3,740

Scmidtcassel alabaster and ivory figure 'Tanzlegende', signed, circa 1910-20, 23.25cm. high. (Sotheby's Belgravia) $800

AMUSEMENT MACHINES

Coin-operated automaton 'The Drunkard's Dream', circa 1935, 66½in. high. (Sotheby's Belgravia) $1,020

Ahrens football game, coin-operated, in oak casing with glazed upper section, circa 1930, 43¾in. wide.(Sotheby's Belgravia) $850

English coin-operated automaton 'The Burglar', circa 1935, 67in. high. (Sotheby's Belgravia) $745

Mutoscope by the International Mutoscope Reel Co., circa 1905, 74in. high. (Sotheby's Belgravia) $710

Great Race game, coin-operated, in oak casing with glazed upper section, 47in. wide, circa 1925. (Sotheby's Belgravia) $850

'Pussy Shooter' amusement machine by British Automatic Co. Ltd., circa 1935, 76in. high. (Sotheby's Belgravia) $635

Zodiac fortune teller, coin-operated machine, circa 1940, 24½in. high.(Sotheby's Belgravia)$235

Allwin De Luxe amusement machine in oak case with glazed front, 27in. high, circa 1935. (Sotheby's) $100

'Laughing Sailor' amusement machine bearing Ruffler & Walker plaque, circa 1935, 68½in. high. (Sotheby's Belgravia) $1,020

AMUSEMENT MACHINES

English coin-operated automaton 'The Haunted House', circa 1935, 70½in. high. (Sotheby's Belgravia) $890

American 'Twenty-one' gambling machine in cast alloy and oak casing, circa 1930, 13½in. wide. (Sotheby's Belgravia) $210

English coin-operated automaton 'The Night Watchman', by the British Automatic Co. Ltd., circa 1935, 66½in. high. (Sotheby's Belgravia) $1,020

American coin-operated mutoscope 'Death Dive', circa 1915, 50in. high. (Sotheby's Belgravia) $680

Early Rowland Pier Head amusement machine 'The Racer', circa 1900, 19in. wide. (Sotheby's) $395

English Green Ray 'television' amusement machine with glass dome above, circa 1945, 75in. high. (Sotheby's Belgravia) $635

Green Ray 'television' amusement machine in wooden casing, circa 1945, 75in. high. (Sotheby's Belgravia) $405

Auto-stereoscope in oak casing with viewer and coin slot at top, circa 1930, 22½in. high. (Sotheby's Belgravia) $320

English 'Pussy Shooter' amusement machine with glazed window, circa 1935, 76in. high. (Sotheby's Belgravia) $595

25

Automaton of a young girl seated at a piano, doll with French bisque head, 41cm. high, restored. (Phillips) $2,880

Continental floral chased and embossed musical singing bird box. (Christie's S. Kensington) $895

Singing bird in cage, in inlaid rosewood case, 18in. high. (Robert W. Skinner Inc.) $750

19th century French magician automaton with plaster head and glass eyes, 28in. high. (Phillips) $2,870

Rare musical tightrope dancer automaton, French, circa 1840, under glass cover. (Sotheby's Belgravia) $985

French ballerina automaton with bisque head impressed SFBJ 801, Paris, circa 1900, 23in. high. (Sotheby's) $1,975

Large French singing bird automaton, 18½in. high, circa 1900. (Sotheby's Belgravia) $610

Automaton magician, 52½in. high, 36½in. wide. (Robert W. Skinner Inc.) $450

French lady conjuror automaton with bisque head and musical movement, circa 1905, 26in. high. (Sotheby's Belgravia) $1,810

French sleeping doll automaton with clockwork and musical movement, 14in. long, circa 1910. (Sotheby's Belgravia) $845

Automaton gum machine in upright oak case, 11½in. wide. (Robert W. Skinner Inc.) $1,200

Early 20th century German singing bird box with timepiece, 10.2cm. long. (Sotheby's Belgravia) $635

Rare French mid 19th century singing bird automaton, 21½in. high. (Sotheby's Belgravia) $10,065

Mid 19th century American dancing negress toy, 7¾in. long, with key. (Sotheby's Belgravia) $130

Dancing negress automaton with key wound mechanism, in good condition, 10½in. high. (Sotheby's) $230

Large magician automaton on ebonized wooden glass-fronted base, 42in. high, circa 1930.(Sotheby's Belgravia) $1,015

Monkey artist automaton with Manievelle musical movement, circa 1900, 13½in. wide. (Sotheby's Belgravia) $915

Automaton 'The Conjuror', of bisque head doll before a pedestal table, 16½in. high. (Robert W. Skinner Inc.) $1,800

27

Mahogany inlaid stick barometer by Curtis & Horsepool, Leicester. (Honiton Galleries) $460

Early 18th century Regency mahogany wheel barometer by Antoni Pilatt, Nottingham, 42in. high. (Sotheby Beresford Adams) $410

Mid 18th century oak stick barometer by F. L. West, London, trunk applied with thermometer, 38in. high.(Sotheby Beresford Adams) $370

Victorian mahogany wheel barometer with hygrometer thermometer, dial signed T. Bedwell, London, 37in. high. (Christie's) $525

19th century mahogany wheel barometer by A. Gallatti, Glasgow, inlaid with marquetry, 98cm. high. (Phillips) $370

Early 19th century mahogany stick barometer by Newman, London, 39in. high. (Sotheby, King & Chasemore) $1,785

19th century mahogany stick barometer by F. Pastorelli, London, 94cm. high. (Phillips) $460

William IV rosewood bow-fronted stick barometer, signed Gardener & Co., Glasgow, 40in. high. (Christie's) $655

28

BAROMETERS

Antique mahogany five dial banjo barometer. (Honiton Galleries) $370

19th century mahogany stick barometer by Jno. Gally & Co., Exeter, silvered plate incorporating a thermometer, 96cm. high. (Phillips)$550

Mid Victorian banjo-shaped barometer by J. Amadio, London, in rosewood case with mother-of-pearl inlay, 40¼in. high.(Sotheby Bearne) $465

Victorian walnut stick barometer signed J. Bassnett & Son, Liverpool, 2ft.10in. high. (Sotheby, King & Chasemore) $1,080

Victorian mahogany stick barometer signed F. W. Clarke, London, with ivory register plates, 38in. high.(Christie's) $635

18th century French Louis XVI carved, gessoed and gilt barometer/thermometer, 37½in. high. (Robert W. Skinner Inc.) $350

Late 18th/early 19th century George III mahogany stick barometer by G. Monolla, London, 38in. high. (Sotheby Beresford Adams)$630

Mid 19th century rosewood wheel barometer by Adie, Liverpool, restored, 38½in. high. (Sotheby Beresford Adams) $445

29

BAROMETERS

Early 19th century rosewood stick barometer with ivory register plate, 36in. high. (Sotheby, King & Chasemore) $530

Banjo-shaped and shell inlaid mahogany barometer by Lione & Co. (Worsfolds) $430

18th century mahogany stick barometer/thermometer by Adams, London, 42in. long. (W. H. Lane & Son) $1,330

Early 19th century wheel barometer by J. M. Ronketti, London, 93cm. high. (Phillips) $470

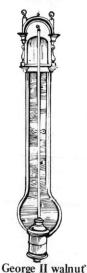

Mahogany wheel barometer in the form of a longcase clock, by J. Hallifax, Barnsley, 45in. high.(Christie's) $2,805

George II walnut stick barometer with arched portico cresting and ribbed bowed base, 42in. high. (Christie's) $2,290

Antique walnut banjo barometer and thermometer by D. Fagioli & Son, Clerkenwell. (Butler & Hatch Waterman) $205

19th century rosewood ship's barometer by Jones, Dublin, 93cm. high. (Phillips) $805

George III banjo barometer by Ortelli & Co., Carmarthen, in mahogany case. (Osmond, Tricks) $580

Oak cased aneroid wheel barometer, circa 1930. (David Symonds)$70

Late Georgian mahogany bow-fronted stick barometer by G. & C. Dixey. (Stride & Son) $1,535

Mid 19th century mahogany wheel barometer by F. Houghton, Chester, 47½in. long. (Sotheby's) $1,065

Mid 19th century mahogany wheel barometer, signed A. Martinelli, London, 37½in. long. (Sotheby's) $295

George III mahogany stick barometer, signed Aliano Fecit, 1800, 95cm. high. (Phillips) $750

19th century mahogany wheel barometer by A. Pastorelli, London, 98cm. high. (Phillips) $505

Late Georgian mahogany bow-fronted stick barometer by Davis of Arbroath. (Stride & Son) $1,665

BRONZE

Late 19th century Japanese bronze group of an eagle and a snake, 14¼in. high. (Sotheby's)
$210

Alliot bronze nude study of a woman, 47.5cm. wide, 1930's, signed. (Sotheby's Belgravia) $635

Small Chiparus and ivory figure of a young girl, 1920's, 24.75cm. high. (Sotheby's Belgravia)
$1,245

Lorenzl bronze dancing figure, nude, holding a drape, 1920's, signed. (Sotheby's Belgravia)
$675

Roland Paris bronze and ivory group of the Devil and a girl accomplice, 40cm. high, 1920's. (Sotheby's Belgravia)
$2,135

Preiss bronze and ivory dancer on green marble tray, 1930's, 29cm. high, signed. (Sotheby's Belgravia) $2,135

Bronze figure of a lady with an asp, signed Phillipe, Ru. M., 19in. high. (R. H. Ellis & Sons) $545

Two 19th century bronze busts, 9in. high. (J. M. Welch & Son)
$155

Oriental bronze vase with two handles, 13in. high. (J. M. Welch & Son) $545

32

BRONZE

Late 19th century Chinese bronze of Guanyin, 18¾in. high.(Sotheby's) $705

Bouraine silvered bronze figure of an Amazon warrior, signed, 1920's, 37cm. wide. (Sotheby's Belgravia) $1,870

One of a pair of Japanese bronze vases with dragon head handles, circa 1900, 25in. high. (Sotheby's)$580

Dyson Smith bronze study of a nude dancer, 1926, 30.5cm. high. (Sotheby's Belgravia) $1,245

Chiparus bronze and ivory dancing girl on brown marble base, 1920's, signed, 56.75cm. high.(Sotheby's Belgravia) $7,655

Bronze figure of a young woman, signed E. Villanis, 80cm. high. (Christie's) $2,055

Sabatier bronze study of a woman carrying flowers, circa 1905, 39.75cm. high. (Sotheby's Belgravia) $855

Japanese bronze figure of an eagle, perched on a rock, 21in. high. (J. M. Welch & Son) $620

Small Preiss bronze and ivory figure of a girl, 14.75cm. high, signed, 1930's. (Sotheby's Belgravia) $500

33

BRONZE

16th century Paduan bronze candlestick of a kneeling satyr, 22.5cm. high. (Christie's) $3,800

Large bronze figure of the Huntsman's Horse after J. Willis Good, 12½in. wide. (Boardman's) $1,360

French gilt bronze bust of a young man, 19cm. high. (Christie's) $1,480

Florentine bronze statuette of Bacchus, 17.5cm. high. (Christie's) $1,690

Bronze and ivory figure of a dancer, inscribed Godard, on brown marble base. (Christie's) $2,260

Late 16th/early 17th century Venetian bronze statuette of Cupid seated, 6.5cm. high. (Christie's) $360

Bronze figure of an Edwardian lady, inscribed I. Blanchot, 32cm. high. (Christie's) $535

Bronze figure of a horse, circa 6th century B.C., 7.5cm. high. (Christie's) $875

Bronze group of Mephistopheles with a girl, inscribed Roland Paris, 40cm. high. (Christie's) $1,645

34

Bronze figure of a coquette, inscribed Bruno Zach, Austria, 34cm. wide. (Christie's) $1,440

Rare 16th century Venetian bronze statuette of the Young Jupiter, 16cm. high. (Christie's) $1,690

Late 16th century Florentine bronze model of a walking bull, 23cm. high. (Christie's) $7,180

Bronze and ivory figure 'Starfish', inscribed D. H. Chiparus, slightly damaged, 38.5cm. high. (Christie's) $2,365

Late 16th century North Italian bronze statuette of Hercules Pomarius, 20cm. high. (Christie's) $8,450

Bronze and ivory figure of a dancer, inscribed J. Philippe, 42cm. high. (Christie's) $2,055

Bronze and ivory figure 'Hoop Girl', by F. Preiss, on marble base, 20.5cm. high. (Christie's) $1,070

17th century Roman gilt bronze group of Marcus Aurelius on horseback, 25.5cm. high. (Christie's) $12,730

Gallo-Roman bronze figure of a Lar, circa 2nd century A.D., 4¾in. high. (Christie's) $1,245

BRONZE

Bronze model of a running hare. (Sotheby, King & Chasemore) $110

Viennese cold-painted bronze model of a woodcock, 6¾in. high. (Sotheby, King & Chasemore)$100

19th century Austrian bronze figure of a whippet, signed H. Muller, 7¼in. long. (Robert W. Skinner Inc.) $300

One of a pair of mid 19th century gilt bronze and porcelain candelabra, 20in. high. (Sotheby Beresford Adams)$335

Pair of spelter figures of warriors in full armour, circa 1900, 20¾in. high. (Sotheby's Belgravia) $220

Bruno Zach bronze figure of a young girl, on square marble base, 46.5cm. high, inscribed Zach. (Phillips) $1,165

One of a pair of ormolu three-branch wall lights, fitted for electricity, 29in. high. (Christie's) $1,105

Bronze group, signed Ch. Raphael Peyre, of a young girl and a dog, 23.5cm. high. (Phillips)$575

One of a pair of gilt bronze mounted urns with curved handles, circa 1870, 8½in. high. (Sotheby's Belgravia) $610

Bronze model of a horse, cast by Morris Singer, after a model by Gainsborough, 9in. long. (Sotheby, King & Chasemore) $275

Mid 19th century bronze figure of Pan, after Eutrope Bouret, 10½in. high. (Sotheby Beresford Adams) $240

Bronze study of a bear, 8¼in. long. (Sotheby, King & Chasemore) $120

One of a pair of parcel gilt bronze candelabra, on pierced rococo bases, 1870's, 22in. high. (Sotheby's Belgravia) $470

Pair of Directoire ormolu busts of Voltaire and Rousseau, 12½in. high. (Christie's) $955

One of a pair of early 19th century parcel gilt bronze candlesticks, 13in. high. (Sotheby's Belgravia) $145

Mid 19th French bronze figure of Pomona, 14in. high. (Sotheby Beresford Adams) $410

Gilt bronze and ivory figure of a girl in pantaloons, possibly by Colinet, 45cm. high. (Phillips) $1,255

Bronze figure of a seated hound, by Emmanuel Fremiet, signed, 10in. high. (Sotheby, King & Chasemore) $410

Bronze group of a standing coursing greyhound with a hare in its mouth, by P. J. Mene, 5in. high. (Sotheby, King & Chasemore) $280

16th century Paduan bronze model of The Capitoline Wolf, by Severo da Ravenna, 14cm. wide. (Christie's) $3,380

Bronze figure of a charging elephant by Barye, 7½in. wide. (Sotheby, King & Chasemore) $1,080

Bronze group of three dogs by Pierre Jules Mene, 1870's, 15in. wide, signed. (Sotheby, King & Chasemore) $805

Bronze figure of a stallion by P. J. Mene, signed, 8½in. long. (Sotheby, King & Chasemore) $930

Bronze and ivory group 'Towards the Unknown', signed Cl. J. R. Colinet, 41cm. wide. (Christie's) $7,200

Bronze figure of a donkey, circa 6th-4th century B.C., 4.2cm. high, sold with another. (Christie's) $540

Pair of ormolu chenets of Louis XV design, stamped Morisot, 13½in. high. (Christie's) $955

16th century Paduan bronze inkstand of a crab attacking a frog, 16cm. wide. (Christie's) $3,380

Japanese bronze model of a crawling monkey, 18in. long. (Hall Wateridge & Owen) $445

Bronze model of a stretching dog, 7½in. long. (Sotheby, King & Chasemore) $485

Bronze figure of a grazing goat by Antoine Louis Barye, 3¾in. long, signed. (Sotheby, King & Chasemore) $520

Bronze figure of a stag and hind by Pierre Jules Mene, 7¼in. wide. (Sotheby, King & Chasemore) $930

Bronze model of the Lion and Serpent, by A. L. Barye, 6¼in. high. (Sotheby, King & Chasemore) $890

Pair of Regency bronze figures of a poodle and a cat on ormolu cushion bases, 14in. high. (Russell, Baldwin & Bright) $2,970

Bronze model of a bull by Rosa Bonheur, signed, 11in. long. (Sotheby, King & Chasemore) $315

Bronze figure of a crouching dog by P. J. Mene, 5¼in. high. (Sotheby, King & Chasemore) $315

American bronze inkwell in the form of a crab, circa 1900, 10½in. long.(Robert W. Skinner Inc.)$325

One of a pair of Japanese bronze models of elephants with ivory tusks, signed, 5½in. high. (Sotheby, King & Chasemore) $480

Unusual gilt bronze model of a winged maiden, signed Adolph, 33cm. high. (Phillips) $1,110

Green patinated bronze figure of a dancer on brown marble base, unsigned, 49cm. high. (Phillips) $465

Stylish bronze figure of a nude girl holding a robe, signed Motto, 46cm. high. (Phillips) $535

Bronze Roman warrior by Gotthilf Jaeger, Germany, born 1871, 26¼in. high. (Robert W. Skinner Inc.) $500

Bronze group of two kittens playing, 7in. wide. (Sotheby, King & Chasemore) $155

Late 19th century French bronze of a seated Breton woman holding an umbrella, 5¾in. high. (Robert W. Skinner Inc.) $200

BRONZE

Cold-painted bronze model of a seated bulldog, 3¾in. high. (Sotheby, King & Chasemore) $185

French cast bronze rabbit on black marble base, signed F. Pautrot, circa 1861, 5½in. long.(Robert W. Skinner Inc.)$600

Viennese cold-painted bronze model of a cat, 6½in. long. (Sotheby, King & Chasemore) $45

Colinet gilt bronze figure of a naked girl, signed Cl. J. R. Colinet, 49.5cm. high. (Phillips)$895

Prof. Poertzel figure 'Snake Dancer', in painted bronze and ivory, signed, 52.5cm. high. (Phillips) $6,800

Frederick Leighton bronze figure of a man 'The Sluggard', signed, 52cm. high. (Phillips) $4,655

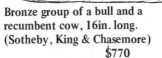

Bronze figure of a seated hare by Barye, 3¼in. high. (Sotheby, King & Chasemore) $240

Bronze group of a bull and a recumbent cow, 16in. long. (Sotheby, King & Chasemore) $770

Striking Polish bronze abstract model of an eagle, 1930, 44cm. high. (Phillips) $750

Mid 16th century Venetian bronze figure of a winged putto, 5in. high. (Sotheby's) $2,495

Late 16th century Italian gilt bronze furniture mount in the shape of a lion's head, 3¼in. high. (Sotheby's) $375

Lorenzl cold-painted bronze dancing girl, 1920's, signed, 40.5cm. high.(Sotheby's Belgravia) $1,240

Hagenauer ebonized wood and bronze gondola, Vienna, circa 1910-20, 44.75cm. wide. (Sotheby's Belgravia) $400

Rosenberg bronze dish, oval, signed Rosenberg 1902, 35cm. wide. (Sotheby's Belgravia) $320

Ouillon Carrere bronze nude study, dated 1919, 54.5cm. high, signed. (Sotheby's Belgravia) $880

Florentine bronze group of the Rape of the Sabines, circa 1690, 20½in. high. (Sotheby's) $1,245

Large gilt bronze figure by Bruno Zach 'The Cigarette', on black marble base, 72.5cm. high. (Christie's)$5,305

BRONZE

French painted bronze statue, of mid-Eastern girl, circa 1898, signed E. Le Guillemin, 26½in. high. (Robert W. Skinner Inc.) $1,800

Early 17th century Flemish bronze mortar with flared lip and base, 5in. high. (Sotheby's) $830

Large Lorenzl bronze dancing girl, signed, 1920's, 69cm. high, on marble base. (Sotheby's Belgravia) $1,560

19th century Japanese bronze figure of a tiger, 20in. long. (J. M. Welch & Son) $380

White metal figure of a partially draped nude, inscribed D. H. Chiparus, 74.5cm. wide. (Christie's) $915

Bronze and ivory group of Cupid and Psyche by G. Omerth, with fitment for electricity, 39.3cm. high. (Christie's) $1,190

One of two similar Gyoko bronze archers, circa 1900, on wood stands. (Sotheby's Belgravia) $1,650

Mid 19th century gilt bronze mounted celadon vase, 22in. high. (Sotheby's Belgravia) $825

BRONZE

One of a rare pair of 17th century Dutch bell-metal pricket candlesticks, 16in. high. (Christie's) $4,025

Limousin Art Deco group in cold painted bronze, ivory and marble, inscribed, central figure 14½in. high. (Lawrence Fine Art) $320

18th/19th century bronze tripod censer with applied dragon handles, wood cover and jade finial, 43cm. wide. (Christie's) $680

Bronze and ivory group 'Les Amis de Toujours', by D. H. Chiparus, inscribed, 64.2cm. wide. (Christie's) $17,385

Bronze figure of a standing nymph, inscribed Pierre Laurel, 58.5cm. high. (Christie's) $785

Oriental bronze group of an elephant being attacked by two tigers. (T. Bannister & Co.) $365

Late 19th century Japanese bronze figure of a falconer, 32cm. high, signed. (H. Spencer & Sons Ltd.)$1,480

16th century Flemish bronze mortar with inscription round rim, 6¼in. high. (Sotheby's) $2,855

Bronze and ivory figure of 'Sonny Boy', inscribed F. Preiss, 8in. high. (Lawrence Fine Art) $1,060

44

BRONZE

19th century English
bronze statuette of
The Norseman, 79cm.
high. (Christie's)
$1,835

Russian bronze figural group,
1870, damaged, 9½in. wide.
(Robert W. Skinner Inc.)
$1,100

Bronze and terracotta
group of two fighting
swordfish by Gaston
Lachaise, 81.5cm.
wide. (Christie's)
$7,320

Bronze and ivory figure
'Hoop Girl' inscribed F.
Preiss, 8in. high.
(Lawrence Fine Art)
$1,135

19th century French cast
bronze quail, signed J.
Moigniez, 9in. high.
(Robert W. Skinner Inc.)
$270

Gilt bronze figural
lamp of Loie Ful-
ler by Raoul Larche,
34cm. high.
(Christie's)
$5,490

Bronze bell with cast
pierced crown, 1633,
12in. diam. (Sotheby's)
$355

Late 19th century Maruki
bronze hawk with detailed
plumage, 28cm. wide.
(Sotheby's Belgravia)
$925

Tokyo School bronze
peasant with a lantern,
circa 1900, 58cm. high,
with wood stand.
(Sotheby's Belgravia)
$1,485

One of a pair of George III brass bound mahogany bottle carriers, 11¼in. high.(Christie's) $3,420

Large 19th century copper bucket with brass swing handle, 13in. diam. (Dickinson, Davy & Markham) $120

One of a pair of George III mahogany plate buckets with brass bands, 14in. diam. (Lawrence Fine Art) $1,505

George III mahogany boat-shaped oyster bucket with brass banding liner and handle, 14in. high, circa 1790. (Sotheby, King & Chasemore) $1,470

Dutch tole-peinte tea bucket decorated with chinoiserie, circa 1800, 1ft.1in. wide. (Sotheby's) $805

Dutch floral marquetry oyster bucket with brass banding and handle, circa 1760, 13in. diam. (Sotheby, King & Chasemore) $1,065

Antique leather fire bucket with coat of arms on front. (J. M. Welch & Son) $75

George III brass bound bucket with swing handle. (Christie's S. Kensington) $835

Gustav Stickley oak waste bucket, banded together with iron, 12in. diam. (Robert W. Skinner Inc.) $950

Early 17th century Jacobean oak casket, lid with crowned Tudor rose, 12½in. long. (Sotheby's) $1,350

Early 19th century American carved and painted trinket box in pine, 10in. wide. (Robert W. Skinner Inc.) $750

Early 19th century American decorated tin document box with domed cover, 13½in. long. (Robert W. Skinner Inc.) $275

Late 17th century carved oak bible box with lock. (J. M. Welch & Son) $210

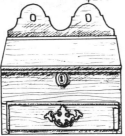

18th century American pine hanging wall candle box with double tombstone crest, 15in. wide. (Robert W. Skinner Inc.) $800

Unusual George IV brass inlaid rosewood medicine cabinet, circa 1825, 11½in. wide. (Sotheby's) $1,160

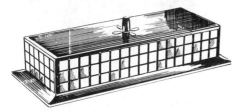

Ebonized wood and marquetry pen box and cover inset with mother-of-pearl, 24.7cm. long. (Christie's) $5,460

Mahogany and inlaid sewing box, 9 x 18in. (J. M. Welch & Son) $110

Papier-mache letter casket, curved top inlaid with mother-of-pearl, circa 1840, 6¼in. wide. (Sotheby's Belgravia) $145

George III ivory veneered tea caddy of oval shape, lid with pineapple finial, circa 1790. (Sotheby, King & Chasemore) $350

Gilt metal jewel casket with pierced hinged lid and sides, 1880's, 16.5cm. long. (Sotheby's Belgravia) $480

19th century mahogany domestic medicine chest with rising top, 30cm. high. (Phillips) $480

Late 18th century George III cutlery urn of ovoid form in mahogany with boxwood and ebony lines, 27in. high. (Sotheby Beresford Adams) $315

Burr-satin birch scent box, containing four scent bottles and stoppers, circa 1850, 5½in. wide. (Sotheby's Belgravia) $315

Mid 19th century Tunbridge-ware coromandel box by Thos. Barton, enclosing three graduated drawers, 8in. wide. (Sotheby's Belgravia) $115

One of a pair of George III mahogany knife boxes with fitted interiors and plated mounts, circa 1780, 9in. wide. (Sotheby, King & Chasemore) $1,105

Electroplated parcel gilt copper electrotype jewel casket by Elkington, Mason & Co., circa 1855, 17cm. long. (Sotheby's Belgravia) $495

48

Tunbridgeware rosewood bookstand with serpentine support, 14in. wide, circa 1860. (Sotheby's Belgravia) $250

George III mahogany and harewood tea caddy, crossbanded in rosewood, 5½in. wide, circa 1790. (Sotheby, King & Chasemore) $230

Regency tortoiseshell two-division tea caddy with serpentine front, 7½in. wide, circa 1820. (Sotheby, King & Chasemore) $315

Mid 19th century papier-mache decanter case of square form, containing four glass scent decanters, 5in. square. (Sotheby Beresford Adams)$165

Mid 19th century coromandel cigar box by Edmund Nye, 8in. wide. (Sotheby's Belgravia) $405

Adjustable Tunbridge-ware bookshelf with two arched ends, circa 1870, 11½in. wide, closed. (Sotheby's Belgravia) $235

George III mahogany and boxwood string-banded tea caddy with Tunbridgeware band. (Sotheby, King & Chasemore)$150

Tunbridgeware coromandel box by Thos. Barton, circa 1870, 9½in. wide. (Sotheby's Belgravia) $450

Early 19th century covered oval quill work box with ivory finial, 5½in. long. (Robert W. Skinner Inc.)$170

Rosewood Tunbridgeware box with floral mosaic lid and fitted interior, circa 1870, 9½in. wide. (Sotheby's Belgravia) $305

Mid 19th century Tunbridgeware ash box with floral mosaic borders, 9½in. wide. (Sotheby's Belgravia)$325

Mid 19th century papier-mache sewing casket, fitted with lift-out tray, 13in. wide. (Sotheby's Belgravia) $325

Tunbridgeware rosewood work box with inlaid top and mosaic border, circa 1840, 10½in. wide.(Sotheby's Belgravia) $740

Mid 19th century rosewood table writing box inlaid with mother-of-pearl, 14in. wide. (Sotheby Beresford Adams) $110

Mid 19th century rosewood Tunbridgeware tea caddy by William Upton, inlaid with cube marquetry, 12½in. wide. (Sotheby's Belgravia) $360

18th century Japanese mother-of-pearl inlaid lacquer, dome topped casket, 9in. wide. (Sotheby, King & Chasemore) $1,340

Tunbridgeware rosewood tea caddy with fitted interior, circa 1840, 13½in. wide. (Sotheby's Belgravia) $665

Mid 19th century Tunbridgeware rosewood pen box by William Upton, 9¾in. long. (Sotheby's Belgravia) $360

Mid 19th century rosewood Tunbridgeware casket with domed top, 10½in. wide. (Sotheby's Belgravia) $245

Regency Tunbridgeware box inlaid with cube pattern, circa 1820, 12in. wide. (Sotheby's Belgravia) $305

Tunbridgeware rosewood box, top inlaid with a view of Penshurst Place, circa 1870, 9in. wide. (Sotheby's Belgravia) $270

Double papier-mache tea caddy, molded top inlaid with mother-of-pearl, 8¼in. wide. (Sotheby's Belgravia) $125

Late 18th/early 19th century satinwood and mahogany tea caddy with two canisters and a mixing bowl, 11½in. wide. (Sotheby Beresford Adams) $130

Papier-mache box by Jennens & Bettridge, circa 1850, 11in. wide. (Sotheby's Belgravia) $180

Rosewood Tunbridgeware writing slope with a view of Hever Castle, circa 1870, 12in. wide. (Sotheby's Belgravia) $485

Regency Tunbridgeware tea caddy of octagonal shape, circa 1820, 6in. wide. (Sotheby's) $470

Mid 19th century French gilt metal jewel casket with five porcelain panels, 20.5cm. long. (Sotheby's Belgravia) $550

Rare George III embroidered tea caddy of hexagonal shape, circa 1775, 7½in. wide. (Sotheby's) $305

One of a pair of George III mahogany knife boxes, circa 1780, 8¾in. high. (Sotheby's) $1,240

Early 19th century English apothecary's chest in rosewood case with boxwood stringing, 6¼in. high. (Sotheby's Belgravia) $140

Red tole painted tea caddy and writing box, circa 1790, 8in. wide. (Robert W. Skinner Inc.)$300

Late 16th century French leather covered casket mounted with crowns and studs, 21½in. wide. (Christie's) $3,295

Georgian satinwood inlaid tea caddy. (Christie's S. Kensington) $185

Regency tortoiseshell-veneered tea caddy with engraved plaque, circa 1820, 7¼in. wide. (Sotheby's) $175

Regency mother-of-pearl inlaid tortoiseshell veneered tea caddy, circa 1820, 6¾in. wide. (Sotheby's) $430

Gilt metal mounted oval ebonized wood jewel casket by Charles Asprey, London, circa 1860. (Sotheby's Belgravia) $345

Mid 19th century American painted wooden folk art box with hinged cover, 12in. long. (Robert W. Skinner Inc.) $275

Victorian coromandel brass bound vanity case with silver mounted bottles, 12in. wide. (Locke & England) $300

Set of three late 18th century George III knive boxes in mahogany, with inlaid lids.(Robert W. Skinner Inc.) $1,550

One of a pair of mahogany cutlery vases in George III style, 28in. high. (Burrows & Day) $360

George III rolled paperwork tea caddy, circa 1785, 6¼in. wide, slightly chipped.(Sotheby's) $370

Canteen of Old English pattern table cutlery by Martin Hall & Co., Sheffield, in oak case. (Dickinson, Davy & Markham) $350

Rare George III maplewood and tortoiseshell tea caddy, 6in. wide, circa 1780. (Sotheby's) $815

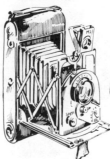

Newman & Guardia Nydia folding plate camera with detachable bellows, circa 1900, 4¼in. high. (Sotheby's Belgravia) $275

Newman & Guardia New Ideal Sibyl folding camera, circa 1925.(Sotheby's Belgravia) $145

Marion's metal miniature camera, 1¼in. high, circa 1884, in mahogany case. (Sotheby's Belgravia) $2,575

Thornton Pickard amber folding field camera, circa 1895. (Sotheby Beresford Adams) $115

Sanders & Crowhurst 'The Birdland' reflex camera in ebonized wood body, circa 1908. (Sotheby's Belgravia) $295

Newman & Guardia Nydia folding plate camera, 4¼in. high, in original leather case, circa 1905. (Sotheby's Belgravia) $310

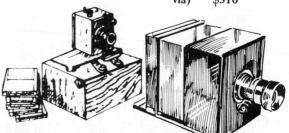

Japanese Canon Model 7 35mm. camera and filter, in leather case, circa 1962. (Sotheby's Belgravia) $550

Mahogany cased stereoscopic camera and six plates by Negretti & Zambra. (Christie's S. Kensington) $7,135

Mid 19th century English sliding box camera, 7½in. square, in mahogany body with brass fittings. (Sotheby's Belgravia) $700

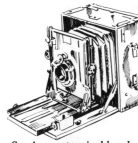

Sanderson tropical hand-and-stand camera, 6½in. high, circa 1910, in teak body with brass fittings. (Sotheby's Belgravia) $590

W. Watson & Sons stereo tailboard camera, 6¾in. wide, circa 1900. (Sotheby's Belgravia) $440

Early Sinclair Una hand-and-stand camera in black leather-covered mahogany body, circa 1905, 4¼in. high. (Sotheby's Belgravia) $165

Ensign tropical special reflex camera in teak body with brass fittings, circa 1930, 4¼in. high. (Sotheby's Belgravia) $275

ICA universal juwel 440 folding plate camera with Zeiss Tessar lens, circa 1925, 18cm. high. (Sotheby's Belgravia) $310

Voigtlander prominent folding camera in original leather case, German, circa 1933. (Sotheby's Belgravia) $405

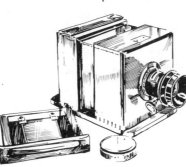

Postcard-size tropical Soho stereoscopic reflex camera. (Christie's S. Kensington) $6,440

English wet-plate camera by W. W. Rouch, London, circa 1864, in mahogany body. (Sotheby's Belgravia) $1,290

Zeiss Ikon contaflex twin lens reflex camera, 36mm. high, circa 1935. (Sotheby's Belgravia) $830

CANE HANDLES

French gold parasol handle set with a watch, by Cartier, 2¾in. high. (Christie's)$2,805

Walking stick with wood shaft and handle and horn ferrule, circa 1900, 88.4cm. long. (Sotheby's Belgravia) $265

Austrian silver gilt walking cane handle, Vienna, 1753, 14.2cm. long. (Sotheby's) $855

Late 19th century malacca walking cane with scrimshaw ball grip set with a compass, 81.5cm. long. (Sotheby's Belgravia) $245

Early 18th century German gilt metal finial from a jester's stick, 4¾in. high. (Sotheby's) $2,285

Gold, silver and enamel mounted parasol handle, initial set with rose-cut diamonds, 2¾in. high. (Christie's) $935

Ebonized wood walking stick with carved ivory handle, circa 1900, 90.3cm. long.(Sotheby's Belgravia) $305

Japanese carved ivory cane top. (Robert W. Skinner Inc.) $75

Silver mounted whip with engraved collar and grip, London, 1864, 92.5cm. long. (Sotheby's Belgravia) $350

56

CAR MASCOTS

Red Ashay glass car mascot in the form of a woman's head, 23cm. wide, 1930's.(Sotheby's Belgravia) $625

Lalique moulded glass car mascot 'Libellule', in the shape of a dragon-fly. (Woolley & Wallis) $1,265

Lalique glass car mascot 'The Spirit of the Wind', in original chromed metal mount, 25.5cm. wide, circa 1925. (Sotheby's Belgravia) $1,985

A standing figure of the Esso man, 5½in. high. (Vernons) $240

Lalique 'Cinq Chevaux' glass car mascot, marked, 1920's, 16.5cm. wide. (Sotheby's Belgravia) $1,215

Mickey Mouse glass car mascot, stamped Walt Disney Productions, circa 1940, 5¼in. high. (Sotheby's Belgravia) $140

Lalique glass dragon-fly car mascot, 20.5cm. long, 1920's, signed. (Sotheby's Belgravia) $1,360

Lalique glass hawk mascot, engraved, 1920's, 16.5cm. high. (Sotheby's Belgravia)$500

A nickel plated Minerva car mascot. (Sotheby's Belgravia) $290

19th century American wooden butter stamp, carved with a ram, 4½in. diam. (Robert W. Skinner Inc.) $350

19th century American butter stamp, carved with a lamb, 3in. diam. (Robert W. Skinner Inc.) $275

19th century American wooden butter stamp showing a bird on a branch, 3in. diam. (Robert W. Skinner Inc.) $225

19th century Japanese carved, gessoed and painted Oriental deity, 29½in. high. (Robert W. Skinner Inc.) $200

Early 18th century Norwegian peg tankard, 8in. high. (Sotheby, King & Chasemore) $310

Fine 14th century French walnut group of the Virgin and Child, 42.5cm. high. (Christie's) $8,450

American pine candle box with carved decoration on all sides, 9¾in. long. (Robert W. Skinner Inc.) $800

One of a pair of Venetian rococo blackamoors, painted and parcel gilt, 4ft. 10in. high. (Sotheby's) $18,000

19th century Scandinavian carved and painted butter tub with flat cover, 13in. diam. (Robert W. Skinner Inc.) $1,450

19th century American wooden handleless butter stamp with incised anchor, 3½in. diam. (Robert W. Skinner Inc.) $75

Early 18th century English fruitwood relief of two cherub heads flanking a chalice, 30cm. high. (Christie's) $505

19th century American wooden butter stamp carved with a cow, 3½in. diam. (Robert W. Skinner Inc.) $150

15th century Umbrian wood statue of St. Sebastian, damaged, 120cm. high.(Christie's) $5,280

Early 16th century French polychrome wood relief of the road to Calvary, 81.5cm. wide. (Christie's) $4,855

17th century Spanish polychrome wood figure of St. John, 12½in. high. (Robert W. Skinner Inc.) $150

19th century American wooden butter stamp carved with a running fox, 2½in. diam. (Robert W. Skinner Inc.) $150

17th century Scandinavian carved burl tankard, thumbpiece in the form of a lion, 8in. high. (Robert W. Skinner Inc.) $700

19th century American wooden butter stamp with incised deer, 4in. diam. (Robert W. Skinner Inc.) $300

59

CARVED WOOD

19th century American wooden butter stamp of shell design, 3½in. diam. (Robert W. Skinner Inc.) $100

Late 19th century lesser yellowleg in original paint, 10½in. high. (Robert W. Skinner Inc.) $475

Scandinavian burrwood peg tankard with carved lid, 8¼in. high. (Burrows & Day) $435

Pair of Elizabethan boxwood nutcrackers, 1583, 4½in. high. (Lawrence Fine Art) $810

19th century Scandinavian painted bride's box of plywood strips, 17½in. long. (Robert W. Skinner Inc.) $450

One of a pair of early George III rococo giltwood wall brackets, circa 1750, 1ft.wide. (Sotheby's) $3,605

One of a pair of antique giltwood candle sconces. (J. M. Welch & Son) $345

17th century Flemish boxwood relief of Adam and Eve in the Garden of Eden, 14.5cm. wide. (Christie's) $2,745

Well-carved 19th century figurehead in the form of a maiden, with twisted iron chains, 42cm. high. (Osmond, Tricks) $545

Old oak wool winder with spindle and folding arm. (Butler & Hatch Waterman) $90

Early 20th century American painted and carved wood seagull, mounted on a board, 16½in. high. (Robert W. Skinner Inc.) $225

North American Indian carved wooden rattle, 1ft. long. (Stride & Son) $6,360

One of a pair of modern painted blackamoor torcheres on molded bases, 41in. high. (Sotheby's Belgravia) $925

One of a pair of 19th century carved carousel horses with brass harnesses and saddles, 46in. long. (Robert W. Skinner Inc.) $850

Scandinavian carved and painted mangling board, circa 1803, 26¼in. long.(Robert W. Skinner Inc.) $100

Adam period carved pine fire surround from Hemsworth Hall. (Phillips) $2,400

19th century American wooden oval butter stamp with carved eagle standing on a globe, initials on either side, 5½in. long. (Robert W. Skinner Inc.) $350

'Swiss Chalet' decanter case with hinged roof, circa 1900, 25½in. wide. (Sotheby's Belgravia) $105

CARVED WOOD

15th century North Italian polychrome oak group of St. Christopher and a child, 25½in. high. (Sotheby's) $1,455

Pair of early 18th century Liege fruitwood plaques, inscribed in ink on the back J. Vognoulle, 10¾in. wide. (Sotheby's) $3,430

Mid 17th century Flemish life-size figure of Cupid, in oak, 29¾in. high, sold with an oak column. (Sotheby's) $2,080

Cherrywood snuff rasp by Bagard of Nancy, circa 1687, 8in. high, grater missing. (Sotheby's) $1,350

Three late 17th century South German polychrome wood Nativity figures dated 1681. (Sotheby's) $1,975

16th century Malines oak group of Anna Selbdritt, 11½in. high, on later base. (Sotheby's) $2,080

One of two 17th century vertical carved wood panels, 16in. and 18½in. high. (Lawrence Fine Art) $305

Continental carved wood figure of a girl, on Victorian carved wood plinth. (Lawrence Fine Art) $1,075

One of three 17th/18th century carved oak panels, 17¾in. high. (Lawrence Fine Art) $195

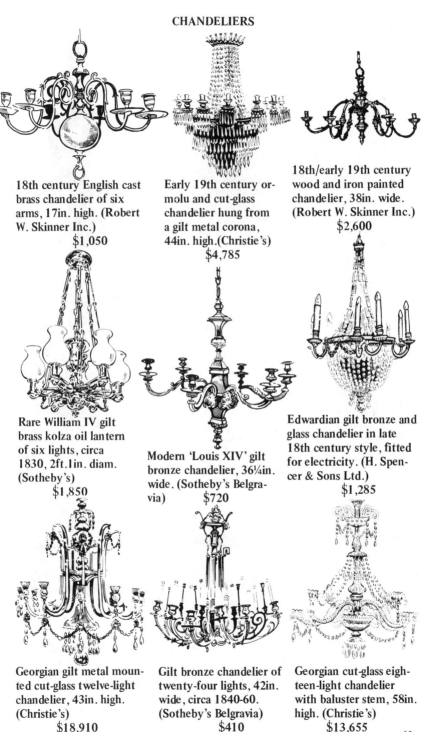

18th century English cast brass chandelier of six arms, 17in. high. (Robert W. Skinner Inc.)
$1,050

Early 19th century ormolu and cut-glass chandelier hung from a gilt metal corona, 44in. high.(Christie's)
$4,785

18th/early 19th century wood and iron painted chandelier, 38in. wide. (Robert W. Skinner Inc.)
$2,600

Rare William IV gilt brass kolza oil lantern of six lights, circa 1830, 2ft.1in. diam. (Sotheby's)
$1,850

Modern 'Louis XIV' gilt bronze chandelier, 36¼in. wide. (Sotheby's Belgravia)
$720

Edwardian gilt bronze and glass chandelier in late 18th century style, fitted for electricity. (H. Spencer & Sons Ltd.)
$1,285

Georgian gilt metal mounted cut-glass twelve-light chandelier, 43in. high. (Christie's)
$18,910

Gilt bronze chandelier of twenty-four lights, 42in. wide, circa 1840-60. (Sotheby's Belgravia)
$410

Georgian cut-glass eighteen-light chandelier with baluster stem, 58in. high. (Christie's)
$13,655

Newcomb pottery vase in blue, artist Leona Nicholson, circa 1903, 10½in. high. (Robert W. Skinner Inc.) $2,100

19th century American Rogers group 'Why Don't You Speak For Yourself John?' (Wm. Doyle Galleries Inc.) $550

Weller Sicardo vase, Fultonham, Ohio, circa 1905, 10½in. high. (Robert W. Skinner Inc.) $400

Newcomb pottery vase, New Orleans, circa 1910, signed A.S.F., 6in. high. (Robert W. Skinner Inc.) $200

19th century American glazed redware pottery jar with cover, 10in. high. (Robert W. Skinner Inc.) $130

Mid 19th century American stoneware decorated water cooler with domed cover, Pennsylvania, 21½in. high. (Robert W. Skinner Inc.) $500

Dedham pottery experimental vase, Massachusetts, circa 1895, 7½in. high. (Robert W. Skinner Inc.) $600

Wheatley pottery vase, Cincinnati, Ohio, circa 1880, 9in. high. (Robert W. Skinner Inc.)$175

19th century American glazed redware pottery jug with handle, 9in. high. (Robert W. Skinner Inc.) $160

Glazed earthenware musical jug, circa 1935, 10in. high. (Sotheby's Belgravia) $205

American double stoneware jug, 1830, with single handle. (Robert W. Skinner Inc.)$1,250

19th century stoneware decorated crock by Fulper Bros., Flemington, N.J., 10in. high. (Robert W. Skinner Inc.) $350

ANSBACH

Ansbach slop-bowl with trailing sprigs of leaves and flowers, circa 1770, 17cm. wide. (Sotheby's) $675

Ansbach shaped circular plate with Ozier rim, circa 1775, 23cm. diam. (Christie's) $590

Ansbach two-handled seau crenelle with gilt dentil rim, circa 1770, 17.5cm. wide. (Christie's) $1,570

ATTIC

Late 6th century B.C. black-figure amphora by the Red Line Painter, 11in. high. (Christie's) $2,910

Attic black-figure Lekythos by the Amasis Painter, circa 550 B.C., 6¾in. high. (Christie's) $4,365

Mid 5th century B.C. Attic red-figure neck amphora, slightly cracked, 10¾in. high. (Christie's) $3,120

BAYREUTH

Royal Bayreuth figural milk jug in the form of an eagle, circa 1900, 6¼in. high. (Robert W. Skinner Inc.)
$350

Royal Bayreuth sunbonnet baby's hair receiver, Germany, circa 1900, 2¾in. diam. (Robert W. Skinner Inc.) $100

Royal Bayreuth figural cream and sugar, circa 1900, 3½in. and 4½in. high. (Robert W. Skinner Inc.) $425

BELLARMINE

Small 17th century tigerware bellarmine bottle with gray beard mask and circular seal, 8½in. high. (Boardman's)
$275

17th century bellarmine flask with plain loop handle, 9¼in. high. (Sotheby, King & Chasemore)
$390

17th century Rhenish saltglaze bellarmine in mottled brown, 9¾in. high. (Sotheby's) $335

BELLEEK

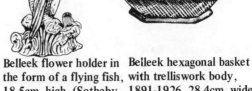

Early Belleek sweetmeat dish in the form of a clam shell, 9.5cm. high. (Sotheby, King & Chasemore) $55

Belleek flower holder in the form of a flying fish, 18.5cm. high. (Sotheby, King & Chasemore)
$185

Belleek hexagonal basket with trelliswork body, 1891-1926, 28.4cm. wide. (Sotheby's Belgravia)
$530

Early 18th century Berlin silver mounted white enamel snuff box, 2½in. wide, in the form of a tricorn hat.(Christie's) $1,350

One of a pair of Berlin royal presentation armorial quatrefoil sauce tureens and covers, circa 1775, 16.5cm. wide. (Christie's) $4,070

Berlin named view plate decorated with harvest scene, 9¾in. diam. (Sotheby's)$560

Mid 18th century Berlin pewter mounted faience tankard, with portrait of Frederick the Great, 23.5cm. high.(Sotheby's) $1,880

Pair of Berlin blackamoor sweetmeat dishes and covers, 18cm. high, late 19th century. (Sotheby, King & Chasemore) $770

Unusual K.P.M. Berlin biscuit porcelain figure 'The Blue Boy', 19in. high. (W. H. Lane & Son) $110

One of a pair of mid 19th century Berlin pot pourri vases and covers, 28cm. high. (Sotheby, King & Chasemore) $520

One of three Berlin armorial shaped circular dishes, circa 1775, 24cm. diam.(Christie's) $2,960

Late 19th century Continental plaque, probably Berlin, 16.5cm. high. (H. Spencer & Sons Ltd.) $675

67

One of a pair of rare Bow 'grotto' candlestick groups, circa 1765-70, 8¾in. high. (Sotheby's)$820

Early Bow group of a ewe and a lamb, circa 1750, 13.5cm. wide. (Sotheby, King & Chasemore) $295

Early Bow figure of a seated monk, circa 1755. (Sotheby, King & Chasemore) $165

Bow figure of a negress in Turkish dress, circa 1760, 18.5cm. high, hand slightly chipped. (Christie's)$1,015

One of a pair of Bow 'Birds in Branches' candlesticks, circa 1755-60, 9in. high. (Sotheby's) $2,645

Rare Bow flower vase and arrangement, circa 1765-70, 7¼in. high. (Sotheby's)$345

Bow figure of Harlequin in chequered suit, circa 1753, 12cm. high. (Christie's)$2,455

One of two Bow white groups of 'Birds in Branches', circa 1755-60, 6¼in. high. (Sotheby's) $775

Bow figure of a dancing girl in yellow hat, circa 1760, 18.5cm. high. (Christie's) $775

Bow figure of a pug dog, circa 1755, 6.5cm. high, (Sotheby, King & Chasemore) $485

Early white Bow figure of 'Hearing', circa 1755-60, 15cm. high. (Sotheby, King & Chasemore) $410

Bow triple salt painted in famille rose style, circa 1753, 13.5cm. wide. (Christie's) $650

One of two Bow hexagonal baluster vases painted in Kakiemon style, circa 1760, 24cm. high. (Christie's)$3,255

Early Bow cream jug with sparrow-beak spout, 3½in. high, circa 1755. (Sotheby's) $285

One of a pair of Bow figures of seated musicians, circa 1765, 18.5cm. high. (Christie's)$1,225

Signed Bow mug of bell shape, circa 1765, 3¾in. high. (Sotheby's) $610

Ormolu mounted Bow figure of a girl flanked by bullrushes, circa 1765, 21.5cm. high. (Christie's)$860

Bow white figure of a girl emblematic of Smell, circa 1755, 13cm. high. (Christie's)$735

Early Bow shell-bowl with ribbed body, circa 1752, 8½in. wide. (Sotheby's) $315

Four Bow figures of the Seasons, circa 1755, 5in. high, Summer and Spring restored. (Sotheby's) $995

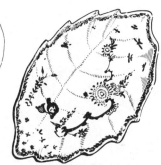

Bow bell-shaped mug with grooved loop handle, circa 1760, 6in. high. (Sotheby's) $795

Bow leaf-shaped dish, molded with ribbing and veining, circa 1760, 11¾in. long. (Sotheby's) $490

Bow mug of cylindrical shape with slightly flared base, circa 1755-60, 5¾in. high. (Sotheby's) $275

Rare Bow garniture of three frill vases and covers, circa 1765, slightly chipped. (Sotheby, King & Chasemore) $1,340

Early Bow coffee pot and cover of the 'Golfer and Caddy' pattern, circa 1752-55, 9in. high, slightly cracked. (Sotheby's) $2,985

English delft bough pot, probably Bristol, 8in. diam., circa 1765-70. (Sotheby's) $935

Bristol oval sauceboat with scroll handle, from Benjamin Lund's factory, 1749-51, 20.5cm. wide. (Christie's) $2,965

Bristol leaf-shaped pickle dish from Benjamin Lund's factory, 1749-51, 10cm. wide. (Christie's) $2,765

Bristol delft Adam and Eve charger with triangle pattern rim, circa 1730, 34cm. wide. (Christie's) $3,665

Bristol delft blue and white inscribed and dated oviform jug, 1730, 23.5cm. high. (Christie's) $2,660

Bristol delft blue and white plate with brick pattern rim, circa 1730, 21.5cm. diam. (Christie's) $385

One of a pair of Bristol pearlware documentary spirit barrels, 1834, 12cm. high.(Christie's) $975

Bristol delft plate with scalloped rim, 9in. diam., circa 1760. (Sotheby's) $205

Bristol delft tea caddy of octagonal form, circa 1760-70, 4¼in. high. (Sotheby's)$1,730

Adams silver mounted blue and white mug with angular handle, London, 1802, 12.5cm. high. (Christie's) $365

English porcelain whistle, circa 1820-30, 4.5cm. wide. (Sotheby, King & Chasemore) $240

Rare Lloyd, Shelton, figure of Queen Victoria and the Princess Royal, circa 1841, 17cm. high. (Sotheby's Belgravia) $245

Early 19th century sporting mug with foliate handle, 5¾in. high. (Sotheby Beresford Adams) $350

Dated creamware box and cover of circular shape, 1773, 3¼in. diam. (Sotheby's) $650

Documentary Billingsley Mansfield jug with two named views, signed, 6¾in. high. (Neales) $1,665

Late 19th century porcelain basket on pedestal, 8¼in. high. (Robert W. Skinner Inc.)$250

'Marriage Pattern' coffee cup, teacup and saucer of fluted form, circa 1775. (Phillips) $465

One of a pair of club-shaped ironstone vases with flared mouths, 15in. high. (Russell Baldwin & Bright)$935

Figure of M. Lind from the Alpha factory, circa 1847, 20cm. high. (Sotheby's Belgravia) $430

James Walford hand modeled pottery group of two figures, 26cm. wide. (Christie's) $350

18th century English creamware leech jar and cover, 40.5cm. high. (Phillips) $1,045

Early 18th century English wet-drug jar, 7¼in. high, slightly chipped. (Christie's)$530

Charger from an English ironstone dinner service of fifty-three pieces, circa 1810. (Sotheby, King & Chasemore) $760

English stoneware silver mounted tankard with grooved handle, circa 1710, 14.5cm. high. (Christie's) $860

Early English delft bowl, probably London, circa 1710-20, 10in. diam., slightly cracked. (Sotheby's) $975

One of a pair of English bough pots, circa 1800, on bun feet, 9½in. high. (Robert W. Skinner Inc.) $900

English delft tulip charger with blue-dash rim, 35.5cm. diam. (Phillips) $890

CANTON

CHINA

Large 18th century Canton blue and white basin, mounted, 28¼in. diam. (Wm. Doyle Galleries Inc.)
$2,900

One of a pair of near matching 19th century Canton candlesticks of inverted trumpet shape, 8½in. high. (Robert W. Skinner Inc.) $1,600

Canton porcelain bowl decorated in famille rose manner, 16in. diam. (Gilbert Baitson)
$605

One of a pair of 19th century Canton vases of flattened baluster form, 31cm. high. (H. Spencer & Sons Ltd.)
$780

One of a pair of 19th century Chinese Canton jars of hexagonal section, 11in. high. (W. H. Lane & Son) $210

One of a pair of Canton vases and covers with domed lids and lion handles, 52cm. high. (Sotheby's Belgravia)
$1,650

Cantonese vase of ovoid form with buddhist lion handles, 25½in. high. (Sotheby's) $810

One of a pair of Canton candlesticks with self tapering columns, 24.5cm. high. (Sotheby's Belgravia)
$405

Late 19th century Cantonese bulb pot and cover of flared form, 9½in. high. (Sotheby's)
$375

Set of four late 19th century Capodimonte figures of the seasons, 13¼in. high. (Sotheby, King & Chasemore) $780

Capodimonte (Carlo III) figure of a Callot dwarf in peaked hat, circa 1750, 8cm. high. (Christie's) $1,665

Capodimonte circular sugar bowl and cover, circa 1758, 10.5cm. diam. (Christie's) $8,165

Large Capodimonte porcelain table lamp with four dancing figures on base. (Honiton Galleries) $315

CAUGHLEY

Part of a Caughley part tea and coffee service of thirty-two pieces, painted in gray black and gilt. (H. Spencer & Sons Ltd.) $670

Part of a thirty-four-piece Caughley dessert service in underglaze blue and gold. (Phillips) $1,445

Chelsea leaf dish molded as two lettuce leaves, circa 1755, 25.5cm. wide. (Christie's) $450

Chelsea baluster coffee cup and saucer with gilt dentil rims, circa 1760. (Christie's) $855

Chelsea fluted leaf-shaped cream jug, red anchor mark, circa 1753, 11cm. wide. (Christie's) $5,290

Chelsea gold mounted baluster scent bottle and butterfly stopper, circa 1755, 9cm. high. (Christie's) $650

Pair of Chelsea sweetmeat dishes in the form of a gallant and his companion, 17.5cm. high. (Sotheby, King & Chasemore) $1,685

Chelsea figure of a begging pug bitch, gold anchor mark, circa 1760, 9cm. high.(Christie's) $1,730

Chelsea molded plate painted with an exotic bird, circa 1758, 22cm. diam (Christie's)$530

One of a pair of Chelsea candlestick figures, circa 1760-65, 11¾in. high. (Sotheby's) $775

Chelsea plate painted with a border of birds, circa 1760, 21.5cm. diam. (Christie's) $530

One of a pair of Chelsea fluted beakers with chocolate line rims, circa 1752, 6.5cm. high. (Christie's) $4,475

Chelsea silver-shaped oval dish, red anchor mark, circa 1753, 21cm. wide. (Christie's) $1,465

One of a pair of Chelsea Derby porcelain shaped circular shallow dishes, 7¾in. diam. (Geering & Colyer) $590

Chelsea 'sunflower' dish, 9in. wide, circa 1752-56. (Sotheby's) $530

Chelsea figure of Pu-Tau Ho-Shang, 1746-49, 8cm. high. (Christie's) $3,070

Chelsea botanical dish painted with a leafy branch, circa 1755, 10½in. diam. (Sotheby's) $2,240

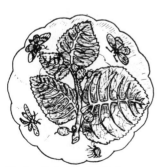

Chelsea lobed botanical dish painted with leaves and insects, circa 1755, 20.5cm. diam. (Christie's) $1,740

Chelsea chinoiserie group of a lady and child scribe, circa 1758, 17.5cm. high. (Christie's) $2,150

Rare Chelsea famille rose fluted dish, 7in. diam., circa 1745-52. (Sotheby's) $1,140

One of two Tongzhi blue and white saucer dishes on wood stands, 15.5cm. diam. (Christie's)
$340

19th century Chinese rose medallion teapot with high domed cover, 10in. high. (Robert W. Skinner Inc.)
$500

Chinese Wanli plate decorated with dragons and flowers, 8in. diam. (J. M. Welch & Son)
$14,105

Mid 19th century rose medallion garden seat of barrel form, 18in. high. (Robert W. Skinner Inc.)
$2,500

One of a pair of 19th century Chinese export porcelain, teak framed panels, 13¾in. square. (Robert W. Skinner Inc.) $900

19th century Chinese garden seat of hexagonal form, sides and top with pierced medallions, 18½in. high. (Robert W. Skinner Inc.) $1,700

19th century Chinese rose medallion vase with flaring top, 13½in. high. (Robert W. Skinner Inc.)$375

Large Doucai dish, encircled Yongzheng six-character mark, 48cm. diam.(Christie's)
$1,350

19th century Chinese Mandarin temple vase with shaped rim, 24½in. high.(Robert W. Skinner Inc.)
$500

One of a pair of late Qing dynasty inlaid black lacquer boxes and covers, 35.5cm. diam. (Christie's) $1,530 ᴕᴕᴜ

One of a pair of antique Chinese containers of flattened gourd shape. (Butler & Hatch Waterman) $380

One of a pair of early 19th century blue and white cache-pots on pedestal bases, 14½in. diam. (Locke & England)$1,020

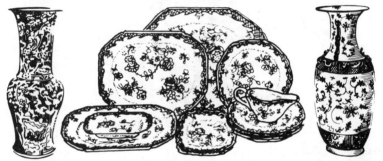

Famille noire vase painted with birds flying amongst flowers, 57cm. high. (Sotheby's Belgravia) $2,685

Fifteen pieces of late 18th/ early 19th century Chinese porcelain. (Lacy Scott) $1,035

19th century Chinese porcelain temple vase of baluster form with flared rim, 24in. high. (Robert W. Skinner Inc.) $650

19th century Chinese pottery garden seat on hexagonal paneled base, 19¾in. high. (Robert W. Skinner Inc.) $150

Tang dynasty unglazed buff pottery figure of a guardian, 40cm. high. (Christie's)$935

Transitional blue and white oviform jar, circa 1640, 24cm. high. (Christie's) $575

CHINESE

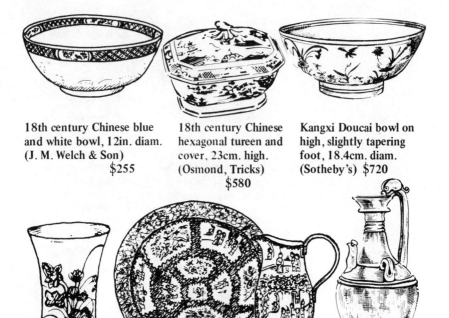

18th century Chinese blue
and white bowl, 12in. diam.
(J. M. Welch & Son)
$255

18th century Chinese
hexagonal tureen and
cover, 23cm. high.
(Osmond, Tricks)
$580

Kangxi Doucai bowl on
high, slightly tapering
foot, 18.4cm. diam.
(Sotheby's) $720

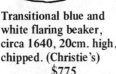

Transitional blue and
white flaring beaker,
circa 1640, 20cm. high,
chipped. (Christie's)
$775

19th century Chinese rose medallion pitcher and bowl decorated
on gold ground.(Robert W. Skinner Inc.) $775

Rare Sui dynasty
'chicken head'
ewer with double
lug handles, 44cm.
high.(Sotheby's)
$34,970

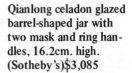

18th/19th century tur-
quoise-glazed pilgrim
bottle applied with scroll
handles, 29cm. high.
(Christie's) $810

Wucai dragon and phoenix
saucer dish with foot rim,
32.1cm. diam., decorated
in famille verte.(Sotheby's)
$3,910

Qianlong celadon glazed
barrel-shaped jar with
two mask and ring han-
dles, 16.2cm. high.
(Sotheby's)$3,085

Newport pottery 'bizarre' crocus vase by Clarice Cliff, 31cm. high, 1930's.(Sotheby's Belgravia)$150

Newport pottery 'Fantasque' two-person breakfast set, designed by Clarice Cliff, 1930's. (Sotheby's Belgravia) $1,280

Newport pottery vase designed by Clarice Cliff, 1930's, 29cm. high.(Sotheby's Belgravia)$260

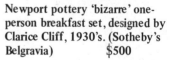

Newport pottery 'bizarre' two-person breakfast set, designed by Clarice Cliff, 1930's. (Sotheby's Belgravia)$535

Newport pottery 'bizarre' one-person breakfast set, designed by Clarice Cliff, 1930's. (Sotheby's Belgravia) $500

Wilkinson Ltd. 'bizarre' lemonade set of seven pieces, 1930's, designed by Clarice Cliff.(Sotheby's Belgravia)$720

Part of an eighteen-piece table set by Wilkinson Ltd., 1930's, designed by Clarice Cliff. (Sotheby's Belgravia) $400

Newport pottery 'biz-arre' coffee pot, desig-ned by Clarice Cliff, 1930's, 19cm. high. (Sotheby's Belgravia) $200

Coalport Election jug, commemorating the Shropshire General Election, of 1841, 23cm. high.(Phillips)$580

Part of a Coalport part dessert service of twenty-one pieces, circa 1910. (Sotheby Beresford Adams)　$775

Coalport lamp base, circa 1900, 5½in. high. (Sotheby's Belgravia)　$280

One of a pair of Coalport named view vases and covers, circa 1910, 17½in. high. (Sotheby Beresford Adams)　$445

Garniture of three English bone china vases in Empire style, probably Coalport. (H. Spencer & Sons Ltd.)　$600

One of a pair of Coalport two-handled vases of ovoid pedestal form, 31cm. high. (H. Spencer & Sons Ltd.)　$730

Part of a Coalport sea-green-ground part dessert service, circa 1820. (Christie's)　$2,850

Teapot from an early Coalport tea and coffee service, early 19th century, twenty-two pieces in all. (Sotheby's)　$425

Coalport blue-ground part dessert service painted with flowers, circa 1820. (Christie's) $3,055

Unusual 'Albert' plate molded in light relief, circa 1840, 18.1cm. diam. (Sotheby's Belgravia) $220

'Queen Caroline' jug bat-printed in black with two portraits, circa 1820, 8.8cm. high. (Sotheby's Belgravia) $255

'Queen Caroline' plaque of rectangular shape, circa 1820, 11.2cm. wide. (Sotheby's Belgravia) $305

Rare 'Victoria R.' jug, possibly Scottish, with faceted body, circa 1838, 17.5cm. high. (Sotheby's Belgravia) $255

One of a rare pair of commemorative children's plates, circa 1840, 13.2cm. diam. (Sotheby's Belgravia) $430

Commemorative mug made for the Coronation of Queen Victoria, 1838, restored, 8.8cm. high. (Sotheby's Belgravia) $890

Mug made to commemorate the Coronation of Queen Victoria. (Sotheby's Belgravia) $1,090

Very rare commemorative bowl made for Seven Incorporations of Dumfries, circa 1820-25, 18.3cm. diam. (Sotheby's Belgravia) $140

Unusual commemorative mug showing Queen Victoria and Prince Albert, 1840, 12.5cm. wide. (Sotheby's Belgravia) $295

18th century Staffordshire slipware dish with dark-brown-ground, 43.5cm. wide. (Sotheby, King & Chasemore)$1,040

Rare Staffordshire pearlware commemorative bowl, circa 1793, 8¾in. diam. (Sotheby's) $435

Commemorative mug made for the Coronation of Queen Victoria, 1838, 8cm. high. (Sotheby's Belgravia) $980

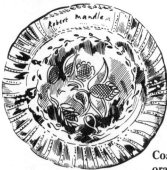

Rare late 18th century American commemorative earthenware dish, 14¾in. diam. (Sotheby's) $235

Coalport jug, commemorating the Shropshire Election of 1841, 29cm. high. (Phillips) $580

Rare Dutch commemorative plate with portraits of William IV, Princess Anne and Princess Caroline, 1747, 22.5cm. diam. (Phillips) $1,545

Rare and very large commemorative punchbowl, 1743, 15½in. diam. (Sotheby's) $690

Very rare commemorative shaving bowl and stand, 1840, for the marriage of Victoria and Albert. (Sotheby's Belgravia) $530

Pearlware teapot and cover depicting the Battle of Trafalgar, circa 1806-10, 4¾in. high. (Sotheby's) $305

Mid 19th century Copeland plaque painted with a view of the Bay of Naples, 30cm. wide. (Sotheby's Belgravia) $345

Copeland cow creamer, date code for 1884, 14.5cm. high. (Sotheby, King & Chasemore) $390

Copeland commemorative tyg painted with panels of Queen Victoria, Britannia, etc., 1900, 14cm. high. (Sotheby's Belgravia) $285

Late 19th century Copeland parian figure of 'Corinna, the Lyric Muse', 55cm. high, slightly cracked. (Sotheby, King & Chasemore) $215

Part of a large 19th century Copeland late Spode dinner service of eighty-three pieces. (Dickinson, Davy & Markham) $195

COPER

Hans Coper stoneware vase of oval section, circa 1970, 21cm. high. (Christie's) $3,660

Hans Coper stoneware vase with spade-shaped body in stone-gray glaze, circa 1968, 49.8cm. high. (Christie's) $12,810

Hans Coper stoneware vase of rectangular oval section, in milky white glaze, 23cm. high. (Christie's) $4,575

DAOGUANG

Daoguang dragon bowl with green enamel decoration, 12cm. diam. (Sotheby's Belgravia) $445

One of a pair of Daoguang famille rose vases, 21.8cm. high. (Sotheby's Belgravia) $375

One of a pair of Daoguang famille rose bowls, 13.7cm. diam. (Sotheby's) $1,335

Daoguang small drum-shaped garden seat in famille rose enamels, 21.5cm. high.(Sotheby, King & Chasemore) $610

Attractive Daoguang cloisonne bowl on blue-ground, 28cm. diam. (Sotheby's Belgravia) $382

Rare Daoguang dated blue and white water jar and cover in bucket shape, 23.2cm. high. (Sotheby's) $14,400

DAVENPORT

Early 19th century Davenport stone china dessert set. (Lacy Scott)$665
86

One of a pair of Davenport oviform vases with caryatid handles, circa 1820, 24.5cm. high. (Christie's) $935

Part of a Davenport pearlware botanical part dessert service, circa 1815, sixteen pieces in all. (Christie's)$2,850

18th century Dutch Delft plate with blue rim, 9in. diam. (Robert W. Skinner Inc.) $100

Dutch Delft tobacco jar painted in blue, circa 1750, 10¾in. high. (Sotheby's) $520

18th century Dutch Delft charger with central reserve of cornflower and fern spray, 13¾in. diam. (Robert W. Skinner Inc.) $325

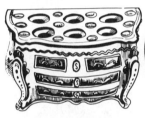

19th century Dutch Delft bulb pot with blue, yellow and green decoration, 9¾in. long. (Robert W. Skinner Inc.) $375

Mid 18th century Dutch Delft 'peacock pattern' dish, 13½in. diam., slightly chipped. (Sotheby's) $165

Mid 18th century Dutch Delft plaque of shaped oval form, 23.5cm. wide. (Sotheby's) $870

One of a pair of Dutch Delft plates in Wanli style, 10in. diam., early 18th century. (Sotheby Beresford Adams) $295

18th century Dutch Delft tobacco jar decorated in blue, 36.5cm. high. (Sotheby's) $695

18th century Dutch Delft charger, 13¼in. diam. (Robert W. Skinner Inc.) $425

87

DELLA ROBBIA

CHINA

Della Robbia vase with three tubular loop handles, galleon D. R. and artist's initials on base, 32cm. high. (Phillips) $250

Della Robbia vase of pear shape with two loop handles, circa 1898, 14¼in. high. (Sotheby's) $605

Della Robbia pottery vase decorated by Cassandia Ann Walker, 1903, 10in. high. (Phillips) $660

DE MORGAN

De Morgan dish painted by Charles Passenger in crimson and mushroom, 39.7cm. diam.(Sotheby's Belgravia) $515

De Morgan two-handled oviform vase with garlic neck, 44cm. high. (Christie's) $60

De Morgan jardiniere, bell body with twin lug handles, 21.5cm. high. (Sotheby's Belgravia) $540

Unusual De Morgan vase, incised by Farini, 1890, 21.3cm. high. (Sotheby's Belgravia) $455

Late Fulham period De Morgan lustre dish painted in ruby and salmon pink, circa 1900, 36.6cm. diam.(Sotheby's Belgravia) $295

William De Morgan oviform vase painted by Joe Juster, 15cm. high. (Phillips) $660

Rare Royal Derby min-
iature coal scuttle of
helmet shape, dated
for 1912, 2¼in. high.
(Sotheby Beresford
Adams) $220

Derby circular basket with
pierced trellis sides and
rope-twist handles, circa
1758, 6¾in. wide.(Sotheby's)
$1,355

Royal Crown Derby min-
iature teapot and cover,
2in. high, dated for 1913.
(Sotheby Beresford
Adams) $205

Set of four Derby porcelain figures of the Four Seasons attributed to Pierre
Stephan, circa 1780, 16 to 17cm. high. (Sotheby, King & Chasemore)
$930

Bloor Derby cow creamer,
15cm. high. (Sotheby,
King & Chasemore)
$390

One of a pair of Derby ice pails
and covers with campana-shaped bodies, circa 1815, 40cm.
high. (Sotheby, King & Chasemore) $645

Derby plate, painted by
William Slater Snr., circa
1825, 23cm. diam.
(Sotheby, King & Chase-
more) $465

89

DERBY

One of a pair of Derby two-handled vases decorated by Richard Dodson, 18cm. high. (Phillips) $925

Early 19th century Derby whistle, 4.5cm. wide. (Sotheby, King & Chasemore) $370

Fine Derby sucrier of deep U-shape, circa 1790, 2¾in. high. (Sotheby's) $1,560

Derby plate, decorated with a view of Worcester. (Christie's S. Kensington) $275

Derby crested mask jug, spout modeled as Admiral Rodney, circa 1770, 24.5cm. high.(Christie's) $735

Derby documentary oval plaque with portrait of Shakespeare, 1839, 10.5cm. high, in giltwood frame. (Christie's) $815

Early 19th century Derby cow creamer, 16cm. high. (Sotheby, King & Chasemore) $370

Pair of Derby figures of a gallant and companion, circa 1760, 22cm. high. (Christie's) $735

Royal Derby Imari miniature vase of pear shape, 4in. high, dated for 1908. (Sotheby Beresford Adams)$240

90

One of a pair of Derby oval sauce tureens and covers, circa 1813, 7.5cm. wide.(Christie's) $1,015

Bloor Derby cylindrical mug decorated with flowers, circa 1815, 12.5cm. high.(Christie's) $755

One of a pair of oval Derby two-handled Monteiths with shell handles, circa 1790, 26.5cm. wide. (Christie's) $915

Derby figure of a street vendor modeled as a girl with a basket, circa 1760, 22cm. high. (Christie's) $895

Early Derby figure of a wild boar, circa 1755, 12.7cm. wide. (Sotheby, King & Chasemore) $160

Derby blue and white shell centerpiece by Wm. Duesbury & Co., circa 1770, 21.5cm. high.(Christie's)$820

Derby centerpiece and stand surmounted by a figure of Neptune, 43.5cm. high, circa 1768.(Christie's) $1,535

Pair of Derby figures of a shepherd and his companion, circa 1765, 23cm. high. (Christie's) $1,630

Unusual Crown Derby pierced vase and cover, 13½in. high. (Hall Wateridge & Owen) $445

DERBY

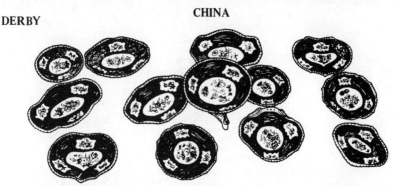

Part of a sixty-three-piece Crown Derby dessert service, circa 1815-30.
(W. H. Lane & Son) $2,115

DOUCAI

Rare Doucai vase of com-
pressed baluster form,
21.8cm. high.(Sotheby's)
$3,700

Early 18th century Doucai
saucer dish, encircled
Chenghua character mark,
15.5cm. diam. (Christie's)
$680

Fine Doucai vase of well
potted pear shape, with
tall narrow neck, 28.6cm.
high. (Sotheby's)
$74,050

DOULTON

Doulton stoneware beaker,
showing golfers, circa
1900, 4¾in. high.
(Sotheby's) $185

Royal Doulton and Rix
patent 'marqueterie'
bowl with lobed rim,
circa 1900, 30.8cm.
diam. (Sotheby's Bel-
gravia) $350

Doulton stoneware fig-
ure of a merry musician
by G. Tinworth, circa
1895, 12cm. high.
(Sotheby, King & Chase-
more) $500

92

Doulton pottery study of Adam and Eve by Mark V. Marshall, signed and dated 1878, 17in. high.(Sotheby's) $3,700

Royal Doulton 'flambe' shallow circular bowl on pedestal foot, 18cm. diam. (Christie's) $275

Doulton stoneware loving cup with cricketing subject, 1882, 6in. high. (Sotheby's) $875

Royal Doulton stoneware slender oviform vase by Frank A. Butler, 41cm. high. (Christie's)$275

Rare Doulton character jug of Field Marshall Smuts, circa 1946-48. (Dee & Atkinson) $980

Rare Royal Doulton Titanianware figure of 'Blighty', 1920's, 29cm. high. (Sotheby, King & Chasemore)$745

One of a pair of Doulton stoneware baluster vases by Hannah Barlow and Francis Lee, 30.5cm. high. (Christie's) $695

Royal Doulton 'flambe' carp, painted by Noke, 31cm. high.(Christie's) $510

One of a pair of Doulton stoneware beakers showing cricketers, circa 1900, 4¾in. high. (Sotheby's)$520

CHINA

Royal Doulton 'flambe' model of a sparrow, 5.5cm. high, roundel mark. (Phillips) $195

Unusual Royal Doulton 'Sung' vase, painted by Arthur Charles Eaton, 25cm. high, impressed 6-25. (Phillips) $1,345

Doulton stoneware figure of a merry musician modeled by George Tinworth, circa 1895, 10cm. high. (Sotheby, King & Chasemore) $1,490

Royal Doulton earthenware vase by Florence Barlow, on muddy brown ground, circa 1910, 20.5cm. high. (Sotheby, King & Chasemore) $220

Doulton figure of Folly, circa 1929-38, 22.5cm. high. (Phillips) $715

One of a pair of 19th century Royal Doulton vases, decorated by Hannah Barlow, 10¼in. high. (Sotheby Beresford Adams) $630

Royal Doulton group 'The Return of Persephone', dated for 1919, 16½in. high. (Sotheby Beresford Adams) $1,480

Royal Doulton figure of Annabella designed by L. Harradine, dated for 1939, 13.5cm. high. (Phillips) $285

Rare Royal Doulton figure 'The Prince of Wales', 19cm. high, dated for 1936. (Phillips)$715

Royal Doulton twin-hand-
led loving cup 'The Three
Musketeers', 25cm. high.
(Phillips) $395

Royal Doulton 'flambe'
model of an alsation
sitting upright, 9cm.
high, roundel mark.
(Phillips) $320

Doulton Lambeth stone-
ware group 'The Cockneys
at Brighton', as a family of
brown mice, 14cm. long,
1886. (Phillips)$570

Doulton Lambeth vase
by Mary Mitchell, 1881,
unsigned, 27cm. high.
(Phillips) $270

Royal Doulton figure of
Lady Anne Nevill, desig-
ned by Margaret Davies,
1948, 25cm. high.
(Phillips) $500

One of a pair of late 19th
century Royal Doulton
vases in Art Deco style,
18¾in. high. (Sotheby
Beresford Adams)
                        $575

Royal Doulton 'Sung'
vase, painted by Arthur
Charles Eaton, 33cm.
high. (Phillips)
                $535

Early Doulton stoneware candlestick group, 1879, 16cm.
high. (Sotheby, King & Chasemore) $485

Rare Royal Doulton
character jug of Field-
Marshall Smuts, 1946,
17cm. high. (Phillips)
$1,110

DRESDEN

One of a pair of Dresden vases by Carl Thierne, 22½in. high. (Sotheby's)
$1,000

Pair of Dresden candlestick figures of a gardener and a laundry maid, 11½in. high. (Dickinson, Davy & Markham)
$295

Late 19th century Dresden gilt metal mounted tankard, 25cm. high. (Sotheby's Belgravia)
$390

Dresden plaque painted with 'The German Bride', circa 1880, framed, 20.8 x 16cm. (Sotheby's Belgravia)
$2,570

One of a pair of late 19th century Dresden 'schneeballen' vases and covers, 57cm. high. (Sotheby's Belgravia) $1,540

Late 19th century Dresden plaque, framed, 24 x 14.4cm. (Sotheby's Belgravia) $1,235

Tall Dresden comport with pierced and shaped circular bowl on a slender stem, 18½in. high. (Dickinson, Davy & Markham) $370
96

Mid to late 19th century Dresden snuff box of bombe shape, with gilt metal mounts. (Sotheby's Belgravia)
$825

Dresden 'Naples' sedan chair, sides and door inset with beveled glass windows, circa 1900, 28cm. high. (Sotheby's Belgravia) $495

Glazed earthenware garden seat modeled as an elephant, in polychrome enamels, 21in. high. (Edgar Horn) $150

Nishida earthenware bowl, interior painted with warriors, circa 1870's, 31cm. diam. (Sotheby's Belgravia) $500

Fine Sylvestrie pottery figure of an eagle owl, 37in. long. (Sotheby, King & Chasemore) $955

Earthenware vase with baluster body, circa 1900, 24.5cm. high. (Sotheby's Belgravia) $240

Hododa Kinkozan earthenware vase in the form of a phoenix, 1890, 14.5cm. high. (Sotheby's Belgravia) $395

One of a pair of earthenware vases, painted and gilt with panels of Samurai, 37cm. high, circa 1900. (Sotheby's Belgravia) $1,040

Mid 19th century Unzan koro and cover in earthenware, with hexagonal body, 13cm. high. (Sotheby's Belgravia) $215

Earthenware kettle and cover painted with panels of Samurai in gardens, circa 1900, 13cm. high. (Sotheby's Belgravia) $325

Amphora earthenware vase with shaped neck, 40.25cm. high, circa 1900. (Sotheby's Belgravia) $260

97

Copenhagen stoneware figure of a child with a cat, modeled by Knud Kyhn. (Christie's) $165

Rare Bottger porcelain bowl decorated in Holland in Kakiemon manner, early 18th century, 21cm. diam. (Sotheby's) $4,790

European majolica covered cheese dish, circa 1880, in the form of a grass hut, 13½in. high. (Robert W. Skinner Inc.) $340

Late 19th century European hand-painted porcelain plate with cobalt blue rim, 15in. diam. (Robert W. Skinner Inc.) $200

Small pair of 19th century Continental porcelain candlesticks depicting Summer and Winter. (May, Whetter & Grose) $340

One of a pair of Companiedes-Indes blue and white plates, painted with a tree peony. (Sotheby, King & Chasemore) $275

One of a pair of large vases by Clement Massier. (Phillips) $35

One of two European porcelain figural groups playing music, 20th century, 7 and 7½in. high. (Robert W. Skinner Inc.) $250

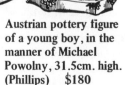

Austrian pottery figure of a young boy, in the manner of Michael Powolny, 31.5cm. high. (Phillips) $180

Mid 18th century European tin-glazed tureen and cover in the form of a bunch of asparagus, 16.5cm. wide. (Sotheby, King & Chasemore) $680

Late 19th century Austrian porcelain plaque, in brass frame, 10in. high. (Robert W. Skinner Inc.) $325

Early 19th century Continental porcelain chocolate pot with angular handle, 8in. high. (Wm. Doyle Galleries Inc.) $350

Continental amphora jardiniere, circa 1900, 16½in. high. (Sotheby Beresford Adams) $150

Pair of Hochst figures of a boy and a girl, circa 1780, 13.5cm. high.(Sotheby's) $1,685

Late 19th century European porcelain ewer with applied figures, 26½in. high. (Robert W. Skinner Inc.) $500

Large Continental vase painted by T. Leroy, signed, 1890's, 87.5cm. high. (Sotheby's Belgravia) $700

One of a pair of oval Berlin dishes with gilt athemion wells, circa 1820, 45cm. wide. (Christie's) $1,200

One of a pair of late 19th century Samson 'Derby' candlesticks, 26cm. high, chipped. (Sotheby's Belgravia) $660

CHINA

FAMILLE NOIRE

Qing dynasty famille noire square tapering vase, enameled on a black ground, 49cm. high. (Christie's)$735

18th century famille noire porcelain vase of baluster form, 52cm. high. (Sotheby's Belgravia) $565

19th century famille noire baluster vase with flaring neck, 59.5cm. high. (Christie's) $695

FAMILLE ROSE

Famille rose lemon-ground globular vase with detachable neck, 27.5cm. high. (Christie's)$1,910

19th century famille rose yellow-ground fish bowl, with wood stand, 46cm. diam. (Christie's) $485

One of a pair of Canton famille rose baluster vases and domed covers, 50.5cm. high.(Christie's) $1,160

One of a pair of famille rose garden seats of hexagonal section, 47cm. high, wood stands. (Sotheby's Belgravia) $1,485

One of a pair of famille rose armorial soup plates, circa 1750, 22.5cm. diam. (Christie's) $635

One of a pair of famille rose vases and covers, enameled with flowers and foliage, 28cm. high. (Sotheby's Belgravia) $595

FAMILLE VERTE

CHINA

FAMILLE VERTE

Large Kangxi famille verte saucer dish, damaged and repaired, 52cm. diam. (Christie's) $1,255

Continental famille verte vase on wood stand, circa 1900, 54cm. high. (Sotheby's Belgravia) $805

Famille verte jardiniere painted with storks among reeds, 50.5cm. diam., on wood stand.(Christie's) $3,500

FRANKENTHAL

Frankenthal mythological figure of the Rape of Prosperine, modeled by J. F. Luck, circa 1756, 28cm. high.(Christie's) $2,035

Rare Frankenthal figure of a poultry girl, by Adam Bauer, 13.5cm. high. (Phillips) $1,000

Rare Frankenthal group of musicians, modeled by J. F. Luck, circa 1755-59, 23cm. high.(Sotheby's) $4,750

Frankenthal ornithological plate painted with a grouse, circa 1756-59, 24cm. diam. (Christie's) $1,185

Early Frankenthal arched rectangular tea caddy and cover painted with large birds, circa 1756, 16cm. high. (Christie's) $830

Frankenthal cup and saucer decorated with landscapes, 1781. (Sotheby's) $405

FRENCH

19th century French plate on blue and gilt ground, Paris, 1823, 9¼in. diam. (W. H. Lane & Son)$110

CHINA

Rare Chantilly figure of a Chinaman, circa 1735-40, 14cm. high, damaged. (Sotheby's) $4,950

One of a pair of French porcelain cache pots, late 19th century, 16cm. high. (H. Spencer & Sons Ltd.) $745

19th century Sevres pedestal ovoid vase with ormolu top, 71cm. high. (H. Spencer & Sons Ltd.) $680

Late 19th century Limoges porcelain tea service with gilt floral details. (Robert W. Skinner Inc.) $200

Late 18th century French faience wine cistern. (Sotheby's) $4,225

One of a pair of Second Empire green fluorspar vases with ormolu mounts, circa 1870, 14½in. high. (Sotheby, King & Chasemore) $1,395

Pair of French figures of a young man and woman, circa 1900, 67.5 and 65.5cm. high. (Sotheby's Belgravia) $1,890

Vincennes jug with elaborate gilt border, circa 1750-55, 23.5cm. high. (Sotheby's) $990

102

One of a pair of late 19th century French vases, 19in. high, slightly damaged. (Sotheby's)$310

Rare mid 18th century Chantilly double salt and pepper box in three sections, 25cm. wide. (Sotheby's) $595

French Art Pottery vase of bulbous form, circa 1910, 10¼in. high. (Robert W. Skinner Inc.) $325

Galle faience seated cat with black glazed body, 33cm. high. (Christie's) $1,340

FUKAGAWA

20th century French porcelain covered urns with domed tops, 13¼in. high. (Robert W. Skinner Inc.) $125

French Doccia figure of a girl on a rock, damaged, circa 1780, 15cm. high.(Sotheby's) $845

One of a pair of Fukagawa vases with colored red enamels, circa 1900, 13in. high. (Sotheby's) $665

Fukagawa bowl of squat form, circa 1900, 9½in. high. (Sotheby's) $560

One of a pair of Fukagawa Imari bottle vases with red grounds, circa 1900, 30cm. high. (Sotheby's) $405

103

CHINA

One of two Loosdrecht shaped oval quatrefoil trencher salts, circa 1770, 9.5cm. wide. (Christie's)$350

Pair of German biscuit figures, 1873, 17in. high. (Sotheby's) $460

One of a pair of late 19th century Helena Wolfsohn seaux crenelles, 27.5cm. wide. (Sotheby's Belgravia) $355

Large late 19th century Potschappel vase, cover and stand, applied with nymphs, 82cm. high. (Sotheby's Belgravia) $1,130

Mid 19th century German plaque painted with two ladies, framed, 17.5 x 13.5cm. (Sotheby's Belgravia) $1,440

Mid 19th century German porcelain egg supported on three scrolled feet, 5in. high. (Robert W. Skinner Inc.) $475

Late 19th century German porcelain epergne, embossed with flowers, 18in. high, damaged. (J. M. Welch & Son) $365

Late 19th century German figure of a seated Maltese terrier, decorated in shades of brown, 19cm. high. (H. Spencer & Sons Ltd.) $595

Late 19th century German porcelain figural piece, slightly damaged, 5½in. high. (Robert W. Skinner Inc.) $350

German sweetmeat dish divided into six sections with ruffled rim, 10¼in. wide. (Robert W. Skinner Inc.) $50

Amstel circular sugar bowl and cover with acorn finial, circa 1780, 11cm. high. (Christie's) $175

19th century German inlaid panel depicting Abraham and Isaac, 61cm. high. (Osmond, Tricks) $220

Mennecy figure of a Turk carrying a cap and two bags, circa 1750, 16cm. high. (Christie's) $740

Plaue-on-Havel frog band of six pieces, circa 1900. (Sotheby's Belgravia) $580

Plaue centerpiece with pierced detachable bowl on a tree trunk stem, circa 1900, 40.5cm. high.(Sotheby's Belgravia) $270

Late 18th century German enameled pocket telescope, 2in. diam.(Christie's) $720

Part of a Furstenberg part coffee service of twelve pieces decorated with flowers, circa 1775. (Sotheby's) $1,880

German stoneware jardiniere and stand. (Allen & May) $615

105

GOLDSCHEIDER

One of two pottery figures of negro musicians, probably by Goldscheider. (Phillips)
$3,170

Goldscheider earthenware figure after a model by Lorenzl, 1920's, 24.25cm. (Sotheby's Belgravia)
$240

Goldscheider cold-painted low-fired figure of a fairy, modeled by E. Tell, circa 1900, 76.25cm. high. (Sotheby's Belgravia)
$640

Goldscheider pottery figure of a young girl with flowers, 39.8cm. high. (Christie's) $785

Small Goldscheider earthenware 'bat girl', 1920's, 21.5cm. high. (Sotheby's Belgravia)
$320

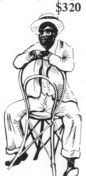

Goldscheider earthenware nude figure holding a blue cloak, 1930's, 41.75cm. high.(Sotheby's Belgravia) $620

Goldscheider earthenware mask, modeled as a woman, 1920's, 30.5cm. high. (Sotheby's Belgravia) $195

Large porcelain figure by Friedrich Goldscheider of a young man seated on a chair, 21in. high. (Phillips & Jolly)
$1,765

Goldscheider 'bat girl' with winged cape, 1930's, 46.25cm. high.(Sotheby's Belgravia) $1,040

Goss model of the birthplace of Thomas Hardy, 4in. long. (Lawrence Fine Art) $395

Late 19th century Goss parian figure of 'The Devil Looking Over Lincoln', 14.5cm. high. (Sotheby's Belgravia) $105

Early 20th century Goss model of the Feathers Hotel, Ledbury, 11.6cm. wide. (Sotheby's Belgravia) $1,065

Goss bust 'My Beautiful Duchess', color decoration, restored. (Phillips) $985

Rare Goss parian bust of 'The Veiled Bride', circa 1865, 26cm. high. (Sotheby's Belgravia) $475

Rare late 19th century Goss figure of Lady Betty with flowers and a shawl, 6¾in. high. (Sotheby's) $125

Early 20th century Goss model of Thomas Hardy's birthplace, 9.9cm. (Sotheby's Belgravia) $285

Early 20th century Goss model of John Bunyan's House, unglazed, 6cm. (Sotheby's Belgravia) $1,025

Early 20th century Goss model of Portman Lodge, 8.5cm. (Sotheby's Belgravia) $325

107

GOSS

CHINA

Early 20th century Goss oven, unglazed, 7.6cm., slightly discolored. (Sotheby's Belgravia) $225

Goss colored parian bust of 'Peeping Tom of Coventry', 11.4cm. high, dated 1893. (Sotheby's Belgravia) $165

Early 20th century Goss model of Dove Cottage, Grasmere, 10.1cm. (Sotheby's Belgravia) $470

Goss parian bust of General Gordon, square base titled, dated 1885, 18.5cm. high. (Sotheby's Belgravia) $185

Early 20th century Goss model of Izaak Walton's birthplace, Shallowford, 9.1cm. wide. (Sotheby's Belgravia)$530

Goss parian bust of Queen Victoria, dated 1881, 15.4cm. high. (Sotheby's Belgravia) $145

Early 20th century Goss oven with red brick and slate roof, green details, 7.4cm. long. (Sotheby's Belgravia) $235

Rare Goss model of The Round Tower, Windsor, 14.4cm., circa 1900.(Sotheby's Belgravia)$695

Early 20th century Goss model of The Abbot's Kitchen, Glastonbury, 8.4cm. high.(Sotheby's Belgravia) $900

108

Gaungxu blue and white
jardiniere painted with
He He erxian, 18in. high.
(Sotheby, King & Chase-
more) $4,090

One of a pair of Guangxu
famille rose bowls with
central panels, 16.5cm.
diam. (Sotheby's Belgravia)
$485

Guangxu blue and white
jar and cover with
panels of flowers, 34cm.
high, slightly chipped.
(Sotheby's Belgravia)
$605

One of a pair of Guangxu
period blue and white
jars and covers, 34cm.
high. (Sotheby's Belgravia)
$845

Guangxu blue and white
fish bowl with wave bor-
der, slightly cracked,
42cm. high.(Sotheby's
Belgravia) $885

One of a pair of Guangxu
blue and white moon
flasks painted with boys,
45.5cm. high.(Sotheby's
Belgravia) $1,410

HAN

Rare Han dynasty green
glazed hill jar and cover
on tripod feet, 22.8cm.
(Sotheby's)$4,525

Han dynasty green
glazed granary jar
with cylindrical
body, 25.4cm. high.
(Sotheby's)
$1,750

Rare Han dynasty green
glazed pottery cauldron
and cover, 20.2cm. wide.
(Sotheby's)$14,400

HOCHST

CHINA

Hochst white figure of a nymph, emblematic of Smell, circa 1765, 14.5cm. high. (Christie's)$260

Hochst figure of a young boy modeled by J. P. Melchior, circa 1770, 12cm. high. (Christie's) $705

Hochst figure of a birdnester by Joh. P. Melchior, 18cm. high, circa 1765-75. (Sotheby's)$1,385

IMARI

One of a pair of rare Chinese Imari bottles with chamfered corners, 27cm. high. (Sotheby, King & Chasemore)$630

One of a set of five late 19th century Imari dishes of shaped octagonal outline, 27cm. diam. (Sotheby's Belgravia) $300

One of a fine pair of heavy bottle-shaped antique Imari vases, richly gilded and decorated, 14¼in. high. (Butler & Hatch Waterman) $280

19th century Japanese Imari vase with ribbed baluster body, 18in. high. (Robert W. Skinner Inc.) $775

One of a set of four late 19th century Imari bowls with pierced rims, 15cm. diam. (Sotheby's Belgravia) $485

19th century large Japanese Imari vase of baluster form, 25¼in. high. (Robert W. Skinner Inc.) $1,200

Late 19th century Imari jardiniere with panels of vases of flowers, 35cm. wide. (Sotheby's Belgravia) $705

19th century Japanese Imari vase with cylindrical neck, 12¾in. high. (Robert W. Skinner Inc.) $475

Imari charger painted in four colors and gilt, 18in. diam. (Russell, Baldwin & Bright) $325

One of a pair of Imari vases and covers, circa 1900, 39cm. high, with ribbed bodies. (Sotheby's Belgravia) $705

Large 19th century Japanese Imari charger, 18½in. diam. (Robert W. Skinner Inc.) $225

Late 19th century Imari jardiniere painted and gilt, 31cm. high. (Sotheby's Belgravia) $360

Late 19th century Japanese Imari charger decorated with cranes, 21in. diam. (Robert W. Skinner Inc.) $375

Late 17th/early 18th century black-ground Imari vase and cover, cracked, 37cm. high. (Sotheby, King & Chasemore)$135

One of a pair of 19th century Imari meat dishes of octagonal form. (J. M. Welch & Son)$325

111

ITALIAN

Dated Italian faenza basket of oval shape, 1613, 23cm. wide. (Sotheby's) $645

Late 19th century Crown Milano cracker jar with plated silver fittings, 7¾in. high. (Robert W. Skinner Inc.)$275

Late 17th century Montelupo dish painted in bright colors, 13in. diam. (Lawrence Fine Art) $1,135

17th century Caltagirone waisted albarello painted with a classical bust, 11in. high. (Lawrence Fine Art) $380

Late 17th century Gubbic lustred vase with waisted neck, 21cm. high, damaged. (Sotheby's) $965

Late 16th century Castel Durante drug jar with strap handle, 21cm. high. (Sotheby's)$1,425

Late 17th century Montelupo dish painted with a man and a banner, 12¾in. diam. (Lawrence Fine Art) $1,360

Early Ginori armorial beaker and saucer, circa 1745.(Christie's) $2,220

Late 17th/early 18th century Castelli plaque of circular shape, 26cm. diam. (Sotheby's) $1,285

Faenza tureen and cover, circa 1760, 29cm. wide, sold with another. (Sotheby's) $1,610

Rare Doccia white glazed figure of a lion, 10cm. high. (Sotheby, King & Chasemore) $295

Vezzi flattened oviform teapot and cover with loop handle, circa 1725, 15cm. wide. (Christie's) $31,450

Naples dancing group of a young man and a girl, circa 1780, 19.5cm. high. (Christie's) $1,665

Early 17th century North Italian drug jar with scrolling grooved handle, 21.5cm. high, damaged. (Sotheby's) $405

Rare Cozzi milk jug and cover with unusual scrolling handle, circa 1767, 12.5cm. high.(Sotheby's) $5,940

One of a pair of Venice puce scale tea bowls and saucers, circa 1770, with shaped borders. (Christie's) $2,035

Venice two-handled beaker vase on spreading foot, circa 1770, 10cm. high. (Christie's) $775

Early 18th century Castelli plate decorated with Fortitude sitting on a tomb, 19cm. diam. (Sotheby's) $1,625

113

JAPANESE

CHINA

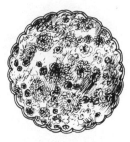

Large late 19th century Japanese cloisonne potiche and cover on three knop feet, 26.5cm. high. (Sotheby, King & Chasemore) $180

19th century Japanese export covered jar with cobalt blue decoration, 13in. high. (Robert W. Skinner Inc.) $125

Japanese earthenware bowl, signed, circa 1900, 9¾in. diam. (Sotheby's) $415

19th century Japanese porcelain vase decorated with peacocks and flowers, 24in. high. (Robert W. Skinner Inc.) $300

Japanese earthenware vase and cover in the form of a rope-tied bag, 22cm. high, circa 1880. (Sotheby's Belgravia) $260

19th century Japanese Imari temple vase with flared top, 24in. high. (Robert W. Skinner Inc.) $650

One of a pair of antique Japanese jars and covers, 19in. high. (Butler & Hatch Waterman)$650

Japanese lacquer circular bowl applied with mother-of-pearl, 21¼in. diam. (Burrows & Day) $224

Chinoiserie hexagonal tea caddy and cover painted with six scenes, circa 1725, 9.75cm. high. (Christie's) $22,200

114

Hododa earthenware bowl painted and gilt, circa 1900, 31cm. diam. (Sotheby's Belgravia) $645

One of a pair of Japanese earthenware vases, circa 1900, 22¼in. high, one damaged. (Sotheby's) $310

Late 19th century Japanese charger painted in colored enamels, 22¼in. diam. (Sotheby's) $560

One of a pair of 19th century Japanese Imari vases with flared tops and handles at necks, 16in. high. (Robert W. Skinner Inc.) $650

One of a pair of Japanese earthenware flasks, 1880's, 28cm. high. (Sotheby's Belgravia) $240

One of a pair of Japanese earthenware vases gilt with panels, circa 1900, 30.5cm. high. (Sotheby's Belgravia) $765

19th century Japanese celadon vase with pierced neck, 23in. high. (Robert W. Skinner Inc.) $300

Late 19th century Kyoto earthenware bowl in the form of a shell, 42.5cm. wide. (Sotheby's Belgravia) $665

Kinkozan earthenware kettle and cover painted and gilt on a blue ground, circa 1900, 13cm. high. (Sotheby's Belgravia) $285

JONES

One of a pair of George Jones & Sons wall plaques, signed Schenek, circa 1875. (Robert W. Skinner Inc.) $600

George Jones jug in Oriental taste, circa 1850, 7½in. high. (Sotheby's)$60

Plate from a sixteen-piece George Jones apple-green-ground dessert service, circa 1900. (Sotheby's Belgravia)　$550

KAKIEMON

Arita porcelain bottle in Kakiemon style, circa 1700.(Sotheby's) $1,800

Kakiemon decorated Meissen bottle of unusual form, circa 1730. (Bonhams) $2,495

One of a pair of late 17th century Dutch-decorated Japanese Kakiemon square bottle vases, 20.5cm. high.(Christie's) $830

KANGXI

Kangxi blue and white beaker vase, 45cm. high. (Christie's)$1,200

Kangxi famille verte saucer dish painted with cranes, 34.5cm. diam., slightly chipped. (Christie's)$1,065

Kangxi blue and white stem cup, 13.5cm. high. (Christie's)$490

Large Kangxi famille verte dish painted with a four-clawed dragon, 39cm. diam. (Christie's) $1,275

Kangxi molded celadon glazed stemcup with wide flaring bowl, 14.7cm. wide. (Sotheby's) $2,055

One of a pair of Kangxi famille verte dishes with central roundels, 37.5cm. diam. (Christie's) $1,165

Kangxi famille verte bowl, decorated in blue, orange, green and yellow, slightly cracked. (W. H. Lane & Son) $720

Kangxi blue and white gu-shaped beaker vase, 45.5cm. high. (Christie's) $1,620

Rare celadon-ground bowl of Kangxi period, enameled in famille verte, 11.8cm. diam. (Sotheby's) $1,850

Kangxi famille verte vase of tapering square section, 40cm. high. (Sotheby's Belgravia) $460

One of a pair of Kangxi famille rose dishes decorated with dragons, 37.5cm. diam. (Sotheby's Belgravia) $360

Kangxi famille verte hexagonal baluster vase and shallow domed cover with flowerhead finial, 63.5cm. high. (Christie's) $4,245

117

One of two Kangxi famille verte furniture bricks, one cracked, 26cm. wide. (Christie's) $1,060

Kangxi blue and white vase of gu form, 14½in. high. (Sotheby, King & Chasemore) $745

Kangxi bowl with everted rim, decorated in blue and white, 8¼in. diam. (W. H. Lane & Son) $795

Kangxi blue and white baluster vase and domed cover, 55cm. high, cover restored. (Christie's)$775

Pair of brightly painted Kangxi parrots. (Christie's S. Kensington) $1,080

One of two Kangxi blue and white flattened pear-shaped ewers and covers, 17.5cm. high. (Christie's)$685

One of a pair of Kangxi famille verte saucer dishes, 25cm. diam. (Christie's) $2,125

Kangxi blue and white baluster jar painted with four panels, 31cm. high, slightly damaged. (Christie's) $385

Kangxi famille verte dish painted at the center with a deer pulling a chariot, 31.5cm. diam. (Christie's) $975

Kutani bijin adjusting her hair, circa 1900, 33cm. high. (Sotheby's Belgravia) $380

One of a pair of late 19th century Kutani tureens and covers in the shape of partridges, 12cm. wide. (Sotheby's Belgravia) $750

Kutani figure of a bijin dressed in a kimono and holding a drum, circa 1900, 31cm. high. (Sotheby's Belgravia) $380

One of a pair of late 19th century Kutani bottle vases with long necks, 31cm. high. (Sotheby's Belgravia) $645

One of a pair of Kutani dishes, circa 1860, 37cm. diam., within diaper borders. (Sotheby's Belgravia) $785

Kutani group of a mother and child, circa 1900, 39cm. high, glaze chipped. (Sotheby's Belgravia) $240

LAMBETH

Lambeth delft polychrome bowl, circa 1710, 30.6cm. diam. (Christie's)$610

Rare dated Lambeth fuddling cup, 1639, slightly chipped, 4¾in. high. (Sotheby's) $5,290

Lambeth delft blue and white ballooning bowl of shallow form, circa 1784, 22cm. diam. (Christie's)$1,015

LEACH

St. Ives preserve pot and cover decorated by Bernard Leach, 11.5cm. high. (Christie's) $275

Bernard Leach stoneware vase with cylindrical body and narrow neck, 34cm. high. (Christie's)$1,465

Bernard Leach stoneware vase of bulbous form, circa 1935, 18.5cm. high. (Christie's) $355

Bernard Leach stoneware circular dish, center incised with an antelope, circa 1968, 34cm. diam. (Christie's) $405

Bernard Leach stoneware vase of oviform, with everted rim, 34cm. high. (Christie's) $1,830

St. Ives stoneware deep bowl decorated by Bernard Leach, 31.5cm. diam., center showing an owl. (Christie's) $1,465

Bernard Leach vase with pinch foot and narrow neck, 8in. high. (W. H. Lane & Son) $350
120

St. Ives stoneware bowl, decorated by Bernard Leach, 31cm. diam. (Christie's) $585

Bernard Leach stoneware slab bottle with narrow neck, 19.4cm. high. (Christie's) $915

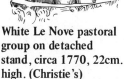

Leeds creamware bonbon-
niere in the form of a
lady's head, circa 1780-90,
3¼in. high. (Sotheby's)
$455

Very rare Leeds creamware
commemorative plate, 1821,
22.7cm. diam. (Sotheby's
Belgravia) $735

Leeds pearlware group of
Venus and Cupid, late
18th century. (Sotheby's)
$190

LE NOVE

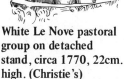

Antonibon period Le
Nove polychrome
group of a shepherd
serenading his compa-
nion, circa 1770, 15cm.
high.(Christie's)
$1,570

Pair of Le Nove figures of a lady
and a gentleman, circa 1790,
15cm. high. (Christie's)
$2,035

White Le Nove pastoral
group on detached
stand, circa 1770, 22cm.
high. (Christie's)
$830

Le Nove group of two
boys and a girl round a
tree stump, circa 1780,
18cm. high. (Christie's)
$1,295

One of three Le Nove tea-
bowls and saucers painted
with famille rose flowers,
circa 1770. (Christie's)
$925

Le Nove figure of a girl,
emblematic of Spring,
circa 1775, 13cm. high.
(Christie's) $830

Liverpool blue and white lobed oval sauceboat, Wm. Reid's factory, 1755-61, 23cm. wide.(Christie's) $895

Liverpool teabowl in 'cannonball' pattern, with saucer, circa 1765-70. (Sotheby's) $160

Liverpool hexagonal creamboat with angular handle, circa 1758, 14.5cm. wide. (Christie's) $2,765

Large Liverpool delft plate, circa 1760, 13in. diam., slightly chipped. (Sotheby's) $935

Liverpool figure of Minerva on circular mound base, 1754-61, 14cm. high. (Christie's) $1,185

Liverpool delft polychrome tile, circa 1760, 13cm. wide, slightly chipped. (Christie's) $265

Liverpool delft octagonal pill slab, mid 18th century, 10½in. square. (Sotheby's) $2,240

Rare Liverpool spoon tray of oval shape, 6in. wide, circa 1770. (Sotheby's) $510

Early 19th century Liverpool Washington memorial pitcher with black transfer printed scene, 9in. high. (Robert W. Skinner Inc.) $700

London delft plate decorated in blue, circa 1710-20, 8½in. diam. (Sotheby's) $860

Rare London 'apollo' drug jar with shouldered ovoid body, 1710-30, 10¾in. high. (Sotheby's)$830

One of a pair of London delft plates painted with cockerels, 6½in. diam., circa 1750. (Sotheby's) $1,730

London delft dated plate, center with initials LIM and date 1688, 21cm. diam. (Christie's)$1,630

Late 17th century London delft charger with cracked rim, 13¾in. diam. (Sotheby's) $305

London delft blue and white plate, circa 1685, 21.5cm. diam., rim slightly chipped. (Christie's) $650

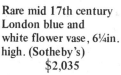

London delftware Royal portrait bowl with deep interior, circa 1690, 22cm. diam. (Sotheby, King & Chasemore) $985

Rare mid 17th century London blue and white flower vase, 6¼in. high. (Sotheby's) $2,035

London delft plate with border pattern, 8½in. diam., circa 1710-20. (Sotheby's) $345

123

CHINA

LONGTON HALL

One of a pair of Longton Hall leaf-dishes, molded as cabbage leaves, circa 1755, 9¼in. wide. (Sotheby's) $815

One of a pair of early Longton Hall vases with double ogee bodies, 6¼in. high. (Sotheby's) $375

Longton Hall blue and white teabowl and saucer, circa 1755. (Christie's) $855

LOWESTOFT

Lowestoft blue and white dated birth-tablet, 1793, 7cm. diam. (Christie's) $2,250

Small Lowestoft teapot and cover, circa 1770-80, 4in. high. (Sotheby's) $425

Rare Lowestoft cylindrical tankard with scrolling handle, circa 1770-80, 4½in. high. (Sotheby's) $490

LUDWIGSBURG

Ludwigsburg ornithological shaped circular plate, circa 1765, 23cm. diam. (Christie's) $430

Ludwigsburg group of Haymakers from a set of the Months, 12.5cm. high, circa 1760-70. (Sotheby's)$1,585

Ludwigsburg figure of a peasant, modeled by Adam Bauer, 11.5cm. high, circa 1760-70. (Sotheby's) $1,030

124

Ludwigsburg oval tea caddy with metal cover, circa 1770, 13.5cm. high. (Christie's) $335

Ludwigsburg porcelain teapot, spherical shape tapering to base, circa 1775, 4¾in. high. (Robert W. Skinner Inc.) $875

Ludwigsburg arched rectangular tea caddy with Ozier border, circa 1765, 12.5cm. high. (Christie's) $685

Ludwigsburg figure of a fish seller modeled by J. J. Louis, circa 1770, 12.5cm. high.(Christie's) $740

Ludwigsburg two-handled ecuelle, cover and stand with Ozier borders, circa 1765. (Christie's) $1,200

Ludwigsburg figure of a huntsman with a dead deer, circa 1765, 16.5cm. high. (Christie's) $1,665

Ludwigsburg figure of a butcher carrying meat on his shoulder, circa 1765, 11.5cm. high. (Christie's) $925

Ludwigsburg group of fruit-pickers from a set of the Months, modeled by Adam Bauer, circa 1760-70, 13.5cm. high. (Sotheby's) $1,190

Ludwigsburg figure of a dancer modeled by J. Nees & C. Fr. Riedel, circa 1765, 14.5cm. high. (Sotheby's)$715

Pilkington's Royal Lancastrian lustre vase, painted by R. Joyce, 16cm. high. (Christie's) $275

Large silver-resist lustre jug, decoration depicting fox hunting and hare coursing, 7½in. high. (Russell, Baldwin & Bright) $360

Pilkington's Royal Lancastrian lustre vase, decorated by R. Joyce, 18cm. high. (Christie's) $330

Lancastrian lustre vase of baluster form, decorated by R. Joyce, circa 1910, 9in. high. (Sotheby Beresford Adams) $335

Royal Lancastrian lustre vase of globular shape, dated for 1912, 7¼in. high. (Sotheby Beresford Adams) $140

Lancastrian lustre vase decorated by R. Joyce, circa 1910, 9in. high. (Sotheby Beresford Adams) $165

Pilkington's Royal Lancastrian lustre waisted cylindrical vase, designed by Wm. S. Mycock, dated 1922, 19.5cm. high. (Christie's) $255

Rare Lancastrian lustre alms dish painted by Charles Cundall, 1908, 22in. diam. (Sotheby's) $1,350

Lancastrian lustre vase of slender ovoid form, circa 1912, 8in. high. (Sotheby Beresford Adams) $110

126

CHINA

MARTINWARE

Martinware terracotta grotesque, signed, 1898, 32cm. wide. (Phillips)
$4,800

Small Martinware jug of flattened oviform shape with loop handle, signed, 9.5cm. high. (Phillips)
$275

Martin Brothers stoneware double-face jug with angular strap handle, 1911, 16.5cm. high. (Christie's)
$825

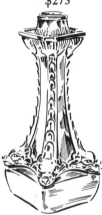

Martin Brothers vase with tapered body, dated 1-1900, 22.4cm. high. (Sotheby's Belgravia)
$775

One of a pair of Martin Bros. candlesticks, signed, 4-1902, 20.5cm. high. (Phillips) $255

Martinware vase of slender oviform shape, with tall cylindrical neck, signed, 24.75cm. high. (Phillips) $255

Small Martin Bros. vase decorated in green and brown with fish, signed, 10.5cm. high.(Phillips)
$310

Martinware terracotta grotesque, signed, 1898, 27cm. wide. (Phillips)
$3,650

Martin Bros. bird vase, in the form of two birds standing back to back, 24.2cm. high. (Sotheby, King & Chasemore)
$4,375

127

MARTINWARE

Martin Brothers vase with globular body, dated 1-1891, 21.5cm. high. (Sotheby's Belgravia) $480

Rare Martin Brothers figure of a pike, by Wallace Martin, circa 1890, 49.3cm. long. (Sotheby, King & Chasemore) $1,930

Martin Brothers gourd vase with ovoid body, speckled in olive, dated 7-1904, 26.2cm. high. (Sotheby's Belgravia) $2,390

Martin Brothers Art Pottery bottle vase of twin-handled ovoid form, 7½in. high. (W. H. Lane & Son) $245

Martinware figure of a bird with large talons, signed on rim, 29cm. high. (Phillips) $5,370

Martin Brothers jug with ovoid body incised with a goat's head, dated 1-1896, 26.3cm. high. (Sotheby's Belgravia) $955

Martin Brothers Art Pottery vase with flared rim and narrow neck, circa 1899. (Robert W. Skinner Inc.) $275

Martin Brothers stoneware bird with wide beak, inscribed, 1906, 21.7cm. high.(Christie's) $1,555

One of a pair of Martin Brothers gourd and lobed shaped vases, 1901, 25.5cm. high. (Christie's) $3,085

One of a pair of Martin
Brothers gourd vases
with hexagonal feet,
dated 6-1904, 27cm.
high. (Sotheby's
Belgravia) $1,690

Martin Brothers jardiniere
with bell body, dated 3-1886,
21.8cm. high. (Sotheby's
Belgravia) $955

Martin Brothers oviform
vase, body with five
panels, 1900, 16cm.
high. (Christie's)
          $535

Unusual 'experimental'
Martin Brothers flask,
signed, 16cm. high.
(Phillips) $70

Martin Brothers stoneware
bird in mottled russet glaze,
inscribed, 22.5cm. high.
(Christie's) $4,025

Martinware jug incised
with fish, 1886, 8½in.
high. (Sotheby Beres-
ford Adams)
          $740

Martin Brothers ewer of
flattened oviform with
loop handle, 25cm. high.
(Christie's) $905

Rare Martin Brothers stoneware bird with long neck,
incised, 41cm. high.
(Christie's) $8,235

Martin Brothers vase
of tapering rectangular
form, 29.1cm. high,
1900. (Christie's)
          $265

MEISSEN

19th century Meissen figure of a cockatoo by J. J. Kaendler, 23cm. high. (Sotheby, King & Chasemore) $180

Meissen chinoiserie miniature globular teapot with scroll handle, circa 1730, 14.5cm. wide. (Christie's)$1,385

Mid 18th century Meissen figure of a sheep, by Paul Reinicke, 10cm. high. (Sotheby, King & Chasemore)$810

19th century Meissen figure of a swan by J. J. Kaendler, 30.5cm. high. (Sotheby, King & Chasemore) $535

Late Meissen tete-a-tete of twelve pieces, crossed swords in blue. (Phillips) $2,590

Rare Meissen Hausmalerei pipe bowl with silver mount and carved wood and antler stem. (Phillips)$775

Late 19th century Meissen group of two sea nymphs and two putti, 31cm. high. (Sotheby, King & Chasemore) $895

Early Meissen teabowl and saucer, painted with quatrelobed panels. (Phillips) $1,850

Part of a late 19th century Meissen part coffee service of eighteen pieces. (Sotheby's) $2,495

130

Late 19th century Meissen group of Amphitrite, on rocky base, 23cm. wide. (Sotheby, King & Chasemore) $325

Part of a late 19th century twenty-four-piece Meissen topographical tea service, with named views. (Sotheby's) $2,805

Early Meissen oval basket with two mask handles, circa 1735-40, restored, 18cm. wide. (Sotheby, King & Chasemore) $395

One of a pair of late 19th century Meissen candelabra, 18¼in. high. (Sotheby's) $1,495

19th century three-piece Meissen garniture of an urn and two candlesticks. (Robert W. Skinner Inc.) $600

Late Meissen table bell. (Christie's S. Kensington) $270

Early Meissen teabowl and saucer, crossed swords in blue marks. (Phillips) $960

Pair of late 19th century Meissen figures, 7½in. high. (J. M. Welch & Son) $530

One of a set of twelve mid 19th century Meissen dessert plates, 21.5cm. diam. (Christie's) $1,120

Meissen arched rectangular tea caddy and cover, borders edged with gilt, circa 1765, 12cm. high. (Christie's) $1,015

Pair of late 19th century Meissen figures of girls, 11.8cm. high. (Sotheby's Belgravia) $790

White Meissen figure of the 'Magic Lantern Carrier', by Kaendler & Reinicke, 15cm. high, circa 1745. (Sotheby, King & Chasemore)$405

One of a set of eight Meissen plates in two sizes, circa 1880, decorated in underglaze blue. (Sotheby's Belgravia)$760

Early 20th century Meissen porcelain urn on stand, 16½in. high. (Robert W. Skinner Inc.) $175

Meissen tea bowl and saucer gilt with chinoiserie figure, birds and plants, circa 1730. (Christie's) $925

Late 19th century Meissen group of two children and a dog, 10¼in. high. (Sotheby Beresford Adams) $795

One of a pair of Meissen figures of prancing horses modeled by J. J. Kaendler, circa 1745, 20.5cm. wide. (Christie's) $1,015

Late 19th century Meissen group of Europa and the Bull, 8¾in. high. (Sotheby Beresford Adams) $705

Early 20th century Meissen figure of a shepherdess and lamb, 24cm. high. (Sotheby's Belgravia) $290

Meissen chinoiserie small baluster teapot and cover painted by Herold, 14cm. wide. (Christie's) $1,940

Meissen chinoiserie hexagonal baluster tea caddy and silver gilt cover, 9.5cm. high. (Christie's) $2,960

Meissen chinoiserie hot milk jug and cover painted by C. F. Herold, circa 1725, 15cm. high. (Christie's) $830

One of a pair of Meissen blue and white tea bowls and saucers painted in the manner of Ferner, circa 1735. (Christie's) $775

Mid 18th century Meissen swan service jug and cover, by J. J. Kaendler, 17cm. high. (Sotheby, King & Chasemore) $2,140

Meissen chinoiserie rectangular tea caddy painted by C. F. Herold. (Christie's) $1,850

Meissen circular two-handled tureen and cover with Ozier borders, circa 1745, 32cm. wide. (Christie's) $1,295

Mid 18th century later decorated Meissen group of dancers, 14cm. high. (Sotheby's Belgravia) $305

Meissen blue and white octagonal baluster tea caddy and cover, circa 1725-30, 9.5cm. high. (Christie's) $890

Meissen brocade pattern circular butter tub and cover with pine cone finial, circa 1735, 12.5cm. wide. (Christie's) $2,960

Meissen arched rectangular tea caddy and cover decorated with scrolls, shells and foliage, circa 1755, 12.5cm. high. (Christie's) $520

Meissen group of apple pickers, 27cm. high, crossed sword mark. (Sotheby, King & Chasemore) $660

Meissen figure of a Sultan riding an elephant, modeled by J. J. Kaendler, circa 1745, 28cm. wide. (Christie's) $27,750

Meissen white figure of a goddess, circa 1741, 30.5cm. high. (Christie's) $405

Meissen oviform jug with pewter mounts and hinged cover, circa 1759, 29cm. high. (Christie's) $925

Meissen Grunes Watteau armorial plate painted in panels, circa 1741, 21cm. diam. (Christie's) $12,950

Mid 18th century Meissen white glazed 'Commedia Dell'Arte' figure of Pantaloon, 12.5cm. high. (Sotheby, King & Chasemore) $835

Meissen arched rectangular tea caddy and cover, circa 1740-50, 13cm. high. (Christie's) $445

Meissen figure of a recumbent sheep modeled by P. H. Reinicke, circa 1750, 17cm. wide. (Christie's) $260

Meissen arched rectangular tea caddy and cover, stippled with cupids, circa 1755, 11cm. high. (Christie's) $520

Meissen figure of a Pandur modeled by J. J. Kaendler, circa 1750, 23cm. high.(Christie's) $4,810

Meissen pot pourri vase and cover with loop handles. (Sotheby, King & Chasemore) $365

Meissen group of three putti emblematic of the Liberal Arts, circa 1760, 30cm. high. (Christie's) $405

Meissen baluster coffee pot and cover with knob finial, circa 1770, 24.5cm. high.(Christie's) $370

Meissen crinoline group of the gout sufferer, modeled by J. J. Kaendler, circa 1742, 19.5cm. wide. (Christie's) $18,500

Meissen rococo scent flask with silver mount and stopper, circa 1750, 13.5cm. high. (Christie's)$645

METTLACH

Mettlach earthenware vase, tapering at base and neck, circa 1905, 25.25cm. high.(Sotheby's Belgravia) $445

One of a pair of Mettlach plaques, signed J. Stahl, 18¼in. diam. (Sotheby Beresford Adams) $945

Mettlach stein with tapering cylindrical body, circa 1910, 22.8cm. high, cover with pewter hinge.(Sotheby's Belgravia) $430

Mettlach flagon of two litres, Germany, 1909, with pewter thumbpiece, 14¾in. high. (Robert W. Skinner Inc.)$525

One of a pair of Mettlach vases decorated with classical maidens, 34.5cm. high, circa 1910. (Sotheby's Belgravia) $515

Large Mettlach ewer decorated with central frieze, 46cm. high, circa 1900. (Sotheby's Belgravia) $370

MING

Late Ming blue and white 'kraak porselein' dish with eight panels, Wanli period, 35.5cm. diam. (Christie's) $580

Late Ming/early Qing dynasty figures of Buddhistic lions in deep aubergine glaze, 19cm. high. (Christie's) $485

Early 17th century Ming blue and white 'kraak porselein' dish, 36.5cm. diam. (Christie's) $345

Late Ming blue and white 'kraak porselein' dish of Wanli period, 50cm. diam.(Christie's) $2,015

Late Ming blue and white box of slender rectangular form, 33cm. long. (Sotheby's) $1,540

Late Ming blue and white broad oviform jar, Wanli, 12.5cm. high. (Christie's) $575

Ming dynasty Cizhou type slender vase painted in brown on white ground, 57.5cm. high. (Christie's)$1,080

One of two late Ming blue and white foliate dishes decorated with hares, 12.5cm. diam. (Christie's) $430

Late Ming dynasty carved jade ewer and cover with pear-shaped body, 21.3cm. high.(Sotheby's) $6,580

One of a pair of Ming dynasty tilemaker's pottery figures of mounted warriors, 33cm. high.(Christie's) $1,440

Rare Ming Wucai box of square section, 13.2cm., with wood cover and stand. (Sotheby's) $5,760

Early 17th century Ming blue and white octagonal baluster jar with short neck, 21.5cm. high. (Christie's)$380

Minton pate-sur-pate plate with pierced border, 23cm. diam., dated for 1902. (Phillips) $590

One of a pair of Minton secessionist candlesticks with two loop handles, circa 1889, 52cm. high. (Christie's) $880

One of ten rare Minton tiles from the Elfin series, 15.5cm. square. (Phillips) $205

Unusual Minton's model of a puma covered in ruby-red glaze, 16cm. high. (Phillips) $130

Minton 'Dresden New Vase' and cover of campana form, circa 1840, 45cm. high. (Sotheby's Belgravia) $1,330

Rare Minton 'malachite' ewer with loop handle, 35cm. high, dated for 1862. (Sotheby's Belgravia) $265

One of a pair of Minton vases and covers in Sevres style, 12¼in. high, circa 1850. (Sotheby's) $730

Minton 'globe pot-pourri' vase, cover and stand, painted with a scene of Hereford, circa 1825-30, 24.5cm. high. (Sotheby's Belgravia) $615

One of a pair of Minton vases with elephant's head and ring handles, dated for 1875, 42cm. high. (Sotheby's Belgravia) $450

138

Moorcroft Hazledene biscuit jar and cover painted in Moonlit Blue pattern, 17cm. high. (Christie's) $330

Moorcroft punch bowl with rolled foot, circa 1911, 14½in. wide, slightly damaged. (Robert W. Skinner Inc.) $250

Unusual Moorcroft vase with lightly ribbed body, circa 1935, 31cm. high. (Sotheby's Belgravia) $495

Moorcroft slender baluster vase, signed, 1914, 30.5cm. high, painted in Claremont pattern. (Christie's) $475

One of a pair of Moorcroft Macintyre vases with gilt details and high loop handles, circa 1900, 12.5cm. high. (Sotheby's Belgravia) $590

One of a pair of Moorcroft Macintyre Florianware vases of double gourd shape, signed, 28cm. high. (Phillips) $320

Moorcroft Art Pottery vase in red brown floral motif, signed and dated, circa 1911, 11¾in. high. (Robert W. Skinner Inc.) $450

Moorcroft loving cup of broad cylindrical shape, flaring at rim, signed, 19cm. high. (Phillips) $215

One of a pair of William Moorcroft vases, signed and numbered, 12in. high. (Geering & Colyer) $505

139

NANTGARW

Stand from a pair of Nantgarw London-decorated sauce tureens, covers and stands, circa 1820, 19cm. wide.(Christie's) $10,275

Nantgarw shaped oval center dish from the Mackintosh service, circa 1820, 35.5cm. wide. (Christie's) $1,730

Nantgarw lobed oval dish painted with flower sprays, 1817-20, 29.5cm. wide. (Christie's) $1,015

NYMPHENBURG

Nymphenburg figure of a Chinese archer modeled by Franz Anton Bustelli, circa 1765, 21.5cm. high. (Christie's) $4,810

Nymphenburg figure of Anselmo or L'Abbe, modeled by Franz Anton Bustelli, circa 1760, 20cm. high. (Christie's) $11,100

Rare Nymphenburg nightlight in the shape of a jug, 19cm. high, circa 1765.(Sotheby's) $1,585

Nymphenburg teacup and saucer with gilt and iron-red scrollwork borders, 1755-65. (Sotheby's) $1,095

One of a pair of Nymphenburg white equestrian figures, 8½in. high. (Coles, Knapp & Kennedy) $270

Nymphenburg snuff box with shaped oval body molded with basketwork, circa 1755-65, 6.5cm. wide. (Sotheby's) $845

One of a pair of Oriental pottery ducks, standing on rocks. (Honiton Galleries) $105

Transitional Jiajing blue and white bowl of hemispherical form, 14.3cm. diam.(Sotheby, King & Chasemore)$610

One of a pair of large Oriental decorated pot pourri vases and covers, on padouk stands. (Gilbert Baitson) $320

Late 16th/early 17th century Swatow polychrome truncated jar, 23cm. high. (Sotheby, King & Chasemore) $295

Sang-de-boeuf vase of baluster form and square section, 30.5cm. high. (Sotheby's Belgravia) $645

One of a pair of modern blue and white garden seats, one cracked, 48cm. high. (Sotheby's Belgravia) $525

Transitional blue and white oviform vase, 17.2cm. high.(Sotheby, King & Chasemore) $860

One of a pair of 18th century clobbered blue and white tureens, covers and stands, 33cm. wide. (Sotheby's Belgravia) $965

19th century Chinese Oriental porcelain bottle with bulbous body and slender neck, 11in. high. (Robert W. Skinner Inc.) $50

PARIS

CHINA

Paris bowl decorated in gilt with birds and flowers, 6½in. diam. (Burrows & Day) $3,740

Rare Paris veilleuse modeled as an 18th century woman, torso detaching to form a teapot, circa 1840, 35cm. high. (Sotheby's Belgravia) $700

Mid to late 19th century Paris oval dish with bleu-celeste-ground, 63cm. wide. (Sotheby's Belgravia) $740

Paris baluster chocolate pot with domed lid and gilt metal thumbpiece, 6½in. high. (Burrows & Day) $7,480

PLYMOUTH

Paris Napoleon portrait coffee can and saucer, circa 1805, saucer repaired. (Sotheby's) $790

One of two Paris jardinieres painted with birds and flowers, 4¾in. diam. (Burrows & Day) $450

One of a pair of Plymouth white figures of seated musicians, 1768-70, 14cm. and 15.5cm. high. (Christie's) $820

Plymouth sauceboat with ribbed scroll handle, circa 1770, 14cm. wide. (Christie's) $1,585

Important Plymouth figure of 'Winter' in the form of a naked boy with a robe, in mint condition. (W. H. Lane & Son) $755

'The Trysting Place' a small lid with plain margin. (Sotheby's Belgravia) $185

Large pot lid showing the Exhibitions Buildings, 1851. (Sotheby's Belgravia) $165

'Bear Hunting' a small pot lid with retailer's inscription and gilt line border. (Sotheby's Belgravia) $325

Large pot lid showing Pegwell Bay, by S. Banger Shrimp Sauce Manufacturer. (Sotheby's Belgravia) $355

Small pot lid 'Bears at School', with base. (Sotheby's Belgravia) $110

Small lid with well-defined print of Bear, Lion and Cock, with base. (Sotheby's Belgravia) $120

Rare medium pot lid 'The Tower of London', in good condition. (Sotheby's Belgravia) $635

'Shooting Bears', a small lid with a clear pring and plain border. (Sotheby's Belgravia) $150

'Shooting Bears' a small pot lid in good condition, with base.(Sotheby's Belgravia)$110

PRATTWARE

Unusual Prattware figure of Lucretia, lying on a couch, circa 1790, 11in. long. (Sotheby's) $460

Late 18th century Prattware Toby jug, shaped base with brown line-border, 9½in. high. (Sotheby's) $405

Comport from an eleven-piece Prattware part dessert service printed with Tyrolean views. (Sotheby's) $355

Rare late 18th/early 19th century 'Collier' Toby jug with Prattware style colors, 10¼in. high. (Sotheby's) $675

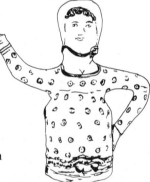

Prattware teapot and cover modeled as a lady in a chair, circa 1785-90, 8¾in. high. (Sotheby's) $715

One of a pair of pot-pourri vases and covers of baluster form, circa 1865, 70cm. high. (Sotheby's Belgravia) $820

Late 18th century Prattware Toby jug, toper seated and holding a tankard of ale, 9½in. high. (Sotheby's) $515

Early 19th century rare Prattware cradle of oval form, 30.5cm. long, cracked. (Sotheby, King & Chasemore) $750

Late 18th/early 19th century Prattware Toby jug in traditional style, 9½in. high, hat restored.(Sotheby's) $440

Early Qianlong famille rose dish painted with a lady beneath a tree, 37cm. diam.(Christie's) $680

One of four Qianlong famille rose deep wine cups, 1776, 6.5cm. diam. (Christie's) $505

Qianlong famille rose deep dish painted with a lady and two small boys, 37.5cm. diam. (Christie's)$805

19th century Qianlong blue and white octagonal vase, 47cm. high. (Sotheby, King & Chasemore)$890

Qianlong famille rose oblong twelve-sided tureen and cover, 34cm. wide.(Christie's) $1,260

Qianlong blue and white ewer with long strap handle, 33.3cm. high. (Sotheby's) $9,255

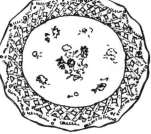

Qianlong blue and white deep dish with complex brocade border, 37.7cm. diam. (Sotheby, King & Chasemore) $230

One of a pair of Qianlong ormolu mounted famille rose beaker vases, 40cm. high. (Christie's) $1,350

One of a set of four late Qianlong Companies-des-Indes dishes of shaped oval form, 23.3cm. wide. (Sotheby, King & Chasemore) $1,110

145

Early earthenware bowl by Lucie Rie, 17cm. diam., dated 1931. (Phillips) $715

Lucie Rie porcelain vase with cylindrical neck and flared rim, 24.8cm. high. (Christie's) $1,100

Lucie Rie porcelain bowl with mustard lime-green glaze, circa 1968, 21.2cm. diam. (Christie's) $640

Early Lucie Rie porcelain deep bowl with crossed linear decoration, circa 1957, 20.8cm. diam. (Christie's) $375

Lucie Rie stoneware bulbous bottle with narrow flattened neck and flared rim, 1979, 30cm. high. (Christie's) $3,145

Lucie Rie porcelain bowl with slightly flattened sides, exterior in dark copper manganese, 14.5cm. wide. (Christie's) $255

Lucie Rie porcelain shallow conical bowl with two concentric bands, 17cm. diam. (Christie's) $880

Early Lucie Rie earthenware vase of slightly flared form, 1932, damaged, 19.7cm. high. (Christie's) $1,005

Lucie Rie porcelain bowl on cylindrical foot, signed, 25.2cm. diam. (Christie's) $1,645

Rockingham leaf-molded basket with overhead twig handle, circa 1830-35, 9in. wide. (Sotheby's) $635

Stand from a twenty-nine-piece Rockingham dessert service, circa 1826-30. (Sotheby's)$2,800

Very rare Rockingham fox mask stirrup cup in plain white glaze, 11.5cm. long. (H. Spencer & Sons Ltd.) $505

One of a pair of Rockingham two-handled vases with flared rims, 4in. high. (Burrows & Day) $75

Part of a Rockingham tea and coffee service of forty-two pieces, early 19th century. (Sotheby Beresford Adams) $925

Rockingham table napkin ring, unmarked, decorated with flowers. (Burrows & Day) $12

Rockingham violeteer of teapot form, circa 1831-42, 2¾in. wide. (Sotheby's) $775

Rare early 19th century Rockingham group of a shepherdess and a sheep, 7in. high.(Sotheby Beresford Adams) $815

Superb Rockingham rococo-shaped porcelain teapot and cover, circa 1830. (John Hogbin & Son) $105

147

ROOKWOOD

Rookwood pottery iris glaze vase, Ohio, circa 1908, 10½in. high, cracked. (Robert W. Skinner Inc.) $475

Rookwood sterling overlay standard glaze jardiniere, Ohio, circa 1907, 5½in. high. (Robert W. Skinner Inc.) $1,500

Rookwood pottery vellum glaze plaque, Ohio, circa 1919, 8¾in. high. (Robert W. Skinner Inc.) $1,600

Rookwood scenic vellum glaze vase, Ohio, circa 1919, 14½in. high. (Robert W. Skinner Inc.) $1,300

Rookwood bisque Spanish water jug, Ohio, circa 1883, 9½in. high. (Robert W. Skinner Inc.) $1,250

Rookwood pottery iris glaze jar, Ohio, circa 1914, probably by Sara Alice Toohey, 7in. high. (Robert W. Skinner Inc.) $400

Rookwood pottery ewer in sage green clay, Ohio, 1900, 8½in. high. (Robert W. Skinner Inc.) $425

Rookwood standard glaze vase, signed A. R. Valentien, circa 1897, 11½in. high. (Robert W. Skinner Inc.) $1,050

Rookwood pottery standard glaze mug, signed for Kataro Shirayamadani, circa 1887. (Robert W. Skinner Inc.)$550

Rosenberg 'eggshell' porce-
lain cup and saucer by
Samuel Schellink, 1903.
(Christie's) $825

Rosenberg 'eggshell' bowl
and cover, decorated by
Roelof Sterken, 12cm. high,
1901. (Sotheby's Belgravia)
$410

Rosenberg 'eggshell' vase
with basket handle.
(Bonham's)$1,410

Rosenberg 'eggshell' por-
celain two-handled vase,
1904, 24.5cm. high.
(Christie's)$1,830

Rosenberg 'eggshell' beaker
and saucer, decorated by
Sam Schellink, 1904.
(Sotheby's Belgravia)
$320

Rosenberg 'eggshell' vase
decorated by Sam Schel-
link, 1908, 22.5cm. high,
with flared neck. (Sothe-
by's Belgravia)$260

Rosenberg 'eggshell' vase,
decorated by R. Sterken,
1903, 10cm. high.(Sothe-
by's Belgravia)$320

Rosenberg 'eggshell' vase,
decorated by Sam Schel-
link, 1904, 21.5cm. high.
(Sotheby's Belgravia)
$1,880

Rosenberg 'eggshell' vase
decorated by Sam Schel-
link, 1904, 34cm. high.
(Sotheby's Belgravia)
$1,440

ROYAL DUX

CHINA

Late 19th century Royal Dux centerpiece with figurine, 12¼in. high. (Robert W. Skinner Inc.) $225

Royal Dux camel group, applied pink triangle, circa 1910, 45.5cm. high. (Sotheby's Belgravia) $780

Royal Dux figure group of a family, circa 1880, 25in. high. (Robert W. Skinner Inc.)$375

Royal Dux earthenware mirror, circa 1900, 54.5cm. high, with scoop dish below. (Sotheby's Belgravia) $800

Royal Dux figure of a boy at a spring filling pitchers, circa 1880, 24in. high. (Robert W. Skinner Inc.)$300

20th century Royal Dux mirror frame, 53cm. high, applied and impressed pink triangle. (Sotheby's Belgravia) $615

20th century Royal Dux figure of a Turkish street vendor, one of a pair, 50.5cm. high. (Sotheby's Belgravia) $985
150

20th century pair of Royal Dux figures 'Farmer's Boy' and 'Farmer's Girl', 16½in. high. (Edgar Horn) $605

Royal Dux figure of a naked girl on a stool, circa 1920, 14½in. high. (Sotheby's) $290

Ruskin high-fired porcelain vase of baluster form, dated 1928, 36cm. high. (Phillips) $550

Ruskin 'high-fired' porcelain shallow bowl and stand, 26cm. diam. (Phillips) $385

Ruskin high-fired porcelain vase, impressed 'Ruskin, England', 36cm. high. (Phillips) $730

RUSSIAN

Biscuit group of a laundress and child by Gardner, Moscow, circa 1880-90, 11cm. high.(Sotheby's) $655

Biscuit group of a mother and child by Gardner, Moscow, circa 1880-90, 23.5cm. high. (Sotheby's) $550

Biscuit group of a woman playing blindman's buff, by Gardner, Moscow, circa 1880-90, 24.5cm. high. (Sotheby's)$410

Porcelain group of Hercules and the Nemean lion by Kozlov, Moscow, circa 1830, 18cm. high. (Sotheby's) $775

One of a pair of urn-shaped vases by Imperial Porcelain Manufactory, circa 1820, 73cm. high.(Sotheby's) $9,820

Biscuit figure of a man playing an accordion by Gardner, Moscow, circa 1880-90, 18cm. high. (Sotheby's) $655

151

SAMSON

One of a pair of Samson nodding mandarins, late 19th century, slightly damaged. (Sotheby's Belgravia) $1,070

One of a pair of late 19th century ormolu mounted Samson 'Meissen' figures of a Shepherd and Shepherdess, 15.8cm. high. (Sotheby's Belgravia) $535

Late 19th century Samson group of putti celebrating the harvest, 36cm. high. (Sotheby's Belgravia) $865

Late 19th century Samson famille rose vase, one of a pair, on wood stands, 29cm. high. (Sotheby's Belgravia) $1,005

Late 19th century Samson tete-a-tete, tray 26.5cm. wide. (Sotheby's Belgravia)$325

Large Samson vase and cover painted in famille verte, 1870's, 60cm. high. (Sotheby's Belgravia) $2,800

Samson 'Chelsea' group modeled as Diana bathing in a stream, circa 1880, 38cm. high. (Sotheby's Belgravia) $455

Samson 'Meissen' comport and stand in the shape of an elephant carrying a basket, circa 1880, 35.5cm. wide. (Sotheby's Belgravia) $1,030

One of a pair of late 19th century Samson 'Derby' candlesticks, 26cm. high, chipped.(Sotheby's Belgravia) $660

One of a pair of Satsuma vases of tapering square section, circa 1900, 38.5cm. high. (Sotheby, King & Chasemore) $445

Late 19th century Japanese Satsuma plate, signed, 8¾in. diam. (Robert W. Skinner Inc.)$300

Large Satsuma koro and cover on three oni supports, 21in. high, slightly damaged. (Lawrence Fine Art) $905

Late 19th century Japanese Satsuma vase of baluster form, 12in. high. (Robert W. Skinner Inc.) $800

Late 19th century barrel-shaped Satsuma vase, 59cm. high, slightly cracked. (Sotheby, King & Chasemore) $145

One of a pair of early 20th century Japanese Satsuma vases with wide necks, 15½in. high. (Robert W. Skinner Inc.) $600

Late 19th century Japanese Ko-Satsuma vase, signed Koto-Togiki Gaisha, 12¼in. high. (Robert W. Skinner Inc.)$1,300

Late 19th century Satsuma figure of a crane with head back, 34.5cm. high. (Sotheby, King & Chasemore) $205

19th century Japanese Satsuma pottery vase with embossed decoration, 12¾in. high. (Robert W. Skinner Inc.) $150

153

Sevres deep green-ground eventail jardiniere, painted by Charles Tandart, 1756-60, 28.5cm. wide. (Christie's)$5,605

Unusual champleve mounted Sevres dish painted and gilt by Hete, signed, circa 1900, 22.5cm. diam.(Sotheby's Belgravia) $215

Sevres bleu-celeste-ground ice pail and cover, painted with scenes of lovers after Watteau, 25cm. high. (Sotheby, King & Chasemore) $730

Rare Sevres shaped circular plate from the service made for Catherine the Great, 23.5cm. diam., dated for 1782. (Christie's) $3,700

One of a pair of Sevres pattern blue-ground ormolu mounted vases, 48.5cm. high. (Christie's)$1,725

Sevres rose pompadour cup and saucer painted with flowers, dated for 1757. (Christie's) $1,200

One of a pair of ormolu and Sevres porcelain vases of Louis XVI design, 20½in. high. (Christie's)$2,760

Sevres hexafoil two-handled seau a verre from the Du Barry service, 16.5cm. wide. (Christie's) $705

Late 18th century Sevres urn of footed baluster form, 17in. high. (Robert W. Skinner Inc.) $1,000

Sevres salad bowl with lobed and shaped border, dated for 1759, 9¼in. diam. (Lawrence Fine Art) $455

Sevres pink-ground cylindrical miniature teapot and cover, circa 1775, 9.5cm. high. (Christie's)$240

Sevres oval jardiniere of lobed outline, 1759, 9in. wide, painted with flowers. (Lawrence Fine Art) $550

Sevres pear-shaped cream jug painted with exotic birds, circa 1755, 10cm. high. (Christie's)
$260

One of a pair of Sevres pattern blue-ground ormolu mounted two-handled vases, 42cm. high. (Christie's)
$610

Sevres coffee cup and saucer with paintings of landscapes and birds, circa 1760. (Christie's)
$175

One of a pair of large Sevres vases and covers, circa 1860, one knop glued, 49cm. high. (Sotheby, King & Chasemore) $1,465

One of a pair of Sevres green-ground shaped rectangular jardinieres, 19.5cm. wide. (Christie's) $5,605

One of a pair of Sevres metal mounted vases, late 19th century, 15¾in. high. (Sotheby's)$435

155

STAFFORDSHIRE

CHINA

Staffordshire figurine of Jumbo, large molded elephant, 10¾in. high. (Robert W. Skinner Inc.) $300

Rare pair of figures of a stag and hind at lodge, circa 1750-55, 17cm. wide. (Sotheby, King & Chasemore) $930

18th century Staffordshire slipware dish, 13¼in. diam. (Sotheby's) $1,320

Staffordshire saltglaze pectin-shell molded teapot and cover with loop handle, circa 1755, 15.5cm. wide.(Christie's) $610

Staffordshire slipware dish by William Simpson, circa 1700, 34cm. diam. (Christie's) $6,545

Pair of late 18th/early 19th century Staffordshire figures of a lion and lioness, 8¼in. and 8in. (Sotheby's) $1,180

Staffordshire pottery group, circa 1820, 20cm. high. (Sotheby, King & Chasemore) $670

Staffordshire washbowl and jug showing Lafayette at Franklin's tomb, circa 1825, 12in. diam. (Robert W. Skinner Inc.) $900

Staffordshire saltglaze polychrome teapot and cover, with crabstock handle, circa 1755, 20.5cm. wide. (Christie's)$1,015

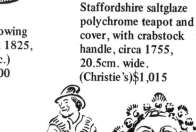

19th century Staffordshire 'barge' teapot, 13in. high. (J. M. Welch & Son) $165

Pair of Staffordshire pottery figures of The Cobbler and his Wife, restored. (Honiton Galleries) $60

One of a pair of Staffordshire furniture rests, late 18th/early 19th century, 6in. high. (Sotheby's) $205

Rare pair of Thomas Parr equestrian figures of the Prince and Princess of Wales, circa 1862, 19.5cm. high. (Sotheby, King & Chasemore) $840

Staffordshire white saltglaze 'house' teapot and cover, 4½in. high, circa 1740-50. (Sotheby's) $570

Staffordshire covered vegetable dish with high domed cover, circa 1825, 12¼in. long. (Robert W. Skinner Inc.) $750

Obadiah Sherratt group 'The Red Barn', 8½in. high. (Edwards, Bigwood & Bewlay) $1,500

Staffordshire pottery box and cover in the form of a tortoise, circa 1820, 13cm. wide. (Sotheby, King & Chasemore) $355

Staffordshire pottery figure of C. H. Spurgeon in straight-sided pulpit, 12in. high. (Russell, Baldwin & Bright) $65

Very rare pair of Staffordshire equestrian figures of Gholab and Ranbir Singh, circa 1846, 22cm. high. (Sotheby, King & Chasemore) $520

Staffordshire pottery figure of John Wesley in scroll-edged pulpit, 11in. high. (Russell, Baldwin & Bright) $115

Staffordshire solid agate model of a cat, circa 1740-50, 4¾in. high. (Sotheby's) $705

Large Staffordshire coffee pot, circa 1825, 11in. high, with C-scrolled handle. (Robert W. Skinner Inc.) $800

Early 19th century Staffordshire pearlware watch stand, 23.2cm. high. (Sotheby, King & Chasemore)$355

Large Staffordshire platter with wide floral border, circa 1825, 19in. wide. (Robert W. Skinner Inc.) $375

Staffordshire pastille burner in the form of a rustic cottage, 7in. high. (Edwards, Bigwood & Bewlay)$455

Early 19th century Staffordshire pearlware pointer by Wood & Caldwell, 11.5cm. wide. (Sotheby, King & Chasemore) $120

Staffordshire equestrian figure of Sir Robert Peel, circa 1850, 31.5cm. high. (Sotheby, King & Chasemore) $560

Staffordshire pottery group of a family, circa 1820, 20cm. high. (Sotheby, King & Chasemore) $670

Rare Staffordshire equestrian figure of Lady Godiva, circa 1870, 25.5cm. high.(Sotheby, King & Chasemore)$855

Two Staffordshire portrait figures of Queen Victoria and Prince Albert, 18in. high. (Edwards, Bigwood & Bewlay) $730

Staffordshire group of the elephant of Siam and Mr Hemming as Prince Almansor, 15.7cm. high, circa 1840-50. (Sotheby, King & Chasemore) $315

Rare Staffordshire porcelain figure of Van Amburgh, 15.5cm. high. (Sotheby, King & Chasemore) $2,945

159

STONEWARE

Henry Hammond stoneware bowl with flared body, circa 1977, 22cm. diam. (Sotheby's Belgravia) $175

Rare dated German stoneware tankard, probably Creussen, 1654, 12.5cm. diam. (Sotheby's) $6,040

Rare Reginald Wells stoneware model of a carthorse, 1930's, 14.5cm. wide. (Sotheby's Belgravia) $300

Burgundian limestone relief of St. James and a donor, circa 1460, 19½in. high. (Sotheby's) $23,910

Tall stoneware flagon with broad strap handle, stamped R. Merkelbach, Grenzhausen, 37.5cm. high.(Phillips) $430

Unusual stoneware vase of hu form, 49cm. high, decorated with imitate bronze. (Sotheby's Belgravia) $1,445

Small Tang dynasty stone head of Buddha, 10.8cm. high. (Sotheby's) $1,645

18th century carved stone bust of Minerva, on black stone plinth, 5¾in. high. (Burrows & Day)$120

Michael Cardew Wenford Bridge stoneware stool, 1970's, 30.8cm. diam. (Sotheby's Belgravia) $265

Miniature Swansea taper-stick, circa 1814-22, 3in. high. (Sotheby's) $345

One of a pair of Swansea creamware sauce tureens, covers and stands, 18.5cm. high. (Phillips)$1,665

Swansea fluted oval two-handled center dish, 35.5cm. wide.(Christie's) $4,475

Circular Swansea dish, impressed mark, 23.5cm. diam. (Christie's) $1,425

Swansea cabinet cup and saucer, painted by Wm. Pollard, circa 1820. (Sotheby, King & Chasemore) $1,210

One of a pair of Swansea deep plates of lobed silver shape, 18.5cm. diam. (Phillips) $1,260

Swansea plate decorated by William Pollard, circa 1820-22, 8¼in. diam. (Sotheby's) $570

Swansea cabinet cup painted by Wm. Billingsley, circa 1820, 12.2cm. high. (Sotheby, King & Chasemore) $520

One of a pair of Swansea square dishes, impressed marks, 24cm. wide. (Christie's)$4,070

161

TANG

CHINA

Small Tang dynasty chestnut glazed jar and cover on solid splayed foot, 17.1cm. high. (Sotheby's)$4,115

Large Tang dynasty cream glazed figure of an unsaddled horse, 59cm.(Sotheby's) $26,740

Sui/early Tang dynasty Changsha glazed stoneware vase and cover with cup-shaped mouth, 13.1cm. high.(Sotheby's) $2,880

Marbled Tang dynasty pottery tray of circular shape, 13.4cm. diam. (Sotheby's)$2,880

Tang dynasty Sancai pottery figure of a court dignitary on pierced plinth, 76cm. high.(Sotheby's) $5,140

Tang dynasty glazed pottery figure of a lady, on wooden stand, 27.3cm. high. (Sotheby's) $2,675

Tang dynasty glazed pottery figure of a groom, wood stand, 27.9cm. high. (Sotheby's) $1,235

Tang dynasty glazed stoneware jar and cover on colorless glaze, 20.4cm. high. (Sotheby's) $3,700

Small Tang dynasty splash glazed pottery jar with short waisted neck, 14cm. high. (Sotheby's) $9,875

162

Celtic Rumanian terra-cotta head, ears pier-ced, circa 1st century B.C., 2¾in. high. (Christie's)$415

Etruscan terracotta sarcopha-gus cover of a reclining man, circa 1st century B.C., 23½in. high. (Christie's)
$9,145

Late 19th/early 20th cen-tury Austrian cold-painted terracotta figure of a negro street vendor, 31in. high. (Sotheby Beresford Adams)
$335

18th century English terra-cotta bust of a girl on a marble plinth, 29cm. high. (Christie's) $635

6th century B.C. Greek terracotta figure of a woman, neck repaired, 11in. high. (Robert W. Skinner Inc.)$175

18th century Flemish terracotta group of two putti by Laurent Delvaux, 39.5cm. high. (Christie's)$5,490

One of a pair of terra-cotta vases and stands with gadrooned bodies, circa 1900, 50in. high. (Sotheby's Belgravia)
$680

Roman terracotta oscillum in the form of a theatre mask, circa 1st-2nd century A.D., 4¼in. high. (Christie's) $1,080

Late 19th century Aus-trian cold-painted terra-cotta figure of a Arab street vendor, 38in. high. (Sotheby Beresford Adams) $225

One of a set of six Tour-
nai soup plates with
molded borders, 9¼in.
diam. (Woolley & Wallis)
$325

Rare Tournai tankard, cover
and saucer in the form of a
hooped barrel, circa 1760,
13.5cm. high. (Sotheby,
King & Chasemore)
$3,130

One of a pair of Tour-
nai white figures of a
boy and his companion,
circa 1770, 14cm. high.
(Christie's)$1,510

One of a pair of Tournai
pot-pourri vases and
covers, mid 18th century,
25.5cm. high.(Sotheby's)
$1,685

Tournai spirally gadrooned
shaped circular plate, circa
1765, 24cm. diam.
(Christie's) $335

Tournai white group of
two boys collecting
flowers, circa 1770,
18.5cm. high.
(Christie's) $646

Tournai spirally gadrooned
soup plate painted in the
manner of Lindemann,
circa 1765, 24cm. diam.
(Christie's) $1,295

Tournai white group
of a young woman and
a pack horse, circa
1765, 13cm. high.
(Christie's)$1,080

Tournai lobed circular
soup plate painted in the
manner of Fidelle Duvi-
vier, circa 1765, 24cm.
diam. (Christie's)
$705

19th century Vienna porcelain cabinet plate with tooled gilt and blue border, 7¼in. diam. (Locke & England) $180

Vienna Du Paquier tall slender beaker, probably by Carl Wendelin Anreiter von Zirnfeld, circa 1725. (Christie's) $1,295

Early Vienna Du Paquier famille rose globular two-handled pot and cover, 1720-25, 22.5cm. high. (Christie's) $25,150

Very rare figure of the Buddha, perhaps by Du Paquier, circa 1740, 13.25cm. high.(Christie's) $1,665

Large Vienna Du Paquier lobed and fluted saucer dish painted in Imari style, circa 1730, 39.5cm. diam. (Christie's) $13,875

Vienna Du Paquier beaker and saucer with silvered rims, circa 1730-35. (Christie's) $3,700

Late 19th century Vienna plate with wavy ribbon border, 9½in. diam. (Sotheby Beresford Adams)$335

One of a pair of early 19th century Vienna porcelain vases, 10½in. high. (W. H. Lane & Son) $690

Vienna Du Paquier plate with lobed rim, circa 1730, 22cm. diam. (Christie's) $2,035

Fine Viennese porcelain sixteen-piece cabaret set, signed Sibl, in mint condition. (Morphets) $4,230

Part of a late 18th century seven-piece Vienna porcelain part service of a dish and six plates. (Wm. Doyle Galleries Inc.) $500

VYSE

Glazed figure by Chas. Vyse, 'The Lavender Seller', signed and dated 1922, 8½in. high. (Geering & Colyer) $370

Charles Vyse stoneware vase of compressed spherical form, incised 1934, 22cm. diam. (Christie's) $640

Charles Vyse figure 'Market Day, Boulogne', 1931, 25cm. high. (Sotheby, King & Chasemore) $560

Charles Vyse pottery figure of a flower seller, signed, 25cm. high. (Christie's)$535

Rare Charles Vyse figure of a shire horse, circa 1920, 28.5cm. (Sotheby, King & Chasemore) $820

Charles Vyse pottery figure 'The Madonna of World's End Passage', dated 1921, 23.5cm. high. (Phillips)$295

Wedgwood Fairyland lustre bowl, printed in gilding, circa 1920, 9in. diam. (Sotheby's) $580

Wedgwood & Bentley white jasper oval portrait medallion of Wm. Shakespeare, circa 1775, 8.5cm. high. (Christie's) $610

Fairyland lustre chalice bowl on pedestal foot, 1920's, 10½in. diam. (Sotheby's)$1,350

Wedgwood blue and white jasper oval desk set with central taperstick, circa 1790, 15cm. wide. (Christie's) $650

Wedgwood blue and white oval medallion, circa 1800, 7cm. wide. (Christie's) $140

Wedgwood three-color jasper circular salt, marked Z. & H., circa 1790, 6.5cm. diam. (Christie's) $735

Wedgwood creamware charger lustered in platinum by Louise Powell, 41.5cm. diam. (Christie's) $365

Wedgwood blue and white jasper oviform scent bottle with cut glass stopper and gold mount, circa 1785, 9.5cm. high. (Christie's) $815

Wedgwood & Bentley blue and white jasper circular plaque showing Medusa, circa 1780, 13cm. diam. (Christie's) $935

167

Wedgwood Fairyland lustre bowl and cover. (Christie's S. Kensington) $695

Mid 18th century Wedgwood basalt covered sugar bowl with two handles, 4¾in. diam. (Robert W. Skinner Inc.) $50

Wedgwood Fairyland lustre vase of flaring square section, 19cm. high. (Phillips) $665

One of a pair of Wedgwood and Bentley vases in black basaltes, circa 1775, 9½in. high. (Sotheby's) $3,460

Wedgwood Fairyland lustre candlemas vase, 23cm. high. (H. Spencer & Sons Ltd.) $710

Wedgwood and Bentley 'Porphyry' vase and cover, circa 1775, 15½in. high. (Sotheby's) $2,240

Wedgwood 'Oriental' Fairyland lustre vase and cover, 9½in. high. (Morphets) $1,200

Plate from a Wedgwood part dinner service of twenty-seven pieces, circa 1815-20. (Sotheby's) $1,535

Wedgwood Fairyland lustre vase, early 1920's, 16½in. high. (Phillips) $2,170

Wedgwood basalt covered bowl of spherical shape, silver encaustic borders, circa 1793, 4¼in. high. (Robert W. Skinner Inc.) $50

Tureen from a Wedgwood pottery dinner and dessert set of ninety-one pieces, circa 1883, signed.(Sotheby Beresford Adams)$390

Wedgwood Fairyland lustre octagonal bowl, 22.5cm. high. (Phillips) $1,075

One of a pair of late 19th century Wedgwood blue jasper vases, 8½in. high. (Sotheby's) $610

Wedgwood encaustic-decorated two-handled bell krater, circa 1820, 35cm. wide. (Christie's) $2,045

Rare late 18th century Wedgwood caneware quadruple bamboo flower vase, 10¾in. high. (Sotheby's) $1,525

Wedgwood Fairyland lustre vase, of baluster form, circa 1920, 26cm. high. (Sotheby, King & Chasemore) $295

Mid to late 19th century Wedgwood blue jasperware oval plaque, 39cm. wide. (Sotheby's Belgravia) $255

One of a pair of Wedgwood Fairyland lustre vases of slender ovoid form, 1920's, 8in. high. (Sotheby Beresford Adams)$925

WEDGWOOD

CHINA

Wedgwood Fairyland lustre bowl, interior painted with the 'Woodland Bridge' pattern, 1920's, 28.5cm. diam. (Sotheby's Belgravia) $1,145

Wedgwood oviform pepper pot with pierced top, circa 1790, 6cm. high. (Christie's) $530

Part of a late 18th century Wedgwood creamware dinner service, some pieces damaged. (Woolley & Wallis) $445

Rare Wedgwood 'Queen's ware' argyle and cover, circa 1780-90, 6¼in. high. (Sotheby's) $630

Wedgwood Fairyland lustre vase and cover, 28.8cm. high, 1920's. (Sotheby's Belgravia) $1,430

Wedgwood Fairyland lustre octagonal bowl, 1920's, 22cm. wide. (Sotheby's Belgravia) $1,145

Wedgwood Fairyland lustre bowl, 1920's, 9in. dram. (Sotheby's) $460

Rare Wedgwood Fairyland lustre plaque decorated with the 'Bubbles' design, 29cm. wide, framed, 1920's. (Sotheby's Belgravia) $1,840

Wedgwood creamware cruet painted by Emile Lessore, circa 1865, 22cm. high.(Christie's) $1,060

Westerwald mug of cylindrical form with chequer pattern, 11cm. high. (Phillips)$260

Mid 18th century Westerwald inkstand of rectangular shape, 19cm. wide. (Sotheby's) $530

Large Westerwald jug of ovoid form, 31cm. high. (Phillips) $465

Mid 17th century Westerwald pewter mounted jug, neck applied with lion's mask, 41cm. high. (Sotheby, King & Chasemore) $895

Rare 18th century Westerwald part writing set modeled as lions, 17.7cm. high. (Sotheby's) $1,105

Westerwald jug with flattened globular body, 1641, with replacement metal handle, 31.5cm. high.(Sotheby's) $1,880

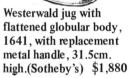

Late 18th century Westerwald stoneware jug applied with the monogram G.R., 25.5cm. high. (Sotheby, King & Chasemore) $250

Rare 18th century Westerwald tankard, inscribed 'London', 18.5cm. high. (Sotheby's) $1,285

Rare Westerwald pewter mounted humpen, circa 1650, 25cm. high. (Sotheby, King & Chasemore) $680

Whieldon oviform teapot and cover with crabstock spout and handle, circa 1755, 19cm. wide. (Christie's) $650

Whieldon lobed globular bottle with garlic neck, circa 1760, 24.5cm. high. (Christie's) $1,260

Mid 18th century Whieldon creamware pot with tortoiseshell glaze, slightly damaged, 4in. high. (Robert W. Skinner Inc.) $175

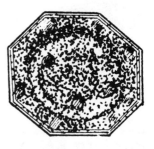

Whieldon model of a ram lying on a grassy base, circa 1760-70, 5½in. wide. (Sotheby's) $1,065

Rare mid 18th century Whieldon type bust of a man, covered with a gray, ochre and manganese glaze, 5¼in. high. (Sotheby's) $1,085

Whieldon octagonal plate in tortoiseshell sponged decoration, 9in. (Edwards, Bigwood & Bewlay) $175

Whieldon teapot and cover with crabstock handle, decorated in tortoiseshell glaze, 4½in. high. (Edwards, Bigwood & Bewlay) $385

Mid 18th century Whieldon model of a swan, 3½in. high, slightly chipped. (Sotheby's) $700

Small Whieldon teapot and cover with crabstock handle and spout, circa 1770, 6½in. diam. (Sotheby's) $470

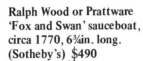

Late 18th century model of a squirrel in the style of Ralph Wood. (Sotheby's) $875

Ralph Wood or Prattware 'Fox and Swan' sauceboat, circa 1770, 6¾in. long. (Sotheby's) $490

Ralph Wood Toby jug of traditional type, circa 1770-80, 9in. high, hat restored. (Sotheby's) $635

Ralph Wood Toby jug, seated, wearing a reddish-brown coat and yellow breeches, 25cm. high. (H. Spencer & Sons Ltd.) $785

Ralph Wood group of St. George and the Dragon, circa 1770, restored, 10¾in. high. (Sotheby's) $905

Late 18th century Ralph Wood Toby jug, 24.5cm. high. (Sotheby, King & Chasemore) $575

Ralph Wood figure of 'The Lost Sheep Found', circa 1775, 21cm. high. (Christie's) $920

Enoch Wood figure of a roaring lion, circa 1790, 12¾in. wide. (Sotheby's) $510

Figure of Mars modeled as a Roman Emperor, by Enoch Wood, circa 1780-90, 9½in. high. (Sotheby's) $305

CHINA

One of a pair of Royal Worcester shell-shaped fruit dishes, decorated by H. Ayrton, 26cm. diam. (H. Spencer & Sons Ltd.) $395

Chamberlain's Worcester reticulated cup and saucer, 1846-50. (Sotheby Beresford Adams) $685

One of a pair of Worcester chinoiserie bowls, circa 1760-65, 9in. high. (Sotheby, King & Chasemore) $200

Late Victorian Royal Worcester porcelain figure 'The Turkish Water Carrier', 18in. high. (Geering & Colyer) $370

Rare set of three Chamberlain's Worcester hunting figures, circa 1820-30, 12cm. and 9cm. high. (Sotheby, King & Chasemore) $1,155

Royal Worcester table lamp as a young girl perched on a tree trunk, 39cm. high. (H. Spencer & Sons Ltd.) $415

Fine Chamberlain's Worcester ice pail, cover and liner, on square marble base, 35cm. wide. (Sotheby, King & Chasemore) $2,195

Royal Worcester 'shot enamel' spill holder, date letter for 1881, 17cm. high.(Sotheby, King & Chasemore) $150

Royal Worcester vase and cover dated for 1919, 7¼in. high. (Sotheby Beresford Adams) $405

Flight, Barr & Barr Worcester fruit bowl of fluted oval form, 14in. wide. (W. H. Lane & Son) $455

One of a pair of Royal Worcester ovoid two-handled vases by C. Baldwyn, 27cm. high. (H. Spencer & Sons Ltd.) $1,115

Worcester comport after Dr. Wall, of shaped oval pedestal design, 13½in. wide. (W. H. Lane & Son) $585

Royal Worcester pot pourri vase and cover painted and signed by J. Stinton, 12in. high, dated for 1924. (Sotheby Beresford Adams) $1,590

Pair of Royal Worcester classical female figures, supported on square gilt socles, 37cm. high. (H. Spencer & Sons Ltd.) $485

Grainger's Worcester vase and cover, dated for 1901, 9¾in. high. (Sotheby Beresford Adams) $335

Royal Worcester bowl painted by Jas. Stinton, signed, 1924, 22cm. diam. (Sotheby's Belgravia) $360

Grainger's Worcester figure of a giraffe, 11cm. high. (Sotheby, King & Chasemore) $295

Royal Worcester vase and cover with ovoid body and mask handles, 1896, 26cm. high. (Sotheby's Belgravia) $325

17

Royal Worcester cracker jar with squat bulbous gadrooned body, 1888, 7in. high. (Robert W. Skinner Inc.) $175

Royal Worcester ewer with squat domed body, 1887, 4½in. high. (Robert W. Skinner Inc.) $225

Royal Worcester vase, circa 1880, with molded woven body, 8in. high. (Robert W. Skinner Inc.) $400

Rare Worcester figure 'The Bather Surprised', modeled by Sir Thos. Brock, 10in. high, 1919. (Sotheby Beresford Adams) $275

Part of a Flight, Barr & Barr period Worcester tea and coffee service. (H. Spencer & Sons Ltd.) $1,225

Royal Worcester cylindrical vase painted and signed by A. Shuck, 1909, 9in. high.(Sotheby Beresford Adams) $220

Worcester Dr. Wall period tea caddy and cover decorated with flowers and insects, 4¾in. tall. (T. Bannister & Co.) $470

One of a pair of Chamberlain Worcester ice pails, covers and liners, circa 1820-30, 37cm. wide. (Sotheby, King & Chasemore) $2,195

Royal Worcester pot pourri vase and cover, 5½in. high, date for 1921, signed G. A. Stinton. (Sotheby Beresford Adams) $370

Royal Worcester jug with lion's profile, circa 1880, 9in. high. (Robert W. Skinner Inc.) $325

Royal Worcester basket in the form of a bird's nest, circa 1890, 6in. high. (Robert W. Skinner Inc.) $250

Royal Worcester ewer with gilt reptile handle, 1881, 11½in. high. (Robert W. Skinner Inc.) $550

Royal Worcester figurine of a woman in 12th century costume, 9in. high, circa 1890. (Robert W. Skinner Inc.) $450

Royal Worcester elephant in gold colored harness and carrying a jardiniere, circa 1882, 6in. high. (Robert W. Skinner Inc.) $150

Royal Worcester vase and cover, signed and painted by H. Stinton, 10½in. high, dated for 1915. (Sotheby Beresford Adams) $515

One of two Royal Worcester vases, circa 1880, 4in. and 6in. high. (Robert W. Skinner Inc.) $200

Royal Worcester squat pot pourri vase and cover, painted and signed by Ricketts, 5in. high, dated for 1926. (Sotheby Beresford Adams) $315

Royal Worcester vase of tankard form, 9in. high. (Robert W. Skinner Inc.) $300

Tureen, cover and stand from a Chamberlain's Worcester pink-ground part dessert service, circa 1825. (Christie's) $1,580

Early Worcester sauceboat of shallow oval form, circa 1754, 6¼in. wide. (Sotheby's) $995

Early Worcester/Lunds Bristol shell-shaped dish with central flower spray, circa 1752, 3¼in. high. (Sotheby's) $995

Royal Worcester centerpiece, stem supported by four cherubs, 14½in. high. (J. M. Welch & Son) $1,490

Worcester teapot, cover and stand painted with 'Bengal Tiger Pattern', circa 1775, 21.5cm. wide. (Christie's) $950

Royal Worcester two-handled oviform vase and cover, painted by F. Roberts, 56cm. high. (Christie's) $1,725

Worcester blue and white bough pot of bombe shape, circa 1765-70, 9in diam. (Sotheby's) $670

Royal Worcester orange-ground two-handled oviform vase and cover, painted by H. Davis, 22cm. high.(Christie's)$530

One of a pair of Worcester lobed oval dishes, circa 1770, 27cm. wide. (Christie's) $990

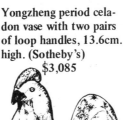

Yongzheng Companie-des-Indes blue and white dish with flanged rim, 35cm. diam. (Sotheby, King & Chasemore) $170

Yongzheng period celadon vase with two pairs of loop handles, 13.6cm. high. (Sotheby's) $3,085

Yongzheng famille rose bowl of double ogee form, wood stand, 17.2cm. diam. (Sotheby's) $4,115

YORKSHIRE

Yorkshire figure of a sportsman, circa 1780, 20cm. high. (Christie's) $490

Yorkshire figure of a cockerel splashed in brown, ochre, yellow and blue, circa 1780, 16.5cm. high. (Christie's) $820

Late 18th/early 19th century Yorkshire Toby jug, face colored deep red, 10in. high, restored. (Sotheby's) $555

Unusual Yorkshire jug and cover, probably Rothwell pottery, circa 1770, 5½in. high. (Sotheby's) $550

Early 19th century Yorkshire Pratt type group of an elephant and rider, 20cm. wide. (Sotheby, King & Chasemore) $3,220

Yorkshire pottery watchholder, modeled as a man and woman on either side of a clock, 9in. high. (Christie's S. Kensington) $930

Mahogany bracket clock in broken arched case with brass fret sides, 16½in. high. (Lawrence Fine Art) $960

Early 18th century bracket clock by Andrew Moran, London, with inverted bell top, 18in. high. (Boardman's) $2,225

Early 19th century ebonized bracket clock, 1ft. 6½in. high. (Sotheby's) $1,450

Late 18th century mahogany bracket clock, dial inscribed Joseph Ismay, London, 22in. high. (Sotheby, King & Chasemore) $1,050

Black lacquer bracket clock signed Marwick Markham, London, 20¾in. high. (Lawrence Fine Art) $1,825

19th century mahogany striking and chiming bracket clock, inscribed Thos. Lace, 24in. high. (Sotheby, King & Chasemore) $2,625

George III ebonized bracket clock by Jno. Starey, London, sides with sunburst grilles, 20in. high. (Sotheby, King & Chasemore) $1,165

Small repeating ebonized bracket clock by J. & W. Mitchell, Glasgow, circa 1850, 8¾in. high. (Sotheby's Belgravia) $2,360

Early 18th century ebonized bracket clock, signed Fromanteel, London. (Christie's) $3,310

Satinwood repeating bracket clock by Desbois & Wheeler, London, 1830's, 16in. high. (Sotheby's Belgravia) $845

Early 19th century bracket clock by John Agar, Malton, in mahogany case, 58cm. high. (Osmond, Tricks) $785

Ebonized bracket clock, signed Barraud, Cornhill, London, 17in. high. (Lawrence Fine Art) $1,150

Small early George III ebonized bracket clock by William Allam, London, 15in. high. (Sotheby's) $4,575

Chain fusee repeating ebonized bracket clock, 1880's, 18in. high. (Sotheby's Belgravia) $1,520

German lacquered bracket clock, case painted with chinoiserie on green-ground, 24in. high, circa 1900. (Sotheby's Belgravia) $825

Early 19th century bracket clock in ornate case, 25in. high. (J. M. Welch & Son) $1,275

Late 19th century bracket clock in ebonized case, retailer's mark of W. H. Collins, Ipswich, 23in. high. (Olivers) $1,430

Late 18th century Continental bracket clock with brass finials. (J. M. Welch & Son) $545

CLOCKS

Early 19th century mahogany brass inlaid bracket clock by George Miles, with double fusee movement. (T. Bannister & Co.) $1,265

Quarter repeating bracket clock by Thos. Tompion, London, signed, on ebonized wall bracket, 12½in. high. (Christie's) $22,440

Regency ebonized striking bracket clock with chamfered top, case with brass inlay, 14in. high.(Christie's)$1,685

Ebonized bracket clock by James McCabe, London, case with brass inlay, 16in. high. (Christie's) $1,870

George III mahogany striking bracket clock, dial signed Wm. Storr, London, 19in. high. (Christie's)$3,555

Late 17th century yew-wood striking bracket clock, signed Jno. Snow, London, 14½in. high. (Christie's)$4,300

George III mahogany striking bracket clock, dial signed James Tregent, London, 15½in. high. (Christie's)$1,495

Fruitwood striking bracket clock, signed Henry Massy, London, case with scroll carrying handle, 17½in. high. (Christie's) $4,490

Late George III fruitwood bracket timepiece alarm, dial signed Duncan, St. James's Street, London, 9½in. high. (Christie's) $1,215

Ebonized bracket clock by Abel Panchaud, London, with brass handles and feet, 16in. high. (Locke & England) $1,790

Walnut bracket clock by A. Miller, Brighton, with enamel dial and Roman numerals. (T. Bannister & Co.) $310

South German ebonized striking bracket clock, dial signed Fr. Hav. Gegenreiner Augsburg, 10¾in. high. (Christie's)$1,495

Early George III chiming bracket clock with automaton, dial signed Thozon Fitter, London, 20in. high. (Christie's) $6,360

George II fruitwood striking bracket clock with inverted bell-top case, dial signed John Fladgate, London, 18½in. high. (Christie's)$2,620

Austrian ebonized quarter striking bracket clock in bell-top case, 19in. high. (Christie's)$1,870

Dark green lacquer striking bracket clock, dial signed Gio. Batta Callin Genoua, mid 18th century, 26in. high. (Christie's)$3,365

Garrard Silver Jubilee clock, designed by F. W. Elliott, 1977. (T. Bannister & Co.) $1,630

Late 17th century ebonized striking bracket clock, signed Wm. Speakman, London, 14½in. high.(Christie's) $5,235

BRACKET CLOCKS

Early 19th century late Regency rosewood bracket clock by John Moore & Son, Clerkenwell, 16in. high. (Sotheby Beresford Adams) $670

George III fruitwood bracket timepiece, dial signed Allam & Caithness, London, 22cm. high.(Phillips)$2,175

19th century bracket clock in heavily carved mahogany case.(Burtenshaw Walker) $1,370

Late George II mahogany bracket clock by Thos. Chappell, London, 55cm. high. (Phillips) $1,700

19th century oak and ormolu bracket clock, 29in. high, with pierced oak wall bracket. (Morphets) $1,185

George III mahogany cased bracket clock by Thos. Wagstaffe, London, 24½in. high. (Burrows & Day) $4,525

Ebonized bracket timepiece by Johan Meyer, Steyer, in glazed case, 15in. high. (Burrows & Day) $450

Tortoiseshell and gilt metal musical bracket clock by G. Prior, London, for the Turkish market.(Sotheby's) $6,550

Georgian mahogany bracket clock with brass and steel dial by Mudge, London, on ogee feet.(Burtenshaw Walker)$1,170

Architectural designed walnut striking bracket clock, marked Frank Giles & Co., Kensington. (Allen & May) $330

18th century Bohemian ebonized quarter striking bracket clock, 19¼in. high. (Sotheby's)$2,600

Late 19th century oak chiming bracket clock in carved case, 28in. high. (Sotheby Beresford Adams) $1,005

Mahogany bracket clock by Thos. Wagstaffe, London, in bell-top case, 19in. high. (Sotheby's) $1,975

19th century bracket clock, painted dial inscribed Thwaites & Reed, London, 37cm. high. (Phillips) $1,360

George III ebonized bracket clock by Matthew Dutton, London, 15in. high. (Sotheby, King & Chasemore) $3,840

Ebonized quarter repeating bracket clock by Marmaduke Storr, London, 18in. high. (Sotheby's) $3,745

George III ebonized bracket clock by S. & C. Joyce, London, 13½in. high. (Sotheby, King & Chasemore) $1,185

Early 19th century Regency mahogany bracket timepiece, enamel dial inscribed Sheppery & Pearce, Nottingham, 16in. high.(Sotheby Beresford Adams) $500

Brass timepiece carriage clock with enamel dial, in one-piece case with hinged rear door, 4¼in. high.(Christie's)$450

English walnut cased chronometer carriage clock, 10in. high. (Christie's)$1,400

Early gilt brass striking chronometer carriage clock by Bolviller, Paris, 7in. high. (Christie's) $2,620

Miniature ivory cased carriage timepiece with enamel dial, 3¼in. high. (Christie's) $335

Early 19th century French brass capucine clock with carrying handle above the bell, 10in. high.(Christie's) $1,400

Large lacquered brass grande sonnerie carriage clock, stamped D. C., in wood traveling case, 8½in. high. (Christie's) $4,115

Miniature lacquered brass carriage timepiece, stamped Payne & Co., Paris, 3in. high. (Christie's) $560

French gilt metal and por-celain mounted striking carriage clock in 'bamboo' case, 6¾in. high.(Christie's) $1,870

Brass carriage clock with Sevres porcelain dial and in gorge case, 6in. high. (Christie's) $1,495

19th century French carriage clock with repeat and alarm, 6½in. high. (Sotheby Bearne) $975

Gilt metal porcelain mounted striking carriage clock, 6¾in. high. (Christie's) $2,245

Miniature silver and enamel carriage clock with porcelain mask and side panels, 3in. high. (Christie's) $1,590

Lacquered brass miniature carriage clock with enamel dial, 3in. high. (Christie's) $260

Gilt metal timepiece carriage clock by Arnold's/Chas. Frodsham, in engraved case, circa 1860, 5in. high. (Christie's) $2,620

Gilt metal porcelain mounted grande sonnerie carriage clock by Drocourt, 5¾in. high. (Christie's) $5,425

Gilt metal petite sonnerie carriage clock, backplate stamped Grohe, London, 5½in. high. (Christie's) $2,805

Brass quarter striking carriage clock, dial signed Leroy et Fils, 5in. high. (Christie's) $970

Gilt metal and champleve enamel striking carriage clock with lever platform, 6in. high. (Christie's) $1,215

CARRIAGE CLOCKS

Silver-cased boudoir clock by William Comyns, London, 1896, 9.5cm. high. (Sotheby's Belgravia) $505

Miniature French brass carriage clock, stamped E. White, Paris, 3¾in. high. (Lawrence Fine Art) $300

Rare silver-cased carriage clock, handle set with shield with coat-of-arms, 6¼in. high. (Christie's) $2,055

Early 20th century gilt brass carriage clock by Russells Ltd., Paris, in red leather case, 6¼in. high. (Sotheby Beresford Adams)$410

Unusual brass carriage clock in the shape of a padlock, 6½in. high. (Lawrence Fine Art) $250

Mid 19th century gilt brass alarm carriage clock by Leroy et Fils, Paris, 6¼in. high. (Sotheby Beresford Adams) $595

Gilt metal miniature carriage clock with enamel side panels, 2½in. high. (Christie's) $4,300

Early 20th century gilt brass carriage clock by A. W. Butt, Chester, 7½in. high. (Sotheby Beresford Adams) $370

French brass carriage clock in gorge type case, 6¼in. high. (Lawrence Fine Art) $595

Enamel mounted carriage clock, signed R. & W. Sorley, Paris, 5¼in. high. (Sotheby's) $1,415

Very rare double striking alarm carriage clock with enamel dial, 5½in. high. (Sotheby's) $4,575

French brass carriage clock dated 1886, 7in. high. (Lawrence Fine Art) $385

Enamel mounted carriage clock with ivorine dial, 6¼in. high. (Sotheby's) $1,455

Gilt metal striking carriage clock in the manner of Thos. Cole, 6¾in. high. (Christie's) $1,870

French brass and porcelain miniature carriage timepiece, in a case, 10cm. high. (Phillips) $2,835

English petite sonnerie brass carriage clock, 31cm. high, signed Edw. Funnell, Brighton. (Phillips) $5,670

French brass carriage clock inscribed Mappin & Webb, French Make, 5½in. high. (Lawrence Fine Art) $190

Good late 19th century French carriage clock with blue enamel dial and side panels, 7¼in. high.(Sotheby Bearne) $1,495

CARRIAGE CLOCKS

Gilt brass hour repeating carriage clock, dial signed Connell, London, circa 1890, 6¾in. high. (Sotheby's Belgravia) $1,030

Ornate French carriage clock with serpentine-shaped front and hinged handle. (Butler & Hatch Waterman) $660

19th century French carriage clock by Magraine in brass oval case, 7in. high. (Dacre, Son & Hartley) $725

Miniature French gilt, brass and enamel carriage clock, 2¾in. high, with canted corners. (Phillips) $1,665

Large French brass repeating carriage clock with day and date dials. (M. Philip H. Scott) $2,864

Gilt bronze and enamel carriage clock, with painted sides, surmounted by a gallery, circa 1890, 4½in. high. (Sotheby's Belgravia) $4,215

Plain faced French brass carriage clock with repeat and alarm. (M. Philip H. Scott) $1,520

French brass carriage clock with alarm, side panels, face and rear door painted. (M. Philip H. Scott) $2,900

Parcel gilt silver miniature carriage clock by Asprey, London, 2½in. high. (Christie's) $655

190

Miniature French brass carriage timepiece with enamel dial, 4in. high. (Lawrence Fine Art) $325

Gilt bronze carriage clock, signed Lucien, Paris, circa 1870, 7¼in. high. (Sotheby's Belgravia) $780

Late 19th century French enameled repeater carriage clock with Sevres face, 5¾in. high. (Robert W. Skinner Inc.) $1,800

English repeating carriage clock by E. White, London, circa 1850. (Bonhams) $7,295

Ebony bracket clock by Thomas Boxell, Brighton, circa 1840, 15½in. high, with key. (Sotheby's Belgravia) $1,440

Fine French gilt metal striking and repeating alarm carriage clock by Leroy et Fils, Paris. (Andrew Grant) $1,090

Small French carriage clock in case with filigree decoration and Corinthian columns. (Butler & Hatch Waterman) $575

Ebony cased striking alarm carriage clock, 7in. high. (Andrew Grant)$475

Large bow-sided brass carriage clock by Elkington & Co. Ltd., in original case. (Worsfolds) $885

CLOCK SETS

French gilt bronze and champleve enamel clock garniture, stamped Japy Freres, 21¼in. high. (Lawrence Fine Art) $1,825

Black and red marble calendar clock garniture, signed Brush & Drummond, circa 1870, clock 23in. high. (Sotheby's Belgravia) $825

Gilt bronze and 'jeweled' Sevres clock garniture by Leroy & Fils, mid 19th century, clock 20in. high. (Sotheby Beresford Adams) $3,535

Gilt spelter and porcelain clock garniture, circa 1890, clock 20½in. high. (Sotheby's Belgravia) $1,130

Mid 19th century composed gilt bronze and porcelain clock garniture by J. Mayer. (Sotheby Beresford Adams) $1,155

Gilt bronze, onyx and champleve clock garniture, signed Mellington Cleton, Boulogne. (Sotheby's Belgravia) $1,400

Three-piece slate garniture de cheminee with urn-shaped vases. (J. M. Welch & Son) $145

Late 18th century clock garniture by Antide Janvier, Paris. (Robert W. Skinner Inc.) $2,000

French parcel gilt green patinated bronze three-piece clock garniture, signed Hry. Marc, Paris. (Sotheby, King & Chasemore) $545

Late 19th century carved walnut sculptural clock garniture, movement stamped Leuenberger Interlaken. (Sotheby's Belgravia) $1,030

19th century French Louis XVI style champleve enamel garniture, clock by Japy Freres. (Robert W. Skinner Inc.) $1,100

Louis XVI style Sevres three-piece clock garniture by Ph. Maurey, France, circa 1870. (Robert W. Skinner Inc.) $1,450

GRANDFATHER CLOCKS

Oak grandmother longcase clock inscribed Tempus Fugit, 5ft.3in. high. (Lawrence Fine Art) $805

Oak longcase clock with square hood surmounted by three brass balls. (Butler & Hatch Waterman) $775

Longcase clock by Anthony Charles. (Cooper Hirst) $3,135

18th century red lacquer and chinoiserie longcase clock by George Washbourne, 2.38m. high. (Phillips) $1,700

18th century walnut veneered and seaweed marquetry longcase clock by Wm. Sellers, Long Acre, 2.16m. high.(Phillips) $7,180

Early provincial walnut longcase clock, signed John Greenhill, Maidstone, 6ft. 11in. high.(Sotheby's) $3,745

Oak longcase clock, signed John Knapp, Reading Fecit, 6ft. 9¼in. high. (Lawrence Fine Art) $1,440

Mahogany eight-day longcase clock with pagoda pediment. (Dee & Atkinson) $740

Grandfather clock in mahogany with domed hood, restored. (Butler & Hatch Waterman) $1,720

George III mahogany striking longcase clock by Isaac Hewlett, Bristol, 7ft.9in. high. . (Woolley & Wallis) $2,590

Rare William IV mahogany equation of time clock, dial signed Wm. Dutton, London, 2.30m. high. (Phillips) $3,305

Carved oak quarter chiming longcase clock, signed Wm. Ferrar, Dundee, 7ft.4½in. high. (Lawrence Fine Art) $1,575

Late 18th century green lacquered longcase clock by John Harris, London, 2.32m. high. (Phillips) $1,285

Oak longcase clock, signed Wm. Graham, London, 6ft.9½in. high. (Lawrence Fine Art) $1,765

Small and rare George III oak regulator, dial signed Wm. Allam, London, 6ft.1in. high. (Sotheby's) $5,200

Mahogany grandmother clock, signed Thos. Hunter, 56½in. high. (Lawrence Fine Art) $1,650

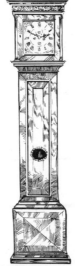

Oak and mahogany longcase clock by Enoch of Warwick, circa 1810. (Locke & England) $665

Early 18th century longcase clock by T. Bacon, Tewkesbury, circa 1720, 79½in. high. (Sotheby, King & Chasemore) $1,315

American Chippendale style mahogany tall cased musical clock, circa 1880, 98in. high. (Robert W. Skinner Inc.) $1,300

Georgian mahogany longcase clock, painted dial signed Robson, N. Shields, 7ft. 9in. high. (Christie's) $2,055

Inlaid mahogany longcase clock with paneled plinth, signed Wm. Evill, Bath, 7ft. 11in. high. (Christie's) $2,990

18th century Dutch walnut longcase clock, signed Fromanteel & Clarke, 6ft. 8½in. high. (Christie's) $3,740

Longcase clock by T. Mudge, London, in later mahogany case, 6ft. 9in. high. (Christie's) $2,150

Late 17th century marquetry longcase clock with concave moldings, 6ft. 8½in. high. (Christie's) $7,105

Fine mahogany long-case clock, by T. Mudge, London, 7ft. 4in. high. (Christie's) $5,235

Mahogany longcase clock with brass face, by T. Meakings, Dublin. (John Hogbin & Son) $315

Dutch striking marquetry longcase clock signed Daniel Quare, London, 6ft. 8½in. high. (Christie's) $21,505

Charles II style simulated tortoiseshell grandmother longcase clock, 6ft. high.(Christie's) $1,685

Victorian mahogany longcase clock with paneled plinth, dial signed 1003 Barrauds, London, 6ft. 3in. high.(Christie's) $4,115

Late 17th century marquetry longcase clock, dial signed Gerrard OverZee Isleworth, 6ft.5in. high. (Christie's) $5,425

Early 19th century eight-day regulator clock by J. Bell, Bath, in mahogany case, 84in. high. (Sotheby Bearne) $2,710

19th century mahogany longcase clock with swan neck pediment, 7ft.3in. high. (Dickinson, Davy & Markham)$735

197

GRANDFATHER CLOCKS

Early 18th century floral marquetry longease clock by Andrew Dunlop, London. (Locke & England) $9,100

Mid 18th century black japanned longcase clock with chinoiserie decoration, 86½in. high.(Sotheby, King & Chasemore) $1,260

Federal mahogany inlaid longcase clock, dial inscribed S. Willard, Roxbury, circa 1790, 87in. high. (Robert W. Skinner Inc.) $4,000

Black japanned longcase clock, dial signed Wm. Allam, London, 6ft.1in. high. (Sotheby's) $5,200

Walnut and marquetry longcase clock by Stephen Wilmot, London, 6ft.9in. high. (Phillips) $4,255

18th century Dutch marquetry longcase clock by Steven Hoogendyk, Rotterdam, 110in. (Wm. Doyle Galleries Inc.) $12,000

German giltwood and porcelain longcase clock, circa 1880, 63½in. high. (Sotheby's Belgravia) $4,730

Eight-day mahogany longcase clock by Hunt of Ludgate Hill. (J. M. Welch & Son) $1,590

17th century William and Mary japanned longcase clock, works by J. Metzell, London, 77½in. high (Robert W. Skinner Inc.)
$1,800

George III mahogany longcase clock by James Lawson, Liverpool, 97in. high. (Sotheby, King & Chasemore)
$1,665

18th century burrwalnut longcase clock by James Snelling, London, 91in. high.(Boardman's)
$2,760

Walnut and marquetry cased month going longcase clock by J. Barnett, London. (Sotheby's)
$7,310

18th century French walnut loncase clock with molded arched pediment, 8ft.8in. high.(Phillips)
$2,035

Mahogany longcase clock with quarter striking on eight chimes, circa 1910, 85in. high.(Sotheby's Belgravia)
$1,220

Early 18th century walnut and herringbone longcase clock by John Wrench, Chester. (Locke & England)
$2,910

Mahogany longcase clock with fret carved hood, 95in. high, circa 1910. (Sotheby's Belgravia)$3,940

199

LANTERN CLOCKS

CLOCKS

19th century, late 17th century style brass lantern clock by Thos. Speakman, London, 15½in. high. (Sotheby Beresford Adams) $520

Wing alarm lantern clock, dial signed J. Windmills, London, circa 1700, 15½in. high. (Sotheby's) $2,080

Late 19th century French lantern clock in brass-sided case, 14½in. high. (Robert W. Skinner Inc.) $325

English brass lantern clock, dial plate signed Edward Stanton, London, 17in. high. (Christie's) $2,805

German brass lantern clock, stamped W. H. Sch., circa 1900, 15in. high. (Sotheby's Belgravia) $615

Small brass lantern clock by Tho. Tompion, London, signed, 6in. high. (Christie's) $7,480

18th century French alarm lantern clock, signature erased, 9in. high. (Sotheby's) $1,765

18th century Continental lantern clock, 27cm. high, with carved walnut bracket. (Phillips) $945

18th century lantern clock, dial signed Step. Harris, Seven Oakes, 13½in. high. (Sotheby's) $1,560

200

Unusual mid 19th century mahogany cased bracket chiming clock, 17in. high. (Sotheby, King & Chasemore) $545

Gilt bronze porcelain mounted mantel clock by Japy Freres, circa 1870, 17in. high. (Sotheby's Belgravia) $845

20th century coppered brass Atmos clock by Jaeger le Coultre, 9¼in. high. (Sotheby's Belgravia) $370

Gilt bronze mantel clock with enamel dial, circa 1870, 15in. high. (Sotheby's Belgravia) $390

Marble and ormolu clock by Achille Brocot, Paris, 23in. high, circa 1850. (Robert W. Skinner Inc.) $1,300

Mid 19th century brass alarm mantel timepiece with glass dome, 9in. high. (Sotheby's Belgravia) $780

Oak quarter chiming bracket clock, signed Pearce & Co., Leeds and Huddersfield, 30½in. high.(Lawrence Fine Art) $940

French Empire ormolu and bronze mantel clock, 54cm. high. (Phillips)$1,170

Mahogany bracket clock, signed Turner, London, in pagoda topped case, 24¼in. high. (Lawrence Fine Art) $540

201

MANTEL CLOCKS

French ormolu mounted enamel faced striking mantel clock. (John Hogbin & Son) $375

Floating-turtle mystery clock, signed Planchon Palais Royale, on ebonized square base, 10in. (Christie's) $2,055

Rococo revival walnut mantel clock, Ansonia, Connecticut, circa 1875, 23½in. high. (Robert W. Skinner Inc.) $175

Late 19th century French enamel and jeweled clock with semi-precious stone and pearl decoration, 8¼in. high. (Robert W. Skinner Inc.) $1,700

French Empire mantel clock in ormolu and black painted case, 12½in. wide. (Sotheby Bearne) $560

Liberty & Co. 'Tudric' pewter timepiece in almost rectangular case and with brass hands, 33.5cm. high. (Phillips) $285

Unusual Art Deco Smith's electric mantel clock on raised black backed glass panel, 15in. high. (Sotheby Bearne) $860

Louis XV style ormolu and boulle bracket clock, signed Courtois a Paris, 34in. high. (Sotheby, King & Chasemore) $1,580

Late 19th century French brass and glass mantel clock in beveled case, 12in. high. (Robert W. Skinner Inc.) $450

202

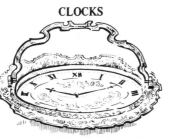

Thomas Cole gilt brass cake basket clock with concave dial, 6¼in. diam. (Christie's) $2,430

Thomas Cole gilt metal strut clock, case signed London & Ryder, London, circa 1859, 4¾in. high. (Christie's) $485

Mid 19th century brass and ormolu French mantel clock with white enamel dial. (T. Bannister & Co.) $290

French gilt metal mantel clock with perpetual calendar, signed Leroy & Fils, 20in. high.(Christie's) $2,055

Exotic English silver gilt quarter striking carriage clock, movement signed Hunt & Roskell, London, 11¾in. high. (Christie's) $5,610

Gilt metal and marble mantel clock, stamped J.B.D., with perpetual calendar dial, 18½in. high. (Christie's) $2,805

Stylish Cartier timepiece case of semi-circular shaped on waisted and stepped base, signed, 25cm. high. (Phillips) $2,865

Unusual Liberty & Co. 'Tudric' timepiece, designed by Archibald Knox, 30.5cm. high. (Phillips)$1,575

French black marble astrological mantel clock with thermometer, calendar dial and barometer, circa 1870, 19¾in. high. (Robert W. Skinner Inc.) $750

MANTEL CLOCKS

18th century Friesland table clock, signed Augustin Linder and Melchior Bruner. (Sotheby, King & Chasemore) $1,690

Ormolu mantel clock by Chas. Frodsham, 18in. high. (Hall Wateridge & Owen) $735

Mid 19th century gilt bronze and porcelain mantel clock, dial inscribed JB Delettrez, Paris, 20in. high. (Sotheby Beresford Adams) $1,155

19th century French clock in boullework case, 2ft.6in. high. (Lacy Scott) $1,060

Late 19th century gilt spelter and porcelain mantel clock by S. Wartenberg, Paris, 14in. high.(Sotheby Beresford Adams) $370

Late 19th century Meissen clock case with movement by Morley, 24½in. high. (Sotheby, King & Chasemore) $3,035

Mahogany cased Edwardian 'balloon' mantel clock. (Alfred Mossop & Co.) $345

French gilt metal four-glass mantel clock by Hry. Marc, Paris, 14in. high.(Sotheby, King & Chasemore) $580

Gilt bronze four-glass battery mantel timepiece, dated 1906, and marked 'Made in England', 12¾in. high. (Sotheby Beresford Adams) $1,040

French gilt metal mantel clock with porcelain mounts, 23½in. high. (Sotheby, King & Chasemore) $805

Regency rosewood mantel clock, silvered dial signed Jas. Tupman, Bloomsbury, 8¾in. high. (Christie's S. Kensington)$1,860

Paris clock case and stand, circa 1840, 43.3cm. high, slightly chipped.(Sotheby's Belgravia) $875

Mid 19th century French red boulle and brass inlaid bracket clock.(Lacy Scott) $1,075

Viennese white metal watch stand, movement inscribed Claydon. (Christie's S. Kensington) $2,380

Gilt metal mounted mantel clock, dial signed Seth Thomas, U.S.A., 13¾in. high. (Sotheby, King & Chasemore)$185

Late George III inlaid mahogany bracket clock with painted dial, 23½in. high. (Sotheby's) $1,665

French gilt and ormolu striking mantel clock. (Alfred Mossop & Co.) $330

19th century red boulle mantel clock signed Martinot, Paris, 15in. high. (Sotheby, King & Chasemore) $780

Gilt bronze and marble clock with silvered dial, circa 1850, 19in. high. (Sotheby's Belgravia) $495

Regency bronze and ormolu mantel clock, dial surmounted by a displayed eagle, 14½in. wide. (Christie's) $2,100

Gilt bronze mantel clock in inlaid case, with key and pendulum, circa 1870, 15¼in. high. (Sotheby's Belgravia) $350

Gilt bronze and porcelain mantel clock, sides flanked with simulated bamboo columns, circa 1870, 14½in. high. (Sotheby's Belgravia) $555

Early Louis XV ormolu mounted boulle bracket clock, signed Dufour a Paris, 44in. high, with bracket. (Christie's) $2,110

Gilt brass mantel clock in bevel-glazed case with pierced columns, circa 1890, 12½in. high. (Christie's) $430

Eight-day mantel chronometer, dial signed Harris, late Hatton & Harris, London, 35cm. high. (Phillips) $1,890

Parcel gilt bronze automaton mantel clock, circa 1860, 17¼in. high. (Sotheby's Belgravia) $1,235

Gilt bronze mantel clock with half-hour striking, in rococo case, 16½in. high, circa 1900. (Sotheby's Belgravia) $640

Ebony mantel clock by
Thomas Boxell, Brighton,
circa 1840, 15½in. high,
with key. (Sotheby's Bel-
gravia) $1,440

German beechwood brac-
ket clock, dial signed T.
Maury, Lisboa, circa
1880, 20in. high. (Sothe-
by's Belgravia)$635

Gilt bronze and porce-
lain mantel clock with
painted dial, circa 1880,
17in. high. (Sotheby's
Belgravia) $1,440

Mahogany mantel time-
piece with gilt bronze
mounts, circa 1870, 14in.
high. (Sotheby's Belgravia)
          $330

Coalbrookdale neo-rococo
clock case, 30cm. high,
circa 1820, movement by
Bennet, Holborn.(Sotheby,
King & Chasemore)
          $500

Architectural champleve
enamel mantel clock
with movement by Japy
Freres, circa 1870, 21in.
high.(Sotheby's Belgravia)
          $1,955

Gilt bronze and porce-
lain 'Gothic' mantel
clock with Roman
numerals, circa 1880,
23in. high. (Sotheby's
Belgravia)$1,005

Louis XVI mantel clock in
brass and ormolu with enamel dial, 20in. high. (Sotheby, King & Chasemore)
          $385

Mid 19th century man-
tel clock by James
McCabe, London, 9½in.
high. (Phillips)
          $1,665

207

CLOCKS

Brass skeleton clock on marble base with wood plinth, 13in. high. (Dickinson, Davy & Markham) $445

Rare three-train brass skeleton clock by J. Defries & Sons, London, 22in. high. (Boardman's)$5,340

Brass skeleton clock on white marble base, circa 1860, 16in. high. (Sotheby's Belgravia) $845

Brass skeleton 'one' at the hour' timepiece, 13½in. high, on mahogany and velvet plinth. (Sotheby's) $775

Rare quarter striking skeleton clock by James Condliff. (Sotheby's) $6,265

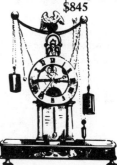

Timepiece skeleton clock, supported on two Tuscan columns flanking a thermometer scale.(Christie's) $3,555

Brass skeleton clock surmounted by a bell, 16in. high, with glass dome. (Sotheby's Belgravia) $845

Small brass skeleton clock under glass dome. (Honiton Galleries) $185

Skeleton clock by Brooking, Clifton, on white marble base and under glass dome, 20½in. high. (Sotheby Bearne) $1,495

Lantern alarm wall clock, face signed Zac Mountfort, St. Albans, 13in. high. (Sotheby, King & Chasemore) $930

18th century blue lacquered Act of Parliament clock by Thos. Watts, Lavenham, 56in. high. (Boardman's) $1,460

Gilt bronze strut timepiece by R. & S. Garrard & Co., London, circa 1870, 4½in. high. (Sotheby's Belgravia) $515

19th century Morbier clock with brass harp pendulum, maker's name M. N. Brecha A Redon. (T. Bannister & Co.) $385

Gilt bronze cartel clock, stamped A. Chapuis A La Gerbe D'Or, Paris, 25in. high, circa 1880. (Sotheby's Belgravia) $865

Friesland wall clock, Holland, circa 1800, 26in. high. (Robert W. Skinner Inc.) $600

Late 19th century French kingwood and ormolu mounted wall clock, 4ft. 7in. high. (Phillips) $2,775

'Regency' gilt bronze cartel clock with enamel dial, 1870's, 29in. high. (Sotheby's Belgravia) $1,480

Walnut wall regulator by E. Howard & Co., 56in. high. (Robert W. Skinner Inc.) $4,500

WALL CLOCKS

CLOCKS

Victorian rosewood trunk wall clock with white dial, 2ft.2in. high. (Dickinson, Davy & Markham) $185

Mid Victorian papier-mache and mother-of-pearl inlaid wall clock, 29in. high. (Coles, Knapp & Kennedy) $325

American mahogany wall acorn timepiece with painted tin dial, 28in. high. (Robert W. Skinner Inc.) $1,200

Late 19th/early 20th century Swiss wall clock in chalet style case, 40in. high. (Sotheby Beresford Adams) $2,140

Friesian oak staartklok surmounted by three brass ball finials, 54in. high. (Lawrence Fine Art) $1,845

Georgian Act of Parliament clock by Thos. Thwaites of Mitcham, in black japanned case, 150cm. high. (H. Spencer & Sons Ltd.) $1,675

Eight-day striking Vienna regulator clock. (J. M. Welch & Son) $545

Drop-dial wall clock in carved case, circa 1840. (J. M. Welch & Son) $435

American Federal mahogany banjo clock, 46½in. high. (Wm. Doyle Galleries Inc.) $2,000

Weight-driven rosewood veneer double dial calendar wall clock, Connecticut, circa 1865, 32in. high. (Robert W. Skinner Inc.) $800

Mid 19th century painted wood automaton wall clock, case painted with flowers, 19in. high. (Sotheby's Belgravia) $3,700

Vienna regulating wall clock, circa 1900. (J. M. Welch & Son) $275

18th century marquetry cased Friesland staartklok. (Anderson & Garland) $1,720

Antique wall clock with fret carving to base and bracket, by Samuel Porter, London. (Butler & Hatch Waterman) $340

Japanese padouk stick clock, trunk with brass chapters, 42cm. high. (Phillips) $755

American Victorian walnut clock, circa 1875, 29½in. high. (Robert W. Skinner Inc.)$500

Pressed wood advertising figure-eight wall clock by Edward P. Baird & Co., New York circa 1880, 31in. long. (Robert W. Skinner Inc.) $450

Victorian inlaid walnut trunk wall clock, dial inscribed 'Fowler', 2ft. 11in. high. (Dickinson, Davy & Markham) $225

Quarter repeating verge pair-cased watch by Benjamin Sidey, hallmarked 1776. (Sotheby Bearne) $785

Lady's Hampden hunting-cased dress watch with white enamel dial and in gold case. (Sotheby Bearne) $580

Silver-cased keyless free sprung reversed escape wheel lever pocket watch, unsigned, 44mm. diam. (Christie's) $300

George III gold lever watch, hallmarked 1816, with diamond end stone. (Sotheby Bearne) $450

Gold hunter-cased minute repeating lever watch, movement signed Falconer & Co., Hong Kong, 52mm. diam. (Christie's) $3,180

Silver pair-cased verge watch movement signed I. Tudham, London, 57mm. diam. (Christie's) $750

Silver pair-cased half quarter repeating verge watch, signed Joseph Martineau Senr., London, 58mm. diam. (Christie's) $1,125

Silver pair-cased verge watch, movement signed George Etherington, London. (Christie's) $895

Silver pair-cased Sun and Moon false pendulum verge watch, signed Regn. Westwood, London, 57mm. diam. (Christie's) $2,055

Gold pair-cased quarter repeating cylinder watch, signed Chas. Haley, London, 1785, 50mm. diam. (Christie's) $2,245

French gold and enamel verge watch, signed Lepaute a Paris, 40mm. diam. (Christie's) $1,400

Silver and gold case lever pocket watch, movement signed W. Ehrhardt, Birmingham, 45mm. diam. (Christie's) $410

George III quarter repeating verge watch by John Ellicott, London, silver case hallmarked 1781. (Sotheby Bearne) $1,125

Swiss gold hunter-cased minute repeating keyless lever calendar chronograph, 55mm. diam. (Christie's) $4,115

French center-seconds chronometer by R. Laurent Jouvenat & Cie, London, in silver case. (Sotheby Bearne) $505

Gold-cased English cylinder pocket watch, cover signed Rundell, Bridge & Rundell, London, 1811, 38mm. diam. (Christie's) $840

Fine gold and enamel duplex watch, signed Vaucher Fleurier, 58mm. diam. (Christie's) $12,155

Silver-cased free sprung lever pocket watch, movement signed Chas. Frodsham, London, 45mm. diam. (Christie's) $390

Open-faced quarter repeating cylinder watch in engine-turned case, 53mm. diam. (Sotheby's Belgravia) $555

14kt. gold hunter pocket watch by the Deutsche Uhrenfabrikation Glashutte. (Sotheby, King & Chasemore) $8,465

Glass calendar desk watch, case with magnifying rear bezel forming the stand, 67mm. diam. (Sotheby's Belgravia) $700

Mid 18th century silver repousse pair-cased 'pendulum' watch by Wolf Burqui, Middleburg, 54mm. diam. (Phillips) $1,510

Late 18th century gilt and enamel calendar verge watch by Joseph Buchegger, Scharnstein, 46mm. diam.(Phillips) $905

Swiss gold and enamel cased cylinder watch, cuvette signed Henry Capt, Geneve, 31mm. diam. (Phillips) $565

Gold hunting cased duplex watch by Barwise, London, 1806, 53mm. diam. (Sotheby's) $1,664

18kt. yellow gold hunter-cased keyless lever pocket watch, movement dated 1888. (Sotheby, King & Chasemore) $690

Silver and horn pair-cased verge alarm watch, signed Conyers Dunlop, London, 53mm. diam. (Lawrence Fine Art) $960

Silver pair-cased verge
watch by Nathaniel
Chamberlain, circa 1720,
58mm. diam. (Sotheby's)
$1,245

Silver hunting cased duplex
watch by Barwise, London,
1820, 55mm. diam.
(Sotheby's Belgravia)
$370

22kt. gold pair-cased
lever watch, signed
Geo. Graham, London,
1734, 49mm. diam.
(Phillips)$1,135

Gold keyless lever dress
watch, dial signed for
Cartier, 45mm. diam.,
with gold and platinum
guard chain. (Phillips)
$1,135

Victorian 18kt. gold case
hunter keyless watch,
London, 1867. (Geering
& Colyer) $2,335

Gold and enamel triple
cased verge watch by
Geo. Prior, London,
1833, 40mm. diam.
(Phillips)$5,480

Gold and enamel verge watch
by Leroy, Paris, circa 1830,
44mm. diam. (Phillips)
$1,665

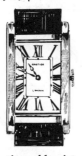

Cartier gold wrist
watch, signed Cartier,
London, 22 x 38mm.,
in presentation box.
(Sotheby's Belgravia)
$2,260

19th century gold and enamel quarter repeating cy-
linder watch, inscribed
Breguet, 47mm. diam.
(Phillips) $3,685

Swiss chronograph with enamel dial, in 18kt. gold case. (Hy. Duke & Son) $345

William IV 18kt. gold open-faced key-wound lever watch by J. & G. Benford, London. (Sotheby Beresford Adams) $335

Slim 18kt. gold open-faced keyless lever watch, movement inscribed Paul Ditisheim, 48mm. diam. (Sotheby Beresford Adams) $355

Slim gold and enamel open-faced key-wound cylinder watch, 40mm. diam. (Sotheby Beresford Adams) $445

Gold half hunting cased keyless lever watch by James McCabe, London, 1878, 52mm. diam. (Sotheby's)$1,415

18kt. gold open-faced verge watch by Grayhurst & Harvey, London, 1810, 45mm. diam. (Sotheby Beresford Adams) $1,080

18kt. gold verge watch by Pilkington, Dublin, 43mm. diam., with engine-turned gold dial. (Sotheby Beresford Adams) $485

18kt. gold hunting cased keyless lever center-seconds watch, Chester, 1898, 57mm. diam. (Sotheby Beresford Adams) $520

18kt. gold open-faced keyless lever watch by Lund & Blockley, London, 1886. (Sotheby Beresford Adams) $335

Early silver keyless watch by John Roger Arnold, 1823, 55mm. diam. (Sotheby's) $1,290

Gilt metal watch and pedometer by Ralph Gout of London, circa 1800, 55mm. diam. (Sotheby's) $1,040

18kt. half hunting cased keyless lever fob watch, signed R. Curtis, Hull, 38mm. diam. (Sotheby Beresford Adams) $335

Enamel and simulated pearl keyless fob watch suspended from ribbon bow. (Lawrence Fine Art) $240

Keyless lever center-seconds half hunter watch by Dent, London, numbered 50425, 18kt. gold case. (Sotheby Bearne) $560

14kt. gold five-minute repeating pocket watch by The American Watch Co., Waltham. (Hy. Duke & Son) $2,880

Silver pair-cased verge watch, signed Josephson, London, mid 18th century, 50mm. diam. (Sotheby Beresford Adams) $485

Swiss gold hunter-cased keyless lever minute repeating watch, 54mm. diam. (Christie's) $1,870

Silver pair-cased alarm verge watch by Thos. Tompion, late 17th century, 58mm. diam. (Sotheby's) $1,870

217

One of a pair of Japanese cloisonne vases decorated in bright colors, circa 1900, 7¾in. high.(Sotheby's) $705

Qianlong cloisonne enamel tripod broad globular censer, 11.5cm. high. (Christie's) $810

Silver gilt and cloisonne enamel cigarette case, Moscow, 1886, 8.6cm. wide. (Sotheby's) $550

Small 19th century Ota Tamasiro cloisonne vase with hexalobed body, 15.2cm. high. (Sotheby, King & Chasemore) $250

Slightly cracked cloisonne vase, with full body enameled with cranes, circa 1900, 13cm. high. (Sotheby's Belgravia) $300

Late 19th century Japanese cloisonne vase with baluster body, 24.8cm. high, signed. (Sotheby, King & Chasemore) $575

Late 19th century Japanese cloisonne opaque and transparent enamel on copper jar, 3½in. high. (Robert W. Skinner Inc.) $150

Late 19th century Chinese cloisonne opaque enamel on copper vase of baluster form, 6in. high. (Robert W. Skinner Inc.) $80

Polish silver gilt and cloisonne enamel cigarette case, circa 1915, 10.2cm. wide. (Sotheby's) $550

18th/early 19th century large cloisonne enamel lobed baluster vase, one of a pair, 72.5cm. high. (Christie's)
$3,395

Silver gilt and cloisonne enamel cigarette case by G.P., St. Petersburg, 1908-1917, 10.7cm. wide. (Sotheby's)
$595

One of a pair of cloisonne enamel jardinieres with blue grounds, 7¾in. diam. (Burrows & Day)
$355

One of a pair of cloisonne vases with silver wire decoration, circa 1900, 25.5cm. high. (Sotheby's Belgravia)
$1,085

One of a pair of cloisonne enamel pilgrim bottles, late 18th/early 19th century, 29.5cm. high. (Christie's) $1,260

Late 19th century Chinese cloisonne opaque and transparent enamel on copper vase, 9¼in. high. (Robert W. Skinner Inc.)
$100

16th century cloisonne enamel censer and cover of squat bombe shape, 15.3cm. (Sotheby's) $740

Cloisonne enamel baluster vase, fitted as an electric lamp, 23cm. high. (Christie's)
$990

Silver gilt and cloisonne enamel bowl by P. Ovchinnikov, Moscow, 12cm. diam., 1899-1908. (Sotheby's) $940

CLOISONNE

Kosen Kyoto cloisonne bowl with ribbed body, 15.5cm. diam., circa 1900, signed. (Sotheby's Belgravia) $465

18th/early 19th century cloisonne enamel globular bottle vase, slightly pitted, 39cm. high. (Christie's) $635

Silver gilt and cloisonne enamel cigarette case, Moscow, 1899-1908, 9.7cm. wide. (Sotheby's) $530

Cloisonne vase with enamelled shouldered body on midnight-blue-ground, 19cm. high, signed Kitsuzan, circa 1900.(Sotheby's Belgravia) $340

Early 20th century Inaba cloisonne vase with beige-ground, silver rim and foot, 16cm. high.(Sotheby's Belgravia) $170

One of a pair of cloisonne vases decorated with birds and branches, 52cm. high. (Sotheby's Belgravia) $2,230

16th/17th century Ming cloisonne enamel censer with bronze lion handles, 12cm. wide.(Christie's) $580

One of a pair of 19th century Japanes deep-blue-ground cloisonne enamel vases, 13in. high. (Lawrence Fine Art) $265

16th/early 17th century late Ming cloisonne enamel two-handled bowl, 13cm. wide across handles. (Christie's) $735

220

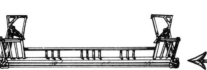

Mid 17th century brass salver with gadrooned edge, 11in. diam. (Sotheby's)
$185

Victorian brass fender with shell corners and railed gallery, 4ft. 5in. wide. (Dickinson, Davy & Markham)
$125

19th century copper eagle weathervane, from Massachusetts, 30in. long. (Robert W. Skinner Inc.)
$600

One of a pair of 17th century Dutch brass candlesticks on stepped and domed bases, 12¼in. high. (Sotheby's)
$1,040

Brass electric kettle designed by Peter Behrens, circa 1920, 22.75cm. high. (Sotheby's Belgravia)
$240

Pair of tall brass temple candlesticks from Bangkok, 38in. high. (Butler & Hatch Waterman)
$115

Italian black fossil limestone gilt brass bound circular table top, 27in. diam. (Christie's)
$2,485

One of a pair of brass fire iron rests, by Christopher Dresser, 1880's, 21.75cm. wide. (Sotheby's Belgravia)
$80

A sheet brass preserve pan with hand wrought iron loop handle, circa 1820, 12in. diam. (Christie's)
$100

221

Brass Imperial bushel measure by Pontifex & Wood, circa 1842, 19in. diam. (Sotheby's Belgravia) $645

Mid 17th century German brass alms dish with engraved rim, 17in. diam. (Sotheby's) $565

Early 19th century English copper bath on wheels, with brass rim, 54in. long. (Sotheby's Belgravia) $625

One of a pair of late 18th century turned brass candlesticks, 9½in. high. (Woolley & Wallis) $100

Late 19th century European cast brass hand mirror decorated with enamel, 8in. long, in fitted case. (Robert W. Skinner Inc.) $175

One of a pair of late 19th century cast brass bear candlesticks, 7¼in. high. (Robert W. Skinner Inc.) $250

One of two copper jugs and cover, 12in. and 18in. high. (Lawrence Fine Art) $65

19th century brass footman, pierced with cabriole shaped front supports, 12½in. high. (Lawrence Fine Art) $185

Early 19th century two-gallon copper measure of circular form, 15in. high. (Sotheby's) $135

COPPER & BRASS

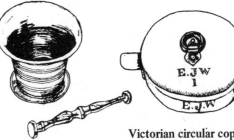

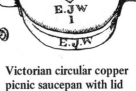

Dutch copper milk pail with snap-over cover, 16in. high. (Lawrence Fine Art) $200

Antique brass mortar with pestle. (Woolley & Wallis) $110

Victorian circular copper picnic saucepan with lid initialed, 5in. diam. (Woolley & Wallis) $80

One of a pair of late 19th century brass medieval revival candlesticks, 38½in. high. (Sotheby's Belgravia) $295

18th century English brass inkstand on trefoil-shaped tray. (Robert W. Skinner Inc.) $700

One of a pair of English 18th century brass candlesticks, 11¾in. high.(Robert W. Skinner Inc.) $400

Early 19th century four-gallon copper and brass measure inscribed R. Cain. (Sotheby's) $146

18th century brass skimmer with iron handle. (Woolley & Wallis) $160

One of two large copper kettles and covers, 12½in. high. (Lawrence Fine Art) $165

16th century German or French gilt brass circlet, 11cm. diam. (Christie's) $465

One of a pair of late 17th/ early 18th century brass andirons with downswept supports and ball feet, 18½in. high. (Sotheby's) $375

Silvered copper ewer and bowl, ewer with riveted curved handle, circa 1904. (Christie's) $2,910

One of a pair of Art Nouveau figural candlesticks, in brass plated white metal, circa 1920, 18½in. high. (Robert W. Skinner Inc.) $325

Three copper jelly molds, one circular and two oval. (Lawrence Fine Art) $220

Large brass witch's hat phonograph horn, 31½in. high, circa 1908. (Sotheby's) $110

Brass 'student's' candlestick on square base. (J. M. Welch & Son) $85

Hagenauer pierced and hammered brass box with flat cover, 1920's, 47.5cm. wide. (Sotheby's Belgravia) $1,780

Victorian brass and gilt metal cotton reel holder with pin cushion. (Butler & Hatch Waterman) $165

19th century globe-shaped copper tea urn. (J. M. Welch & Son) $230

20th century wrought iron and copper pea fowl weathervane, American, 30½in. wide. (Robert W. Skinner Inc.) $700

Antique copper kettle with domed lid and wooden handle. (Alfred Mossop & Co.) $100

Mid 15th century Persian base brass candlestick, one of a pair, 9½in. high.(Sotheby's) $2,160

Set of three graduated antique copper jugs, 8in. to 11in. high. (J. M. Welch & Son)$235

One of a pair of Charles II brass candlesticks with ribbed stems, circa 1660, 7½in. high. (Sotheby's) $3,395

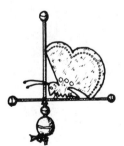

Late 19th century sheet metal butterfly weathervane, American, in copper. (Robert W. Skinner Inc.) $1,100

Art Deco brass sparkguard carved with a peacock. (J. M. Welch & Son) $90

One of a pair of early 19th century American Federal brass George Washington figural andirons, 21in. high. (Robert W. Skinner Inc.) $500

Brass mounted copper coal helmet. (Morris, Marshall & Poole) $190

One of three American copper plaques, signed Raymond Averill Porter, circa 1913-19.(Robert W. Skinner Inc.) $250

One of a pair of 17th century French brass candlesticks, 20in. high. (Boardman's) $1,245

Dutch brass warming pan with pierced lid, dated 1619, 44in. long.(Sotheby, King & Chasemore) $220

15th century German brass alms dish with slightly flaring rim, 10½in. diam. (Robert W. Skinner Inc.) $1,650

One of a pair of brass candlesticks, European, circa 1870, 10¼in. high. (Robert W. Skinner Inc.) $250

19th century circular copper kettle with ringed cover and acorn finial, 11in. high. (Dickinson, Davy & Markham)$110

Large 19th century seamed copper kettle with cover, cast iron handle and brass tap, 12in. high. (Dickinson, Davy & Markham) $75

19th century Japanese patinated brass teapot of bulbous form with wrapped handle grip, 6in. diam.(Robert W. Skinner Inc.)$80

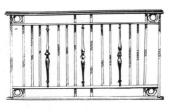

Large 19th century sea-
med copper kettle with
cover and curving han-
dle, 1ft.1in. high.
(Dickinson, Davy &
Markham) †
$75

One of a set of seven brass railings,
circa 1910, each 50in. wide.
(Sotheby's Belgravia) $845

One of a pair of 16th
century Flemish tur-
ned brass candlesticks,
16in. high. (Board-
man's) $2,420

Jeweled and enameled gilt
copper monstrance, designed
by John Francis Bentley,
circa 1864, 65.8cm. high.
(Sotheby's Belgravia) $2,590

Limoges enameled
copper dish with trans-
parent red border, circa
1870, 6¾in. long.
(Robert W. Skinner Inc.)
$300

Benham & Froud copper
and brass kettle, designed
by Christopher Dresser,
77cm. high. (Phillips)
$230

American Art Deco cop-
per water jug with sphe-
rical body, circa 1930,
12in. high. (Robert W.
Skinner Inc.) $45

Pair of early 19th century
Federal brass and wrought
iron steeple-top andirons,
21in. high.(Robert W.
Skinner Inc.)$1,150

Georgian copper choco-
late pot with fitted tur-
ned fruitwood side han-
dle, 18cm. high. (Sotheby,
King & Chasemore)
$205

Late 19th century Kesi informal robe on saxe-blue ground, bordered with indigo and white. (Sotheby's Belgravia) $820

Pair of early 17th century gauntlets of white kid, cuff applied with ivory silk and sequins. (Phillips)$335

Rare late 19th century Kesi formal robe woven with colored silks on indigo ground. (Sotheby's Belgravia) $2,045

Black georgette dress with vertical lines of black beads and red plastic 'gems', 1920's. (Sotheby's Belgravia) $205

Paisley pattern shawl with central lobed medallion, circa 1860, 106 x 134½in.(Sotheby's Belgravia) $250

Red beaded georgette dress bordered with trailing scrolls, 1920's. (Sotheby's Belgravia) $370

Chinese robe of midnight blue silk, deep sleeves lined with cream and beige Afghan fox. (Phillips) $1,015

Early 17th century uncut velvet fragment with initials 'CR' surmounted by a crown.(Phillips) $185

Early 19th century Chinese robe of midnight blue silk, embroidered with colored silks, lined. (Phillips)$405

COSTUME

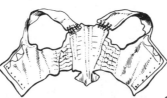

19th century lady's Kesi informal robe on rose-pink ground. (Sotheby's Belgravia) $615

Pair of late 18th century stays of white linen with silk binding, circa 1790. (Phillips) $1,075

20th century Moroccan Pasha's robe edged with heavy gold braid. (Sotheby's Belgravia) $615

Silver and white beaded georgette dress, sold with a suede bag, 1920's. (Sotheby's Belgravia) $185

19th century Norwich shawl with ivory silk ground, fringed, 1.46m. square. (Phillips) $205

Gold, white and black beaded dress and jacket, 1920's. (Sotheby's Belgravia) $570

Late 19th century Algerian silk scarf with embroidered ends, on lemon ground.(Sotheby's Belgravia) $100

Kid jerkin with overlay of late 17th century French brocade, silk and cotton lined. (Phillips)$150

Finely embroidered silk shawl in polychrome silks on a black ground, circa 1900, 48 x 51in. (Sotheby's Belgravia) $185

Christian Dior two-piece evening dress, labeled, circa 1950. (Sotheby's Belgravia) $125

Gold, black, silver and white beaded dress with V-neck, 1920's. (Sotheby's) $580

Printed silk two-piece bodice and skirt, with purple violet sprigs, circa 1895.(Sotheby's Belgravia) $205

Unusual polychrome and gold thread long satin evening dress with cross-over bodice, 1920's. (Sotheby's Belgravia) $455

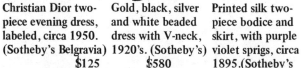

Gold sequinned and beaded black strapless satin evening dress, probably by C. Dior, circa 1960. (Sotheby's Belgravia) $115

Maroon and black shot silk dress, circa 1865, with later lace collar. (Sotheby's Belgravia) $105

Nini Ricci full-length black velvet evening dress, labeled, 1940's. (Sotheby's Belgravia) $205

Shaded blue and silver beaded dress probably by Chanel, circa 1923, on a black satin ground. (Sotheby's Belgravia)$205

230

Black, white and eau-de-nil beaded dress with overlapping leaf design, 1920's.(Sotheby's Belgravia) $580

Painted and printed brown chiffon dress and cape painted by Elaine Bodley, 1920's. (Sotheby's Belgravia)$175

Fortuny 'Delphos' dress of black satin, circa 1920, unlabelled. (Sotheby's Belgravia)$580

Coco Chanel black satin and tulle evening dress, labeled, circa 1930.(Sotheby's Belgravia) $730

Gold lace long evening dress and jacket with roses down the side, 1930's.(Sotheby's Belgravia) $355

Chanel sequinned long evening dress, labeled, circa 1930, zip and bodice added. (Sotheby's Belgravia) $625

French beaded dress with slate blue muslin ground, 1920's, skirt with vandyked hem. (Sotheby's Belgravia) $625

Black taffeta short evening dress by Christian Dior, 1950's. (Sotheby's Belgravia) $70

COSTUME

Woven shawl of Paisley design, 64 x 137in., circa 1870. (Sotheby's Belgravia) $305

19th century Chinese triangular panel of yellow silk, designed with a dragon, 2.30 x 1.15m. (Phillips) $520

Unusual printed cockade fan, 1876, Viennese, 24.5cm. long. (Sotheby's Belgravia) $290

Mid 19th century dress of printed cotton in check pattern, circa 1840's. (Phillips) $295

19th century Paisley shawl of 'moon shawl' design, with ivory cashmere ground, circa 1840's, 1.60 x 1.72m. (Phillips) $85

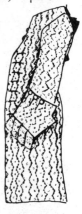

Coat from an 18th century French gentleman's three-piece suit, in moire silk. (Sotheby's Belgravia) $1,245

Chinese mandarin's coat of turquoise silk with orange lining, embroidered in gilt thread. (Woolley & Wallis) $140

Two-piece green and cream silk jacket and trained skirt, sold with belt and bag, circa 1867. (Sotheby's Belgravia) $115

Late 19th century lady's embroidered informal robe with indigo satin ground. (Sotheby's Belgravia) $540

232

19th century Chinese waistcoat of gray silk embroidred in colored and ivory silks, lined. (Phillips) $370

19th century Brussels triangular shawl of bobbin and needlepoint applique.(Phillips) $445

Late 18th century Persian jacket of stamped brocade, sleeves with loop fastenings, lined. (Phillips) $665

Length of mid 17th century gros point de Venise designed with curled flowers, 0.09 x 1m. (Phillips) $350

19th century Russian priest's vestment and robe in brocade with metallic thread.(Robert W. Skinner Inc.) $425

Cheruit evening coat of bright yellow, edged with black velvet, circa 1920. (Sotheby's Belgravia) $105

19th century Paisley shawl of striped design, circa 1840's, fringed, 1.55m. square. (Phillips)$350

Clear beaded black georgette dress with fringed panels, 1920's. (Sotheby's)$165

19th century Paisley shawl of 'moon shawl' design, with olive green cashmere ground, 1.62m. square. (Phillips) $390

Heubach bisque head doll, Germany, circa 1900, 15½in. high, original dress and hat. (Robert W. Skinner Inc.) $175

Kammer & Reinhardt bisque head character baby doll, Germany, circa 1900, 17in. long. (Robert W. Skinner Inc.) $350

20th century Heubach dusky bisque character doll, with glass eyes, 6¾in. long. (Robert W. Skinner Inc.)$80

German yellow plush teddy bear with elongated body, circa 1925, 20½in. high. (Robert W. Skinner Inc.) $60

Victorian waxed shoulder composition doll in original ivory satin and lace bridal dress, 24in. high. (Sotheby Beresford Adams) $280

Bisque doll, stamped Jumeau d'Or Paris, 20in. high, lacking wig, in original navy blue and wine red peasant costume. (Sotheby Beresford Adams) $2,525

Armand Marseille bisque 'My Dream Baby' doll in original ensemble. (Sotheby's Belgravia) $235

Bisque character doll, possibly by Heubach, 13½in. high, with molded hair. (Sotheby Beresford Adams) $335

Simon & Halbig bisque headed doll, Germany, circa 1880, 12½in. high. (Robert W. Skinner Inc.) $950

234

DOLLS

S.F.B.J. bisque headed doll, Paris, early 20th century, stamped Made in France, 15¼in. high. (Robert W. Skinner Inc.) $170

Rare clockwork swimming doll with celluloid head and cork body, 15in. long. (Sotheby's Belgravia) $815

Kammer & Reinhardt bisque headed character baby doll, Germany, 1909, 11in. long. (Robert W. Skinner Inc.) $200

German bisque head doll with composition body, circa 1900-10, 24in. long, thumb missing. (Robert W. Skinner Inc.) $300

Fine French bisque fashion doll, impressed F, circa 1870, 18in. high. (Sotheby's Belgravia) $2,750

German bisque head character doll, circa 1900, 15in. long, slightly chipped. (Robert W. Skinner Inc.) $375

Early 20th century German lithographed tin wind-up newsboy, 7¼in. high. (Robert W. Skinner Inc.) $80

Large Kestner bisque head doll, circa 1900, 32in. long, with sleeping glass eyes. (Robert W. Skinner Inc.) $475

Late 19th century German beige bisque head doll, 11¼in. high, with glass eyes. (Robert W. Skinner Inc.) $350

Armand Marseille bisque headed doll with kid body, 13in. high. (Burrows & Day) $260

Late Victorian wax doll in pink silk dress and leather shoes. (Woolley & Wallis) $485

Rare mid 19th century German triple faced bisque headed doll with fabric body, 13½in. high. (Locke & England) $1,260

Rare Heubach 'Whistling Jim' character boy doll with cloth body, 15in. high. (Sotheby's Belgravia) $890

Kammer & Reinhardt/Simon & Halbig 'My Darling' doll with jointed body, 22in. high. (Sotheby's Belgravia) $3,355

Bruno Schmidt 'Tommy Tucker' bisque character doll, circa 1910, 13in. high. (Sotheby's Belgravia) $890

Barr & Proschild bisque character doll with curved limb body, 13in. high. (Sotheby's Belgravia) $340

Armand Marseille bisque 'Oriental' baby doll in printed 'Japanese' robe, 8in. high. (Sotheby's Belgravia) $680

Good French bisque 'Parisienne' doll with gusseted kid body, circa 1875, 16in. high. (Sotheby's Belgravia) $610

DOLLS

Bisque character headed baby doll marked K*R, S. & H., 114/A, 18in. high. (Christie's S. Kensington) $2,325

Late Victorian wax doll in pale blue silk dress and straw hat. (Woolley & Wallis)$485

Victorian china doll in cream silk dress. (Woolley & Wallis) $150

Fine 'long face' Jumeau Bebe doll, 28in. high, circa 1870. (Sotheby's Belgravia)$3,560

Ges. Gesch shoulder bisque character boy doll with cloth body, 14in. high. (Sotheby's Belgravia) $510

Kammer & Reinhardt/ Simon & Halbig bisque doll with jointed body, 26in. high. (Sotheby's Belgravia) $635

Simon & Halbig walking/ talking doll with jointed body, 20in. high. (Sotheby's Belgravia) $635

Alt. Beck & Gottschalck bisque doll, 24in. high, with jointed body. (Sotheby's Belgravia) $340

Tinplate somersaulting figure, probably by F. Martin, France, circa 1905, 7½in. high. (Sotheby's Belgravia) $405

DOLLS

French cloth doll, circa 1920's, 2ft.3in. high. (Sotheby's Belgravia) $65

Bisque 'Bald' head doll with perished lambswool wig, in original dress, circa 1880, 10½in. high. (Sotheby's Belgravia) $725

Simon & Halbig doll with jointed body and opening eyes, 5in. high. (Woolley & Wallis) $115

Kammer & Reinhardt bisque character doll with painted blue eyes, circa 1915, 16½in. high. (Sotheby's Belgravia) $2,820

Victorian waxed shoulder-papier-mache pumpkin head doll, 20in. high, circa 1860, in box. (Sotheby's Belgravia) $360

George III wooden doll with pink kid arms, 18½in. high, in original dress. (Sotheby's) $1,400

Wax shoulder doll with stuffed fabric body, 18in. high, in white cotton dress. (Sotheby's) $415

China headed Nanny doll with original clothes and child doll, 5in. high. (Woolley & Wallis) $115

Jumeau bisque doll, head marked, with glass eyes and blonde wig, 16½in. high. (Sotheby's Belgravia) $1,410

238

DOLLS

Ernst Heubach boy doll with bisque head and composition body, 18in. high, in pyjamas. (Sotheby's) $250

Large early 19th century female Hina festival doll, right hand detached, 16in. high. (Sotheby's Belgravia) $260

Kammer & Reinhardt character bisque doll, 15in. high, head repaired, in white cotton dress. (Sotheby's Belgravia) $525

Mid 19th century poured shoulder wax lady doll, possibly by Pierotti, 18in. high. (Sotheby's) $415

Pair of Armand Marseille bisque 'Red Indian' dolls, 9in. high, in original costumes. (Sotheby's Belgravia) $405

Fine Bru bisque doll with original clothing and shoes, circa 1875, 21in. high.(Christie's) $7,650

Strobel & Wilken 'googly-eyed' bisque doll, in green cotton dress, 7in. high.(Sotheby's Belgravia)$440

S.F.B.J. Bebe doll with jointed body, 26in. high, in red silk dress. (Sotheby's Belgravia) $565

'Googly-eyed' bisque doll by JDK Ges. Gesch, 11in. high, in knitted pullover and cap. (Sotheby's Belgravia) $1,610

Model doll's house of 'Harethorpe Hall' with painted brick front, 47in. long. (Sotheby's Belgravia) $725

Late 19th/early 20th century wooden model of a stable with two papier-mache horses, 23in. wide. (Robert W. Skinner Inc.) $250

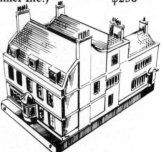

Early 20th century American wooden gabled roof doll's house with glass windows, 24¾in. high. (Robert W. Skinner Inc.) $200

Triang custom built doll's house, replica of 45 Kensington Square, London, 51in. wide, complete with accessories. (Sotheby's) $605

Late Victorian wooden doll's house, circa 1890, 33in. wide, with hinged front. (Sotheby's Belgravia)$850

Late 19th century doll's house with opening front, 47in. high x 37in. wide. (Woolley & Wallis) $385

American diorama of an early 19th century hallway, circa 1950, fitted with dolls and furniture, 19½in. wide. (Robert W. Skinner Inc.) $125

19th century wooden Mansard roof doll's house with painted brick front, 23¾in. high. (Robert W. Skinner Inc.) $200

ENAMEL

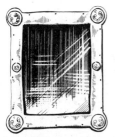

Liberty & Co., silver and enamel frame, 29cm. high, Birmingham, 1905. (Sotheby's Belgravia) $1,030

German enamel snuff box decorated with hunting scenes, circa 1760, 8.5cm. wide. (Sotheby's) $610

17th century Limoges enamel hexalobate dish by Jacques Laudin, 6½in. wide.(Sotheby's) $1,245

Unusual circular German enamel snuff box with lobed bombe-shaped sides, circa 1750, 7.5cm. diam. (Sotheby's) $3,460

Mid 19th century enameled double-handled vase with gilt handles, 48.5cm. high. (Sotheby's Belgravia)$300

Late 19th century French enamel dish with dark-blue-ground, 9in. diam. (Sotheby's) $890

German enamel snuff box painted by Andreas Bech-dolff of Ellwangen, 1763, 7.5cm. wide. (Sotheby's) $4,475

Mid 18th century German gold and enamel mounted walking stick with mush-room-shaped handle. (Christie's) $1,355

German enamel comme-morative snuff box with portrait of Frederick the Great, circa 1760, 8cm. wide. (Sotheby's) $2,035

19th century Swiss gold and enamel box formed as a barrel, 1¾in. high. (Christie's) $5,820

Continental rectangular enamel snuff box, probably Vienna, circa 1760, 3¼in. wide. (Christie's)$960

Bilston green-ground mustard pot with loop handle and detachable cover, circa 1770, 3½in. high. (Christie's) $455

Late 18th century Bilston enamel frog bonbonniere, 2in. diam. (Christie's) $665

Late 19th century small Viennese enamel standing cup and cover, 16cm. high. (Sotheby's Belgravia)$730

17th century Limoges grisaille and polychrome enamel fluted bowl by Jean Laudin, 14.5cm. across. (Christie's) $380

Birmingham fine enamel tea caddy of oval form, circa 1765, 4¾in. wide.(Christie's) $6,235

17th century Limoges polychrome enamel water stoup by Pierre Nouailher, 27.5cm. high. (Christie's) $950

Late 19th/early 20th century small Viennese enamel bowl with fluted oval body, 12.3cm. wide. (Sotheby's Belgravia) $580

ENAMEL

Early 20th century Norwegian plique-a-jour cup and saucer decorated with enamel. (Sotheby's Belgravia) $995

Chinese rectangular famille rose porcelain snuff box, circa 1760, with silver gilt mounts, 3in. wide. (Christie's) $1,295

Swiss jeweled gold and enamel vinaigrette with split pearl border, early 19th century, 3.8cm. wide.(Sotheby's) $1,910

Modern Limoges enamel vase designed by Camille Faure, 27.2cm. high. (Sotheby's Belgravia) $605

One of a pair of Bilston enamel cassolettes on plinth bases, circa 1770. (Christie's)$4,575

Late 19th century Viennese enamel nef with gilt metal mounts, 14cm. high. (Sotheby's Belgravia) $825

Framed enamel on copper plaque of Neptune, signed E. Sieffert, circa 1910, 36½in. high. (Robert W. Skinner Inc.) $1,900

Louis XVI oval gold and enamel snuff box by Joseph Etienne Blerzy, Paris, 1776, 3¼in. wide. (Christie's) $20,790

Large pair of French or Swiss enameled opera glasses, 11.5cm. high, circa 1875. (Sotheby's Belgravia) $660

FANS

Late 19th century Japanese ivory fan decorated in Shibayama style, 38cm. long. (Sotheby's Belgravia) $195

French mother-of-pearl fan with pierced sticks, circa 1860, signed Mabel, 26.8cm. long. (Sotheby's Belgravia) $265

Fan painted with a watercolor and with gilt and mother-of-pearl sticks, 1895, 34cm. long. (Sotheby's Belgravia)$370

Late 18th century ivory fan with pierced and carved sticks with chinoiserie figures, 23cm. long. (Sotheby's Belgravia)
$130

18th century chinoiserie 'peep-hole' fan decorated with mother-of-pearl, 29cm. long. (Sotheby's Belgravia) $370

Late 19th century French mother-of-pearl fan, leaf painted with a water-color, 25.2cm. long. (Sotheby's Belgravia) $165

Mid 19th century lacquered Chinese brise fan, 23.5cm. long. (Sotheby's Belgravia) $270

Framed Chinese ivory brise fan with finely pierced and draped central shield, circa 1795, 19in. wide. (Robert W. Skinner Inc.) $160

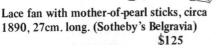

Lace fan with mother-of-pearl sticks, circa 1890, 27cm. long. (Sotheby's Belgravia) $125

Early 18th century Vernis Martin brise fan, 21cm. long. (Sotheby's Belgravia) $1,345

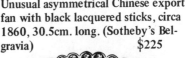

Early 19th century Chinese lacquer brise fan, black sticks painted in shades of blue, red and green, 20cm. long. (Sotheby's Belgravia) $1,135

Unusual asymmetrical Chinese export fan with black lacquered sticks, circa 1860, 30.5cm. long. (Sotheby's Belgravia) $225

Late 19th century Chinese ivory brise fan with carved bead, 28cm. long. (Sotheby's Belgravia) $405

Mid 19th century Chinese parcel gilt filigree brise fan, 19.5cm. long. (Sotheby's Belgravia) $660

Mid 19th century Chinese silver filigree and enamel fan, slightly damaged, 28.5cm. long. (Sotheby's Belgravia) $455

Chinese ivory and feather fan with pierced and carved sticks and guards, 23cm. long, circa 1830. (Sotheby's Belgravia) $185

FURNITURE

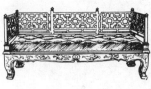

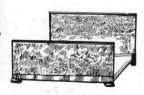

19th century Chinese red-wood day bed with carved frame, 214cm. wide. (H. Spencer & Sons Ltd.) $1,380

Late 19th century bed from a Renaissance revival walnut suite of five pieces. (Robert W. Skinner Inc.) $1,050

Bed from a three-piece set of Art Deco burl and ash bedroom suite, American, circa 1930. (Robert W. Skinner Inc.) $250

Hepplewhite four-poster with domed top and fluted and carved pillars, 6ft. wide. (Russell, Baldwin & Bright) $2,970

Late 19th/early 20th century giltwood double bed with caned headboard and carved toprail, 54in. wide. (Sotheby's Belgravia) $985

Early 17th century James I oak tester bed with leaf-carved panels, 4ft.8in. wide. (Sotheby's) $4,320

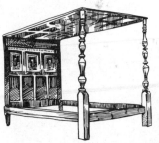

Oak four-poster bed made from Jacobean timbers, with triple paneled head-board, 57in. wide. (Locke & England) $1,275

Bed from a late 19th century American Renais-sance revival walnut bed-room suite, with burl panels. (Robert W. Skin-ner Inc.) $1,900

American Renaissance revival walnut and burl veneer bed with carved arch, sold with a match-ing commode, circa 1870. (Robert W. Skin-ner Inc.) $1,500

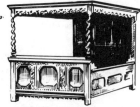

Oak swinging cradle with carved side panels. (Dee & Atkinson) $160

Brass and mother-of-pearl three-sided double bed, circa 1880, 75¼in. wide. (Sotheby's Belgravia) $740

17th century German oak four-poster bed with paneled canopy and foot-boatd. (Boardman's) $2,685

Bed from a late 19th century American three-piece walnut bedroom set. (Robert W. Skinner Inc.) $900

Superbly carved Spanish walnut four-poster bed on carved animal feet. (John Hogbin & Son) $3,600

Early 17th century Jacobean carved oak tester bed with carved arcading, 4ft.9in. wide. (Sotheby's) $3,085

Mahogany Hepplewhite style four-poster bed with carved arcaded frieze. (Edward, Bigwood & Bewlay)$1,645

19th century American bed frame with paneled ends, 3ft.11½in. wide.(Sotheby's) $1,455

Four-poster bed of Hepplewhite style, with finely reeded front pillars and cornice, 4ft.6in. wide. (Butler & Hatch Waterman) $1,850

William IV rosewood book-
case with raised back portion having a brass gallery,
65in. wide. (Lawrence Fine
Art) $2,505

One of a pair of Regency
satinwood veneered
open bookcases, 30in.
wide. (Woolley & Wallis)
          $3,160

Edwardian mahogany re-
volving bookcase on
brass castors. (J. M.
Welch & Son)$280

Walnut breakfront bookcase
of Chippendale style with
satinwood inlay, 90in. high.
(Hy. Duke & Son)
          $2,975

Late 19th century maho-
gany bookcase of Adam
style with pierced trellis,
3ft.6in. wide. (Sotheby,
King & Chasemore)
          $3,905

Mid 19th century mahogany
library bookcase with molded pediment, 75in. wide.
(Sotheby Beresford Adams)
          $3,070

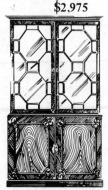

George III mahogany
bookcase with molded
cornice, 55in. wide.
(Christie's) $2,980

George III mahogany double breakfront library bookcase with broken
scrolled pediment, 157in. wide.
(Christie's) $11,840

George IV mahogany
cabinet bookcase,
circa 1825, 3ft.2in.
wide. (Sotheby, King
& Chasemore)
          $650

Gustav Stickley oak bookcase, New York, circa 1912, 39in. wide.(Robert W. Skinner Inc.)
$1,550

Mahogany bookcase on French bracket feet, top with glazed tracery doors, 4ft.6in. wide. (Gilbert Baitson) $710

Eastern United States Renaissance revival walnut bookcase, circa 1870, 46in. wide, with two glazed doors. (Robert W. Skinner Inc.)$425

George III mahogany bookcase with molded cornice, 40in. wide. (Burrows & Day)
$1,265

Mid 19th century William IV mahogany breakfront library bookcase with molded pediment, 95in. wide. (Sotheby Beresford Adams) $2,510

George II mahogany bookcase with egg and dart molding, circa 1735, 69in. wide. (Sotheby, King & Chasemore) $6,990

Mahogany breakfront bookcase, top with four glazed Gothic tracery doors, 6ft . wide. (Gilbert Baitson)
$1,700

William IV mahogany breakfront bookcase with decorated cornice, 108in. wide. (Boardman's)$4,345

George III mahogany breakfront bookcase, 9ft.3in. wide, circa 1770.(Edwards, Bigwood & Bewlay)
$12,810

Early George II mahogany bureau with gilt bronze rococo handles, 43in. wide. (Christie's) $3,235

Satinwood cylinder bureau with three short drawers above, 55¼in. wide. (Christie's) $1,590

Early 18th century South German or Austrian walnut bureau with raised superstructure, 50in. wide. (Christie's) $4,970

Rosewood and marquetry cylinder bureau by James Shoolbred & Co., circa 1890, 38in. wide. (Sotheby's Belgravia) $1,475

Mid 18th century Louis XV kingwood bureau de dame, 3ft. wide, with ormolu mounts. (Sotheby, King & Chasemore)$16,370

Unusual oak standing desk with fall flap enclosing fitted interior, 3ft. wide, circa 1720. (Sotheby, King & Chasemore) $2,415

Chippendale maple and birch slant top desk, New England, circa 1780, 39¼in. wide. (Robert W. Skinner Inc.) $1,900

Dutch floral marquetry bombe bureau with four drawers, 44in. wide. (Christie's)$5,520

George III mahogany bureau, inlaid with oval shell and stringings, 42in. wide. (Burrows & Day) $2,220

Early Georgian walnut bureau with oyster veneered sloping flap, 36in. wide. (Christie's)
$2,590

Dutch tulipwood and marquetry bombe bureau with solid cylinder, 47½in. wide. (Christie's) $4,785

Late 18th century George III mahogany bureau on bracket feet, with swan neck carrying handles, 30in. wide.(Sotheby Beresford Adams)
$1,210

George I walnut bureau inlaid with herringbone stringing and crossbanded, 30in. wide. (Locke & England)$3,515

Queen Anne tiger maple slant front desk, circa 1760, 36in. wide. (Robert W. Skinner Inc.)
$24,570

George I walnut and burr-walnut bureau, on later ogee bracket feet, 39in. wide. (Christie's)
$2,775

Mahogany bureau with brass drop handles and escutcheons, on ogee feet, 39in. wide. (Dee & Atkinson)
$1,115

Mid 18th century North Italian serpentine walnut bureau with ebonized upper section, 46in. wide. (Christie's) $19,320

18th century Dutch walnut bureau of bombe shape, with four drawers. (John Hogbin & Son)
$3,240

Dutch mahogany bureau in two parts, circa 1780, 3ft.5½in. wide. (Sotheby's)$2,260

Mahogany cylinder bureau with pull-out writing slide, 1840-60, 53½in. wide. (Sotheby's Belgravia) $660

18th century Massachusetts Chippendale reverse-serpentine mahogany bureau, 43½in. wide. (Wm. Doyle Galleries Inc.) $4,750

Late George I walnut bureau, flap inlaid with chequered lines, on ogee bracket feet, 32½in. high. (Christie's) $6,290

Small Edwardian banded mahogany bureau with floral marquetry panel to lid, 2ft.6in. wide.(Russell, Baldwin & Bright) $1,170

George I walnut and feather-banded bureau on later shaped bracket feet, circa 1720, restored, 3ft. wide.(Sotheby, King & Chasemore) $2,235

Georgian oak fall-front bureau with brass handles and escutcheons. (J. M. Welch & Son)$765

Sheraton rosewood tambour front bureau, outlined with boxwood stringing, 36in. wide. (Wm. Doyle Galleries Inc.) $5,750

German marquetry cylinder bureau, lowest drawer inlaid with parquetry, circa 1780, 3ft.5½in. wide. (Sotheby's) $3,085 ·

Lombard walnut bureau with three graduated serpentine drawers, circa 1740, 3ft.6in. wide. (Sotheby's)$3,395

18th century New England Chippendale reverse-serpentine birchwood bureau, 41in. wide. (Wm. Doyle Galleries Inc.) $5,500

George I walnut bureau, circa 1720, 2ft.7½in. wide. (Sotheby's) $5,730

Federal cherry inlaid slant top desk, circa 1790, 40½in. wide. (Robert W. Skinner Inc.) $4,250

19th century rosewood cylinder top writing desk, 32in. wide. (J. M. Welch & Son) $875

American Chippendale mahogany slant top bureau on bracket feet, circa 1780, 41¼in. wide. (Robert W. Skinner Inc.) $2,400

George III mahogany and crossbanded bureau with brass drop handles and ivory escutcheons, 42in. wide. (Dacre, Son & Hartley) $1,640

Painted satinwood cylinder bureau with oval medallion, circa 1900, 23in. wide. (Sotheby's Belgravia) $785

Georgian walnut fall-front bureau on bracket feet, 38in. wide. (J. M. Welch & Son) $1,400

BUREAU BOOKCASES

Queen Anne oak bureau bookcase with double domed cornice, circa 1710, 3ft. wide.(Sotheby, King & Chasemore) $3,145

18th century South German walnut bureau cabinet. (Sandoe, Luce Panes) $11,400

Queen Anne walnut and featherbanded bureau bookcase, circa 1710, 3ft.3in. wide.(Sotheby, King & Chasemore) $6,005

Walnut bureau bookcase with molded cornice, doors inlaid with herringbone bands, 80in. high. (Christie's) $2,715

Dutch bleached mahogany bureau bookcase with domed pediment, with silvered metal handles and escutcheons, 4ft.3in. wide. (Geering & Colyer) $3,145

Mahogany bureau bookcase with swan neck cresting, fall front with beaded molding, circa 1880, 44in. wide.(Sotheby's Belgravia) $3,310

Dutch walnut and floral marquetry bureau cabinet with double domed cornice, 43in. wide. (Christie's)$14,720

Early George III mahogany bureau bookcase with broken pediment having center shell finial, 39in. wide. (Locke & England) $10,415

Walnut and featherbanded Queen Anne bureau cabinet, circa 1710, slightly damaged, 3ft.3in. wide. (Sotheby, King & Chasemore)$6,070

Dutch walnut and marquetry bureau cabinet with bombe base, 53in. wide. (Christie's) $16,930

Queen Anne walnut bureau bookcase with mirror glazed doors, 40in. wide. (Christie's)$7,400

Queen Anne figured walnut bureau bookcase, on a later stand. (Anderson & Garland) $9,700

Early 18th century walnut, crossbanded and feather inlaid bureau bookcase on bracket feet, 3ft.2in. wide. (Geering & Colyer) $4,810

George III mahogany bureau bookcase with swan neck pediment, on ogee bracket feet, 44in. wide. (Sotheby, King & Chasemore)$4,970

George I walnut bureau cabinet with molded cornice and two paneled and fielded doors, 37½in. wide. (Christie's) $9,990

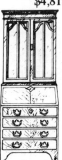

Maples walnut bureau bookcase with arched astragal doors, on bracket feet. (T. Bannister & Co.) $1,355

American Chippendale style mahogany secretaire bookcase, circa 1920, 37in. wide. (Robert W. Skinner Inc.) $1,100

Mahogany and oak bureau bookcase with molded dentilled cornice, 79½in. wide. (Christie's) $2,775

BUREAU BOOKCASES

American Chippendale veneer secretary bookcase, circa 1770, 41in. wide. (Robert W. Skinner Inc.) $5,500

George III mahogany bureau cabinet with shaped cornice and lancet frieze, circa 1790, 3ft.9in. wide. (Sotheby's) $7,030

18th century New England tiger maple secretaire bookcase with bonnet top, 38½in. wide. (Wm. Doyle Galleries Inc.) $20,000

Late 19th century bureau bookcase in Sheraton manner with astragal glazed doors.(Pearson) $1,765

Mahogany bureau cabinet with two glazed cupboard doors, 34in. wide. (Christie's) $2,995

Queen Anne burr-walnut bureau cabinet with molded double domed cornice, 41½in. wide. (Christie's) $9,620

Small George II mahogany bureau bookcase on bracket feet, circa 1755, 2ft.8½in. wide. (Sotheby's) $2,455

Unusual George III pine breakfront bureau bookcase, 6ft.9in. wide, circa 1765, restored.(Sotheby's) $6,410

George I walnut bureau bookcase with broken arched pediment, 38in. wide. (Lawrence Fine Art) $8,450

256

19th century small mahogany bureau bookcase with Gothic glazed doors, 76cm. wide. (Osmond, Tricks) $2,000

George III mahogany bureau cabinet on bracket feet, circa 1770, 4ft.1½in. wide. (Sotheby's) $3,515

18th century German walnut and fruitwood bureau cabinet with brass knob handles, 32½in. wide. (Wm. Doyle Galleries Inc.) $6,250

Early 20th century George III style mahogany cylinder bureau bookcase, 44in. wide. (Sotheby Beresford Adams) $1,155

German mid 18th century rococo walnut parquetry bureau cabinet, 47½in. wide. (Robert W. Skinner Inc.) $7,500

Queen Anne style burrwalnut bureau bookcase, top with single mirror paneled door, 34in. wide. (Wm. Doyle Galleries Inc.) $9,500

Early Georgian oak double-domed bureau cabinet with shaped base apron. (Graves Son & Pilcher) $1,860

Late Georgian bureau bookcase with glazed trellis doors, molded cornice and broken pediment, 45in. wide. (Locke & England) $2,275

George III mahogany bureau bookcase, circa 1800, 3ft.8in. wide. (Sotheby, King & Chasemore) $1,920

BUREAU BOOKCASES

19th century mahogany bureau bookcase with glazed doors. (Graves Son & Pilcher) $2,325

Mahogany and satinwood crossbanded bureau bookcase, 1900, 43in. wide. (Sotheby's Belgravia) $1,235

Mid Georgian mahogany bureau cabinet with broken scrolled pediment, 39in. wide. (Christie's) $7,590

Mid 18th century Dutch walnut and marquetry bureau bookcase with shaped cornice, 3ft.6in. wide. (Sotheby's) $7,900

Black and gold lacquer bureau cabinet with double domed cornice and gilt metal hinges, 39in. wide. (Christie's) $10,810

Mid 18th century Dutch fruitwood bureau cabinet, 44in. wide. (Wm. Doyle Galleries Inc.) $12,000

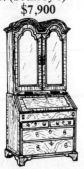

George I walnut bureau cabinet with double domed cornice, 37¾in. wide. (Christie's) $9,150

George I walnut and feather-banded bureau bookcase, circa 1720, 2ft.7½in. wide. (Sotheby, King & Chasemore) $4,835

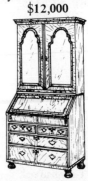

George I walnut bureau bookcase with two arched beveled cupboard doors, 41in. wide. (Christie's) $10,395

258

Victorian burr-walnut side cabinet inlaid with satinwood and with ormolu mounts, 32½in. wide. (Morphets) $755

19th century lacquer and chinoiserie cabinet, 15in. wide. (J. M. Welch & Son) $290

Late 19th century rosewood veneered writing table with inlaid decoration, 40in. wide. (W. H. Lane & Son) $830

Satinwood and marquetry display cabinet on stand by Edwards & Roberts, circa 1900, 45in. wide. (Sotheby's Belgravia)$1,750

Bronze mounted Louis Philippe inlaid whatnot-cabinet. (Wm. Doyle Galleries Inc.) $2,300

George I burr-walnut cabinet with cavetto frieze drawer, 41¼in. wide. (Christie's) $5,820

One of a pair of walnut and marquetry side cabinets with grained tops, circa 1870, 33½in. wide. (Sotheby's Belgravia) $2,160

Edwardian satinwood breakfront cabinet with burr-walnut inlay, 74in. wide. (Dee & Atkinson) $1,075

Walnut and marquetry side cabinet with bow-front, circa 1870, 46½in. wide. (Sotheby's Belgravia) $2,015

259

Mid 19th century ebony and ivory inlaid cabinet on stand, 33in. wide, probably Spanish. (Sotheby Beresford Adams) $1,395

17th century Flemish tortoiseshell and ebonized cabinet with later hinged top, 24in. wide. (Christie's) $2,210

Swedish walnut serpentine bombe voting box on carved legs and ball and claw feet, 34in. wide. (Christie's) $1,325

Late 17th century carved oak standing cabinet. (Lacy Scott) $1,370

Small 16th century German oak stollenschrank, probably Westfalian, 37in. wide. (Boardman's) $4,070

Walnut and ebonized Renaissance cabinet, late 17th century, 33in. wide. (Lacy Scott) $2,110

17th century Flemish rosewood, walnut and marquetry cabinet on stand, 76in. wide. (Christie's) $3,496

17th century Flemish silver mounted ebony and tortoiseshell cabinet on scrolled legs and paw feet, 55½in. wide. (Christie's) $9,200

17th century Goanese ivory and tortoiseshell inlaid rosewood table cabinet, 20½in. wide. (Christie's) $1,235

17th century Dutch oak cabinet on stand with ebony inlay, 57in. wide. (Edwards, Bigwood & Bewlay) $5,215

Regency rosewood dwarf cabinet with brass gallery, 44½in. wide. (Christie's) $5,965

Arts & Crafts music cabinet. (Capes, Dunn & Co.) $1,040

18th century German scarlet and gold lacquer cabinet on chest with broken scrolled pediment, 46½in. wide. (Christie's) $1,840

William and Mary oyster veneered chest on stand, late 17th century with later stand, 32½in. wide. (Sotheby Beresford Adams) $1,860

Dutch carved marquetry cabinet on chest, circa 1790, 6ft. wide. (Sotheby, King & Chasemore) $3,990

Writing cabinet on stand in satinwood and harewood with marquetry inlay, 19th century, by A. Chalmers, 20in. wide. (Morphets)$1,860

Fine late 19th century Sheraton design silver cabinet veneered in amboyna with satinwood banding, 2ft.7in. wide. (Locke & England) $930

Late 17th century Dutch cabinet on stand with marquetry medallions, 6ft. 3in. wide.(Phillips & Jolly's)$7,320

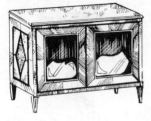

Early 19th century Louis XVI influence two-door cabinet in mahogany with mottled marble top. (Robert W. Skinner Inc.) $750

Rosewood side cabinet, superstructure with pierced gallery and mirror panel, circa 1840, 57in. wide. (Sotheby's Belgravia) $740

Walnut side cabinet with central cupboard door inlaid with flowers, circa 1870, 59in. wide. (Sotheby's Belgravia) $1,170

Giltwood cabinet on stand, door applied with a mid 18th century Soho tapestry, 40in. wide.(Sotheby's Belgravia) $920

19th century Spanish vargueno in mahogany and mahogany veneer, 14in. wide. (Robert W. Skinner Inc.) $150

Ebonized wooden cabinet by Gillows & Co., Lancaster, dated for 1871, 138cm. wide. (Phillips) $805

Burr-walnut and marquetry side cabinet with D-shaped top, cupboard door inlaid with flowers, circa 1870, 67in. wide. (Sotheby's Belgravia) $2,070

One of a pair of 19th century French Napoleon III boulle mounted meubles a hauteur d'appui, 33in. wide. (Robert W. Skinner Inc.) $4,500

Burr-walnut porcelain mounted side cabinet with gilt bronze mounts, circa 1870, 71½in. wide. (Sotheby's Belgravia) $3,680

Ebonized burr-walnut small side cabinet, door with Wedgwood plaque, circa 1870, 49in. wide.(Sotheby's Belgravia) $790

Late 18th/early 19th century Japanese lacquered traveling cabinet on stand, 3ft.2in. wide. (Dickinson, Davy & Markham) $2,115

19th century Georgian style two-door cabinet, painted black with gilt decoration, 40in. wide. (Robert W. Skinner Inc.) $600

Victorian bamboo cabinet with gilt black lacquered panels and open undertier, 17½in. wide. (John Hogbin & Son)$130

Marquetry side cabinet with carara marble top, circa 1860, 89in. wide. (Sotheby's Belgravia) $2,520

Art Nouveau mahogany cabinet with gallery top and railed sides, 3ft. 4½in. wide.(Dickinson, Davy & Markham) $660

Breakfront walnut side cabinet applied with five Sevres plaques, circa 1870, 65½in. wide. (Sotheby's Belgravia) $1,690

19th century boulle cabinet, ebonized with simulated tortoiseshell and brass, 29in. wide. (Locke & England) $465

17th century South German ebony and bone marquetry table cabinet, 27in. wide. (Boardman's)$1,945

Good mid Victorian walnut and marquetry side cabinet with gilt metal mounts, 147.5cm. wide. (H. Spencer & Sons Ltd.) $1,450

Walnut and marquetry serpentine display cabinet, 35½in. wide, circa 1860. (Sotheby's Belgravia) $2,165

Ebony veneered side cabinet with inlaid frieze, circa 1880, 84¼in. wide. (Sotheby's Belgravia) $1,655

Mid 18th century Dutch walnut veneered and oak cabinet on chest, 4ft. wide. (Woolley & Wallis) $3,160

Regency mahogany side cabinet with well-figured crossbanded bowed breakfront top, 52½in. wide. (Christie's)$4,810

One of a pair of walnut and marquetry side cabinets, circa 1870, 31in. wide. (Sotheby's Belgravia)$1,955

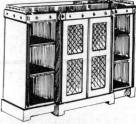

Rosewood side cabinet with mirrored back, 1890's, 24½in. wide. (Sotheby's Belgravia) $510

William IV rosewood breakfront side cabinet, circa 1830, 5ft.3½in. wide. (Sotheby's) $2,035

Late Regency painted and parcel gilt breakfront side cabinet, 5ft. wide, circa 1820. (Sotheby's) $1,200

Mid 19th century tulipwood, gilt bronze, porcelain and marquetry side cabinet, 72in. wide. (Sotheby Beresford Adams) $3,905

Aesthetic movement mahogany hanging cabinet, signed CWM, dated 1888, 44cm. wide. (Christie's) $370

17th century Goanese ivory and tortoiseshell inlaid rosewood table cabinet, 20½in. wide. (Christie's) $1,235

Early 18th century Chinese black lacquer cabinet on stand, 3ft.2½in. wide. (Sotheby's) $3,310

Edwardian walnut glazed back display cabinet. (Alfred Mossop & Co.) $405

Mid 19th century Italian Renaissance ebony and ivory cabinet with broken arch pediment, 38in. wide. (Sotheby Beresford Adams) $1,675

17th century style Flemish carved oak cabinet, 4ft.9in. high, circa 1860. (Sotheby, King & Chasemore) $920

William and Mary black and gold lacquer cabinet on chest, 23½in. wide. (Christie's)$8,025

Regency rosewood side cabinet with three-quarter brass gallery, circa 1810, 2ft.6½in. wide.(Sotheby's) $3,825

William IV mahogany canterbury with four divisions, circa 1835, 21in. wide.(Sotheby's Belgravia) $685

Fine Regency rosewood music canterbury of four compartments. (Dee & Atkinson) $645

Mid 19th century mahogany canterbury of three divisions, 22½in. square. (Sotheby Beresford Adams)$895

Simulated rosewood canterbury with three compartments, circa 1840, 20½in. wide. (Sotheby's Belgravia) $640

Mid 19th century walnut canterbury, top tier with fretwork pierced gallery, 25in. wide. (Sotheby's) $1,015

Early Victorian rosewood canterbury of four compartments, 43cm. wide. (H. Spencer & Sons Ltd.) $805

Walnut canterbury in well-figured wood, circa 1850, 19in. wide. (Sotheby's Belgravia) $505

Walnut canterbury with pierced gallery, circa 1860, 24in. wide.(Sotheby's Belgravia) $765

Early 19th century bird's eye maple canterbury, circa 1825, 1ft.8in. wide. (Sotheby's) $850

William and Mary banister back side chair, America, circa 1720, 43in. high. (Robert W. Skinner Inc.) $140

One of a set of six mid 19th century unusual country-made chairs with spade-shaped backs, restored. (Sotheby's) $735

One of a pair of 18th century Chippendale mahogany side chairs with pierced splats. (Wm. Doyle Galleries Inc.) $1,600

One of a pair of early 18th century mahogany chairs with shaped backs. (W. H. Lane & Son) $400

One of a pair of walnut side chairs with leather seats and backs, circa 1680. (Sotheby's) $800

Ebonized hall chair, back with horizontal splats and with rush seat, by Chas. Rennie Mackintosh, circa 1903. (Christie's) $4,370

One of an early 19th century set of ten elmwood and beechwood children's school-room chairs. (Sotheby's) $1,425

One of a set of six William IV mahogany dining chairs, circa 1835. (Sotheby's Belgravia) $1,195

One of a set of six rosewood framed chairs with squab seats. (Arthur G. Griffiths & Sons) $1,090

DINING CHAIRS

One of a set of four mahogany dining chairs with carved, arched toprails, circa 1870. (Sotheby's Belgravia) $325

One of a pair of Renaissance revival side chairs in ebonised wood, walnut and burl veneer, circa 1865, 34½in. high. (Robert W. Skinner Inc.) $175

One of a set of five mid 19th century walnut drawingroom chairs with balloon backs. (Sotheby's Belgravia) $685

American Queen Anne child's ladder back side chair with rush seat, circa 1765. (Robert W. Skinner Inc.)$300

Mid Georgian mahogany dining chair with pierced splat and wavy toprail. (Christie's)$1,450

One of a set of eight 19th century baroque style carved side chairs in oak, backs 53in. high. (Robert W. Skinner Inc.) $800

One of a set of four walnut dining chairs with pierced and carved backs, circa 1860, on cabriole legs. (Sotheby's Belgravia) $810

One of a set of four mid 18th century George III mahogany dining chairs.(Sotheby Beresford Adams) $485

New England Queen Anne maple Spanish foot side chair with vase-shaped splat, circa 1730, back of chair 41½in. high. (Robert W. Skinner Inc.) $700

One of a set of twelve late William IV mahogany dining chairs with drop-in seats. (Sotheby Beresford Adams) $1,210

One of a set of three thumb back side chairs, signed H. Cook, New England, circa 1820. (Robert W. Skinner Inc.) $650

One of a set of six Georgian Chippendale style dining chairs with pierced splats. (Dickinson, Davy & Markham) $1,240

One of a set of six early George III mahogany dining chairs with pierced waved ladder backs. (Christie's)$5,365

One of a pair of antique black papier-mache chairs with mother-of-pearl inlay, and cane seats. (John Hogbin & Son) $590

One of a set of eleven 18th century mahogany dining chairs with cane seats, possibly Anglo-Chinese. (Christie's) $1,755

Gustav Stickley oak side chair, New York, circa 1905, back 39in. high. (Robert W. Skinner Inc.) $140

One of a set of ten mahogany dining chairs with pierced Gothic pattern baluster splats and needlework seats. (Christie's) $5,550

One of a set of six George III provincial mahogany dining chairs with Gothic pierced vase splats. (H. Spencer & Sons Ltd.) $1,955

269

DINING CHAIRS

One of a set of seven Dutch marquetry dining chairs with solid vase-shaped splats, sold with a settee. (Christie's) $5,150

Two of a set of six Hepplewhite period mahogany fluted frame carved back dining chairs, circa 1785. (Neales) $2,140

One of a set of eight 18th/19th century French Provincial side chairs, 42½in. high. (Robert W. Skinner Inc.) $1,500

One of a set of six 19th century oak Jacobean style high back chairs, heavily carved. (Dickinson, Davy & Markham) $1,120

Two of a set of eight late Victorian mahogany dining chairs in Chippendale style. (H. Spencer & Sons Ltd.) $1,955

One of a pair of Regency ebonized mahogany dining chairs with cane seats and sabre legs. (John Hogbin & Son) $240

Victorian mother-of-pearl inlaid papier-mache occasional chair with cane seat. (Hy. Duke & Son) $220

Two of a set of twelve late 19th century 'George III' mahogany dining chairs with shield backs. (Sotheby's Belgravia) $2,790

18th century French transitional Louis XV chaise with canted rectangular back, 43½in. high. (Robert W. Skinner Inc.) $150

One of a set of six
Victorian mahogany
balloon back dining
chairs on shaped
reeded legs.(Burten-
shaw Walker) $1,395

Two of a set of eight Chippendale
style dining chairs with pierced
splats, and leather covered seats.
(Locke & England)$1,850

One of a pair of Chip-
pendale period maho-
gany single chairs
with pierced splats.
(Edwards, Bigwood &
Bewlay) $785

One of a pair of Dutch
walnut and marquetry
chairs with baluster-
shaped splats and cab-
riole legs. (Christie's)
$2,945

Two of a set of ten carved oak
and inlaid Elizabethan style chairs,
20th century. (Sotheby, King &
Chasemore) $2,310

19th century Ger-
man carved oak
hall chair.
(Christie's S. Ken-
sington) $560

One of a pair of
George II walnut
framed dining
chairs. (Sotheby
Bearne)
$2,230

Two of a set of ten mahogany dining
chairs with carved toprails and molded crossbars, circa 1840. (Sotheby's
Belgravia) $3,310

George I walnut
dining chair with
solid splat.
(Sotheby, King &
Chasemore)
$255

271

DINING CHAIRS

One of a set of four walnut dining chairs with oval backs, circa 1860.(Sotheby's Belgravia) $865

One of a set of three late 18th century fan back Windsor chairs with shaped crest rails. (Robert W. Skinner Inc.) $3,800

One of a set of six walnut dining chairs with balloon backs and serpentine seats, circa 1860. (Sotheby's Belgravia) $1,655

One of a set of six Regency simulated rosewood beech-framed chairs, circa 1810. (Sotheby, King & Chasemore) $1,630

One of a set of eight mahogany dining chairs of mid Georgian design with pierced and carved splats. (Christie's) $8,140

One of a set of six George III mahogany dining chairs with arched toprails and pierced bar-shaped splats. (Christie's) $1,630

One of a pair of late 18th century Chippendale period Gothic design chairs with pierced lancet backs. (Locke & England) $360

One of a set of six walnut dining chairs with waisted balloon backs, circa 1860. (Sotheby's Belgravia) $1,080

One of a set of eight William IV rosewood dining chairs with leaf-carved crossbar, circa 1835. (Sotheby's Belgravia) $3,060.

One of a set of four mid 19th century walnut dining chairs with molded oval backs. (Sotheby Beresford Adams) $855

One of a set of six early 19th century George III mahogany dining chairs, molded splats centered by vases. (Sotheby Beresford Adams) $1,525

One of a set of six mid 19th century William IV rosewood dining chairs with drop-in seats. (Sotheby Beresford Adams)$595

One of a set of seven George III provincial mahogany dining chairs with Gothic pierced vase splats. (H. Spencer & Sons Ltd.) $2,230

One of a set of six Gillows ebonized dining chairs designed by Bruce J. Talbert. (Phillips) $715

One of a set of six Heal's walnut dining chairs, 1914, with curved lattice backs. (Phillips) $1,255

One of a pair of early 19th century Regency mahogany hall chairs with carved and molded shell backs. (Sotheby Beresford Adams) $520

One of a set of twelve mahogany dining chairs of George III design with pierced splats. (Christie's) $6,290

Viennese beech chair, designed by Josef Hoffmann, with fluted toprail. (Phillips) $215

273

DINING CHAIRS

One of a set of five early 19th century painted side chairs, 35½in. high. (Robert W. Skinner Inc.) **$1,000**

Two from a set of eight Chippendale style mahogany dining chairs with vase-shaped splats. (Jackson-Stops & Staff) **$4,850**

One of a set of four mid 19th century rosewood drawing-room chairs, on cabriole legs.(Sotheby's Belgravia)**$720**

One of a set of four mid 19th century beechwood drawing-room chairs. (Sotheby's Belgravia) **$425**

Two from a set of eight carved mahogany dining chairs, circa 1910. (Sotheby, King & Chasemore) **$2,225**

One of a set of eight red painted and gilded dining chairs in early Georgian style. (Christie's) **$2,990**

One of a set of ten Regency simulated rosewood and parcel gilt dining chairs. (Christie's) **$4,320**

Two of a set of ten Reproduction dining chairs in Chippendale style. (Hall Wateridge & Owen) **$3,420**

One of a set of eight walnut balloon-back dining chairs with carved toprails, circa 1870.(Sotheby's Belgravia)**$1,870**

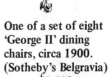

One of a set of four early 18th century Dutch walnut marquetry chairs. (Edwards, Bigwood & Bewlay) $1,830

Two of a set of eight George III Hepplewhite design chairs with camel-shaped backs. (Boardman's)$3,215

One of a set of six George III mahogany dining chairs with X-pattern splats. (Christie's) $2,470

One of a set of ten 'George III' mahogany dining chairs with three-stick splats, circa 1880. (Sotheby's Belgravia) $1,805

Two from a set of eight 19th century mahogany framed Hepplewhite style dining chairs with carved frames. (W. H. Lane & Son) $1,585

One of a set of eight 'George II' dining chairs, circa 1900. (Sotheby's Belgravia) $1,590

One of a pair of Victorian papier-mache chairs with mother-of-pearl inlay and cane seats. (Dee & Atkinson) $560

One of four Victorian mahogany dining chairs with open backs. (Dickinson, Davy & Markham) $205

Two of a set of twelve mahogany dining chairs in Sheraton style. (Hall Wateridge & Owen) $3,385

DINING CHAIRS

One of a set of twelve Victorian walnut cabriole leg dining chairs with oval backs. (Boardman's) $3,780

Two from a set of six carved mahogany dining chairs and one carver, with openwork splats. (Brogden & Co.) $630

One of a set of six Regency mahogany hall chairs, circa 1805, with squab cushions. (Sotheby's) $1,200

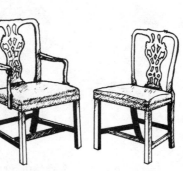

William and Mary carved side chair, early 18th century New England, 47½in. high. (Robert W. Skinner Inc.) $4,000

Two from a set of ten George III mahogany dining chairs, circa 1775, on square molded legs. (Sotheby's) $5,320

Early 19th century Dutch walnut standard chair with carved frame, with paw feet.(Jackson-Stops & Staff) $550

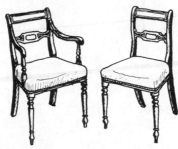

One of a set of six George III mahogany dining chairs with pierced vase-shaped splats, circa 1760. (Sotheby's)$2,045

Two from a set of eight Georgian mahogany dining chairs with reeded bar backs. (Lawrence Fine Art) $2,390

One of a set of five late George II mahogany side chairs, circa 1760. (Sotheby's) $5,375

One of a set of eight
Hepplewhite dining
chairs with shield-
shaped backs.
(Messenger, May &
Baverstock)
$7,680

Two of a set of six Hepplewhite
style dining chairs with shield
backs. (Lawrence Fine Art)
$1,435

One of a pair of
mahogany dining
chairs on fluted
tapering legs.
(Gilbert Baitson)
$170

One of a set of four
Flemish beechwood
and walnut side
chairs with carved
and pierced toprails.
(Sotheby's) $1,150

Two of a set of six Hepplewhite
mahogany dining chairs on sabre
legs. (Lawrence Fine Art)
$1,750

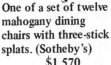

One of a set of twelve
mahogany dining
chairs with three-stick
splats. (Sotheby's)
$1,570

One of a set of six
George III mahogany
dining chairs with
buttoned backs and
seats. (Sotheby's)
$4,550

Two of a set of ten Chippendale
style mahogany dining chairs
with pierced and waved ladder-
backs. (Lawrence Fine Art)
$2,945

One of a set of five
George III mahogany
chairs with stick backs,
circa 1785. (Sotheby's)
$1,330

EASY CHAIRS

One of a pair of mahogany armchairs with padded backs and wing sides, circa 1900. (Sotheby's Belgravia) $550

Early Victorian period ornately carved walnut salon chair with spoon back. (Locke & England) $1,340

Queen Anne red walnut wing arm easy chair on cabriole legs, circa 1710. (Sotheby, King & Chasemore) $2,115

One of a pair of carved giltwood and Aubusson tapestry bergeres. (Sotheby, King & Chasemore) $7,810

17th century Queen Anne high-backed open armchair with turned front legs and stretchers. (Butler & Hatch Waterman) $650

One of a pair of mid 19th century carved giltwood bergeres of Louis XVI style, covered in Aubusson tapestry. (Sotheby, King & Chasemore) $4,090

Mid 19th century European oak campaign chair on collapsible and adjustable frame. (Sotheby's Belgravia) $250

One of a set of two walnut chairs, one an armchair, with padded oval backs, circa 1860. (Sotheby's Belgravia) $1,620

Mid 19th century carved giltwood bergere, covered in Aubusson tapestry. (Sotheby, King & Chasemore) $2,790

Mid 18th century George III wing armchair with padded back, sides and seats, 42in. high. (Sotheby Beresford Adams) $315

Superb Victorian walnut lounge chair with buttoned back, upholstered in tapestry. (Allen & May)
$700

Modern George II style wing armchair with slightly arched padded back. (Sotheby Beresford Adams)$175

One of a pair of library armchairs with padded backs and arm supports, circa 1770. (Sotheby's)
$2,695

Late 17th/early 18th century walnut wing armchair on cabriole legs with hoof feet. (Christie's)
$1,850

Late 17th century walnut armchair with curved and molded arms, Flemish. (Sotheby, King & Chasemore)
$1,490

Mid 19th century George II elm wing armchair with tall padded back, arms and serpentine seat, 42in. high.(Sotheby Beresford Adams)
$595

20th century early George III style mahogany cock-fighting chair with adjustable writing slope. (Sotheby Beresford Adams) $425

Late 18th century George III armchair with out-turned arms, back 46in. high. (Robert W. Skinner Inc.)
$1,650

Early George III mahogany elbow chair with carved arm supports. (Lawrence Fine Art) $1,000

Leather upholstered reclining armchair by J. Foot, London, 1880-1900. (Sotheby's Belgravia) $1,070

Arts & Crafts lady's oak spindle Morris chair by Gustav Stickley, circa 1905. (Robert W. Skinner Inc.) $2,300

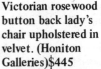

17th century Flemish walnut armchair with X-stretcher. (Sotheby, King & Chasemore) $550

Pair of walnut framed Victorian grandfather and mother chairs with scroll feet. (Worsfolds) $2,055

Victorian rosewood button back lady's chair upholstered in velvet. (Honiton Galleries)$445

One of a pair of French 'Louis XVI' beechwood armchairs on stop-fluted turned tapering legs, circa 1880. (Sotheby's Belgravia) $660

Victorian walnut spoon back lady's chair with carved top and cabriole legs. (Dickinson, Davy & Markham)$630

Queen Anne walnut armchair with shaped wings and out-curved arms, circa 1710.(Sotheby's) $1,945

Victorian mahogany
framed tub chair on
turned front legs.
(J. M. Welch & Son)
$115

Swedish laminated plywood chaise
longue, by Bruno Mattsson, 1930's,
82cm. high. (Sotheby's Belgravia)
$605

Carved mahogany arm-
chair upholstered in
green hide. (Brogden &
Co.) $185

Victorian carved rose-
wood framed easy
chair on cabriole legs.
(Geering & Colyer)
$820

Two rococo Revival walnut chairs,
America, circa 1860, with carved
crests, 45in. and 40½in. high.
(Robert W. Skinner Inc.)
$550

19th century rose-
wood lady's chair
with carved frame.
(J. M. Welch & Son)
$475

One of a pair of rosewood
button-upholstered arm-
chairs, circa 1860.
(Sotheby's Belgravia)
$1,170

19th century rosewood
framed lady's chair.
(J. M. Welch & Son)
$690

Mid 19th century walnut
lady's chair with button-
back and carved legs.
(T. Bannister & Co.)
$560

281

EASY CHAIRS

Victorian rosewood lady's chair with button back. (Honiton Galleries) $520

18th century English open armchair with mahogany frame, circa 1750. (W. H. Lane & Son) $2,710

Victorian spoon back nursing chair with scrolling arms and cabriole legs. (Lawrence Fine Art) $425

George III mahogany armchair, stamped B. Harmer, circa 1770, with bow-fronted seatrail. (Sotheby's) $980

Victorian gentleman's chair in mahogany frame with button back. (Alfred Mossop & Co.) $810

Chair from a three-piece suite of drawingroom furniture, circa 1870. (Sotheby's Belgravia) $1,050

Georgian style library armchair with shaped top and wings. (Lawrence Fine Art) $590

One of a pair of French 18th century Louis XV style fauteuil en cabriolet, in fruitwood, 34in. high. (Robert W. Skinner Inc.) $1,450

One of a pair of mahogany framed Gainsborough armchairs. (Gilbert Baitson) $225

George III mahogany library armchair, legs with blind Chinese fret, circa 1770. (Sotheby's) $2,560

One of a pair of Victorian grandfather chairs with mahogany frames. (Hall Wateridge & Owen) $715

William IV tulipwood reclining armchair, circa 1835. (Sotheby, King & Chasemore) $800

George II mahogany armchair in French style, circa 1750, with carved front legs. (Sotheby's) $980

Queen Anne walnut and upholstered chair on pad feet, circa 1715. (Sotheby, King & Chasemore) $1,730

Victorian lady's button back chair in mahogany frame. (Alfred Mossop & Co.) $885

Victorian walnut carved spoon back chair with serpentine-fronted seat and cabriole legs. (John Hogbin & Son) $380

One of a pair of 19th century French Louis XV style fauteuils a la Reine, 38in. high. (Robert W. Skinner Inc.) $650

Queen Anne walnut wing frame easy chair, circa 1710. (Sotheby, King & Chasemore) $2,945

283

EASY CHAIRS

One of a pair of Dutch mahogany armchairs with horseshoe-shaped toprails, circa 1790. (Sotheby's) $2,865

Herman Miller lounge chair designed by Charles Eames, 1956, 81cm. high.(Sotheby's Belgravia) $1,040

Victorian spoon-back chair in carved walnut frame, upholstered in brown tapestry. (Butler & Hatch Waterman) $610

One of a pair of 17th century restored walnut open armchairs. (Christie's)$1,800

Chair from an eleven-piece suite of bamboo porch furniture, circa 1930, 30in. high. (Robert W. Skinner Inc.) $5,900

One of four oak hall chairs with carved and pierced backs, on scroll form supports. (Outhwaite & Litherland)$830

Victorian walnut elbow chair with buttoned back upholstered in pink velvet. (Lawrence Fine Art) $665

Mid Victorian papier-mache occasional chair by Jennens & Bettridge, decorated in mother-of-pearl. (Dacre, Son & Hartley) $930

Victorian elbow chair, walnut frame with oval back, upholstered in orange velvet.(Lawrence Fine Art) $555

Oak turner's chair, back with pierced horizontal and vertical baluster splats. (Christie's) $1,425

Regency mahogany library step chair with cane seat, folding to reveal four baize covered steps. (Lawrence Fine Art)$1,575

18th century elm, oak and beechwood Windsor armchair with pierced Gothic pattern splats.(Christie's) $620

Early 18th century mahogany, beech and oak framed elbow chair with vase-shaped splat. (W. H. Lane & Son) $275

Rare mid 17th century wainscot armchair with shaped cresting above a paneled back.(Sotheby's) $490

Late 18th century Windsor armchair in elm, ash and beech, with shaped pierced splat. (W. H. Lane & Son)$290

One of a set of six Dutch marquetry chairs with pierced splats, circa 1765. (Sotheby's) $1,800

Late 18th century Windsor stick-back armchair in elm, ash and beech, with crinoline stretchers. (W. H. Lane & Son) $125

Early 18th century country-made beech and oak framed elbow chair with vase-shaped splat. (W. H. Lane & Son) $255

American Art Nouveau laminated mahogany and maple armchair, circa 1910, back 44½in. high. (Robert W. Skinner Inc.) $350

One of a pair of 'George III' satinwood armchairs with Prince of Wales's feathers carved on backs, 1910-20. (Sotheby's Belgravia) $1,510

Laminated mahogany armchair by the Paine Furniture Co., Boston, circa 1920, back 45in. high. (Robert W. Skinner Inc.) $250

One of a set of twelve Regency mahogany open armchairs with reeded frames. (Christie's) $6,660

French carved walnut 'caqueteuse' chair upholstered in rose red velvet. (Butler & Hatch Waterman) $520

One of a pair of Regency mahogany armchairs with reeded toprails, circa 1805. (Sotheby's) $2,420

Mid 18th century knuckle arm Windsor chair with bow back and bobbin turned stretchers. (Robert W. Skinner Inc.) $825

One of a set of eight late Regency mahogany dining chairs with concave rails and padded seats. (Sotheby Beresford Adams) $2,230

Late 19th century Japanese carved oak armchair with serpentine cloud form apron, 34½in. high.(Robert W. Skinner Inc.) $375

FURNITURE

One of a set of eight mid 20th century George III style mahogany dining chairs by Waring & Gillow Ltd. (Sotheby Beresford Adams) $1,580

19th century French Empire armchair with barrel-shaped backrail and with cast brass mounts, 31½in. high. (Robert W. Skinner Inc.) $500

Federal mahogany lolling chair with serpentine back, Massachusetts, circa 1780. (Robert W. Skinner Inc.) $9,500

One of a set of eight George IV mahogany dining chairs, circa 1820, with pierced scroll crossbars. (Sotheby's) $3,535

Early 18th century Dutch East Indies Colonial burgomaster's armchair, back flanked by mask finials. (Sotheby Beresford Adams) $1,860

One of a set of seven early 20th century Queen Anne style mahogany dining chairs, with vase-shaped splats. (Sotheby Beresford Adams) $1,765

American Elizabethan revival walnut platform rocker, New York, circa 1884. (Robert W. Skinner Inc.) $275

American Arts & Crafts oak armchair with corniced rail, circa 1900, back 51in. high. (Robert W. Skinner Inc.) $175

Gustav Stickley oak Morris chair with slanted arms, New York, circa 1906, 33in. wide. (Robert W. Skinner Inc.) $10,000

ELBOW CHAIRS

One of a pair of Chinese padouk framed armchairs with carved backs and arms. (W. H. Lane & Son) $935

Arts & Crafts oak armchair with padded back rest and pierced apron, 83cm. high. (Christie's) $225

One of a pair of Regency painted armchairs with cane seats, circa 1805. (Sotheby's) $2,130

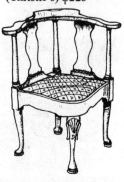

One of a set of seven mahogany elbow chairs of Hepplewhite design with wheel backs. (Jackson-Stops & Staff) $2,760

Walnut corner chair on slight cabriole legs and pad feet. (Alfred Mossop & Co.) $365

One of a set of eight mahogany dining chairs. (Rowland Gorringe) $4,115

One of a set of eight 'George I' mahogany dining chairs with solid splats, circa 1900. (Sotheby's Belgravia) $3,290

19th century elm high back Windsor chair with turned legs and stretcher. (Dickinson, Davy & Markham) $230

One of a set of eight early 18th century ash and oak ladderback dining chairs. (Lacy Scott) $2,540

One of a pair of Hepplewhite design mahogany wheel back dining chairs. (Jackson-Stops & Staff) $505

One of a pair of Regency painted and parcel gilt caned bergeres, circa 1815. (Sotheby's) $3,410

Late Victorian mahogany occasional elbow chair. (Gilbert Baitson) $190

One of a set of eight Hepplewhite design mahogany dining chairs. (Woolley & Wallis) $2,510

Hepplewhite style carver chair in mahogany frame with floral upholstery. (Alfred Mossop & Co.) $270

One of a set of four late George II mahogany dining chairs with vase-shaped splats, circa 1755. (Sotheby's) $1,850

Mahogany elbow chair with shield back and wheat-ear decoration. (Gilbert Baitson) $105

Small 19th century high back Windsor chair with pierced splat and crinoline stretcher. (Dickinson, Davy & Markham) $295

One of a set of eight mahogany ladderback dining chairs in Chippendale style, with leather seats. (Woolley & Wallis) $1,490

19th century Scandinavian carved and painted armchair on spiral supports. (Lawrence Fine Art) $700

Russian poplar armchair, heavily carved, circa 1900. (Sotheby's Belgravia) $455

One of a set of six George III mahogany dining chairs with arched toprails, circa 1780. (Sotheby's) $2,220

18th century armchair in fruitwood and beech with pierced crest, 45in. high. (Robert W. Skinner Inc.) $225

Second Empire armchair, France, circa 1855, with carved arms and legs. (Robert W. Skinner Inc.) $850

One of a set of eight Regency mahogany dining chairs with rope-twist toprails, circa 1805. (Sotheby's) $4,765

One of a set of eight Regency mahogany dining chairs with bowed toprails, circa 1810. (Sotheby's) $4,705

One of a set of four Charles II beechwood armchairs, circa 1660, with carved toprail and backs. (Sotheby's) $5,350

Late George II mahogany armchair with carved toprail, circa 1755. (Sotheby's) $735

One of a pair of Regency armchairs with caned seats and black and gilt decoration. (J. M. Welch & Son) $290

One of a set of six late 19th/early 20th century mahogany dining chairs with shield backs. (Sotheby's Belgravia) $660

One of a set of four Georgian period mahogany elbow chairs with pierced splat backs. (Woolley & Wallis) $16,655

High-back Essex elbow chair on square legs. (J. M. Welch & Son) $290

Flemish carved walnut armchair with gadrooned scrolled back, circa 1690, legs joined by waved X-stretchers. (Sotheby's) $1,480

Spindle-backed 19th century rocking chair with rush seat. (J. M. Welch & Son) $90

Small early 19th century comb-back chair on turned legs. (J. M. Welch & Son) $335

Edwardian Art Nouveau satinwood armchair with slender padded back, circa 1910. (Sotheby's Belgravia) $865

One of a set of ten George III mahogany dining chairs including two armchairs, circa 1765. (Sotheby's) $5,170

18th century comb-back elbow chair with shaped toprail. (J. M. Welch & Son) $565

Painted satinwood armchair with caned back and sides, circa 1900. (Sotheby's Belgravia) $265

One of a set of eight Charles II style oak dining chairs, six single and two carvers. (J. M. Welch & Son) $1,275

Chippendale style elbow chair with pierced splat. (J. M. Welch & Son) $245

One from a set of eight country style rail and wheel back dining chairs. (Butler & Hatch Waterman) $455

One of a rare pair of late George II mahogany corner armchairs, circa 1760, with pierced Gothic splats. (Sotheby's) $1,580

One of a set of six late 19th century 'George III' mahogany dining chairs. (Sotheby's Belgravia) $430

Late 19th century carved oak elbow chair with cane seat and back. (J. M. Welch & Son) $455

One of a set of eight mahogany dining chairs, including two armchairs, circa 1880. (Sotheby's Belgravia) $1,400

19th century yew-backed child's Windsor chair. (J. M. Welch & Son) $180

19th century child's high chair with tray and foot rest. (J. M. Welch & Son) $125

Early 17th century yew-wood Turner's chair with T-shaped back. (Sotheby's) $3,190

Mid 18th century George III oak and elm wainscot armchair with solid seat. (Sotheby's) $440

Antique open armchair with carved splat and apron, with squab cushion. (J. M. Welch & Son) $300

One of a pair of formerly caned Guangxu rosewood armchairs. (Sotheby's Belgravia) $505

George II mahogany corner armchair with arched upholstered back, circa 1735. (Sotheby's) $786

French giltwood fauteuil with reeded legs and upholstered seat and back. (J. M. Welch & Son) $290

One of a pair of 'George III' armchairs with serpentine backs, circa 1920. (Sotheby's Belgravia) $615

English Colonial solid camphorwood and ebony military secretaire chest in two parts, 42in. wide, circa 1840. (Sotheby's Belgravia) $2,250

George III serpentine mahogany chest of drawers, circa 1780, 3ft. wide.(Sotheby's) $4,340

Early Georgian mahogany chest of five drawers with brass handles, 3ft. wide. (Allen & May)$605

Chinese export camphorwood military secretaire chest with brass fittings, circa 1900, 36in. wide. (Sotheby's Belgravia) $1,655

New England Chippendale tiger maple tall chest of drawers with applied molded cornice, 36in. wide, circa 1760. (Robert W. Skinner Inc.) $2,200

Charles II oak chest of four long drawers on stand with a ball turned frame, 40in. wide. (Sotheby, King & Chasemore) $900

Late 17th century William and Mary walnut chest, on four ball feet. (Robert W. Skinner Inc.) $950

Chest of four short and two long drawers with turned wood handles. (Honiton Galleries) $300

Early 18th century herringbone walnut chest of four long drawers with brass knob handles, 30in. wide. (Burtenshaw Walker) $1,635

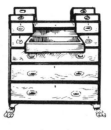

Victorian mahogany bow-fronted chest of four drawers, 36in. wide. (J. M. Welch & Son) $345

Mid 19th century camphor-wood military chest of drawers with brass bindings, 44in. wide. (Eldon E. Worrall & Co.) $1,730

Georgian mahogany chest of five drawers with brass drop handles and escutcheons, on ogee bracket feet. (John Hogbin & Son) $340

Charles II oak chest with applied moldings and paneled ends, 29in. wide . (Burrows & Day) $460

Charles II oak chest of drawers with walnut veneered drawer fronts. (H. C. Chapman & Son) $1,900

Edwardian style inlaid mahogany chest of five drawers with brass ring handles and on bracket feet. (John Hogbin & Son) $215

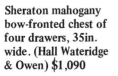

Sheraton mahogany bow-fronted chest of four drawers, 35in. wide. (Hall Wateridge & Owen) $1,090

Louis XV kingwood parquetry chest of drawers with ormolu mounts, 4ft.3in. wide, with red marble top. (Turner, Rudge & Turner) $9,100

George III mahogany serpentine chest of four drawers, circa 1775, 3ft.5½in. wide. (Sotheby's) $3,620

CHESTS OF DRAWERS

Mahogany and ebony banded chest of five drawers with brass drop handles. (John Hogbin & Son) $130

American Federal maple inlaid chest with rectangular top and bow front, circa 1790, 38½in. wide. (Robert W. Skinner Inc.) $1,200

George II mahogany chest of four long drawers, circa 1750, 2ft.6in. wide. (Sotheby's) $1,700

18th century George II walnut commode with brass handles and escutcheons, 38in. wide. (Robert W. Skinner Inc.)$950

19th century French Empire semainier in mahogany and mahogany veneer, 61in. high. (Robert W. Skinner Inc.)$1,200

Late 19th century walnut chest with herringbone inlay to top, drop loop handles and bracket feet. (T. Bannister & Co.) $1,175

Early Georgian walnut chest, top inset with a panel of burr-maple, 37½in. wide. (Christie's) $2,080

19th century French ebonized boullework chest with tortoiseshell and brass drawer fronts, 2ft.2in. wide.(Dickinson, Davy & Markham) $440

Regency mahogany dressing chest with bowed top crossbanded with rosewood, 39½in. wide. (Christie's) $2,405

George I walnut chest of four long drawers and quartered crossbanded top, 31½in. wide. (Christie's) $2,775

Mid 19th century square front mahogany chest of drawers with shaped apron. (T. Bannister & Co.) $305

George III gentleman's plum pudding mahogany dressing chest, circa 1790, 37in. wide. (Sotheby, King & Chasemore) $1,920

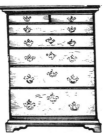

American Chippendale pine two drawer blanket chest, with simulated five drawer front, circa 1765, 37in. wide. (Robert W. Skinner Inc.) $1,500

Country Chippendale tiger maple chest of drawers, 48in. high, circa 1770, on dovetailed bracket feet. (Robert W. Skinner Inc.) $1,800

American Queen Anne pine lift-top blanket chest with simulated drawer front, circa 1740, 38¾in. wide. (Robert W. Skinner Inc.) $10,500

Country William and Mary pine and maple painted chest of drawers, Deerfield, Massachusetts, 1700-1715, 40in. wide. (Robert W. Skinner Inc.)$14,000

19th century Louis XVI style five drawer chiffonier with marble top, 43½in. high. (Robert W. Skinner Inc.) $425

Late 18th century serpentine-fronted mahogany dressing chest, circa 1770, 43½in. wide. (Sotheby, King & Chasemore) $11,345

CHESTS OF DRAWERS

Charles II walnut chest of drawers with dentil molding, circa 1680, 3ft.2in. wide.(Sotheby's) $1,260

Mid 19th century teak military chest of five drawers, in two sections, 39in. wide. (Lawrence Fine Art) $590

Late Georgian mahogany bow-fronted chest of three graduated drawers, 36in. wide. (Lawrence Fine Art) $590

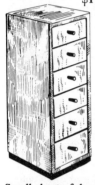

Small chest of drawers, designed by Marcel Breuer, 1920's, 30cm. wide. (Sotheby's Belgravia) $1,425

19th century Far Eastern five drawer chest, 55in. long. (Robert W. Skinner Inc.) $850

William IV mahogany Wellington chest of eight drawers, 24in. wide. (Lawrence Fine Art) $590

Late 17th century oak chest of four long drawers, restored, 37in. wide. (Sotheby's) $670

Mid 17th century oak chest of four long drawers, 2ft. 10in. wide. (Sotheby's) $855

Georgian mahogany chest of drawers with ivory escutcheons and brass handles, 33in. wide. (Lawrence Fine Art) $625

18th century Massachusetts mahogany chest of drawers with brass handles and escutcheons. (Wm. Doyle Galleries Inc.) $21,000

Charles II chest of drawers in oak with walnut veneered front, circa 1670, feet later, 3ft.8in. wide. (Sotheby's)$2,340

Jacobean oak chest of four long drawers, 36in. wide, in need of restoration. (J. M. Welch & Son) $800

18th century figured walnut chest of five drawers, 37in. wide. (Lawrence Fine Art) $2,210

Early 19th century black lacquer and chinoiserie chest of drawers, 3ft.6in. wide. (J. M. Welch & Son) $420

Mid 18th century Dutch walnut and marquetry chest with molded top, 3ft.2in. wide.(Sotheby's) $4,730

'George III' serpentine-fronted chest of drawers in mahogany, circa 1880, 54in. wide. (Sotheby's Belgravia) $1,530

Queen Anne walnut chest of six drawers on bracket feet, 36in. wide. (J. M. Welch & Son)$400

18th century George III oak chest on ogee bracket feet, 33½in. wide. (Sotheby's)$1,045

CHESTS ON CHESTS

Georgian walnut tallboy with oak crossbanding, brass plate handles and molded cornice, 41in. wide. (Lawrence Fine Art) $1,010

George III provincial chest on chest veneered in mahogany, 100cm. wide. (Osmond, Tricks) $1,090

Georgian mahogany tallboy with molded cornice, 47in. wide. (Lawrence Fine Art)$3,130

18th century walnut tallboy with brass handles and bracket feet, 3ft.4in. wide. (Dickinson, Davy & Markham) $2,990

George I walnut tallboy with cavetto cornice, circa 1720, 3ft.5in. wide. (Sotheby's)$4,225

Queen Anne walnut and chevronbanded chest on chest, circa 1710, restored, 3ft.5in. wide. (Sotheby, King & Chasemore) $2,595

George I black japanned tallboy, circa 1725, 3ft. wide. (Sotheby's) $2,895

Early 18th century walnut and burr-walnut chest on chest with contemporary brass handles, 42in. wide. (W. H. Lane & Son) $1,365

George I walnut secretaire tallboy with cavetto cornice, restored, circa 1720, 3ft.8in. wide. (Sotheby's) $2,455

18th century American Chippendale cherrywood bonnet top chest on chest, 53in. wide. (Wm. Doyle Galleries Inc.)
$5,250

Late 18th/early 19th century George III provincial walnut and fruitwood chest on chest, 41in. wide. (Sotheby Beresford Adams)
$820

Mid 18th century Chippendale tiger maple chest on chest, New Hampshire, 36in. wide. (Robert W. Skinner Inc.)
$4,500

Mahogany tallboy chest of eight drawers, with turned wood handles. (J. M. Welch & Son)
$525

Late 19th century walnut chest on chest with brass key plates and drop loop handles, on bracket feet. (T. Bannister & Co.)
$2,760

American Chippendale maple chest on chest, 40in. wide, circa 1780. (Robert W. Skinner Inc.)
$2,500

Late 18th century Queen Anne maple chest on chest, 38in. wide, with original brasses. (Robert W. Skinner Inc.)
$18,000

Early 18th century American Queen Anne walnut bonnet top highboy, 39in. wide. (Robert W. Skinner Inc.)
$6,000

18th century mahogany two-section tallboy with brass swan neck handles, 42in. wide. (W. H. Lane & Son) $520

301

CHESTS ON STANDS

19th century William and Mary style black lacquered chest on stand, 38in. wide. (Dee & Atkinson) $1,300

German walnut veneered chest inlaid with ivory and boxwood, 3ft.5in. wide. (Woolley & Wallis) $2,605

George II mahogany chest on stand on cabriole legs, circa 1740, 3ft.0½in. wide. (Sotheby's) $2,070

American Chippendale style mahogany bonnet top highboy, circa 1930, 38½in. wide. (Robert W. Skinner Inc.) $800

George II oak chest on stand with cavetto cornice, 39in. wide. (Lawrence Fine Art) $1,345

Queen Anne walnut, mahogany and cherrywood highboy, circa 1770, 38¾in. wide. (Robert W. Skinner Inc.) $15,000

American Queen Anne maple highboy, circa 1760, 38¼in. wide, with flat molded cornice. (Robert W. Skinner Inc.) $5,250

Late 18th century black lacquer and chinoiserie chest on stand, 3ft.6in. wide. (J. M. Welch & Son) $2,910

Queen Anne tiger maple chest on stand, late 18th century, 38in. wide. (Robert W. Skinner Inc.) $4,100

Late 17th century walnut marquetry chest on stand on five barley-sugar twist legs, 42in. wide.(Edwards, Bigwood & Bewlay) $6,405

Reproduction Jacobean chest of five drawers, on stand with five pear-shaped feet, 39in. wide. (Gilbert Baitson) $455

Mid 18th century George III chest on stand with molded pediment, 44in. wide. (Sotheby's)$1,880

20th century American Chippendale style mahogany tallboy with broken arch top, 39in. wide. (Robert W. Skinner Inc.) $1,650

Queen Anne walnut chest on stand, drawers framed by herringbone bands, 39in. wide. (Christie's) $4,015

18th century New Jersey Queen Anne stained wood chest on stand on cabriole legs, 42in. wide. (Wm. Doyle Galleries Inc.) $10,000

Early Georgian oak chest on stand on later short baluster supports, 40in. wide. (Lawrence Fine Art) $690

Queen Anne cherrywood highboy, American, circa 1730, 36in. wide. (Robert W. Skinner Inc.)$8,000

Late 17th century Portuguese chest on stand with elaborately paneled fronts, 3ft.10½in. wide. (Sotheby's) $3,820

CHIFFONIERS

Victorian black lacquered and japanned chiffonier with plate glass top, 48in. wide. (Dee & Atkinson) $1,955

One of a pair of Regency mahogany chiffoniers with pleated silk panels, 33in. wide. (Boardman's) $1,890

William IV rosewood veneered chiffonier, with mirrored galleried top, circa 1830, 3ft.9½in. wide. (Sotheby's) $2,480

George III Sheraton design chiffonier with shaped gallery and silk-lined glazed panel doors, 31in. wide. (Locke & England) $3,220

Regency ormolu mounted rosewood chiffonier with raised superstructure, 36in. wide. (Christie's) $3,990

Regency ormolu mounted rosewood and parcel gilt chiffonier, 41½in. wide, with three-quarter galleried top.(Christie's) $3,330

19th century chiffonier with carved back, 44in. wide. (W. H. Lane & Son) $420

Dutch mahogany chiffonier inlaid with fan medallions, circa 1790, 3ft.3in. wide.(Sotheby's) $1,275

Unusual mid 19th century Colonial satinwood chiffonier on gadrooned turned feet, 40in. wide. (Sotheby Beresford Adams) $745

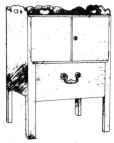

18th century mahogany bedside cupboard with tray top, on square legs, 1ft.11in. wide. (Jackson-Stops & Staff)$185

Georgian mahogany boudoir cabinet with tray top and tambour front, on bracket feet. (Gilbert Baitson) $815

Georgian mahogany tray top commode with shaped apron. (Cooper Hirst) $325

One of a pair of satinwood petite commodes with marble tops, 17½in. wide. (Christie's) $3,590

A George III mahogany tray top commode with sliding drawer. (Phillips) $575

Early 19th century Georgian mahogany pot cupboard, top with three-quarter gallery, 14in. wide. (Sotheby's) $155

Late 19th century Georgian mahogany pot cupboard with serpentine-shaped door, 16in. wide. (Sotheby's)$920

Antique mahogany tray top pot cupboard on square legs. (Farrant & Wightman) $175

Victorian fluted mahogany pot stand with inset marble top.(Phillips) $190

Italian style rosewood, walnut and marquetry inlaid serpentine commode chest, 4ft.8½in. wide. (Geering & Colyer) $2,300

Mid 18th century South German pewter inlaid walnut serpentine commode, 48in. wide. (Christie's) $8,280

One of a pair of late 18th century fruitwood and parquetry commodes, Italian or Austrian, 40½in. wide. (Christie's) $2,945

Louis XV provincial walnut commode with serpentine molded top, 53in. wide. (Christie's) $6,255

Early 19th century provincial Louis XV commode in serpentine case, 36in. wide. (Robert W. Skinner Inc.) $1,350

Louis XV transitional marquetry breakfront commode with molded white marble top, circa 1775, 3ft. wide. (Sotheby, King & Chasemore) $2,230

One of a pair of 'Chippendale' mahogany commodes with serpentine-shaped tops, circa 1900, 28¼in. wide. (Sotheby's Belgravia) $2,390

19th century provincial oak three drawer commode with applied molding, 34in. wide. (Robert W. Skinner Inc.) $625

George III serpentine-fronted mahogany commode chest, on ogee bracket feet, 42in. wide, circa 1780. (Sotheby, King & Chasemore) $5,890

306

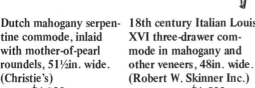

Dutch mahogany serpentine commode, inlaid with mother-of-pearl roundels, 51½in. wide. (Christie's) $4,230

18th century Italian Louis XVI three-drawer commode in mahogany and other veneers, 48in. wide. (Robert W. Skinner Inc.) $1,500

18th century North Italian rosewood commode with molded serpentine top, 48½in. wide. (Christie's) $6,990

Mid 18th century Italian tulipwood and rosewood bombe commode with marble top, 50½in. wide. (Christie's) $5,890

19th century French Louis XVI style bombe commode in mahogany and burl veneers, 38in. wide. (Robert W. Skinner Inc.) $1,250

Mid 18th century Swedish kingwood bombe commode with molded marble top, 41½in. wide. (Christie's) $7,360

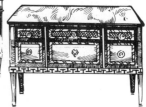

18th century French Louis XV provincial commode in fruitwood, with overhanging serpentine top, 47in. long. (Robert W. Skinner Inc.) $3,000

Late Louis XVI mahogany commode with eared rectangular marble top, 51½in. wide. (Christie's) $2,390

18th century Italian Louis XVI two drawer commode with gray marble top, 46½in. wide. (Robert W. Skinner Inc.) $1,500

COMMODE CHESTS

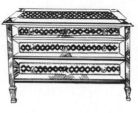

18th century North Italian walnut commode, inlaid with rosewood banding, 48in. wide. (Wm. Doyle Galleries Inc.) $15,000

18th century Swiss parquetry commode with three long drawers, in zig-zag pattern.(Graves, Son & Pilcher) $3,185

Hungarian 'transitional' mahogany parquetry commode with marble top, circa 1930, 45¾in. wide. (Sotheby's Belgravia) $1,050

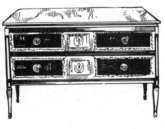

William IV mahogany commode with raised back and carved decoration, 2ft.9in. wide. (Butler & Hatch Waterman) $695

18th century Louis XVI two-drawer marquetry commode in harewood and fruitwood, 41in. long. (Robert W. Skinner Inc.) $1,700

Late18th/early 19th century double serpentine-fronted burr-walnut and crossbanded Continental commode, 36in. wide. (Locke & England) $2,885

Dutch block front walnut commode, 18th century, with cabriole legs, 32in. wide. (Lawrence Fine Art) $955

German serpentine-fronted walnut commode, circa 1750, 3ft.10in. wide. (Sotheby's) $3,025

George III serpentine mahogany commode chest, circa 1775, 3ft. 8½in. wide.(Sotheby's) $5,115

18th century Continental walnut serpentine commode on short cabriole legs. (Graves, Son & Pilcher) $965

Neapolitan parquetry commode in quarter veneered kingwood, with serpentine front, circa 1770, 4ft.6in. wide. (Sotheby's) $3,025

Continental bow-fronted mahogany commode, 18th century, 49½in. wide. (Lawrence Fine Art) $3,130

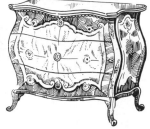

Mid 18th century Dutch walnut commode chest of four drawers, on bracket feet, 2ft.9½in. wide. (Sotheby's) $2,865

Hepplewhite mahogany serpentine-fronted commode with reeded pilaster corners, circa 1790, 3ft.2½in. wide.(Sotheby, King & Chasemore) $2,455

North Italian walnut parquetry commode with serpentine top, circa 1760, 3ft.11½in. wide. (Sotheby's) $11,930

Mid 18th century Louis XV provincial walnut commode with inverted serpentine top, 4ft.2in. wide. (Sotheby's) $3,705

One of a pair of 18th century Italian walnut commodes on bracket feet. (Capes, Dunn & Co.) $5,795

18th century French provincial walnut commode, 4ft.1in. wide, with serpentine front. (Turner, Rudge & Turner) $3,310

309

CORNER CUPBOARDS

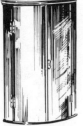

Late 18th century bow-fronted corner cupboard, 2ft. wide. (Dickinson, Davy & Markham) $295

Louis XV kingwood and marquetry encoignure with serpentine marble top, 38in. wide. (Christie's) $1,730

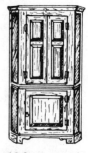

Late 18th century American Chippendale basswood corner cupboard, 45in. wide. (Robert W. Skinner Inc.)$1,400

Good late 18th century Dutch walnut and marquetry encoignure with bowed front, 72cm. wide. (H. Spencer & Sons Ltd.) $670

George III mahogany corner cupboard with molded cornice and canted corners, circa 1770, 4ft. 2½in. wide. (Sotheby's) $1,210

George III mahogany standing corner cabinet in two parts, circa 1760, 3ft.10in. wide.(Sotheby, King & Chasemore) $2,955

Dutch walnut bow-fronted corner cabinet, top inlaid with harewood, 37½in. high. (Lawrence Fine Art) $955

Late 18th century oak standing corner cupboard with plain pediment, 4ft.3in. wide (Dickinson, Davy & Markham)$680

One of a pair of Louis XV black and gold lacquer encoignures with marble tops, 28in. wide. (Christie's) $9,505

310

18th century oak corner cupboard with double paneled doors, with brass key escutcheons, 40in. wide. (Gilbert Baitson) $285

Mahogany corner cabinet by Wright & Mansfield, door crossbanded in tulip-wood, 1880's, 27½in. wide. (Sotheby's Belgravia) $1,510

Mid 18th century George III oak corner cupboard with fluted canted sides, 36in. wide. (Sotheby's) $835

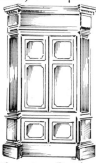

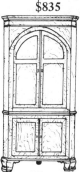

18th century Dutch architectural double corner cupboard with dentil cornice, 55in. wide.(Boardman's) $1,780

Mid 18th century Dutch walnut and marquetry corner cupboard with ogee-fronted base, 3ft.5in. wide. (Sotheby's) $10,830

George III mahogany corner cupboard in well-figured wood, circa 1780, 3ft.10in. wide. (Sotheby's) $1,475

Late 19th century maho-gany and inlaid double corner cupboard on brac-ket feet, 36in. wide. (Lacy Scott)$2,305

George III Chippendale mahogany corner cup-board with scroll-shaped pediment, 43in. wide. (Boardman's) $4,345

Late 18th/early 19th cen-tury George III oak stand-ing corner cupboard with glazed doors, 42in. wide. (Sotheby's) $960   311

COURT CUPBOARDS

Mid 17th century oak buffet with carved frieze and doors, 56in. wide. (Christie's) $2,560

Late 17th century carved oak court cupboard with recessed top cupboard, 5ft.4in. wide. (Russell, Baldwin & Bright) $990

Mid 17th century oak cupboard with recessed upper section, 56in. wide. (Edwards, Bigwood & Bewlay) $3,295

Heavily carved 19th century oak court cupboard, 4ft.9in. wide. (J. M. Welch & Son) $730

17th century oak buffet with carved frieze and doors, 48½in. wide. (Christie's) $4,390

Early 18th century oak court cupboard with pendant finials, 59in. wide. (Sotheby's) $1,800

George II oak tridarn with molded cornice, 4ft.4½in. wide. (Sotheby's) $3,105

Mid 17th century Charles II oak court cupboard, 5ft.5in. wide, probably Westmorland. (Sotheby's) $3,120

Mid 17th century oak court cupboard with fluted frieze, 60in. wide. (Sotheby's) $1,360

Italian Renaissance walnut credenza, heavily carved, basically 16th century, 70in. wide. (Boardman's) $3,700

Victorian burr-walnut and kingwood banded ormolu mounted credenza, 3ft. 10½in. wide, circa 1865. (Sotheby, King & Chasemore) $3,170

Early 17th century Tuscany Provincial walnut credenza with canted ends, 59in. wide. (Robert W. Skinner Inc.) $3,000

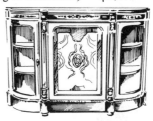

Victorian burr-walnut credenza with marquetry panels in kingwood surround, 65in. wide. (Boardman's) $2,405

Victorian walnut credenza with inlaid satinwood stringing and ormolu beading, 5ft.5in. wide. (Dickinson, Davy & Markham) $2,160

Mid Victorian ebonized and ormolu mounted credenza with burr-walnut frieze, 65in. wide. (Dacre, Son & Hartley) $735

Victorian walnut credenza crossbanded in rosewood, 70in. wide. (Dee & Atkinson) $1,860

Mid Victorian ebonized and ormolu mounted credenza with inlaid frieze, 54in. wide. (Dacre, Son & Hartley) $820

CUPBOARDS

George II oak wall cupboard with shaped panel doors, circa 1730, 2ft. 5¼in. wide. (Sotheby's) $405

Partly 17th century carved oak cupboard in two parts, 48in. wide. (Lawrence Fine Art) $1,805

George I oak press cupboard with paneled dornice and front, circa 1725, 4ft.11in. wide. (Sotheby's) $4,070

Small mid 17th century North Holland oak four door cupboard on pearshaped bun feet, 47in. wide. (Boardman's) $4,625

Unusual Regency mahogany clothes press in the manner of George Smith, 55in. wide. (Christie's) $4,255

19th century Louis XI style chinoiserie decorated lingere, in mahogany with marble top, 38in. wide. (Robert W. Skinner Inc.) $1,800

Georgian oak press cupboard with molded cornice, 57in. wide. (Lawrence Fine Art)$1,565

17th century oak zeeuwschekast, doors inlaid with a marquetry of palisander, 63in. wide. (Boardman's) $4,070

Joined oak press cupboard, circa 1670, 5ft. 5in. wide, on stile feet. (Lawrence Fine Art) $2,485

17th century German walnut schrank with original pewtered lock and keys, 8 lin. wide. (Boardman's) $3,235

Mid 18th century George III oak wall cupboard with two arched fielded paneled doors, 41in. wide. (Sotheby's) $355

Rare West Country painted and carved oak cupboard with molded cornice, circa 1640, 5ft. 3½in. wide. (Sotheby's) $5,350

Chinese Chippendale mahogany linen press with dentil cornice, on ogee feet, 3ft. 8in. wide. (Gilbert Baitson) $630

Early 18th century South German serpentine walnut kommodenschrank with domed top, 55in. wide. (Boardman's) $3,795

19th century Anglo-Indian padoukwood cupboard with gadroon paneled doors, 46in. wide. (Sotheby Beresford Adams) $705

Large 19th century Continental oak hall cupboard with wrought iron hinges and handles. (Butler & Hatch Waterman) $925

18th century oak breakfront linen press with brass handles and escutcheons. (J. M. Welch & Son) $1,600

Early 18th century Namuroise oak armoire with breakfront pediment, 6ft. 3in. wide. (Boardman's) $2,960

17th century press with overhanging molded cornice, on block feet, 60in. wide. (Christie's) $1,370

Mid 17th century oak hanging cupboard with arcaded upper section, 33¾in. wide. (Christie's) $1,280

Early 18th century oak hanging cupboard with triangular pediment, 50in. wide. (Christie's) $560

Mid 17th century oak press with overhanging cornice carved with lozenges and rosettes, 55½in. wide. (Christie's) $2,470

Fine North German oak cupboard, doors applied with octagonal molded panels, 65½in. wide. (Christie's) $3,795

17th century oak food cupboard with molded cornice, 49in. wide. (Christie's) $1,190

South German or Swiss walnut and fruitwood veneered cupboard with serpentine cornice, 1760, 3ft.9in. wide.(Sotheby's) $3,740

Early 17th century Tuscan walnut cupboard with molded projecting top, 4ft.6in. wide. (Sotheby's) $3,645

Swiss pewter-inlaid walnut standing cupboard, circa 1700, 1ft.9½in. wide. (Sotheby's) $1,180

316

Victorian inlaid walnut Davenport with carved 'dolphin' supports, 23in. wide. (Burtenshaw Walker) $1,255

Rococo revival rosewood Davenport desk with pierced brass gallery, 22½in. wide. (Robert W. Skinner Inc.) $500

Late Regency rosewood Davenport with galleried top, 19in. wide. (Christie's)$2,260

Unusual walnut Davenport in well-figured and burr-wood, circa 1870, 22½in. wide.(Sotheby's Belgravia) $1,335

Early 19th century George III mahogany Davenport with three-quarter gilt metal gallery, 20in. wide. (Sotheby's) $4,785

Victorian walnut Davenport with shaped front and finely molded supports. (M. Philip H. Scott) $2,430

Burr-walnut Harlequin Davenport, superstructure with pierced gallery, circa 1860, 23in. wide. (Sotheby's Belgravia) $1,750

American Victorian bird's-eye maple veneer bamboo Davenport desk, circa 1870, 32in. wide. (Robert W. Skinner Inc.) $1,800

Victorian walnut piano top Davenport with wood gallery, 22in. wide. (Woolley & Wallis) $1,520

DAVENPORTS

Walnut Davenport, circa 1860's, 22¼in. wide, on molded cabriole legs. (Sotheby's Belgravia) $945

William IV mahogany Davenport with galleried top, circa 1830, 1ft.9in. wide. (Sotheby's) $2,035

Early Victorian burr-walnut Davenport with boxwood stringing, 1ft.10in. wide. (Capes, Dunn & Co.) $1,160

Victorian inlaid walnut Davenport. (Honiton Galleries) $880

Victorian walnut Davenport with pierced fret gallery, 2ft. 3in. wide, circa 1855. (Sotheby, King & Chasemore) $1,385

Burr-walnut Harlequin Davenport with sprung superstructure, circa 1870, 22in. wide. (Sotheby's Belgravia) $1,485

Mid 19th century walnut Davenport with gallery, 22in. wide. (Locke & England) $800

Unusual japanned Davenport with waisted top and pierced gallery, circa 1900, 27in. wide. (Sotheby's Belgravia) $1,280

Victorian Davenport in inlaid burr-walnut, in good condition. (Way, Ridet & Co.) $980

Burr-maple and ebonized wood Davenport with leather surface, circa 1870, 22¾in. wide. (Sotheby's Belgravia) $595

Mid 19th century Anglo-Indian walnut Davenport with irregular black graining, 49½in. wide. (Sotheby's Belgravia) $925

Walnut Davenport with hinged stationery compartment, circa 1870, 21in. wide. (Sotheby's Belgravia) $1,195

Mid 19th century mahogany pedestal desk with inset writing surface, 62in. wide, restored. (Sotheby's Belgravia) $1,295

English Renaissance revival bird's-eye maple veneer and inlaid Davenport desk, circa 1870, 22in. wide. (Robert W. Skinner Inc.) $750

19th century walnut Davenport desk with raised superstructure. (J. M. Welch & Son)$490

Mahogany Davenport, superstructure with hinged lid, 1880's, 22½in. wide. (Sotheby's Belgravia) $460

19th century walnut Davenport desk on turned legs. (J. M. Welch & Son)$435

Walnut Harlequin Davenport with secret rising section, in very good condition. (Allen & May) $1,700

DISPLAY CABINETS

Double-domed walnut display cabinet, 19th century, 45in. wide. (Lawrence Fine Art) $2,390

Dutch walnut display cabinet, circa 1760, with molded serpentine cornice, 5ft.6½in. wide. (Sotheby's) $3,290

Mahogany and marquetry small display cabinet, circa 1900, 26in. wide. (Sotheby's Belgravia) $740

Late 19th century Chippendale style display cabinet on stand. (J. M. Welch & Son)$475

Mid 18th century Portuguese rosewood display cabinet on stand, 39½in. wide.(Christie's) $1,590

One of a pair of late 19th century French vitrines with pierced brass galleries and ormolu mounts, 2ft.2in. wide.(Sotheby, King & Chasemore) $5,395

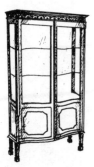

Display cabinet of Hepplewhite design in mahogany frame, 39in. wide. (W. H. Lane & Son) $770

Giltwood Vernis Martin display cabinet in Louis XV style, circa 1900, 44in. wide. (Sotheby's Belgravia) $2,230

Edwardian 'Sheraton' display cabinet framed in mahogany with satinwood inlay, 36in. wide. (W. H. Lane & Son) $735

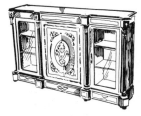

Mid 19th century walnut and marquetry display cabinet with gilt metal mounts, 75in. wide. (Sotheby Beresford Adams) $1,860

Early 19th century Dutch mahogany and boxwood inlaid display cabinet, 73in. wide. (Boardman's) $1,985

Late 19th century mahogany and giltwood bronze display cabinet in the manner of Francois Linke, 50in. wide. (Sotheby Beresford Adams) $1,395

'William and Mary' burr-walnut display cabinet with double-domed top, circa 1900, 53in. wide. (Sotheby's Belgravia) $1,700

20th century Louis XV style French vitrine in harewood and other veneers, 49in. wide. (Robert W. Skinner Inc.) $1,500

Art Nouveau mahogany breakfront display cabinet on tapering octagonal legs, 169cm. wide. (Christie's) $2,055

Mahogany display cabinet with glazed astragal doors and running frieze, 3ft.9in. wide. (Brogden & Co.) $665

Dutch oak and marquetry display cabinet with molded cornice, 85½in. wide. (Christie's) $8,830

Art Nouveau mahogany display cabinet inlaid with mother-of-pearl, 135cm. wide. (Christie's) $2,880

Burr-walnut display cabinet with domed top above a glazed door, 19in. wide. (Hy. Duke & Son)
$480

Satinwood display cabinet, superstructure with a pierced gallery, circa 1890, 58in. wide. (Sotheby's Belgravia)
$1,195

Two-tier glazed display cabinet, on cabriole legs. (Honiton Galleries)
$205

Mid 19th century satinwood display cabinet with molded cornice, crossbanded with rosewood, 38in. wide. (Sotheby's Belgravia)
$1,190

18th century Dutch marquetry vitrine, cornice rising to carved center, 35in. wide. (Boardman's) $4,440

Mid 20th century 'Charles II' giltwood rectangular cabinet on stand with glazed top, 43in. wide. (Sotheby's Belgravia)
$1,655

Dutch walnut display cabinet with scrolled pediment and bombe base, 84in. wide. (Christie's)
$11,040

Mahogany and marquetry Art Nouveau display cabinet with bow-fronted glazed doors, circa 1900, 55in. wide. (Sotheby's Belgravia) $645

Mahogany display cabinet with arched top frieze and open mirror back, 58½in. high. (Locke & England)
$1,200

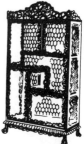

19th century French kingwood small display cabinet with colored marble top, 2ft.2½in. wide. (Dickinson, Davy & Markham) $2,850

Early 20th century Edwardian mahogany and marquetry display cabinet with gilt metal gallery, 49in. wide. (Sotheby Beresford Adams) $930

Carved and stained hardwood display cabinet with open shelves. (Phillips) $810

Small French display cabinet, 1920's, 110cm. high. (Sotheby's Belgravia) $680

Early 20th century satinwood display cabinet with bow-front, 46in. wide. (Sotheby Beresford Adams) $930

19th century French vitrine in Louis XV style, with serpentine-front and bow sides. (John Milne) $1,840

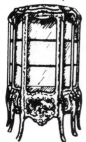

19th century French kingwood vitrine with serpentine-fronted glass door, 3ft.9in. wide. (Edwards, Bigwood & Bewlay) $5,305

Large 18th century Dutch walnut and marquetry vitrine with dome-shaped top, 80in. wide. (Boardman's) $8,510

Mahogany display cabinet with gilt bronze moldings, circa 1880-1900, 46½in. wide. (Sotheby's Belgravia) $885

18th century Welsh oak dresser with baluster turned front supports, 5ft. 6in. wide, with potboard below. (Russell, Baldwin & Bright) $3,060

18th century Normandy dresser with canted corners and carved moldings. (Locke & England) $1,430

18th century oak Shropshire dresser with brass swan neck handles and pierced carved canopy. (Burtenshaw Walker) $1,550

Queen Anne oak tridarn, dated 1722, 4ft. 6in. wide. (Sotheby, King & Chasemore) $1,940

18th century oak dresser with brass handles and lockplates. (Sotheby, King & Chasemore) $1,455

Early 19th century oak dresser with ogee pediment, 80in. wide.(Sotheby's)$2,715

Georgian oak high dresser with divided open shelves and shaped apron, 82in. wide. (Lawrence Fine Art) $3,650

17th/18th century oak dresser base with three Gothic paneled doors and iron hinges, 51in. wide. (Andrew Grant)$3,625

Late 18th century American pine cupboard with flat cornice, 48in. wide. (Robert W. Skinner Inc.) $1,400

George III three drawer oak dresser with shaped apron, 6ft.11in. wide. (Wyatt & Sons with Whitehead's) $1,820

Oak Shropshire dresser on cabriole legs, 63in. wide. (Hall Wateridge & Owen) $1,940

Partly 18th century oak dresser with wavy pediment and apron, 88in. wide. (Sotheby's) $1,045

Antique oak dresser base, three deep drawers fitted with brass swan neck handles, on four turned legs with shaped frieze. (Butler & Hatch Waterman) $230

Early 20th century James I style oak dresser base, 72in. wide. (Sotheby's) $795

19th century oak dresser with cyma recta pediment and bracket feet, 74in. wide. (Sotheby's) $1,360

Charles II oak and elm dresser, circa 1680, 5ft. wide, restored. (Sotheby, King & Chasemore) $1,730

George I oak dresser on stem feet, 5ft.6in. wide, circa 1725. (Sotheby, King & Chasemore) $1,445

18th century oak Welsh dresser with plain pediment, triple delft rack and paneled back, 5ft. 8in. wide. (Dickinson, Davy & Markham) $2,575

DRESSERS & BUFFETS

Georgian oak high dresser with brass handles, 68in. wide. (Lawrence Fine Art) $1,510

Charles II oak dresser with brass pear-drop handles, molded understretchers, 75in. wide. (Dacre, Son & Hartley)$1,820

Georgian oak high dresser with shaped frieze, 55in. wide. (Lawrence Fine Art) $2,575

George II oak dresser with ogee top, circa 1740, 4ft.8½in. wide, later cornice. (Sotheby's) $8,315

18th century open back oak dresser with scaloped frieze and lower pot shelf, 70in. wide. (W. H. Lane & Son) $1,090

Late Elizabethan oak buffet, circa 1600, 4ft.10½in. wide. (Sotheby's) $5,820

Oak dresser with raised solid back with molded top, 5ft. wide. (Coles, Knapp & Kennedy) $535

George II oak and pollard elm dresser with shaped apron, circa 1740, 7ft.8in. wide. (Sotheby, King & Chasemore) $4,650

Early oak dresser with plain canopy and wrought iron hinges, 5ft.1in. wide. (Butler & Hatch Waterman) $1,965

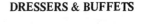

19th century French provincial oak dresser base, 56in. wide, on cabriole legs. (Lawrence Fine Art) $1,140

Late Georgian oak dresser with brass handles and escutcheons. (Biddle & Webb) $1,395

George II oak and elm dresser with three-quarter gallery, circa 1740, 5ft.9½in. wide. (Sotheby's) $1,730

18th century oak dresser on square legs united by pot board, original iron hooks, 61in. wide. (Locke & England) $1,185

Georgian oak joined dresser with inlaid frieze, 63in. wide. (Lawrence Fine Art) $2,025

Early 19th century Welsh dresser on cabriole legs. (V. & V's.) $1,730

Late 18th century Georgian oak joined dresser with brass knob handles, 60in. high. (Lawrence Fine Art) $1,195

Late 17th/early 18th century oak dresser base on turned supports and feet, 79in. long. (Sotheby's) $1,880

Oak dresser with later rack and molded cornice above an ogee-cut frieze, 6ft.2½in. wide. (Sotheby's) $1,670

Regency mahogany two-tier dumb waiter with graduated shelves, 25in. diam. (Christie's)
$1,110

One of a pair of George III mahogany dumb waiters on tripod bases, circa 1800, 1ft.11in. diam. (Sotheby's)
$1,585

Regency mahogany two-tier dumb waiter on molded tripod base, 25½in. diam. (Christie's)
$910

Unusual William IV mahogany concertina whatnot on reeded column, circa 1835, 20¾in. wide. (Sotheby's Belgravia)
$515

George III mahogany three-tier circular dumb waiter with ebony stringing, circa 1800, 30in. diam. (Edwards, Bigwood & Bewlay) $1,060

Satinwood three-tier tea table with leaf-cast bronze handle, circa 1920. (Sotheby's Belgravia)
$330

Modern George III style mahogany dumb waiter with two foliate molded tiers, 24in. diam. (Sotheby's) $405

328

Satinwood dumb waiter with circular top and four further trays, circa 1900, 22in. diam. (Sotheby's Belgravia)
$905

Hepplewhite period mahogany three-tier dumb waiter on three cabriole legs, 24in. high. (Woolley & Wallis)
$4,900

George II red walnut lowboy, circa 1750, 2ft.4in. wide. (Sotheby, King & Chasemore) $1,825

Queen Anne oak lowboy with molded edged top, shaped apron and square cabriole legs, 36in. wide. (Dacre, Son & Hartley) $490

Georgian oak lowboy, top with molded edge, 30in. wide. (Lawrence Fine Art) $1,290

One of two similar late George II mahogany lowboys, circa 1755, 2ft. 10in. wide. (Sotheby's) $1,570

Mid 18th century oak lowboy with brass handles. (Lacy Scott) $1,405

William and Mary lowboy in mahogany and mahogany veneer, 30½in. wide. (Robert W. Skinner Inc.) $850

George II oak lowboy, crossbanded borders and inlaid stringing, pierced brass loop handles, circa 1730, 31½in. wide. (Neales) $1,860

George I mahogany lowboy with brass butterfly plates and swan-neck handles, 83.5cm. wide. (Jackson-Stops & Staff)$915

Queen Anne cherrywood dressing table with central fan carved drawer, 30in. wide, circa 1760. (Robert W. Skinner Inc.) $14,000

329

PEDESTAL & KNEEHOLE DESKS

Mid 19th century mahogany pedestal desk with inset writing surface, 62in. wide, restored. (Sotheby's Belgravia) $1,295

Victorian solid mahogany roll-top desk on bracket feet. (Parkinson, Son & Hamer) $1,455

18th century walnut kneehole desk with crossbanded and featherbanded top, 31in. wide. (Hy. Duke & Son) $2,590

Mid 19th century mahogany pedestal desk with leather-lined top, 60in. wide. (Sotheby's Belgravia) $1,010

Mid 20th century mahogany pedestal desk with rope-carved molded edge, 60in. wide. (Sotheby's Belgravia) $700

George III mahogany kneehole writing table on bracket feet, circa 1770, 3ft. 7in. wide. (Sotheby's) $835

Mahogany chest of drawers with molded top, circa 1770, 3ft.3½in. wide. (Sotheby's) $3,145

George III mahogany double-sided writing table with crossbanded top, circa 1790, 4ft.7in. wide. (Sotheby's) $2,480

Desk by Howard & Sons on four bamboo legs with brass castors, mid 19th century, 49½in. wide. (Sotheby's Belgravia) $700

George III mahogany partner's desk with nine drawers, 56½in. wide. (Christie's) $4,440

Victorian mahogany cylinder front desk with maplewood drawers, 5ft. wide. (Capes, Dunn & Co.) $1,045

Queen Anne walnut kneehole desk with crossbanded top, 31in. wide. (Christie's) $2,245

Mahogany secretaire desk with leather-lined interior, circa 1850. (Sotheby's Belgravia) $1,045

George III mahogany kneehole pedestal writing table with leather top, circa 1770, 3ft.8in. wide. (Sotheby's) $4,135

Mid 19th century mahogany pedestal desk stamped T. Willson, London, 54in. wide. (Sotheby Beresford Adams) $1,080

George III satinwood kneehole desk with oval inlaid top, 32in. wide. (Christie's) $2,150

Pedestal kneehole desk in mahogany, with leather top, circa 1880, 72in. wide. (Sotheby's Belgravia) $1,955

George III mahogany kneehole writing desk, 3ft.3in. wide. (Sotheby's) $2,250

20th century mahogany pedestal desk with green leather top, 60in. wide. (Sotheby's Belgravia) $825

Victorian satinwood bow-fronted desk, cupboards with panels of maidens, 44in. wide. (Morphets) $1,755

19th century walnut Wootton Patent Office desk with galleried top, 58in. wide. (Dacre, Son & Hartley) $6,370

19th century Georgian mahogany desk of kneehole shape, with oak linings, 38½in. wide. (Lawrence Fine Art) $995

Late 18th century mahogany twin pedestal kneehole desk, 37½in. wide. (W. H. Lane & Son) $625

Chippendale style partner's desk with red leather top, inset with fan corners. (Coles, Knapp & Kennedy) $1,255

George II mahogany kneehole writing desk, top with canted corners, circa 1750, 3ft. 1½in. wide.(Sotheby's) $5,115

Mid 19th century oak Jacobean revival pedestal desk, 84in. wide. (Sotheby's Belgravia) $3,395

Walnut and marquetry pedestal desk, 48in. wide. (J. M. Welch & Son) $1,345

Mid 19th century oak partner's desk with red tooled leather top, 68in. wide. (Sotheby's) $1,255

George III mahogany library writing table of kneehole form, 46in. wide. (Wm. Doyle Galleries Inc.) $4,400

George III mahogany kneehole writing and toilet chest, circa 1775, 3ft.1in. wide. (Sotheby's) $1,385

Dutch or German inlaid mahogany writing desk, circa 1790, 4ft.4in. wide. (Sotheby's) $1,195

Victorian mahogany roll-top pedestal desk with writing slope. (J. M. Welch & Son) $910

Mid 18th century mahogany kneehole writing desk with center cupboard, 32in. wide. (Lacy Scott) $2,590

William IV rosewood partner's desk, top inset with red American cloth. (Woolley & Wallis) $4,115

333

SCREENS

18th century Dutch black and gold lacquer six-leaf screen decorated in raised gilt, 95½in. high. (Christie's) $7,565

Large Chinese screen inlaid in ivory and hardstones, circa 1900, 130cm. wide. (Sotheby's Belgravia) $3,850

Guangxu four-fold embroidered screen with carved frame, 70cm. high. (Sotheby's Belgravia) $5,435

Shibayama two-fold table screen, each leaf divided into two panels, 10½in. high.(Phillips)$865

19th century Chinese six-panel Oriental screen, 67½in. high. (Robert W. Skinner Inc.) $7,750

Late 18th/early 19th century Chinese Export black and gold lacquer eight-leaf screen, 95in. high. (Christie's) $5,455

Two mid 19th century Burmese carved wood panels from a screen, each 23½in. wide. (Sotheby's)$790

17th century four-leaf screen formed from an oil painting in the style of P. Snayers, 72in. high. (Christie's) $3,955

SCREENS

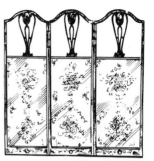

Three-fold lacquer screen by M. Lattry, Paris, circa 1930, 165.5cm. high. (Sotheby's Belgravia) $1,000

Walnut firescreen, central panel showing a mother and three children, circa 1860, 33in. wide. (Sotheby's Belgravia) $650

Satinwood three-fold screen, each fold with arched glazed top, circa 1900, 69in. high. (Sotheby's Belgravia) $700

19th century six-fold Chinese screen showing a junk. (Robert W. Skinner Inc.) $7,750

'Moorish' four-fold polychrome and parcel gilt screen in walnut, 1890's, 73¾in. high.(Sotheby's Belgravia) $2,560

Very rare three-fold Regency screen of nine japanned panels on copper, circa 1810, 81in. wide. (Sotheby, King & Chasemore) $19,215

Early 20th century painted three-fold screen in mahogany frames, 71in. high. (Sotheby's Belgravia) $205

Early 19th century Chinese Export lacquer eight-leaf screen decorated in black and gold, 85in. high. (Christie's)$8,480

335

Georgian mahogany secretaire chest, 45in. wide. (J. M. Welch & Son)$675

Unusual Georgian mahogany secretaire with pierced brass gallery, 3ft.8in. wide. (Lawrence Fine Art) $1,195

Mahogany secretaire chest of three drawers with brass drop handles. (John Hogbin & Son) $1,890

Georgian walnut secretaire a abattant with pear drop handles, 41in. wide. (Lawrence Fine Art) $955

Continental mahogany escritoire with pierced gallery back, on turned and reeded trestle ends and stretcher. (Locke & England)$965

Mahogany secretaire a abattant with raised superstructure. 1840's, 42in. wide. (Sotheby's Belgravia) $595

Queen Anne secretaire a abattant, outlined with herringbone banding. (Neales) $7,135

William and Mary walnut secretaire cabinet on later bun feet, circa 1700, 3ft. 5in. wide. (Sotheby's) $3,930

Late Georgian mahogany secretaire with turned wood handles, 30in. wide. (Lawrence Fine Art) $810

Mahogany secretaire
Wellington chest, circa
1880, 28in. wide.
(Sotheby's Belgravia)
$1,540

Late Georgian mahogany
secretaire chest of drawers
with brass handles. (J. M.
Welch & Son)$1,600

Gustav Stickley oak fall
front desk with pine
compartments, New
York, circa 1905, 31¾in.
wide. (Robert W. Skinner
Inc.) $550

Mid/late 19th century
French walnut and mar-
quetry inlaid secretaire a
abattant. (Lacy Scott)
$3,935

Late 19th century American
Victorian walnut butler's
desk, 40in. wide. (Robert W.
Skinner Inc.) $1,000

Regency black and
gold lacquer secre-
taire, fitted with
Bramah lock, 33½in.
wide. (Christie's)
$1,030

Dutch satinwood secre-
taire a abattant with
crossbanded mahogany
top, 35in. wide.
(Christie's)$2,025

George I period burr-elm
and crossbanded secre-
taire tallboy chest, 3ft.
6¼in. wide. (Geering &
Colyer) $2,335

Fine Sino-Dutch Lac Bur-
gaute secretaire a abattant,
circa 1820, 3ft.2in. wide.
(Sotheby's)$3,705

337

SECRETAIRES & ESCRITOIRES

Early George III mahogany secretaire cabinet with waved three-quarter gallery, 34½in. wide. (Christie's) $1,530

19th century Dutch marquetry secretaire on block feet, 42in. high. (Olivers)$1,890

Late Louis XVI mahogany, rosewood and boulle secretaire with galleried top, 20in. wide. (Christie's) $3,170

George I walnut secretaire on chest with molded cornice and convex frieze drawer, 42½in. wide. (Christie's) $2,700

German mahogany secretaire a abattant, circa 1760, 38½in. wide, by Abraham Roentgen. (Christie's) $18,240

Louis XVI mahogany and brass inlaid secretaire with galleried top, 31in. wide. (Christie's) $6,335

Italian marquetry secretaire a abattant, inlaid on rosewood ground, circa 1835, 37½in. wide. (Sotheby's Belgravia) $4,935

Regency camphorwood military secretaire chest on turned knob feet, 36in. wide. (Burtenshaw Walker) $1,385

Mahogany secretaire tallboy with brass handles and side carrying handles, circa 1800. (J. M. Welch & Son) $2,365

George III mahogany
secretaire bookcase,
circa 1790, 4ft. wide.
(Phillips)
$2,685

Late George III mahogany
secretaire bookcase, circa
1820, 4ft.1½in. wide.
(Sotheby's)$2,935

Mid Georgian mahogany
secretaire cabinet with
dentilled cornice, 50in.
wide. (Christie's)
$2,390

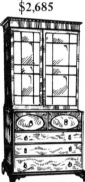

Late Georgian maho-
gany secretaire book-
case with reeded astra-
gal glazed doors, 45½in.
wide. (Lawrence Fine
Art) $2,865

Large Victorian mahogany
bookcase-secretaire with
three glazed doors, circa
1860, 61in. wide. (Neales)
$2,805

George III secretaire
bookcase in mahogany
and satinwood, circa
1770, later cresting,
3ft.3½in. wide.(Sothe-
by's) $7,245

Regency mahogany and
calamanderwood secre-
taire cabinet with narrow
cornice, 31¼in. wide.
(Christie's)$6,460

Antique secretaire book-
case with adjustable
bookshelves, 3ft.5in.
wide. (Brogden & Co.)
$4,440

George III mahogany
secretaire bookcase,
circa 1770, 3ft.1in.
wide. (Sotheby's)
$4,540

SECRETAIRE BOOKCASES

Mahogany tallboy with secretaire, brass fittings, 3ft.6in. wide. (Gilbert Baitson) $1,135

George III mahogany secretaire tallboy, circa 1780, 50in. wide. (Sotheby, King & Chasemore)$4,050

Mid 19th century mahogany secretaire bookcase with two arched glazed doors, 58in. wide. (Sotheby Beresford Adams) $1,490

George III mahogany secretaire bookcase, circa 1790, 3ft.7½in. wide. (Sotheby's) $2,325

Tall 19th century secretaire bookcase with glazed astragal doors, 3ft.9in. wide. (Dickinson, Davy & Markham) $1,105

Late Regency mahogany secretaire cabinet with molded ribbed cornice, 50in. wide. (Christie's) $2,960

George III mahogany secretaire cabinet, circa 1785, 3ft.8½in. wide. (Sotheby's) $3,720

Pollard oak secretaire bookcase, heavily carved, 3ft.9in. wide. (Gilbert Baitson) $1,560

Regency mahogany secretaire bookcase, circa 1810, 3ft.5¼in. wide. (Sotheby, King & Chasemore) $1,090

Late 18th century mahogany secretaire bookcase with swan-neck cresting, 4ft. wide. (Sotheby's) $1,455

Wellington secretaire chest of drawers with fitted interior. (Butler & Hatch Waterman) $825

George III secretaire cabinet, circa 1800, 3ft.7in. wide, with dentil cornice. (Sotheby's)$2,035

Mahogany secretaire bookcase with double glazed doors, 35½in. wide, 1840's. (Sotheby's Belgravia) $1,620

Sheraton style mahogany secretaire bookcase with satinwood crossbanding. (Phillips)$8,370

Late 18th/early 19th century mahogany secretaire bookcase with satinwood veneered frieze, 44½in. wide. (Sotheby Beresford Adams) $1,860

Gothic mahogany secretaire bookcase with glazed doors, 19th century, 50in. wide. (Lawrence Fine Art) $1,010

Georgian style mahogany secretaire bookcase with astragal doors, 37½in. wide. (Lawrence Fine Art) $1,140

William IV mahogany secretaire bookcase, circa 1830, 55in. wide, plinth remade.(Sotheby's Belgravia) $2,160

SETTEES & COUCHES

Superb mid 19th century American settee by John H. Belter of New York, in laminated rosewood frame. (Edwards, Bigwood & Bewlay) $38,430

18th century curved oak settle with panel seat and high paneled back, 6ft.1in. wide. (Edwards, Bigwood & Bewlay) $935

One of a pair of matching rosewood chaise longues, circa 1840, 84in. long. (Sotheby's Belgravia) $1,980

Small late Victorian mahogany two-seat settee, on cabriole legs, 4ft.6in. wide. (Dickinson, Davy & Markham) $515

Walnut sofa with padded back, upholstered in 18th century gros and petit point needlework, 52in. wide.(Christie's) $2,775

19th century German Provincial carved oak settle with hinged seat, 70in. wide. (Robert W. Skinner Inc.) $450

Fine 17th century oak four panel settle on baluster turned supports, 6ft. wide. (Andrew Grant) $1,115

Walnut settee with button back, circa 1860, 87in. wide. (Sotheby's Belgravia) $560

Mid 19th century American rococo revival walnut sofa with carved arm supports and apron. (Robert W. Skinner Inc.) $600

18th century Portuguese jacarandawood settee with triple chair back, 69in. wide. (Christie's) $4,970

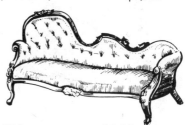

18th century French Provincial Louis XVI canape on square molded frame, 50½in. wide. (Robert W. Skinner Inc.) $800

Walnut settee on molded frame carved with flowers, 1860's, 73in. long. (Sotheby's Belgravia) $1,225

19th century Japanese carved teak settle, 65in. long. (Robert W. Skinner Inc.) $850

One of a pair of early 19th century Regency hall benches in the manner of Thos. Tatham, 54in. long. (Sotheby Beresford Adams) $1,710

One of a pair of late 19th century American rococo revival rosewood reclamiers, 51in. long. (Robert W. Skinner Inc.) $1,150

Late 19th century American Renaissance revival finger carved walnut sofa, 68in. long. (Robert W. Skinner Inc.) $300

SETTEES & COUCHES

'George III' painted small settee with arched padded back, circa 1890, 44in. wide. (Sotheby's Belgravia)$445

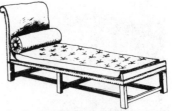

Early George III mahogany day bed, 6ft.11in. long, circa 1765. (Sotheby's) $3,070

Mid 20th century 'Louis XV' parcel gilt and caned settee from a suite, 46in. wide. (Sotheby's Belgravia) $410

'George II' mahogany settee with triple chair back, circa 1880, 59in. wide. (Sotheby's Belgravia) $1,655

19th century George III style 'satyr and mask' settee, in mahogany, 51in. long. (Robert W. Skinner Inc.)$3,600

Settee from a mahogany inlaid Edwardian seven-piece drawingroom suite, with carved backs and brocade seats. (Outhwaite & Litherland)$1,800

19th century French Louis XVI style tapestry covered canape, 67in. long. (Robert W. Skinner Inc.) $600

Mid 18th century George III elm settle with paneled concave back, 68in. wide. (Sotheby's) $1,880

19th century Chinese carved rosewood settee with triple paneled back, 76in. long. (Robert W. Skinner Inc.) $800

Fine Victorian sofa with serpentine front in walnut frame. (Butler & Hatch Waterman) $2,745

Victorian rosewood framed small couch with single scroll end, 154cm. long. (H. Spencer & Sons Ltd.) $700

George II walnut and parcel gilt day bed with scrolled arm supports, 76in. long. (Christie's) $1,605

Rare Queen Anne walnut double chair settee. (Bonham's) $14,510

Rosewood conversation settee with three padded chair backs, 54in. wide, 1880's. (Sotheby's Belgravia)$730

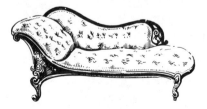

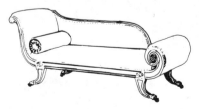

Victorian walnut framed chaise longue, on short cabriole legs. (J. M. Welch & Son) $675

Early 19th century Regency painted day bed with scroll end, 8ft. long. (Sotheby's) $1,415

SETTEES & COUCHES

Silk upholstered and beechwood chaise longue by Betty Joel, of gondola form, circa 1930, 194cm. long. (Christie's) $1,185

American Renaissance revival walnut and burl walnut settee, circa 1870, 61in. wide. (Robert W. Skinner Inc.) $325

Victorian walnut small settee with pierced and carved frame, 50in. wide. (Lawrence Fine Art) $1,255

One of a pair of George III blue painted and gilded hall seats, 55in. wide. (Christie's) $3,845

Early 20th century rosewood and fruitwood settle with rush matted seat, 98cm. wide. (Sotheby's Belgravia) $1,740

Walnut center seat of three addorsed chairs, 44in. wide, approx., 1870's. (Sotheby's Belgravia) $680

Regency simulated rosewood and white painted day bed, 85in. wide. (Christie's) $985

Mid 19th century cast-iron and brass campaign bed with hinged back. (Sotheby's Belgravia) $410

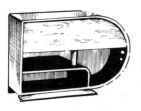

One of a pair of D-shaped mahogany shelf-sofa ends, 1930's, 69cm. high. (Sotheby's Belgravia) $300

Regency ebonized and parcel gilt set of shelves, circa 1815, 4ft.4in. wide. (Sotheby's) $2,585

Early 19th century mahogany cartonnier with carrying handles, 41cm. wide. (H. Spencer & Sons Ltd.) $605

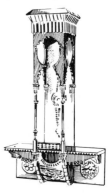

One of a pair of Regency bookcases with two shelves, two cupboard doors and a drawer each. (Capes, Dunn & Co.) $9,350

Rococo revival walnut etagere, American, circa 1865, with pierced, carved crest, 45½in. wide. (Robert W. Skinner Inc.) $1,500

Ebonized and mahogany hanging shelf by Carlo Bugatti, 101cm. high. (Christie's) $730

William IV small rosewood bookcase with three shelves, molded supports applied with gilt rosettes, circa 1835, 36in. wide. (Sotheby's Belgravia) $505

Early George III pine chimneypiece with later carved shelf, 66in. wide. (Christie's) $6,765

Late 19th century mahogany book trough. (J. M. Welch & Son) $200

347

SIDEBOARDS

Georgian mahogany breakfront sideboard, 68in. wide, with satinwood crossbanding. (Lawrence Fine Art) $1,565

George III semi-lunar sideboard inlaid with harewood, 89in. wide. (Lawrence Fine Art) $2,390

Late 18th century George III demi-lune sideboard in mahogany, 71in. long. (Robert W. Skinner Inc.) $1,650

'George III' ebonized bow-front sideboard with a superstructure, 58in. wide, applied with Sevres panels. (Sotheby's Belgravia) $625

Sheraton sideboard in figured mahogany with shell inlay, 5ft. wide, top with brass rail and curtain. (Gilbert Baitson) $2,835

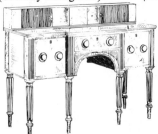

Late George IV mahogany breakfront sideboard with tambour-fronted superstructure, circa 1825, 4ft.11½in. wide. (Sotheby's) $890

Late 18th century Sheraton design mahogany and boxwood inlaid breakfront sideboard, 66in. wide. (Locke & England) $1,835

George III serpentine-fronted mahogany sideboard on square tapering legs, 78in. wide, circa 1790. (Sotheby, King & Chasemore) $1,470

Pollard oak sideboard with carved panels on cupboards and drawers, 6ft. wide. (Gilbert Baitson) $815

George III Sheraton mahogany sideboard with ebony inlay, 84in. wide. (Boardman's) $2,930

Regency mahogany bow-fronted sideboard with inlaid blackwood stringing, 6ft.4½in. wide. (Jackson-Stops & Staff) $1,380

George III apsidal sideboard in 'plum-pudding' mahogany, circa 1780, 5ft.4in. wide. (Sotheby's) $5,320

George III mahogany serpentine-fronted sideboard, top set with an oval, circa 1790, 6ft.1in. wide. (Sotheby's) $6,290

Mid 19th century William IV mahogany sideboard with arched and carved back panel, 96in. wide. (Sotheby Beresford Adams) $445

Late 18th/early 19th century George III bow-front mahogany sideboard, 72in. wide. (Robert W. Skinner Inc.) $1,500

American Federal style mahogany inlaid sideboard with bowed front, circa 1920, 45½in. wide. (Robert W. Skinner Inc.) $950

Italian 1950's upright mahogany sideboard, with vellum-covered upper cabinet, 139.5cm. high. (Sotheby's Belgravia) $320

George III mahogany and kingwood crossbanded sideboard of Sheraton design, 5ft.10in. wide, circa 1800. (Sotheby, King & Chasemore) $1,315

Unusual small George III serpentine mahogany sideboard, circa 1790, 2ft.11½in. wide. (Sotheby's) $1,950

American Louis XV influence rosewood and rosewood veneer sideboard, circa 1930, 50in. wide. (Robert W. Skinner Inc.) $800

Gustav Stickley oak sideboard with rectangular top and ledge back, 178cm. wide.(Christie's) $1,820

One of a pair of American custom oak sideboards with galleried cornice top, circa 1920, 43½in. wide. (Robert W. Skinner Inc.) $1,350

George III mahogany breakfront sideboard with brass curtain rails, 4ft.11½in. wide. (Lawrence Fine Art) $1,655

Mahogany Sheraton sideboard with inlay and serpentine front, 5ft. wide. (Brogden & Co.)$555

Late 18th century bowfronted sideboard framed and veneered in mahogany, 66½in. wide. (W. H. Lane & Son) $920

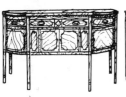

American Federal mahogany and mahogany veneer sideboard, circa 1790, 68¾in. wide. (Robert W. Skinner Inc.)
$1,800

Late Georgian mahogany and string and shell inlaid serpentine-fronted sideboard, 84½in. wide. (Dacre, Son & Hartley)
$910

Chinese carved teak sideboard, circa 1930, 56in. wide, with glazed center door. (Robert W. Skinner Inc.)
$400

Eastlake cherry sideboard with carved bee and brickwork, circa 1875, 45in. wide. (Robert W. Skinner Inc.)
$650

American baroque style oak sideboard with carved crest, circa 1900, 64½in. wide. (Robert W. Skinner Inc.)
$1,150

Victorian oak sideboard, American, with mirror back, circa 1900, 48in. wide. (Robert W. Skinner Inc.)
$250

Late 19th century American Renaissance revival ebonized inlaid sideboard, 67in. wide. (Robert W. Skinner Inc.)
$700

Regency mahogany sideboard crossbanded in satinwood, 7ft.2in. wide, circa 1800. (Sotheby's)
$2,715

17th century oak sideboard with paneled cupboard doors and brass handles, 3ft. 9in. wide. (J. M. Welch & Son)
$1,865

FURNITURE

Chinese carved teak and marble stand with lobed top, 33in. high, circa 1880. (Robert W. Skinner Inc.) $375

Mid 19th century papier-mache book or music stand inlaid with mother-of-pearl, 12¼in. wide. (Sotheby's Belgravia) $160

Sheraton style inlaid mahogany urn stand with shell inlay to lower shelf. (Gilbert Baitson) $225

One of a pair of Regency rosewood pedestal music stands with lyre-shaped insets. (Worsfolds) $1,535

Walnut jardiniere in well-figured wood with removable lid and liner, 1860's, 26in. wide. (Sotheby's Belgravia) $575

William and Mary tripod stand with octagonal top, circa 1680, 1ft.2½in. wide. (Sotheby's)$895

One of a pair of 19th century French ebonized pedestal cabinets with marble tops. (J. M. Welch & Son) $1,820

Early 18th century American pine and maple cross stretcher base candlestand, 27in. high. (Robert W. Skinner Inc.) $425

George II bottle rack on walnut stand, circa 1750, 2ft.2in. wide. (Sotheby's) $1,570

One of a pair of Regency burr-yew diningroom pedestals on bronze paw feet, 19½in. wide. (Christie's) $1,645

Late Empire French jardiniere stand on cabriole legs. (J. M. Welch & Son) $275

Folding circular telescopic lectern table with swivel action, by Swan & Milligan. (Butler & Hatch Waterman) $430

One of a pair of mid 19th century giltwood and burr-walnut torcheres, 52in. high. (Sotheby's Belgravia) $2,545

William IV mahogany folio stand with railed adjustable sides, 28in. wide. (Christie's) $1,355

William and Mary oak tripod stand with spiral-twist stem and baluster base, circa 1680, 1ft. 1½in. wide. (Sotheby's) $935

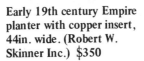

17th century Flemish ebony and rosewood press on spirally turned legs and cross stretcher, 32in. wide. (Christie's) $2,390

Early 19th century Empire planter with copper insert, 44in. wide. (Robert W. Skinner Inc.) $350

Edwardian mahogany shaving stand on square tapering legs. (J. M. Welch & Son) $125

Chinese hardwood urn stand with marble top, 18in. diam. (Lawrence Fine Art) $205

One of a pair of Irish Georgian mahogany lecterns with sloping tops, 26½in. wide. (Christie's) $1,560

One of a pair of Chinese hardwood urn stands with marble tops, 23in. high. (Lawrence Fine Art) $285

Bugatti stand with square top and lower shelf, circa 1900, inlaid with pewter, 112cm. high. (Sotheby's Belgravia) $680

Early 19th century Dutch mahogany tea kettle stand with cover or cellarette, 26in. high. (Lawrence Fine Art) $700

17th century Spanish walnut lectern with molded book-rest, 44in. high. (Christie's) $360

George IV mahogany reading table with adjustable top, 2ft.11½in. wide, circa 1820. (Sotheby's) $1,010

18th century elm candle-stand with circular top and splayed pine legs, 17¼in. diam.(Christie's) $600

Fine quality beechwood spinning wheel. (J. M. Welch & Son) $635

Regency style rosewood X-framed stool with tapestry seat. (J. M. Welch & Son) $235

Victorian 12in. foot stool, with copper warmer inside. (J. M. Welch & Son) $90

Herman Miller stool, designed by Charles Eames, 41cm., 1956. (Sotheby's Belgravia) $340

One of a pair of early George II fruitwood stools with drop-in seats in floral needlework, 21½in. wide. (Christie's)$9,250

Rare set of late George III mahogany bed steps, circa 1805, 2ft. 10in. long. (Sotheby's) $1,475

One of a pair of late 16th century Gothic oak stools, 1ft.10in. wide.(Sotheby's) $1,645

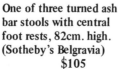

George III mahogany window seat with scroll ends, circa 1765, 2ft. 10in. wide. (Sotheby's) $2,380

One of three turned ash bar stools with central foot rests, 82cm. high. (Sotheby's Belgravia) $105

Dressing stool with petit point seat and carved cabriole legs in mahogany. (John Hogbin & Son) $160

STOOLS

Victorian mahogany framed piano stool with revolving top. (Vernons)$100

One of a pair of mid 19th century rosewood footstools with cut plush tops, 13½in. wide. (Sotheby's) $170

19th century mahogany framed stool on turned and fluted legs. (Vernons) $45

One of a pair of Swedish giltwood stools with slightly dipped padded tops, 1ft.10in. wide, circa 1805. (Sotheby's)$2,865

Oak coffin stool with carved frieze and reeded legs. (Butler & Hatch Waterman) $985

Late 19th century elm stool on turned legs. (Vernons) $35

One of a pair of 17th century oak joint stools with molded rectangular tops, 18in. wide. (Christie's)$730

Pair of Regency period stools with dish-shaped seats, on turned and fluted mahogany legs, 18in. wide. (Woolley & Wallis) $980

17th century design oak joint stool. (Biddle & Webb) $295

Bugatti vellum and beaten metal on wood stool, circa 1900, 43cm. high. (Sotheby's Belgravia) $570

19th century French Empire banquette in mahogany with upholstered seat, 32in. wide. (Robert W. Skinner Inc.) $750

One of a pair of early George III giltwood stools with serpentine seats, 21in. wide. (Christie's) $5,465

Early Georgian Chippendale mahogany stool on four boldly carved cabriole legs, 23in. wide. (Boardman's) $2,250

Victorian rosewood piano stool on carved legs. (Phillips) $135

Victorian rosewood square stool on cabriole legs, 1ft. 7in. square. (Dickinson, Davy & Markham)$125

American William and Mary joint stool, circa 1700, 26in. wide, on stretcher base. (Robert W. Skinner Inc.) $3,000

One of a pair of late 16th century Gothic oak stools, 1ft.10in. wide. (Sotheby's) $1,645

Charles II walnut stool with needlework upholstered seat, 15in. wide. (Boardman's)$660

Part of a 20th century French Louis XVI giltwood parlor set of five pieces in tapestry upholstery. (Robert W. Skinner Inc.) $3,900

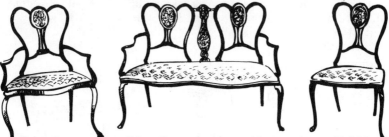

Part of a seven-piece Edwardian mahogany and ivory satinwood inlaid boudoir suite, upholstered in silk damask. (Dacre, Son & Hartley) $1,545

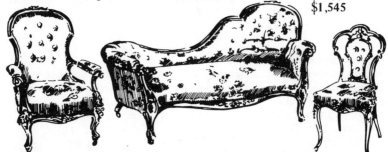

Part of a mid 19th century walnut drawingroom suite of thirteen pieces covered with floral ivory damask. (Sotheby Beresford Adams) $3,625

Part of a ten-piece drawingroom suite with oval carved backs, circa 1860. (Sotheby's Belgravia) $5,705

Three-piece bergere lounge suite with front cabriole legs. (Allen & May)
$700

Three-piece Art Nouveau fruitwood parlour set, France, circa 1910, with carved crests. (Robert W. Skinner Inc.) $600

Part of a four-piece walnut drawingroom suite, circa 1860, in gold upholstery. (Sotheby's Belgravia) $4,245

Part of a six-piece Victorian rosewood salon suite with oval backs and floral upholstery. (Dickinson, Davy & Markham) $1,860

19th century French walnut fold-over card table with inlaid shaped top, 3ft.1½in. wide. (Dickinson, Davy & Markham) **$1,215**

Ebony and rosewood envelope card table, swivel top inlaid with boxwood and ivory motifs, circa 1900, 21¾in. wide. (Sotheby's Belgravia) **$535**

Rosewood card table by Gillows, top with beaded border, circa 1840, 36in. wide. (Sotheby's Belgravia) **$755**

Marquetry card table with serpentine top on kingwood ground, circa 1870, 32½in. wide. (Sotheby's Belgravia) **$1,655**

One of a pair of mid 19th century rosewood tea tables with hinged tops, 39in. wide. (Sotheby's Belgravia) **$1,330**

Chippendale mahogany serpentine-fronted tea table with fold-over top and blind fret carving to frieze, 36in. wide, circa 1760. (Sotheby, King & Chasemore) **$2,850**

George III demi-lune tea table on tapering fluted legs. (Capes, Dunn & Co.) **$935**

20th century American Federal style mahogany card table with shaped top, 35in. wide. (Robert W. Skinner Inc.) **$350**

George III satinwood card table, top crossbanded with tulipwood and inlaid with a lunette, 38in. wide. (Christie's) **$2,265**

One of a pair of Victorian shaped rosewood folding top tea tables on quadruple supports, 36in. wide. (Lewes Auction Rooms)
$2,325

Early 20th century Maple & Co., mahogany and marquetry envelope card table, crossbanded in satinwood, 22in. wide.(Sotheby Beresford Adams) $855

One of a pair of fairly plain Regency card tables with fold-over tops. (Stride & Son)
$3,035

Burr-walnut games table with hinged swivelling top, circa 1860, 35in. wide. (Sotheby's Belgravia) $990

George II folding top tea table in red walnut, on slender cabriole legs, shell carved at knees. (Christie's & Edmiston's)
$8,235

Early Victorian burr-walnut card table with boxwood string inlay and folding flap top. (Capes, Dunn & Co.)
$1,215

New England Federal mahogany inlaid card table, top with ovolu corners, circa 1700, 34¾in. wide.(Robert W. Skinner Inc.)
$1,600

George II red walnut triple flap card and tea table with lobed top, 36in. wide. (Christie's)
$4,255

Federal mahogany card table with demi-lune top on square tapered legs, 35in. wide.(Robert W. Skinner Inc.)
$400

Victorian walnut card table of serpentine shape with fold-over swivel top, 36in. wide. (Lawrence Fine Art) **$1,035**

Rosewood card table on central octagonal-shaped pillar on shaped platform with bun feet, 35½in. wide. (Butler & Hatch Waterman) **$450**

Chinese Chippendale fold-over top card table with carved frieze. (Morris, Marshall & Poole) **$1,410**

One of a pair of late George III mahogany card tables, circa 1805, 2ft.10in. wide. (Sotheby's)**$1,850**

Regency rosewood tea table inlaid with brass stringing, on quadruple splay feet, 3ft. wide. (Jackson-Stops & Staff)   **$955**

One of a pair of George III mahogany D-shaped breakfront card tables, 3ft. wide. (Sotheby's) **$4,625**

Small George II mahogany tea or games table on cabriole legs, circa 1740, 2ft.1in. wide. (Sotheby's) **$4,295**

Late 18th century George III mahogany demi-lune tea table with satinwood crossbanding, 39in. wide. (Sotheby Beresford Adams)   **$965**

Early Georgian solid mahogany circular tea table, 30in. diam. (Hall Wateridge & Owen) **$1,110**

Regency rosewood and brass parquetry card table on four turned supports, 36in. wide. (Boardman's) $1,360

Victorian figured mahogany fold-over break-fast table on gun barrel stem. (Gilbert Baitson) $470

One of a pair of George III semi-circular mahogany card tables, circa 1785, 3ft. wide. (Sotheby's) $2,310

Victorian walnut French style card table, top crossbanded in kingwood, 36in. wide. (Hy. Duke & Son) $1,380

George I walnut games table with rounded corners, circa 1725, 2ft. 8in. wide. (Sotheby's) $980

Mid 18th century George III satinwood card table with fold-over top and tulipwood crossbanding, 37in. wide. (Sotheby Beresford Adams) $1,265

Regency coromandel card table, circa 1815, 3ft. wide, with hinged top.(Sotheby's) $825

George III mahogany tea table on chamfered square legs, circa 1760, 2ft.11in. wide. (Sotheby's) $1,040

One of a pair of William IV rosewood-veneered card tables with burr-elm scroll feet, circa 1830, 3ft. wide. (Sotheby's) $925

CONSOLE TABLES

Louis XVI console table with serpentine marble top, on pierced scroll supports, 51½in. wide. (Christie's)$2,485

One of a pair of George III console tables in satinwood veneers, 33in. long. (Robert W. Skinner Inc.) $2,400

German giltwood serpentine-fronted console table with carved cabriole legs, circa 1750, 3ft.9½in. wide. (Sotheby's) $3,085

Regency console table with mottled gray marble top, circa 1815, 2ft.9¼in. wide.(Sotheby's)$1,685

One of a pair of 18th century giltwood pier glasses with matching side tables, 3ft.10in. wide.(Dickinson, Davy & Markham) $1,520

20th century American Federal style mahogany console table with inlaid edge, 35in. wide.(Robert W. Skinner Inc.)$125

One of a pair of George IV rosewood and grained rosewood console tables, circa 1820, 2ft.0½in. wide. (Sotheby's) $635

George III console table with Carrara marble top, circa 1775, 4ft.6½in. wide. (Sotheby's) $2,585

Louis XV giltwood console table with serpentine rosso Levanto marble top, 27in. wide. (Christie's) $2,050

364

Regency rosewood and amboyna breakfast table with rectangular top, 51in. wide. (Boardman's) $2,455

Regency mahogany circular dining table on arched sabre legs. (Lawrence Fine Art) $7,175

Rosewood veneered circular tip-top breakfast table on paw feet, 1840's, 48in. diam. (Sotheby's Belgravia) $850

German mahogany center table with gray veined marble top, circa 1840. (Sotheby's Belgravia) $845

19th century mahogany breakfast table with oval top. (J. M. Welch & Son) $345

Late Georgian mahogany revolving drum table on turned column and four swept legs, 41in. diam. (Locke & England) $1,820

Rosewood and marquetry breakfast table, top inlaid with satinwood border, circa 1840, 48in. diam. (Sotheby's Belgravia) $3,085

19th century Regency tilt-top breakfast table in mahogany, 59in. long. (Robert W. Skinner Inc.) $850

Mid Victorian walnut and inlaid loo table with boxwood and amboyna top, 52in. wide. (Dacre, Son & Hartley) $655

Rectangular mahogany breakfast table with molded top, circa 1850, 45in. wide. (Sotheby's Belgravia) $735

Burr-walnut center table with quarter-veneered molded top, circa 1860, 48in. wide. (Sotheby's Belgravia) $665

Walnut oval breakfast table with tip-top, circa 1870, 46½in. wide. (Sotheby's Belgravia) $770

Walnut dining table with oval quarter-veneered top, 1860's, 52in. long. (Sotheby's Belgravia) $660

Mahogany breakfast table on platform base with splay feet and brass paw castors, 3ft.6in. wide. (Allen & May) $720

Regency mahogany extending dining table in the manner of Gillows, 100½in. wide. (Christie's) $9,620

Burr-walnut center table with oval top on four fluted columns, 1860's, 42in. wide. (Sotheby's Belgravia) $560

Flemish oak and walnut center table with parquetry inlaid motifs, on bulbous-shaped legs, 43¾in. wide. (Geering & Colyer) $570

Pollard oak and parcel gilt breakfast table, circular tip-top inlaid with flowers, 53¼in. diam., 1840's. (Sotheby's Belgravia) $2,150

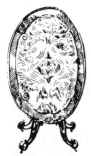

Walnut loo table in well-figured and burr-wood, top inlaid with stringing, circa 1860, 51in. long. (Sotheby's Belgravia) $1,115

George IV mahogany and rosewood crossbanded circular tilt-top pedestal table, 4ft. diam., circa 1825. (Sotheby, King & Chasemore) $1,570

Mid 19th century rosewood breakfast table on faceted baluster stem, 48in. diam. (Sotheby Beresford Adams) $595

20th century walnut and parcel gilt breakfast table in well-figured wood with dolphin supports, 50in. diam. (Sotheby's Belgravia) $1,840

Regency rosewood and satinwood crossbanded library table with ebonized and reeded border, circa 1800, 4ft.3in. diam. (Sotheby's) $860

William IV rosewood breakfast table with circular tip-top, circa 1835, 52½in. diam. (Sotheby's Belgravia) $1,380

Mid 19th century rosewood breakfast table, 49in. diam. (Sotheby Beresford Adams) $630

Oak coaching table with oval folding top, 3ft.6in. wide, circa 1800. (Sotheby, King & Chasemore) $930

Walnut and rosewood marquetry center table with circular tip-top, circa 1850, 39in. diam. (Sotheby's Belgravia) $2,340

Rosewood circular breakfast table with molded border, circa 1850, 53in. diam. (Sotheby's Belgravia) $1,485

Large oval George IV mahogany breakfront or dining table, 5ft.4in. diam., circa 1820. (Sotheby's) $3,930

George IV mahogany two pedestal dining table of unusual form, circa 1820, 3ft.5in. wide. (Sotheby's)$1,385

Regency rosewood and cut brass inlaid pedestal table, circa 1810. (Sotheby, King & Chasemore) $2,375

Victorian walnut center table on carved pillar and quadruple scroll legs. (Hall Wateridge & Owen) $600

George IV mahogany three pillar extended dining table, circa 1820, 11ft.4in. wide. (Sotheby's) $7,240

Georgian mahogany triple pedestal dining table with reeded edge, 11ft.6in. wide, open. (Jackson-Stops & Staff)
          $1,885

Victorian walnut loo table with oval top inlaid with birds, on quadruple base. (Hall Wateridge & Owen) $770

Georgian mahogany D-end dining table with extending leaf, 9ft.3½in. wide extended. (Dickinson, Davy & Markham) $1,100

Victorian burr-walnut and marquetry center table, 54in. wide.(Boardman's) $4,535

Circular Regency brass inlaid rosewood snap-top breakfast table, 48in. diam. (Burtenshaw Walker) $3,025

Large George III serpentine-fronted dining-room side table, circa 1785, 9ft.1½in. wide. (Sotheby's) $1,665,

Early 20th century 'George III' mahogany dining table with intersection, 112in. long extended. (Sotheby's Belgravia) $1,805

Early Victorian walnut breakfast table with oval top veneered in well-figured wood, 152.5cm. wide. (H. Spencer & Sons Ltd.) $1,210

Rare George III drop-leaf pedestal dining table with circular top, 3ft.11in. diam., circa 1805. (Sotheby's) $2,560

William IV four-pedestal dining table, circa 1835, 13ft.2in. wide.(Sotheby's) $9,000

DRESSING TABLES

One of a pair of Regency mahogany dressing tables with galleried tops, 39in. wide. (Lawrence Fine Art) $1,380

Rococo revival walnut mirrored bureau, circa 1860, with arched top mirror, 47½in. wide. (Robert W. Skinner Inc.) $475

American rococo revival rosewood and rosewood veneer dressing table, circa 1860, 24½in. wide. (Robert W. Skinner Inc.) $600

19th century dressing table veneered in thuyawood with tulipwood crossbanding, 48in. wide. (W. H. Lane & Son) $1,635

George V lady's toilet cabinet, fitted with silver brushes, bottles and manicure implements. (Locke & England) $340

Dressing table from a satinwood bedroom suite in six pieces, circa 1910. (Sotheby's Belgravia) $1,080

Regency mahogany dressing table in the manner of Gillows, 48in. wide. (Christie's) $3,700

Hindley & Wilkinson painted satinwood dressing table with shield mirror, circa 1890, 40¼in. wide. (Sotheby's Belgravia) $4,935

19th century mahogany and inlaid dressing table, 38in. wide. (J. M. Welch & Son) $890

Late 18th century George III mahogany and satinwood dressing table with opening folding top, 25in. wide. (Sotheby Beresford Adams) $895

George III bow-fronted mahogany dressing chest with boxwood inlay, 39in. wide. (Boardman's) $1,625

Amboynawood and parcel gilt decorated Art Deco dressing table by W. & T. Lock Ltd., 63in. wide. (Boardman's)$1,435

Renaissance revival walnut and burl veneer princess bureau with carved crest, circa 1870, 63½in. wide. (Robert W. Skinner Inc.) $950

Late Victorian/early Edwardian Sheraton design oval dressing table surmounted by an oval mirror. (Locke & England) $750

Victorian bamboo writing desk/dressing table, lacquered with birds and flowers, with brass drop handles. (John Hogbin & Son) $295

19th century French Louis XVI transitional style marquetry poudreuse, in harewood, mahogany and other woods, 32in. wide. (Robert W. Skinner Inc.)$950

Late 18th century German Directoire mahogany dressing table with arched swing mirror plate, 21in. wide. (Sotheby Beresford Adams) $670

Mid 19th century mahogany Sheraton revival dressing table with satinwood crossbanded top, 35in. wide. (Sotheby Beresford Adams) $595

FURNITURE

19th century oak Sutherland table on turned legs. (J. M. Welch & Son) $155

George III D-end mahogany dining table with center portion, restored, 106in. wide, extended. (Lawrence Fine Art) $2,325

Gustav Stickley oak drop-leaf table, circa 1909, 32in. diam., open. (Robert W. Skinner Inc.) $1,100

Cherrywood inlaid dining table with drop leaves, circa 1790, 48in. wide. (Robert W. Skinner Inc.) $1,800

Early 18th century William and Mary butterfly table, 38½in. diam. (Robert W. Skinner Inc.)$3,970

Rare George II solid yewwood drop-leaf table with one flap, 2ft.3½in. wide, circa 1755. (Sotheby's) $2,240

Rare Victorian bird's-eye maple Sutherland table on bobbin turned supports, 22in. wide. (Locke & England) $475

Federal painted harvest table, New England, circa 1810, 72in. long. (Robert W. Skinner Inc.) $4,725

Early 19th century Shaker cherrywood drop-leaf table, 29in. wide. (Robert W. Skinner Inc.) $3,000

Early 19th century mahogany writing table on quadruple turned pillars and four sabre legs, 56in. wide. (W. H. Lane & Son) $540

Late George III mahogany Cumberland-action drop-leaf dining table, circa 1810, 5ft.5½in. wide. (Sotheby's)$1,880

George II mahogany drop-leaf table with D-shaped flaps, circa 1740, 6ft. wide extended. (Sotheby's)$2,865

George III mahogany drop-leaf dining table on tapering legs. (Warren & Wignall) $445

Early 19th century painted maple and pine hutch table, 41in. diam. (Robert W. Skinner Inc.) $1,900

Inlaid Edwardian mahogany Sutherland table, top with inlaid oval. (Warren & Wignall) $305

Irish Georgian mahogany supper table with two-flap top, 52½in. wide extended. (Lawrence Fine Art) $865

Rare George II oak gate-leg table with unusual hipped legs on paw feet, circa 1730, 5ft.4½in. wide. (Sotheby's)$7,935

Early 19th century mahogany drop-leaf dining table with tapering legs on pad feet. (T. Bannister & Co.) $380

GATELEG TABLES

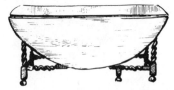

Early 19th century oval gateleg table in solid walnut, fitted with a single drawer. (Edwards, Bigwood & Bewlay) $4,970

William and Mary oak gateleg table, late 17th century, 4ft.6in. wide. (Sotheby's) $1,665

Late 17th century oak gateleg table with oval top, 57in. wide, extended. (Sotheby's) $1,465

17th century oak gateleg table with later oval twin-flap, 71in. wide, open. (Christie's) $2,105

17th century oak eight/ten seater gateleg dining table with oval top, 68in. wide, open. (Boardman's) $2,590

Oval gateleg table in oak on baluster turned legs, 5ft. wide, extended. (Andrew Grant) $1,535

William and Mary walnut gateleg table with oval top, circa 1690, 4ft.10in. wide. (Sotheby's) $1,000

Charles II oval oak gateleg table on bobbin-turned legs, circa 1670, 5ft. 4in. wide, open. (Sotheby's) $2,775

Late 19th century oak gateleg table with oval top. (J. M. Welch & Son) $345

Small oval dining table with turned legs and stretchers in oak. (Alfred Mossop & Co.) $540

Mid 17th century oak gateleg dining table with molded apron, 62½in. long. (Dacre, Son & Hartley) $1,820

Late 17th century oak gateleg table on columnar supports, 52in. wide, extended. (Sotheby's) $670

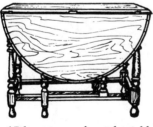

Late 17th century oak gateleg table with oval top, 63in. wide, extended. (Sotheby's) $1,545

18th century George III walnut gateleg table on block and baluster turned supports, 30in. wide. (Robert W. Skinner Inc.) $3,000

Early Georgian period red walnut oval twin flap top gateleg table, 3ft.8in. wide. (Woolley & Wallis) $1,280

17th century Charles II oak gateleg table with oval top, on turned baluster supports, 58in. wide, extended. (Sotheby's) $1,715

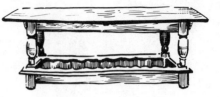

Georgian mahogany D-end dining table on turned supports, 9ft.4in. long extended. (Dickinson, Davy & Markham) $1,700

17th century German oak refectory table with two-plank top and four turned legs. (Boardman's) $2,220

Walnut and oak banded dining table, 4ft. 4in. wide, legs carved with figures of lions. (Allen & May) $2,835

Walnut dining table of elongated rectangular form, mid 1960's, 90in. long. (Sotheby's Belgravia) $830

17th century Flemish oak drawleaf table, 90in. wide, open. (Sotheby, King & Chasemore) $2,850

Early 20th century George III style mahogany three-pillar dining table, 147in. long open. (Sotheby Beresford Adams) $2,140

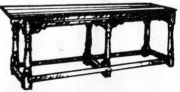

Early 19th century convertible mahogany dining table. (Clarke Gammon) $8,830

17th century oak side table with four-plank top, 98in. long, on six turned tapering legs. (Edwards, Bigwood & Bewlay) $3,385

Sheraton period mahogany dining table with boxwood and ebony stringing, 5ft. 11in. wide. (Capes, Dunn & Co.) $1,045

Early oak refectory dining table on four turned legs joined by plain stretcher rails. (Butler & Hatch Waterman) $2,520

Early 17th century oak refectory table with four-plank top, 8ft.2in. long. (Edgar Horn) $3,660

16th century Gothic walnut and oak trestle table with plank top, 120in. wide. (Boardman's) $6,290

Unusual late Victorian mahogany patent extending dining table, 68in. diam., closed. (Christie's S. Kensington) $22,320

Oak refectory table with rectangular plank top on bulbous cup and cover legs, 74in. wide. (Christie's) $915

Oak serving table on turned baluster supports, 8ft. long. (Sotheby, King & Chasemore) $2,605

Period oak side table on carved and bulbous stretcher supports, 52in. wide. (John Hogbin & Son) $250

377

19th century French kingwood and marquetry center table on cabriole legs, 2ft.11in. wide. (Dickinson, Davy & Markham) $370

Set of three satinwood tea tables on four fluted turned supports joined by trestle bases, circa 1920.(Sotheby's Belgravia) $550

Georgian mahogany circular tilt-top occasional table on triple splay support, 3ft. diam. (Geering & Colyer) $590

One of a pair of mid 19th century rosewood tripod tables with gadrooned borders. (Sotheby Beresford Adams) $1,675

Octagonal-shaped drum-top table in mahogany, with tooled leather inset, 36in. wide. (Sotheby, King & Chasemore) $830

Late 19th century French tulipwood parquetry gueridon, on tapering cabriole legs, 1ft.11in. wide. (Sotheby, King & Chasemore)$1,025

Rosewood and marquetry occasional table, with circular top, circa 1830, 22½in. diam. (Sotheby's Belgravia) $450

Regency mahogany reading table on easel support and quadripartite base, 34in. wide. (Christie's) $1,665

Mid 19th century mahogany oblong tripod tip-up wine table. (T. Bannister & Co.) $160

Late 19th century American rococo revival rosewood marble top table, 34in. wide. (Robert W. Skinner Inc.)$400

French Art Nouveau mahogany table in the manner of Majorelle, 107cm. wide. (Phillips) $785

George II mahogany tripod table, circa 1740, 2ft.6in. diam. (Sotheby's) $750

French marquetry table d'accoucher of serpentine form, circa 1840, 1ft.11in. wide.(Sotheby, King & Chasemore) $2,885

Oval mahogany table ambulante, inlaid with flowerhead trellis, 16½in. wide. (Sotheby, King & Chasemore) $1,395

Unusual Regency mahogany tray-top table with two galleried tiers, the upper lifting off, 31¼in. wide. (Christie's) $890

French table ambulante, circular top with pierced gallery, 2ft.4in. diam., circa 1900. (Sotheby, King & Chasemore) $780

Set of three Regency brass inlaid rosewood quartetto tables in the manner of Louis Le Gaigneur, 18½in. to 14in. wide. (Christie's) $3,515

Gilt plaster and mosaic center table by Morant of London, 1850's, 27in. diam. (Sotheby's Belgravia) $3,330

OCCASIONAL TABLES

19th century Louis XV style kingwood occasional table, stamped Edwards & Roberts, 17½in. wide. (Hy. Duke & Son) $770

Early 19th century Irish George III style wine tasting table with attachable tray. (Robert W. Skinner Inc.) $3,300

20th century American Chippendale style pie crust tip table, top with carved edge, 30in. diam. (Robert W. Skinner Inc.) $225

Early 19th century Shaker cherry and birch candlestand, Massachusetts, 26¾in. high. (Robert W. Skinner Inc.) $700

Late George III mahogany oval occasional table on turned and ringed supports with undertier, circa 1800, 2ft. wide. (Sotheby, King & Chasemore) $1,330

Chippendale pine bird cage candlestand, New England, circa 1780, 14½in. diam. (Robert W. Skinner Inc.) $1,795

One of a pair of Victorian mahogany tables, carved to simulate linen folds and feathers. (Sotheby's Belgravia) $1,355

19th century boulle center table. (Christie's S. Kensington) $2,930

Late 19th century Italian carved white marble table with round top, 37in. diam. (Robert W. Skinner Inc.) $450

18th century French Louis XV provincial one-drawer table with shaped apron, 49in. wide. (Robert W. Skinner Inc.) $1,500

George III mahogany reading stand with folding top, 2ft. wide, circa 1770. (Edwards, Bigwood & Bewlay) $1,115

Victorian papier-mache pedestal occasional table with plate glass top, 40in. wide. (Dee & Atkinson) $670

Continental rectangular top occasional table in floral marquetry, 22in. wide. (Edwards, Bigwood & Bewlay) $660

Mid 19th century boulle center table of serpentine outline, 36in. wide.(Sotheby Beresford Adams) $630

19th century black lacquered pedestal table with circular top, 20in. diam. (Dee & Atkinson) $630

Federal mahogany tip table, New England, circa 1790, 28¼in. high. (Robert W. Skinner Inc.) $675

Rectangular marquetry table with brass stringing, on rosewood cluster column, 40in. wide. (Edwards, Bigwood & Bewlay) $2,290

American Federal mahogany inlaid tip-top candlestand, circa 1790, 28½in. high. (Robert W. Skinner Inc.)$575

William and Mary style birch tavern table, circa 1930, 50in. wide. (Robert W. Skinner Inc.) $350

Hepplewhite period satinwood table with banded and inlaid decoration. (J. M. Welch & Son) $985

Elm kneading trough with shaped apron and trestle legs, 3ft.6in. wide. (J. M. Welch & Son) $130

19th century provincial French style center table in rosewood and walnut, 53in. wide. (Coles, Knapp & Kennedy) $715

Early Victorian mahogany teapoy with sarcophagus-shaped top, 20in. wide. (Lawrence Fine Art) $440

Center table with circular top on square stem and spiral geometric quadripartite base, 104cm. diam. (Christie's) $690

Victorian burr-walnut stretcher table on carved and fluted underframe, 43in. wide. (Burtenshaw Walker) $700

Florentine mosaic marble top table on walnut tripod stand, 1860's, 19½in. diam.(Sotheby's Belgravia)$1,685

Regency mahogany dressing table with bowed top, 44in. wide. (Christie's)
                  $1,965

Rare Sheraton period satinwood and mahogany lady's dressing cabinet, 34½in. high. (Edgar Horn) $1,630

17th century Spanish chestnut side table on baluster legs and square stretchers, 61in. wide. (Christie's) $1,315

Mid 17th century oak box table with hinged lid, on turned baluster legs, 31½in. wide. (Christie's) $880

George III mahogany dressing table with divided double-flap top crossbanded in rosewood, 27in. wide, closed. (Christie's) $2,950

Mid 18th century George III rosewood tripod table with dished snap top, 16in. diam. (Sotheby's) $845

Regency rosewood four-tier occasional table on turned supports, 25in. wide. (Christie's) $2,515

William and Mary maple and pine tavern table, circa 1750, 31in. wide. (Robert W. Skinner Inc.) $850

Early George III mahogany stand, circular recess with scalloped border, 23in. high. (Christie's) $2,865

Late 19th century rosewood and inlaid display table. (J. M. Welch & Son) $710

George III mahogany and satinwood Pembroke table with serpentine top, 37¾in. wide, open. (Christie's) $6,060

Late Georgian mahogany Pembroke table with kingwood crossbanding, 21½in. wide. (Lawrence Fine Art) $520

George III mahogany Pembroke table, top crossbanded with satinwood and rosewood, 39½in. wide, open. (Christie's) $3,440

One of a pair of Federal mahogany Pembroke tables, circa 1808-16, 39¾in. wide. (Robert W. Skinner Inc.) $7,000

Small mahogany Pembroke table with rounded flaps, now on square pillar with rectangular base, 17.5cm. wide. (Lawrence Fine Art) $270

Late George III mahogany Pembroke table with oval crossbanded top, circa 1790, 2ft.6in. wide. (Sotheby, King & Chasemore) $705

George III satinwood Pembroke table in the manner of Ince & Mayhew, 39in. wide, top crossbanded with rosewood. (Christie's) $1,755

American Federal style inlaid mahogany Pembroke table with shaped top and leaves, circa 1920, 31in. wide. (Robert W. Skinner Inc.) $225

Antique oval inlaid dropleaf table on square tapering legs. (Farrant & Wightman) $395

George III satinwood Pembroke table, top bordered with a broad plumwood band, 40½in. wide, open. (Christie's)$7,355

19th century French rosewood and marquetry occasional table with four oval drop leaves, 21in. square. (Morphets)$855

Sheraton period satinwood veneered oval Pembroke table with mahogany and harewood crossbanding, 31in. wide. (Woolley & Wallis) $11,815

Small Georgian mahogany Pembroke table with inlaid top, 1ft. 4in. wide. (Dickinson, Davy & Markham) $520

Late 19th century painted Pembroke table on square tapering legs, 35in. wide. (Sotheby's Belgravia) $1,130

Late Georgian mahogany Pembroke table with two-flap top, 34in. wide, extended. (Lawrence Fine Art) $625

George III mahogany Pembroke table, top with central shell patera and tulipwood crossbanding, 2ft. 6in. wide, circa 1785. (Sotheby's)$1,300

Late Georgian mahogany Pembroke table with fluted edge, 18in. wide. (Lawrence Fine Art) $480

George III mahogany Pembroke table with serpentine top crossbanded with satinwood, 41½in. wide. (Christie's) $1,965

385

18th century crossbanded mahogany serving table with serpentine front, 4ft.2in. wide. (Russell, Baldwin & Bright) $1,080

George I Irish walnut tray top side table, circa 1720, 31in. wide. (Sotheby, King & Chasemore) $3,845

Regency mahogany diningroom side table, circa 1805, 7ft.6in. wide. (Sotheby's) $805

Mid 18th century Irish beechwood side table with gadrooned border, 58½in. wide. (Christie's) $1,630

George III mahogany serpentine-fronted side table, circa 1790, 36in. wide. (Sotheby, King & Chasemore) $590

George II mahogany side table with gray marble top, on cabriole legs, 2ft.10in. wide, circa 1740.(Sotheby's) $1,860

Early George III grained side table with later mahogany eared serpentine top, 54in. wide. (Christie's) $2,035

One of a pair of George I style gilt gesso side tables, 39in. wide.(Sotheby, King & Chasemore) $3,295

Late 18th century fruitwood side table with quarter mirror-figured top, 50½in. wide. (Christie's) $1,290

Adam style serpentine-fronted serving table decorated with urns and husks, 60in. wide. (Edwards, Bigwood & Bewlay) $1,100

Edwards & Roberts walnut and marquetry writing table, 1860's, 52in. wide. (Sotheby's Belgravia) $1,435

Late 17th century oak side table on chamfered legs, 35in. long. (Andrew Grant) $855

Mid 18th century Dutch walnut and marquetry side table, demi-lune top with shaped edge. (Sotheby Beresford Adams) $2,510

French Regency style large mahogany side table of serpentine form, 6ft.1in. wide. (Dickinson, Davy & Markham) $690

One of a pair of George III style giltwood side tables with marble tops, 3ft. 7in. wide. (Sotheby's) $4,835

Painted and gilded side table in Adam style with brass-bordered top, 49¼in. wide. (Christie's) $1,355

FURNITURE

One of a pair of 'George III' satinwood side tables with D-shaped tops, circa 1880, 47in. wide. (Sotheby's Belgravia) $2,570

Oak side table with single drawer under, 29in. wide. (J. M. Welch & Son) $175

One of a pair of Edwardian mahogany side tables with decoration in colored woods, 4ft.wide.(Russell, Baldwin & Bright)$1,620

William and Mary oak side table with molded top, circa 1690, 2ft. 8in. wide. (Sotheby's) $955

George II walnut side table with shaped frieze, 35½in. wide. (Christie's) $4,935

19th century walnut and inlaid side table, 24in. wide. (J. M. Welch & Son) $420

Mahogany side table with marble top, circa 1740, possibly Irish, 4ft.3in. wide. (Sotheby's) $4,090

Late George I walnut side table with cross-banded top, circa 1720, 2ft.5in. wide.(Sotheby's) $4,705

Mid 19th century giltwood pier table with marble top, 53in. wide. (Sotheby's Belgravia) $905

Mahogany bow-fronted side table with drawer, on turned and stretchered legs, 34in. wide. (John Hogbin & Son) $145

Sheraton style serpentine front serving table in crossbanded and inlaid mahogany, 152cm. wide. (Osmond, Tricks) $820

Early 18th century oak lowboy on slender cabriole legs, 28½in. wide. (Locke & England) $545

Sheraton style mahogany semi-circular side table, crossbanded in kingwood, 22in. wide. (Hy. Duke & Son) $770

George III serving table with fretwork frieze, 72in. wide. (Christie's) $3,495

One of a pair of Regency rosewood side tables in the manner of George Smith, 27¼in. wide. (Christie's) $3,290

Mid 19th century giltwood side table, one of a pair, with serpentine marble top, 53½in. wide. (Sotheby's Belgravia) $2,570

Tubular steel and zebrawood side table with circular drum top, 1930's, 73.5cm. high. (Sotheby's Belgravia) $840

Late 18th century oak and fruitwood Continental table with carved apron, on cabriole legs. (Gilbert Baitson) $490

Regency rosewood sofa table crossbanded with calamanderwood and satinwood, 57in. wide. (Christie's) $2,470

Late George III mahogany sofa table, crossbanded in rosewood, 5ft.1½in. wide. (Sotheby's) $2,895

Regency padoukwood sofa table with baluster turned stretcher, on reeded sabre legs, 62in. wide. (Lawrence Fine Art) $2,025

George IV mahogany sofa table, circa 1825, 40in. wide. (Sotheby, King & Chasemore) $1,005

Regency mahogany sofa table, top crossbanded in rosewood, circa 1830, 37in. wide. (Sotheby, King & Chasemore) $3,865

Regency mahogany sofa table with 'plum pudding' top and kingwood crossbanding, 57in. wide, extended. (Lawrence Fine Art) $1,730

Georgian mahogany sofa table with reeded edge and ebony line inlay, 5ft. 3in. wide, extended. (Lawrence Fine Art) $3,680

Regency rosewood veneered sofa table in well-figured wood, circa 1805, 4ft. 11in. wide. (Sotheby's) $7,365

Late Regency rosewood sofa table, inlaid with brass motifs, 58in. wide,
extended. (Lawrence Fine Art)
$1,610

Late George III mahogany sofa table
with D-shaped ends, circa 1820, 5ft.
10½in. wide. (Sotheby's)
$5,585

Late George III satinwood small sofa
table with satinwood banding, 63cm.
wide. (H. Spencer & Sons Ltd.)
$1,025

George III mahogany sofa table, top
crossbanded with rosewood, 57in. wide.
(Christie's) $2,055

Small Regency rosewood sofa table, inlaid with brass lines, on trestle end
supports, 42in. wide, extended. (Lawrence Fine Art) $1,700

Early 19th century Regency mahogany
sofa table inlaid with ebony lines,
50in. wide. (Sotheby Beresford Adams)
$1,265

Regency mahogany sofa table, top banded with satinwood and inlaid with
ebony stringing, 62½in. wide, extended.
(Lawrence Fine Art) $2,235

Regency mahogany sofa table with inlaid ebony stringing, legs joined by an
arched stretcher, 148.6cm. long.
(Jackson-Stops & Staff) $730

391

WORKBOXES & GAMES TABLES

Mid 19th century walnut combined sewing and games table with fold-over top, 30in. wide. (Sotheby Beresford Adams) $1,265

Burr-walnut combined games and work table with swivel oval-ended top, 1860's, 27in. wide. (Sotheby's Belgravia) $1,115

Georgian mahogany games table with shaped corners, on cabriole legs, 33in. wide. (Hall Wateridge & Owen) $1,110

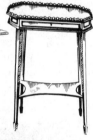

George III mahogany work table with two-flap top, circa 1800, 2ft.4in. wide. (Sotheby's) $1,345

'Louis XVI' brass inlaid mahogany games table for chess and backgammon, 1880-1900, 29½in. wide. (Sotheby's Belgravia) $720

18th century George III sewing table in rosewood, burl and other veneers, with hinged lid, 18¾in. wide. (Robert W. Skinner Inc.) $1,900

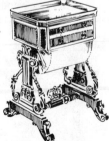

Unusual papier-mache work table with domed top, circa 1850, 19in. wide. (Sotheby's Belgravia) $1,170

Victorian walnut games and work table on carved and baluster end standard, 27in. wide. (Hy. Duke & Son) $920

William IV rosewood and mahogany work table, top with solid gallery, circa 1835, 1ft.9in. wide. (Sotheby's) $775

Victorian rosewood work table with marquetry inlay, 1ft.8in. wide. (Dickinson, Davy & Markham) $615

19th century Regency bow-fronted sewing table in mahogany and mahogany veneer, 36in. wide. (Robert W. Skinner Inc.) $900

Regency partridge-wood and mahogany work table, lid inset with satinwood oval, 1ft.1½in. wide, circa 1810. (Sotheby's) $725

Rosewood work table with hinged top on octagonal stem on concave-sided base, circa 1840, 19in. square. (Sotheby's Belgravia) $990

Northern New England Federal birch work table, circa 1800, 19in. wide. (Robert W. Skinner Inc.) $755

Fine Regency walnut tea-poy of tapering octagonal paneled form, 29in. high. (W. H. Lane & Son) $505

Small Georgian walnut work box on square tapering legs with X-stretcher. (Pattison Partners & Scott) $675

Regency mahogany and satinwood banded work table with inlaid motifs, circa 1810, 1ft. 10in. wide. (Sotheby, King & Chasemore) $1,445

Mid Victorian sewing and games table in walnut strung with boxwood, 61cm. wide. (H. Spencer & Sons Ltd.) $965

German or Flemish mahogany work table, 19½in. wide, 1840's. (Sotheby's Belgravia) $515

One of a pair of rare New York City Empire rosewood and grain painted games tables, 36½in. wide. (Wm. Doyle Galleries Inc.) $10,500

Late Regency mahogany work table with two-flap top, 28in. wide, extended. (Lawrence Fine Art) $660

George III mahogany writing and work table with hinged leather top, circa 1790, 1ft.11in. wide. (Sotheby's) $1,665

19th century figured mahogany work table with satin work box, 20½in. wide. (Lawrence Fine Art) $845

Mid 19th century rosewood sewing table with fitted swing top and wool well, 20in. wide. (W. H. Lane & Son) $310

George IV mahogany work table of teapoy shape, circa 1815, 1ft. 8½in. wide. (Sotheby's) $1,025

Damascus combined chess and backgammon table with hinged lid, 1920's, 33¼in. wide. (Sotheby's Belgravia) $865

Georgian mahogany work table with satinwood edging, 36in. wide, extended. (Lawrence Fine Art) $645

Early George II maho-
gany games table with
double-hinged top,
circa 1720, 2ft.9½in.
wide. (Sotheby's)
$1,810

Burr-walnut work table
with tulipwood cross-
banding, circa 1860,
25in. wide. (Sotheby's
Belgravia) $805

Anglo-Dutch mid Georgian
walnut games table with
sliding tray top, 35½in.
wide. (Christie's)
$1,560

Georgian mahogany
work table with
reeded edge, on ring
turned supports,
32in. wide, extended.
(Lawrence Fine Art)
$830

Irish mid Georgian tea and
games table with double
folding top, 30½in. wide.
(Christie's)$1,510

Viennese mahogany and
cherrywood work table
with hinged top, circa
1830, 1ft.7in. wide.
(Sotheby's) $780

19th century Burmese hardwood and rosewood work
table with carved border,
30in. wide. (Coles, Knapp
& Kennedy) $285

Small Victorian rose-
wood work table with
glazed panel doors to
the top. (Butler &
Hatch Waterman)
$400

19th century rosewood
games table on turned
and carved legs. (J. M.
Welch & Son)
$945

Pollard oak writing table with tooled leather writing surface, circa 1840, 43¼in. wide. (Sotheby's Belgravia) $3,900

Mid 19th century giltwood center table by C. Hindley & Son, London, 52in. wide. (Sotheby's Belgravia) $595

William IV parcel gilt rosewood writing table with leather inset top, circa 1835, 60in. wide. (Sotheby's Belgravia) $1,530

Edwards & Roberts walnut and marquetry writing table, 1860's, 52in. wide. (Sotheby's Belgravia) $1,435

Small mahogany bonheur du jour with lion-head handles and on ring turned legs, 22in. wide. (Aldridge's) $2,715

Kingwood bonheur du jour with amboyna interior, 42in. wide, circa 1860. (Sotheby's Belgravia) $1,290

Rosewood writing table, top inset with writing surface, circa 1860, 46in. wide. (Sotheby's Belgravia) $1,400

George IV rosewood veneered library table on paneled trestle supports, circa 1820, 3ft.9in. wide. (Sotheby's) $1,075

One of a pair of George I style gilt gesso side tables, 39in. wide. (Sotheby, King & Chasemore) $3,295

Ormolu mounted kingwood bureau plat with leather-lined top, 56in. wide. (Christie's) $6,255

George III mahogany library table, circa 1780, 66in. wide, with writing slope. (Sotheby, King & Chasemore) $7,685

Unusual painted papier-mache center table inlaid with mother-of-pearl chipping, circa 1850, 57in. wide. (Sotheby's Belgravia) $4,500

American Art Deco sycamore and mahogany desk with V-shaped top surrounded by walnut banding, 36¼in. wide, circa 1920. (Robert W. Skinner Inc.) $600

Regency mahogany writing table, top crossbanded with rosewood and on ring-turned beechwood supports, 54in. wide. (Christie's) $2,960

Regency rosewood writing table on spindle-filled trestle ends, 41in. wide. (Christie's) $1,515

George III oval mahogany library table, circa 1820, 67in. wide. (Sotheby, King & Chasemore) $27,450

Mahogany writing desk with hinged flap and on trestle base, circa 1840, 22in. wide. (Sotheby's Belgravia) $515

French Second Empire rosewood library table on bobbin turned pedestals, 65in. wide. (W. H. Lane & Son) $1,120

Victorian satinwood writing desk painted with cherubs, flowers and portraits, 39in. wide. (Morphets) $1,580

Edwardian lady's shaped rosewood marquetry kneehole desk on cabriole legs, 36in. wide. (Burtenshaw Walker) $1,285

George IV rosewood writing table with pierced brass gallery, 107cm. wide. (H. Spencer & Sons Ltd.) $780

Reproduction lady's burr-walnut writing desk with slant front, on cabriole legs. (T. Bannister & Co.) $415

Mahogany library table with rectangular top, circa 1840, 54in. wide. (Sotheby's Belgravia) $685

French Art Deco bureau de dame painted in relief, 120cm. high. (Christie's) $820

Regency mahogany writing table with leather-lined top with ebonized borders, 60½in. wide. (Christie's) $6,660

Satinwood Carlton House desk with fitted superstructure, circa 1910, 53in. wide. (Sotheby's Belgravia) $2,340

Early 20th century Maple & Co. mahogany and marquetry writing desk, 48in. wide. (Sotheby Beresford Adams) $1,675

Edwardian inlaid mahogany cylinder top kneehole desk on square tapering legs, 48in. wide. (Burtenshaw Walker) $2,080

Victorian lady's small bonheur du jour with gilt metal gallery and inset leather top, 41½in. wide. (Butler & Hatch Waterman) $745

Lady's Eastlake walnut and burl veneer desk with mirrored top, circa 1870, 31in. wide. (Robert W. Skinner Inc.) $625

Rosewood and bone inlaid Regency Carlton House desk. (Christie's S. Kensington) $1,325

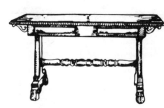

Late Georgian mahogany library table with rosewood crossbanding and beaded decoration, 56in. wide. (Locke & England) $1,395

George III mahogany and satinwood strung cheveret with detachable superstructure, 55cm. wide. (Phillips) $2,700

19th century French walnut bureau plat with serpentine-shaped top crossbanded in kingwood, 4ft. wide. (Edwards, Bigwood & Bewlay) $2,470

WRITING TABLES & DESKS

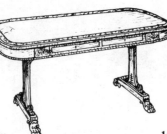

German mahogany combined writing and dressing table, inlaid with satinwood stringing, 43¼in. wide. (Sotheby's Belgravia) $550

Regency rosewood writing table with rounded rectangular top, on splayed trestle ends, 60in. wide. (Christie's) $9,280

19th century French provincial mahogany bonheur du jour, with serpentine fall-front, 35½in. wide. (Coles, Knapp & Kennedy) $895

Early 20th century fruitwood writing desk with shelved superstructure, 141cm. high. (Sotheby's Belgravia) $1,045

Regency mahogany architect's table with rising top, circa 1815, 3ft.6in. wide. (Sotheby, King & Chasemore) $1,400

Walnut writing desk, superstructure with pierced gallery, drawer inset with porcelain plaques, circa 1860, 40½in. wide.(Sotheby's Belgravia)$2,675

Walnut and burr-walnut bonheur du jour with gilt bronze mounts, circa 1870, 35in. wide. (Sotheby's Belgravia) $2,335

Rare lacquer and giltwood kneehole table on cabriole legs, 5ft.2½in. wide, restored. (Sotheby's) $7,220

Edwardian rosewood writing table with shaped front and baluster gallery, 109cm. wide. (H. Spencer & Sons Ltd.)$1,105

Louis XV kingwood bureau plat, stamped Criaerd, 57in. wide. (Wm. Doyle Galleries Inc.) $30,000

Mid 19th century Dutch marquetry side table with oval center panel, 52cm. wide. (H. Spencer & Sons Ltd.) $2,430

Late 19th century Louis XV style bureau plat in ebonized wood, 42in. long. (Robert W. Skinner Inc.) $1,000

Inlaid Edwardian mahogany two-tier table with fret sides, on thimble and castor legs. (John Hogbin & Son) $430

19th century mahogany folding desk of unusual design, 24in. wide. (Lawrence Fine Art) $790

George I walnut side table with chamfered crossbanded and quartered top, 32in. wide. (Christie's) $2,360

Inlaid mahogany desk with rising top and on tapered legs. (John Hogbin & Son) $635

Walnut partner's desk with brass drop handles and leather inset top, 60in. wide. (John Hogbin & Son) $990

Victorian pollard elm writing table, stamped Howard & Sons, with raised superstructure, 43in. wide. (Christie's) $1,935

Early 18th century four-paneled coffer, inscribed A.H. 1723, 50in. long. (Andrew Grant) $335

Oak dower chest with three-panel front, 48in. wide. (Hall Wateridge & Owen) $425

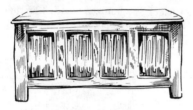

16th century oak linenfold chest with rising plank lid, 52in. wide. (Boardman's) $890

Late 18th century pine decorated dower chest, Pennsylvania, 48in. wide. (Robert W. Skinner Inc.) $1,700

Mid Georgian mahogany coffer on chest with brass carrying handles, 44in. wide. (Christie's) $1,630

17th century oak chest with plain rising top and carved front panels, 4ft.9in. wide. (Edwards, Bigwood & Bewlay) $515

Small 16th century oak linenfold chest with rising paneled lid and iron hasp and hinges, 39½in. wide. (Boardman's) $2,035

Country Federal grain painted blanket chest with lift top, 44¼in. wide, circa 1810. (Robert W. Skinner Inc.) $350

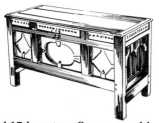

Mid 17th century Commonwealth oak coffer with four-panel top and carved frieze rail, 50in. wide. (Sotheby's) $900

Large mid 17th century oak coffer with hinged top in two parts, 74in. wide. (Sotheby's) $880

Mid 17th century oak mule chest with carved frieze rail, restored. (Sotheby's) $795

George I walnut coffer on stand with brass carrying handles, circa 1715, 4ft. wide. (Sotheby's) $2,480

Small 18th century oak coffer with triple paneled top and front, 3ft.2in. wide. (Dickinson, Davy & Markham) $295

Rare carved pine child's blanket box, New England, 1788, 21¼in. wide. (Robert W. Skinner Inc.)$4,300

Mid 16th century Charles I oak coffer with triple panel front, 51in. wide. (Sotheby's) $460

German stained and painted pine chest, circa 1670, 4ft.9in. wide. (Sotheby, King & Chasemore) $780

15th century North Italian pine casket carved on three sides, 53cm. wide. (Sotheby's) $1,245

Alto Adige cedarwood chest with three-paneled front, circa 1680, 6ft.4½in. wide. (Sotheby's) $1,480

North Italian cedarwood 'Cyprus chest', 63in. wide. (J. M. Welch & Son) $365

17th century coffer, front with four arcaded panels and original lock, 50in. wide. (W. H. Lane & Son) $370

Early 18th century William and Mary oak and pine chest on frame, with lift top, 30in. wide. (Robert W. Skinner Inc.) $6,500

Plymouth pine blanket chest, circa 1700, 49½in. wide. (Robert W. Skinner Inc.) $2,455

Early 18th century paneled oak chest, with carved frieze, 44in. wide. (J. M. Welch & Son) $400

17th century leather covered trunk, domed lid inlaid with gilt brass nailheads, 45½in. wide. (Christie's) $880

Late 16th century Italian walnut cassone with deeply paneled top, 4ft. 2½in. wide. (Sotheby's) $925

Breton Louis XV provincial inlaid elmwood chest, front inlaid in light and dark wood, circa 1770, 5ft.10in. wide. (Sotheby's) $710

Decorated pine blanket box, New York, dated 1816, 39¾in. wide, with hinged molded top. (Robert W. Skinner Inc.) $4,100

17th century Dutch or North German iron strong box with rustic landscape panels, 33in. wide. (Christie's) $770

Small 17th century steel strong box, overlaid with riveted iron strapwork, 2ft.5in. wide. (Sotheby's)$1,220

Early 18th century black and gold lacquer casket on stand, 29½in. wide. (Christie's) $1,195

Late 16th century North Italian painted and gilded cassone, restored, 5ft.3in. wide. (Sotheby's) $1,110

18th century oak coffer with plank top and paneled front, 3ft.9in. wide.(J. M. Welch & Son) $365

18th century Dutch walnut armoire in marquetry with double paneled doors, on ogee bracket feet, 60in. wide.(Edwards, Bigwood & Bewlay) $7,500

Wardrobe, designed by Marcel Breuer, in pale wood, 1920's, 186cm. wide. (Sotheby's Belgravia) $375

18th century French provincial oak armoire with overhanging cornice, 4ft. 8in. wide. (Edwards, Bigwood & Bewlay) $1,555

Dutch mahogany armoire with broken pediment, circa 1780, 5ft. 9in. wide. (Sotheby's) $2,225

Mid 18th century Dutch walnut and marquetry wardrobe, 5ft.7½in. wide. (Sotheby's) $10,080

Quartered mahogany wardrobe in Chippendale manner with carved key pattern cornice. (Gilbert Baitson) $320

Gentleman's mahogany wardrobe with dentil cornice and two inlaid and crossbanded doors, 4ft.3in. wide. (Butler & Hatch Waterman) $530

Mid 18th century Liegeois carved armoire on stand with serpentine top, 6ft. 7in. wide. (Sotheby's) $2,580

20th century oak wardrobe by JPC with carved frieze panel, 42½in. wide. (Sotheby's Belgravia) $445

19th century German rose-
wood wardrobe, 7ft.5in.
wide. (Phillips & Brooks)
$3,640

Large early oak armoire
with fan and rose carv-
ing and geometric mol-
ding. (Butler & Hatch
Waterman) $1,190

Flemish rosewood and
ebony armoire with
molded overhanging
cornice, 95½in. wide.
(Christie's) $4,415

Dutch mahogany armoire
with molded arched
broken pediment cente-
red by a vase stand, 76in.
wide. (Christie's)$2,575

17th century Dutch oak
four door cupboard with
scrollwork frieze, 58in. wide.
(Boardman's) $7,770

Anglo-Dutch walnut and
burr-walnut armoire
with crossbanded pane-
led doors, 67½in. wide.
(Christie's) $4,785

Late 18th/early 19th cen-
tury George III mahogany
breakfront wardrobe with
dentil cornice, 92in. wide.
(Sotheby Beresford Adams)
$1,210

Louis XVI provincial
oak armoire with
molded cornice and
carved frieze, 64½in.
wide. (Christie's)
$3,130

George III inlaid maho-
gany breakfront ward-
robe. (Sotheby Bearne)
$1,795

WASHSTANDS

Georgian mahogany washstand with folding top and unusual cross stretcher support, in original condition. (Gilbert Baitson) $150

19th century mahogany washstand on turned legs. (Phillips) $190

Georgian mahogany inlaid corner washstand with center drawers, on splay legs, 29in. wide. (Dee & Atkinson) $295

18th century American painted pine water bench, upper shelf with splashback, 26½in. wide. (Robert W. Skinner Inc.) $400

Mid 18th century George III mahogany circular washstand with Copeland Spode basin, 32in. high. (Sotheby Beresford Adams) $540

Victorian marble topped washstand on a walnut veneered base.(Phillips) $160

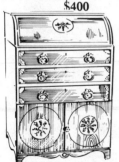

Late 18th/early 19th century mahogany and marquetry washstand with cylinder front, 26½in. wide. (Sotheby's) $535

Antique mahogany corner washstand with brass handles. (Farrant & Wightman)$150

Liberty oak washstand with green-tiled top, labeled, circa 1900, 141cm. high. (Sotheby's Belgravia) $225

Kingwood and parquetry etagere with three serpentine tiers, circa 1880, 14in. wide. (Sotheby's Belgravia) $425

Victorian whatnot in polished rosewood with six serpentine-fronted tiers. (Aldridge's) $525

Mahogany whatnot with four tiers joined by baluster turned supports, circa 1840, 48½in. high. (Sotheby's Belgravia) $940

Late Georgian mahogany four-tier whatnot on turned supports with brass castors, 18in. wide. (Locke & England) $465

Mid 19th century mahogany whatnot, top with adjustable book rest, 16in. wide. (Sotheby's) $770

Late George III mahogany whatnot with turned and ringed spindles, 18½in. wide.(Lawrence Fine Art) $1,430

Early 20th century mahogany whatnot, one of a pair, 23½in. wide. (Sotheby's Belgravia) $820

19th century three-tier bird's-eye maple and rosewood whatnot, crossbanded in satinwood, 20in. wide. (W. H. Lane & Son) $435

Late 19th century American Renaissance revival carved walnut whatnot, over cupboard base, 40in. wide. (Robert W. Skinner Inc.)$525

409

Georgian brass bound mahogany wine cooler of octagonal shape and with lead liner. (Dacre, Son & Hartley)$2,640

Late Regency sarcophagus form wine cellaret in cross-banded mahogany with lead lining. (Locke & England) $780

Late 18th century mahogany and inlaid cellaret of Sheraton design, with brass carrying handles. (Locke & England) $1,075

One of a pair of 'George III' mahogany wine coolers with hexagonal bodies, mid 19th century, 19in. wide. (Sotheby's Belgravia)$5,710

Georgian oval mahogany wine cooler, with brass carrying handles and reeded base and legs. (D. M. Nesbit & Co.) $1,575

George III mahogany and brass bound octagonal wine cooler, lead lined, 17½in. wide. (Burrows & Day) $990

Mahogany wine cellaret of canted form, with fitted lead interior, 12in. wide. (W. H. Lane & Son) $295

George IV mahogany cellaret, 2ft. wide, with brass bound body. (Sotheby's)$1,035

George III oval mahogany wine cooler with brass carrying handles, circa 1790, 1ft.9in. wide. (Sotheby's) $1,240

Early 19th century William IV mahogany wine cooler of tapering rectangular form, 22in. wide. (Sotheby Beresford Adams)$445

William IV mahogany cellaret, circa 1820, 2ft.2in. wide. (Sotheby's) $1,795

Late 18th/early 19th century George III mahogany wine cooler of hexagonal outline, 20½in. wide. (Sotheby's)$1,290

George III mahogany brass bound hexagonal wine cooler, lined in lead, 45cm. diam. (Osmond, Tricks) $945

Late 18th century George III mahogany wine cooler with brass handles and bands, 19in. wide. (Sotheby's)$2,300

George III mahogany wine cooler with three brass bands, 1ft.9in. wide, circa 1790. (Sotheby's) $2,215

George III mahogany cellaret of hexagonal form with brass handles and bands, 50cm. wide. (H. Spencer & Sons Ltd.) $1,030

George III oval mahogany cellaret with brass bands, 61.5cm. wide. (Jackson-Stops & Staff) $2,655

Mahogany cellaret with domed lid and side carrying handles, on turned legs with casters.(Alfred Mossop & Co.) $1,090

French opaque-opaline
glass flared octagonal
beaker, circa 1725, 9cm.
high. (Christie's)
$505

Yellowish green glass
beaker with straight
flaring sides, circa 3rd
century A.D., 3¼in.
high. (Sotheby's)
$440

Bohemian Zwischengold
fluted dice beaker in two
parts, circa 1740, 8.5cm.
high. (Christie's)
$970

Bohemian amber-flash
waisted hexagonal bea-
ker, engraved in the
manner of Hoffmann,
12.5cm. high, circa
1840. (Christie's)
$1,110

Transparent enameled topographical beaker by Carl von
Scheidt, circa 1815, 12cm.
high. (Sotheby's)$11,740

One of a pair of rare
'Zwischengold-und-
Silberglas' beakers by
Johann Mildner, 1799,
12cm. high.(Sotheby's)
$9,715

German enameled and
dated Kurfurstenhumpen,
32.7cm. high, 1620.
(Phillips) $1,630

German dated enameled
Reichsadler humpen,
Bohemia, 1624, 28cm.
high. (Christie's)$8,510

German enameled bea-
ker of tapering bucket
shape, inscribed Vive
Mamie anne, 1743.
(Phillips) $220

412

Small late 19th century cameo glass bottle, body etched with chinoiserie scene, 5.7cm. high. (Sotheby's Belgravia) $415

Etched and polished internally decorated bottle and stopper, incised Marinot, 13.2cm. high. (Christie's) $5,825

Glass wine bottle of squat mallet shape, neck with string rim, 20cm. high. (Phillips) $40

Dutch engraved bottle by Willem van Heemskerk with dark emerald green body, 1689, 33cm. high. (Sotheby's) $11,740

19th century Indian glass hookah bottle with bell-shaped sides, 7in. high. (Sotheby's) $175

17th century Dutch sealed wine bottle, shoulder applied with armorial seal, 9½in. high. (Sotheby's) $2,430

Northern Indian rich purple glass hookah bottle, circa 1700, 7¼in. high. (Sotheby's) $395

17th century Nether-landish blue-tinted glass bottle with slim tapering neck, 13.5cm. high. (Sotheby's) $1,375

18th/19th century Indian blue glass hookah bottle with flaring ridged neck, 7½in. high. (Sotheby's) $435

413

Early 20th century Tiffany Favrile blue iridescent glass bowl, New York. (Robert W. Skinner Inc.)$300

Mt. Washington cameo glass bowl, late 19th century, in opaque pink on white, 9in. diam. (Robert W. Skinner Inc.) $375

Late 19th century glass bowl by Stevens & Williams, with gold and silver applied decoration, 5¾in. diam. (Robert W. Skinner Inc.)$275

Iridescent bluė Favrile glass flower center by Tiffany & Co., early 20th century, 11in. diam. (Robert W. Skinner Inc.) $550

Galle cameo glass bowl, marked, after 1904, 7.75cm. (Sotheby's Belgravia) $520

One of a pair of early 19th century covered pedestal bowls, 31cm. high. (Sotheby's Belgravia) $380

Enameled dated Baccarat opaline bowl of thistle shape, 1867, 30.4cm. diam., on wood stand. (Sotheby's Belgravia) $1,080

One of a set of six Tiffany iridescent glass bowls and saucers, circa 1900, 6cm. high. (Sotheby's Belgravia) $1,700

One of a pair of early 20th century
Tiffany Favrile glass finger bowls, with
undertrays. (Robert W. Skinner Inc.)
$425

South Bohemian lithyalin flared octagonal two-handled bowl, circa 1835,
Count Buquoy's Glassworks, 19cm.
wide. (Christie's) $1,390

Daum etched and gilded glass bowl,
marked, 1890's, 8.25cm. high.
(Sotheby's Belgravia) $570

Amberina shade by the New England
Glass Co., Massachusetts, circa 1880,
7¾in. diam. (Robert W. Skinner Inc.)
$200

Early 20th century European crystal,
brass and enamel bowl with portrait
base, 5¼in. diam. (Robert W. Skinner
Inc.) $350

One of a pair of cut glass bowls, covers
and stands, circa 1780, stands 19.5cm.
diam. (Christie's) $275

One of nine Steuben Rosaline cased
bowls, New York, circa 1925, signed,
5in. diam. (Robert W. Skinner Inc.)
$650

Golden iridescent Favrile glass rose
bowl by Tiffany Studios, 25cm. diam.
(Christie's) $820

415

BOWLS

American cut-glass Monteith bowl, circa 1880, 10in. diam. (Robert W. Skinner Inc.) $225

Galle etched and enameled cameo glass bowl, circa 1900, 11.5cm. wide. (Sotheby's Belgravia)$560

Opalescent glass bowl by R. Lalique, France, 8in. wide. (Lawrence Fine Art) $110

Argy Rousseau pate de cristal bowl, molded with leaves and arrowheads, 7.75cm. wide. (Sotheby's Belgravia) $875

Lalique opalescent glass bowl, 1920's, 30.25cm. diam., marked. (Sotheby's Belgravia) $710

Argy Rousseau pate de cristal bowl with bell-shaped body, 9.75cm. high, 1920's. (Sotheby's Belgravia)$1,670

1st century A.D. dark-blue cast glass pillar molded bowl with ribbed body, 19.5cm. diam.(Sotheby's) $8,870

Lithyalin foot bowl in marbled glass, Bohemian, circa 1840, 14.5cm. high.(Sotheby's Belgravia) $500

Lalique opalescent glass bowl with frieze of budgerigars, 24.5cm. diam., 1930's. (Sotheby's Belgravia) $525

Pate-de-verre rectangular box and cover by G. Argy Rousseau, 13.2cm. wide. (Christie's) $4,730

Frosted and opalescent glass bonbonniere and cover, by R. Lalique, 16cm. diam. (Christie's) $275

Fire-polished overlay glass bonbonniere and cover of spherical form, 17cm. diam. (Christie's)$1,235

White glass box cover, molded by R. Lalique, 11.5cm. diam. (Christie's) $275

Galle cameo glass box and cover with squat tapering body, circa 1900, 7.5cm. wide. (Sotheby's Belgravia) $1,000

17th century Venetian glass box and cover, 8in. high. (Robert W. Skinner Inc.) $100

Opalescent circular glass box and cover with bluish finish, molded by R. Lalique, 26cm. diam. (Christie's) $640

Double overlay triangular box and cover, signed, 11.5cm. high. (Christie's) $2,675

Small Walter pate-de-verre box and cover with waisted body, 1920's, 7cm. diam. (Sotheby's Belgravia) $520

CANDLESTICKS

One of a pair of early 20th century Tiffany Favrile glass candlesticks, New York, 7¼in. high. (Robert W. Skinner Inc.) $400

One of three circular glass candle holders, marked R. Lalique, 14.4cm. diam. (Christie's) $220

One of a pair of cobalt blue glass candlesticks, Massachusetts, circa 1840, 9½in. high. (Robert W. Skinner Inc.) $700

Glass taperstick with slim nozzle, circa 1730, 6¾in. high. (Sotheby's) $660

Airtwist taperstick with beaded knop and domed foot, circa 1750, 17.5cm. high. (Christie's) $705

Silesian stemmed candlestick, nozzle set on three collars, 22.5cm. high, circa 1730. (Sotheby, King & Chasemore) $230

Georgian cut glass candlestick on domed and faceted foot, circa 1780, 20cm. high. (Sotheby, King & Chasemore) $340

Early 20th century Aurene candlestick, signed, 10in. high. (Robert W. Skinner Inc.) $225

Unusual glass taperstick of hollow section and with pear-shaped knop, circa 1740, 4½in. high. (Sotheby's) $370

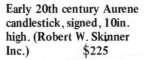

18th century Chinese
ruby glass wine cup,
7.5cm. high. (Vernons)
$90

17th century Facon de Venise
engraved cup with shallow
body, opposed auricular handles, 10cm. diam.(Sotheby's)
$1,175

German milchglas
mug with strap
handle and barrel-
shaped body, 12cm.
high. (Phillips)
$420

Mid 18th century Bohe-
mian milchglas mug deco-
rated with a roundel en-
closing a figure. (Christie's)
$875

A Facon de Venise ice
glass standing cup, South
Netherlands, 16th cen-
tury, 16.5cm. high.
(Christie's)
$3,300

Gutenbrunn Mildner cy-
lindrical mug with oval
plaque, dated 1792,
9.5cm. high.(Christie's)
$1,920

A small opaque glass cy-
lindrical mug, South
Staffordshire, circa 1760,
7cm. high. (Christie's)
$675

Late 19th century plated
amberina punch cup,
ribbed, with shaped rim,
2¾in. high. (Robert W.
Skinner Inc.)
$1,300

Pressed glass ale mug
with geometric deco-
ration, circa 1860.
(Vernons) $24

DECANTERS

GLASS

Burmese glass spirit decanter in the shape of a pig. (Christie's S. Kensington)

$275

One of a pair of clear glass and brown stained decanters and stoppers, inscribed Lalique, 27.3cm. high. (Christie's) $495

Cobalt blue bar bottle, cork stopper with pewter and cobalt stopper, circa 1850, 12in. high. (Robert W. Skinner Inc.) $250

One of a pair of cut-glass decanters and stoppers of club form, circa 1820, 26.5cm. high. (Christie's)$705

Clear glass flattened spherical decanter, etched R. Lalique, France, 34cm. high.(Christie's) $550

One of a rare pair of white enameled electioneering decanters and one stopper, circa 1765-68, 22cm. high. (Christie's) $10,175

One of a rare pair of rock crystal engraved decanters and stoppers, by Stevens & Williams, circa 1885. (Sotheby's Belgravia) $5,405

Lalique glass decanter, bulbous body with tapering neck, 32cm. high, 1920's. (Sotheby's Belgravia) $300

Overlay decanter and stopper by A. Bohm, signed, 38cm. high. (Sotheby's Belgravia) $2,495

Lalique glass decanter, signed, 1920's, 25.5cm. high, sides molded with masks. (Sotheby's Belgravia)$340

One of a pair of Regency cut-glass decanters and stoppers with concentric horizontal grooves, circa 1820, 26.5cm. high. (Sotheby, King & Chasemore) $375

One of a pair of diamond-cut crystal ship's decanters with mushroom stoppers, 24.5cm. high. (Jackson-Stops & Staff) $290

Late 19th century American two-color green cut-glass decanter of conical shape, 16¾in. high. (Robert W. Skinner Inc.) $200

Cut-glass wine set of two decanters and stoppers and a claret jug and stopper. (Dee & Atkinson) $410

Lalique glass decanter and stopper with slender cylindrical neck, 1920, 39.5cm. high. (Sotheby's Belgravia) $980

Large cut-glass decanter and stopper, circa 1820, 11¾in. high, chipped. (Sotheby's) $385

Enameled decanter and stopper for 'Port', by Wm. and Mary Beilby, circa 1765. (Christie's)$4,440

German enameled decanter jug with pewter cap, possibly Franconian, 1664, 28.5cm. high. (Sotheby's) $2,055

Enameled glass dish and cover, attributed to Fachschule Szwiesel, circa 1910, 17cm. high. (Sotheby's Belgravia) $160

Galle cameo glass dish of squat tapering form, circa 1900, 28cm. wide. (Sotheby's Belgravia) $790

Galle enameled glass pot and cover with barrel-shaped body, 1890's, 19cm. high. (Sotheby's Belgravia) $1,600

Opalescent circular glass dish molded with a sea nymph, 36.5cm. diam., by R. Lalique.(Christie's) $825

17th century Facon de Venise sweetmeat dish with flat bowl, 13.5cm. diam. (Sotheby's) $405

Walter pate-de-verre glass dish, incised mark, circa 1920's, 23.5cm. diam. (Sotheby's Belgravia) $795

Venetian footed dish of straight-sided form, circa 1500, 26.5cm. diam. (Sotheby's)$3,170

Late 18th century Irish canoe-shaped footed glass dish, 30cm. high. (Sotheby, King & Chasemore)$315

Daum cameo glass dish and cover, circa 1900, 9.5cm. diam. (Sotheby's Belgravia) $785

Massive Daum glass dish in clear yellow glass, engraved, 1930's, 25cm. wide. (Sotheby's Belgravia) $440

One of a pair of American glass compotes, circa 1845, with pointed scalloped rims, 4¾in. high. (Robert W. Skinner Inc.) $750

Double overlay triangular glass dish with inverted rim, 24.5cm. wide. (Christie's)$1,030

Crested amethyst circular shallow glass dish, gilt by Isaac Jacobs, circa 1800, 17.5cm. diam. (Christie's) $460

Unusual sweetmeat glass with cup-shaped bowl, circa 1750, 5½in. high. (Sotheby's)$190

Clear and opalescent glass dish by R. Lalique, France, 38cm. wide. (Christie's) $585

Unusual Galle cameo glass dish in the form of a leaf, circa 1900, 27.75cm. long. (Sotheby's Belgravia) $835

Sweetmeat dish on pedestal stem, 6in. high, circa 1730. (Sotheby's) $165

Good Almeric Walter pate-de-verre dish of scallop shell-shape, signed, 19cm. wide. (Phillips)$3,400

DRINKING SETS

Boxed set of six Lalique glasses, panels stained brown, 1920's, 9.8cm. high. (Sotheby's Belgravia) $1,030

Part of a late 19th century Stourbridge glass table service of fifty-two pieces. (Sotheby's Belgravia) $800

Three-bottle tantalus in brass bound case. (Honiton Galleries) $250

Three from a set of thirty 20th century drinking glasses with enameled bands. (Sotheby's Belgravia) $520

Part of a one hundred and twenty-eight-piece gilt glass table service, circa 1900. (Sotheby's Belgravia) $830

Suite of table glass by R. Lalique, France, thirty-five pieces in all. (Coles, Knapp & Kennedy) $330

424

Unusual parquetry table decanter set with globe body, circa 1860-80, 13¼in. high. (Sotheby's Belgravia)$2,920

Clear and amber stained glass carafe and stopper with six glasses en suite, inscribed R. Lalique, France. (Christie's) $740

GLASS

DRINKING SETS

Etched enameled and applied glass ewer and glasses by E. Galle, signed. (Christie's) $1,850

Mid 19th century Black Forest tantalus of table cabinet form, 19in. high. (Sotheby's) $465

Unusual gilt water set of eight pieces, circa 1900, jug 30.5cm. high. (Sotheby's Belgravia) $420

Boulle and ebonized rosewood serpentine decanter box with glasses, 13in. wide, circa 1850. (Sotheby's Belgravia) $1,025

Part of a set of seventeen Lalique glasses, 1930's, with square stems and rectangular panels. (Sotheby's Belgravia) $1,360

Late Victorian blue glass decanter and six glasses with silver and gilt decoration. (Sotheby's) $585

Galle enameled glass liqueur set in smoked glass with gold foil inclusions, 1880's. (Sotheby's Belgravia) $4,025

Oak tantalus, inscribed Betjemanns Patent, with silver plated mounts and cut glass whisky decanters, 12in. high. (Dickinson, Davy & Markham) $130

425

GLASS

German enameled flask of octagonal shape, 14cm. high. (Phillips) $405

Aubergine translucent glass flask with ribbed decoration, circa 3rd/4th century A.D., 6¼in. high. (Christie's) $1,765

Iridescent blue translucent glass date flask, 1st century A.D., 3¼in. high. (Christie's) $705

German enameled flask with pewter mounted neck, 17.5cm. high. (Phillips) $1,145

Late 17th century Bohemian enameled pewter mounted square spirit flask with pewter cover, 21.5cm. high.(Christie's) $1,110

German enameled flask of canted rectangular form, with pewter mounted neck, 18.5cm. high. (Phillips) $850

Mid 18th century Central European enameled silver mounted flask with canted corners, 14.5cm. high, (Christie's) $565

Interesting German enameled flask with pewter mounted neck and screw stopper, 14.5om. high. (Phillips) $665

Mid 18th century Armorial middle-European enameled glass flask with pewter rim, 16.7cm. high. (Sotheby, King & Chasemore) $465

Clear glass and grey stained rectangular scent flask, signed R. Lalique, 13.8cm. high.(Christie's) $730

Translucent yellowish-green glass flask, circa 3rd century A.D., 3¼in. high. (Christie's) $875

Aubergine translucent glass date flask, 1st century A.D., 3in. high. (Christie's)$520

17th century Spanish Facon de Venise flask with hexalobed body, 18.5cm. high. (Sotheby's) $485

Mid 18th century Armorial middle-European enameled glass flask, with pewter rim, 16.8cm. high. (Sotheby, King & Chasemore) $360

Glass flask in the form of bellows, the clear glass combed in blue and white, circa 1840, 33cm. high. (Sotheby's Belgravia) $160

German enameled glass flask of chamfered rectangular form, with pewter mounted neck. (Phillips) $310

German dated locksmith's rectangular pewter mounted spirit flask, 1788, 13cm. high. (Christie's) $360

German enameled flask with pewter mounted neck, 12.5cm. high. (Phillips) $500

One of four early 20th century Tiffany iridescent gold glass goblets, 5¾in. high. (Robert W. Skinner Inc.) $475

One of a pair of engraved goblets, circa 1870, 16.4cm. high. (Sotheby's Belgravia) $190

Wine goblet with rounded funnel bowl, circa 1700, 5¾in. high. (Sotheby's) $525

Dutch-engraved Newcastle goblet, shoulder knop with air-thread inclusions, circa 1750, 7¾in. high. (Sotheby's) $1,275

Engraved wine goblet with large ovoid bowl, circa 1780, 7in. high. (Sotheby's) $505

Bohemian cut and engraved goblet on baluster knopped stem, circa 1710, 21cm. high. (Christie's) $295

Baluster wine goblet with pointed funnel bowl, circa 1700, 7¾in. high. (Sotheby's) $605

Early lead glass goblet in Venetian style, supported on wrythen serpentine stem, circa 1680, 9¾in. high. (Sotheby's) $1,215

Bohemian ruby flashed faceted goblet of thistle shape, circa 1850, 28cm. high. (Sotheby's Belgravia) $380

Masonic goblet with bucket-shaped bowl on knopped stem, circa 1830, 15.5cm. high. (Sotheby, King & Chasemore) $270

French hyalith goblet, by Hautin & Cie, circa 1840, 11cm. high. (Christie's) $205

Early 19th century glass rummer with large square bowl, etched with initials J.B., 6½in. high. (Dacre, Son & Hartley) $370

Late 18th century Dutch-engraved goblet, Scandinavian or Lauenstein, 23.5cm. high. (Christie's) $335

Bohemian ruby stained goblet and cover on faceted knopped stem, circa 1850, 55cm. high. (Sotheby's Belgravia) $720

Engraved Paris Exhibition goblet and cover on knopped stem and stepped foot, 29cm. high, 1878. (Sotheby's Belgravia) $875

One of six early 20th century American cut-glass goblets, with starburst bases, 6in. high. (Robert W. Skinner Inc.) $400

Bohemian armorial goblet with funnel bowl, engraved with a coat-of-arms, circa 1700, 23cm. high. (Christie's) $405

17th century Facon de Venise goblet with cup-shaped bowl, 12.8cm. high. (Sotheby's) $385

429

Baluster goblet with round funnel bowl, circa 1700, 23cm. high. (Christie's) $740

Baluster goblet with round funnel bowl, on domed and folded foot, circa 1720, 17cm. high. (Christie's) $315

Unusual goblet with deep ribbed ovoid bowl, circa 1750, 8¼in. high. (Sotheby's) $185

Mid 18th century Williamite goblet with engraved bucket bowl, circa 1760, 17cm. high. (Christie's) $2,035

Unusually large engraved air-twist goblet, circa 1750, 12in. high. (Sotheby's) $205

Thuringian engraved goblet with funnel bowl, circa 1740, 19.5cm. high. (Christie's) $645

Dutch engraved goblet with funnel bowl, lower part cut on facets, circa 1760, 18cm. high. (Christie's) $425

Early 18th century Bohemian engraved goblet with widely flared funnel bowl, 15cm. high.(Christie's) $295

Very fine Dutch-engraved Newcastle goblet with funnel bowl, circa 1750, 8in. high. (Sotheby's) $3,290

Baluster goblet with deep rounded funnel bowl, circa 1700, 8¼in. high. (Sotheby's) $865

Engraved facet stemmed goblet, with inscribed bowl, circa 1780, 18.5cm. high. (Christie's) $370

Baluster goblet with flared bowl and domed and folded foot, circa 1700, 6¾in. high. (Sotheby's) $1,235

German armorial goblet engraved with a coat-of-arms, circa 1730, 18cm. high. (Christie's) $405

Dutch engraved goblet with slightly waisted funnel bowl, stem enclosing a large tear, circa 1750, 22cm. high. (Christie's) $705

Dutch-engraved wine goblet with pointed round funnel bowl, circa 1750, 8¼in. high. (Sotheby's) $945

Baluster goblet with large flared bucket bowl, circa 1700, 9¼in. high. (Sotheby's) $390

Rare wine goblet, funnel bowl with solid base, circa 1715, 7in. high. (Sotheby's) $615

Mammoth baluster goblet with round funnel bowl, circa 1700, 29cm. high. (Christie's) $335

JUGS & EWERS

Cased wheeling peach blow pitcher, 5½in. high. (Robert W. Skinner Inc.) $650

GLASS

Early 19th century glass champagne jug with trefoil rim, diagonal ice funnel, 11½in. high. (Dacre, Son & Hartley) $140

Daum etched and enameled miniature jug with applied glass handle, 8.9cm. high. (Christie's) $535

Lobmeyr engraved jug with strap handle, 33.6cm. high, 1870's. (Sotheby's Belgravia) $1,145

18th century Spanish or Bohemian jug and cover with applied scroll handle, 31.5cm. high. (Sotheby's) $675

Engraved glass claret jug with loop handle. (Christie's S. Kensington) $525

One of a pair of green glass eagle claret jugs with electroplated mounts, 10¼in. high. (Christie's S. Kensington) $705

Olive-green glass jug with spherical body and flaring mouth, 11cm. high, circa 3rd-4th century A.D. (Sotheby's) $200

Eastern United States cut glass footed pitcher with paneled pouring spout, circa 1880, 9in. high. (Robert W. Skinner Inc.) $200

432

Galle enameled glass jug in smoked glass, 1880's, 35.5cm. high.(Sotheby's Belgravia) $1,225

Late 19th century cameo glass metal mounted jug in cranberry colored glass. (Sotheby's) $585

Small Daum etched and enameled glass jug, marked, circa 1900, 7.25cm. high. (Sotheby's Belgravia) $835

Early Ravenscroft 'crizzled' decanter jug, circa 1674, 20cm. high. (Christie's) $710

Heath & Middleton silver mounted jug, Birmingham, 1893, 30.25cm. high. (Sotheby's Belgravia) $1,255

Ravenscroft 'crizzled' decanter jug with tapering oviform body, circa 1685, 23.5cm. high. (Christie's)$890

Glass water pitcher by Hawkes, Corning, New York, circa 1900, 8½in. high. (Robert W. Skinner Inc.) $200

Blown three mold glass jug with wide flaring rim and pouring spout, circa 1828, 6¼in. high. (Robert W. Skinner Inc.) $425

American cut glass champagne jug, circa 1890, 13½in. high with flared rim. (Robert W. Skinner Inc.) $300

433

GLASS

Late 19th century amberina basket, floral decorated, 10½in. high. (Robert W. Skinner Inc.) $275

Pair of ormolu mounted two-branch cut glass candelabra, 41cm. high. (Sotheby, King & Chasemore)$2,560

Mid 19th century vaseline glass bell with diagonally ribbed body, and clear handle, 27cm. high. (Sotheby's Belgravia) $70

Clear glass etched and enameled basket with gilded metal handle, by Emile Galle, 18cm. diam. (Christie's) $2,260

Late 19th century ruby and white cameo glass knife handle, 9.2cm. long. (Sotheby's Belgravia) $165

Gilt and enameled cut glass stemmed jar and cover, attributed to Faschule Haida, circa 1910-20, 25cm. high. (Sotheby's Belgravia) $240

Pate-de-verre figure of a seated girl, by A. Walter, signed, 20.5cm. high. (Christie's) $2,455

Lalique glass cockerel's head on wood stand, 1930's, signed, 16.5cm. high.(Sotheby's Belgravia) $390

One of a pair of mid 19th century amber bells with white rims, 29.5cm. high. (Sotheby's Belgravia) $170

One of a pair of cut glass candelabra, circa 1900, 25½in. high. (Robert W. Skinner Inc.) $450

Pate-de-verre tray by A. Walter, modeled by Henri Berge, 20.8cm. wide. (Christie's) $2,185

One of a rare pair of early 19th century Irish cut glass butter piggins, 13cm. high. (Sotheby, King & Chasemore) $395

Lalique frosted glass figure of a mermaid, 10cm. high, 1920's, marked. (Sotheby's Belgravia) $265

Cameo glass biscuit barrel, electroplated mounts by W. W. Harrison & Co., Sheffield, circa 1885, 17cm. high. (Sotheby's Belgravia) $830

Early 20th century Burmese double-handled urn by Mt. Washington Glass Co., Massa., 13½in. high. (Robert W. Skinner Inc.) $675

American Gothic revival walnut and glass terrarium with peaked top, 29½in. wide, circa 1840. (Robert W. Skinner Inc.) $200

Unfinished cameo glass plaque in translucent ruby, 1880's, 30.8cm. diam. (Sotheby's Belgravia) $415

Lalique glass frog molded with angular features, 1930's, 6.25cm. high. (Sotheby's Belgravia) $1,335

435

Signed St. Louis concentric millefiori weight with mauve cane, 6.3cm. diam. (Sotheby's) $1,195

Daum pate-de-verre paperweight modeled as a moth, signed, 12cm. wide. (Christie's) $945

Rare St. Louis color ground weight in salmon pink, green and white, 8cm. diam. (Sotheby's) $1,030

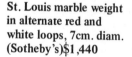

St. Louis marble weight in alternate red and white loops, 7cm. diam. (Sotheby's)$1,440

Clear pale amethyst glass and gray stained paperweight by R. Lalique, 21cm. high. (Christie's) $1,645

Baccarat butterfly and garland weight with star-cut base, 6.5cm. diam. (Sotheby's) $1,110

American flower weight cut with circular windows, in pink, white and green, 8.2cm. diam. (Sotheby's) $1,750

Paperweight in clear and frosted glass by R. Lalique, France, 10.8cm. high. (Christie's)$985

One of a rare pair of St. Louis doorknobs in the form of paperweights, 5cm. diam. (Sotheby's) $1,705

St. Louis mushroom paper-
weight in white, blue, pink
and green, 7.3cm. diam.
(Sotheby's) $1,070

Pate-de-verre paper-
weight by A. Walter,
11cm. wide.
(Christie's)$1,130

St. Louis mushroom paper-
weight of concentric canes,
8cm. diam. (Sotheby's)
$535

St. Louis flat-bouquet
weight of swirling latt-
cinio threads, 7.8cm.
diam. (Sotheby's)
$1,150

Clear and frosted glass
paperweight by R.
Lalique, France, 20.5cm.
high. (Christie's)
$1,235

Rare Baccarat snake paperweight, sides with diamond
facets, 7.5cm. diam.
(Phillips) $9,100

Rare Baccarat camomile
and garland weight with
star-cut base, 7.5cm. diam.
(Sotheby's) $1,480

Venetian millefiori weight by
Bigaglia in red, white and
turquoise, 7.8cm. diam.
(Sotheby's) $700

Clichy swirl weight in
green, white and pink,
7.9cm. diam. (Sotheby's)
$495

Brown stained glass scent bottle, molded Lalique, 8.1cm. diam. (Christie's) $455

Cameo glass and gilt metal mounted scent flask modeled as a curled dolphin, circa 1885, 13cm. wide. (Christie's)
$2,220

Brown glass scent bottle with dome-shaped stopper, R. Lalique, 7.6cm. high. (Christie's)
$510

Lalique glass perfume bottle and stopper for Worth's 'Dans la Nuit', 1920's, 10cm. high. (Sotheby's Belgravia)
$250

Unusual Daum cameo glass perfume bottle and stopper, signed, 13.5cm. high. (Phillips) $645

Late 19th century unfinished cameo glass scent bottle, 6.5cm. (Sotheby's Belgravia) $85

Double-overlay atomizer scent bottle with metal fitting, signed, 19.8cm. high. (Christie's)
$290

Clear glass and amber stained cologne bottle and stopper, molded R. Lalique, 17.6cm. high. (Christie's) $245

Clear and gray stained glass scent bottle and stopper, by Lalique, 11.2cm. high. (Christie's) $730

Worth perfume bottle
by R. Lalique, France,
with amber glass stop-
per, 10.6cm. high.
(Christie's)$275

Lalique glass perfume bottle
and stopper in original box,
1920's, 13.5cm. high.
(Sotheby's Belgravia)
$730

Frosted glass globular
scent bottle and stop-
per, molded as a
nymph, by Lalique,
9.8cm. high.
(Christie's) $545

Cameo glass silver moun-
ted scent bottle of tear-
drop form, circa 1885,
11cm. long. (Christie's)
$520

One of a pair of French 19th
century lime green opaline glass
square-shaped scent bottles,
4¾in. high. (Geering & Colyer)
$260

Late 19th century
molded overlay scent
bottle shaped as a per-
ching owl, 11.5cm. high.
(Sotheby's Belgravia)
$62

Lalique glass perfume
bottle and stopper,
signed, 1930's, 14cm.
high. (Sotheby's Bel-
gravia) $745

French 'gorge de pigeon' opaline globular scent bottle and
stopper, circa 1830, 11.5cm.
high. (Christie's)$2,220

Lalique heart-shaped per-
fume bottle with crescent-
shaped flat stopper, 1920's,
10.5cm. high. (Sotheby's
Belgravia) $745

439

GLASS

STAINED GLASS

One of a set of nine stained glass panels with arched tops, 27in. wide. (Sotheby's Belgravia) $1,260

TANKARDS

Art Deco cameo and stained glass window, circa 1930, 49½in. long. (Robert W. Skinner Inc.) $1,300

One of a set of four late 19th century stained glass panels, 16¼in. wide. (Sotheby's Belgravia) $410

18th century Central European enameled milchglas tankard painted in polychrome, 14.5cm. high. (Sotheby's) $485

Bohemian Hausmalerei opaque-opaline glass tankard and cover of barrel shape, circa 1750, 16.5cm. high.(Christie's) $1,515

Mid 18th century Bohemian enameled milchglas mug with convex body, 11cm. high. (Sotheby's) $485

Mid 18th century Bohemian enameled milchglas tankard, applied strap handle, 16cm. high. (Sotheby's) $605

Saxon dated cylindrical tankard with engraved body, dated 1763, 13.5cm. high. (Christie's) $1,010

Mid 18th century Bohemian enameled milchglas tankard with masonic symbols, 15cm. high. (Sotheby's) $305

440

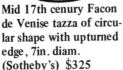

Unusual 16th/17th century turquoise tinted tazza with wide tray, 25cm. diam. (Sotheby's) $305

Mid 17th cenury Facon de Venise tazza of circular shape with upturned edge, 7in. diam. (Sotheby's) $325

16th/17th century Facon de Venise tazza of amber-tinted metal on blue-tinted base, 24cm. diam. (Sotheby's) $690

TUMBLERS

Early 18th century Bohemian evangelist's flared tumbler, engraved with four portraits, 10.5cm. high. (Christie's)$775

North Bohemian engraved and fluted waisted tumbler with everted lower part, circa 1840, 12cm. high. (Christie's)$910

French 'bleu lavende' opaline cylindrical tumbler gilt with a figure of Napoleon, circa 1825, 9cm. high. (Christie's) $335

Bohemian Zwischengold fluted dice tumbler in two parts, circa 1740, 8.5cm. high. (Christie's) $970

Early 18th century Bohemian glass engraved tumbler with slightly flared sides, 15.5cm. high. (Christie's) $555

Bohemian engraved tumbler attributed to Franz Gottstein, circa 1825, 10.5cm. high. (Christie's) $1,515

VASES

Loetz silver and iridescent glass oviform vase, signed, 11cm. high. (Christie's) $450

Early oviform locust vase in translucent opalescent glass, inscribed Lalique, France, 27cm. high. (Christie's) $1,440

Two-color cameo vase, circa 1880, in opaque white cut to blue, 10in. high. (Robert W. Skinner Inc.) $3,200

Daum etched and enamelled slender oviform vase, signed, 36cm. high. (Christie's) $1,235

One of a pair of 19th century Bohemian cranberry tinted glass vases with lustre drops, 12¼in. high. (Geering & Colyer) $795

Daum double overlay cameo glass vase, signed Daum Nancy, circa 1900, 13½in. high. (Sotheby's) $705

Attractive Austrian glass vase with short trumpet neck, circa 1900, 5¾in. high, sold with another. (Sotheby's) $375

Daum etched and enamelled vase of rectangular section, 11.7cm. high. (Christie's) $820

Early oviform locust vase in clear and frosted glass, inscribed R. Lalique, France, 27.5cm. high. (Christie's) $1,195

442

Early 20th century Tiffany
Favrile iridescent gold vase,
New York, 5½in. high.
(Robert W. Skinner Inc.)
$375

St. Louis shot vase on scram-
bled paperweight base, 8cm.
high. (Sotheby's) $700

Wheel carved and etched
boat-shaped vase by
Emile Galle, signed, 16cm.
wide. (Christie's)
$1,030

Vase from a late
19th century cran-
berry glass garniture
of four pieces with
enameled paintings.
(Sotheby's)
$500

Pair of George Jones pate-sur-
pate vases with white relief
decoration, 24cm. high, circa
1875. (Sotheby, King & Chasemore) $610

Green glass amphora
with trailed decora-
tion, 3rd century
A.D., 11½in. high.
(Christie's)
$1,560

Loetz gourd-shaped vase
with dimpled neck, 16cm.
high. (Christie's)
$225

Thick-walled flared cylindrical
vase with two broad loop handles,
engraved R. Lalique, France.
(Christie's) $1,235

Handel cameo glass
vase, circa 1920,
signed Mosher,
9¾in. high.
(Robert W. Skinner
Inc.) $400

443

GLASS

Tiffany paperweight aqua-marine vase, New York, circa 1910, 5in. diam. (Robert W. Skinner Inc.) $3,500

Cameo glass vase in topaz with white overlay, 11cm. high, 1880's, slightly chip-ped. (Sotheby's Belgravia) $800

Webb glass overlay vase, amber on clear glass, signed. (Capes, Dunn & Co.) $150

Legras cameo glass vase with gray glass body, circa 1900, 25.4cm. high. (Sotheby's Belgravia) $390

Galle cameo glass land-scape vase with original bronze light fitment, circa 1900, 24.75cm. high. (Sotheby's Belgravia) $800

Mid 19th century ruby overlay vase, 25.2cm. high. (Sotheby's Belgra-via) $190

Flared cylindrical vase, inscribed R. Lalique, France, 24.5cm. high. (Christie's) $825

One of a pair of Loetz iridescent glass vases of baluster form, inscribed Loetz, Austria, circa 1900, 9½in. high. (Woolley & Wallis) $1,575

Galle enameled amber glass vase with squat square body, 1890's, 16.5cm. high.(Sotheby's Belgravia) $1,515

One of a pair of amethyst tulip glasses with scaloped rims, circa 1845, 10in. high. (Robert W. Skinner Inc.) $725

Unusually decorated cameo glass vase, circa 1880. (Sotheby's Belgravia) $2,550

Loetz pale golden iridescent glass vase of spiraled triangular section, 20.8cm. high.(Christie's) $165

Multi-colored Peking glass brushpot of cylindrical shape, 12cm. high, on wood stand. (Sotheby, King & Chasemore) $170

Galle carved and applied glass vase with spiraling grooves, 1890's, signed, 27.5cm. high.(Sotheby's Belgravia) $1,780

Etched and polished internally decorated shaped oviform vase, incised Marinot, 13.5cm. high. (Christie's) $5,095

Galle cameo glass vase with teardrop body, signed, circa 1900, 26cm. high. (Sotheby's Belgravia) $1,245

Iridescent glass vase attributed to Loetz, circa 1900, 24.74cm. high. (Sotheby's Belgravia) $925

Cameo fire-polished double baluster vase with milky amber ground, 23.2cm. high. (Christie's) $1,365

445

Late 19th century miniature Tiffany blue iridescent vase of baluster form, 2¾in. high, signed. (Robert W. Skinner Inc.) $350

Legras winter landscape cameo vase of square section, signed, 11cm. high. (Phillips) $535

Early 20th century gold iridescent vase by Tiffany, New York, 3½in. high. (Robert W. Skinner Inc.) $425

Galle cameo glass 'landscape' vase of tapering cylindrical form, signed, 25cm. high. (Phillips) $1,005

Loetz iridescent glass vase with flared neck decorated with silver and pale blue banding, signed, 20cm. high. (Phillips) $715

Late 19th/early 20th century Webb cameo glass vase in blues and white, 13in. high. (Robert W. Skinner Inc.) $3,900

Late 19th century peachblow vase with coral decoration, 12in. high. (Robert W. Skinner Inc.) $250

Lalique vivid turquoise glass vase molded with budgerigars, signed, 25.5cm. high. (Phillips) $1,970

Galle cameo glass vase, signed, circa 1910, 12in. high. (Robert W. Skinner Inc.)$850

Walter pate-de-verre vase by Henri Berge, circa 1920, 18cm. high. (Sotheby, King & Chasemore) $3,050

Loetz iridescent glass vase of compressed form with silver colored metal rim, 10.5cm. high. (Phillips) $785

Moss agate vase by Steuben, Corning, New York, circa 1920, 10¾in. high. (Robert W. Skinner Ltd.) $800

Large late 19th/early 20th century Galle cameo glass vase, 23¼in. high. (Robert W. Skinner Inc.) $825

Daum cameo glass vase of goblet shape with three petals at rim, signed, 15cm. high. (Phillips) $1,215

Daum cameo glass vase of tall slender shape, applied with white wheel-cut with flowers, 33.5cm. high, signed. (Phillips)$1,255

Early 20th century etched and cut glass vase with flaring top and bottom. (Robert W. Skinner Inc.) $1,150

Webb 'ivory' cameo glass baluster vase in Oriental style, circa 1890, 14cm. high. (Christie's) $1,200

Late 19th century blue iridescent glass vase by Tiffany, New York, 11¾in. high. (Robert W. Skinner Inc.)$975

447

Unfinished cameo glass vase by J. B. Hill, signed, 1918, 11cm. high. (Sotheby's Belgravia) $290

Late 19th century cameo glass vase of globular form with short clear glass neck, 5.7cm. high. (Sotheby's Belgravia) $185

Yellow and black cameo vase with flared mouth, 10cm. high. (Sotheby's Belgravia) $625

One of a pair of green overlay vases with ovoid bodies, circa 1850, 35.8cm. high. (Sotheby's Belgravia) $1,225

Daum cameo glass vase of compressed conical shape, signed, 18.5cm. high. (Phillips) $930

French cameo glass vase, signed A. Delatte Nancy, circa 1925, 15in. high. (Sotheby Beresford Adams) $775

Double overlay cameo vase with flared neck, 1880's, 11.7cm. high. (Sotheby's Belgravia) $580

Unusual French iron and glass lamp in the form of a flower, signed Roby, Paris, circa 1900, 60cm. high. (Sotheby, King & Chasemore) $275

One of a pair of opaline enameled vases with flared necks, circa 1880, 46cm. high. (Sotheby's Belgravia) $705

Early 20th century Quezal iridescent Art Glass vase, New York, 12½in. high. (Robert W. Skinner Inc.) $550

Lalique opalescent vase with flat flared rim, France, circa 1925, 9in. high. (Robert W. Skinner Inc.) $375

Unusual early 20th century unfinished chinoiserie cameo glass vase in Art Nouveau style, 10cm. high. (Sotheby's Belgravia) $310

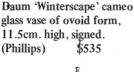

Eastern United States tall cut glass vase with ruffled rim, circa 1890, 16in. high. (Robert W. Skinner Inc.) $325

Daum 'Winterscape' cameo glass vase of ovoid form, 11.5cm. high, signed. (Phillips) $535

Late 19th century American cranberry overlay cut glass vase with scaloped top, 10in. high. (Robert W. Skinner Inc.) $200

Late 19th century cameo glass vase with pear-shaped body and flared neck, 11.7cm. high. (Sotheby's Belgravia) $580

One of a pair of portrait overlay vases, covers and stands, mid 19th century, 63cm. high. (Sotheby's Belgravia)$3,015

One of a pair of mid 19th century enameled gray glass vases, with shouldered ovoid bodies, 41.4cm. high. (Sotheby's Belgravia) $205

449

One of a set of twelve late 19th century two-color brilliant cut champagne glasses, American, 4½in. high. (Robert W. Skinner Inc.) $600

Beilby Masonic firing glass, ogee bowl enameled in white and iron-red, circa 1770, 8cm. high. (Christie's) $1,565

One of four late 19th century two-color cut glass wine glasses, American, 4½in. high. (Robert W. Skinner Inc.) $850

Engraved color twist wine glass, ogee bowl with border of fruiting vine, circa 1770, 15cm. high. (Christie's) $275

Mixed twist wine glass with waisted bucket bowl, on conical foot, circa 1760, 17cm. high. (Christie's) $240

Beilby opaque twist wine glass, funnel bowl enameled in white, circa 1765, 15.5cm. high. (Christie's) $890

Facet stemmed dated wine glass with inscribed bowl, 1752, 16cm. high. (Christie's) $110

Mead glass with bucket bowl having gadrooned lower part, circa 1715, 15cm. high. (Christie's) $480

Beilby opaque twist wine glass, funnel bowl enameled in white, circa 1765, 15cm. high. (Christie's) $925

One of ten American cut glass wine glasses with knopped stems, circa 1910, 4in. high.(Robert W. Skinner Inc.)$75

Heavy baluster toast-master's glass with thick funnel bowl, circa 1700, 13.5cm. high.(Christie's) $260

One of four late 19th century American two-color cranberry cut glass wine glasses, 5in. high.(Robert W. Skinner Inc.) $250

Balustroid wine glass of drawn trumpet shape, circa 1745, 16cm. high. (Christie's) $165

Opaque twist champagne glass with double ogee bowl, circa 1770, 15.5cm. high. (Christie's) $275

Dutch engraved wine glass on inverted baluster stem, circa 1740, 17cm. high. (Christie's) $295

One of six late 19th century American green overlay cut glass liqueur glasses, 5¼in. high, on long stems. (Robert W. Skinner Inc.) $175

Baluster wine glass with bell bowl supported on a cushion knop, circa 1720, 16cm. high. (Christie's) $370

Lynn opaque twist wine glass, funnel bowl molded with horizontal ribs, circa 1770, 14.5cm. high. (Christie's) $260

451

One of a rare set of six wine glasses with round funnel bowls, 14cm. high. (Phillips) $665

One of a set of six wine glasses with bell bowls, 17cm. high. (Phillips) $1,110

Baluster deceptive glass with thick trumpet bowl, circa 1710, 5in. high. (Sotheby's) $450

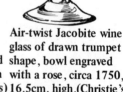

Engraved air-twist wine glass of Jacobite significance, circa 1750, 15cm. high. (Christie's)$390

Opaque twist cordial glass, funnel bowl with hammered flutes, on conical foot, circa 1765, 16cm. high.(Christie's) $185

Air-twist Jacobite wine glass of drawn trumpet shape, bowl engraved with a rose, circa 1750, 16.5cm. high.(Christie's) $220

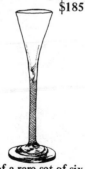

Beilby enameled wine glass with petal-molded bowl, circa 1770, 5in. high. (Sotheby's) $825

One of a rare set of six slender toasting glasses on conical feet, 19cm. high. (Phillips) $1,390

Engraved cordial wine glass with small funnel bowl, circa 1750, 6¾in. high. (Sotheby's) $165

Baluster wine glass of dark brilliant metal on domed and folded foot, circa 1700, 5¾in. high. (Sotheby's) $780

17th century Lowlands diamond Facon de Venise wine glass, 14cm. high. (Sotheby's) $185

Dutch-engraved Newcastle glass decorated in the manner of Jacob Sang, circa 1745-55, 7½in. high. (Sotheby's)$1,440

Color-twist wine glass with funnel bowl, on conical foot, circa 1770, 15.5cm. high. (Christie's) $370

Jacobite wine glass with engraved flared bowl, circa 1750, 7in. high. (Sotheby's) $575

Color-twist wine glass with waisted bucket bowl, circa 1770, 5¾in. high. (Sotheby's) $945

Wine glass with cylinder knop, circa 1700, 6in. high, with flared bowl. (Sotheby's)$2,055

Cordial glass with small bucket bowl, circa 1770, 7in. high, with corkscrew stem. (Sotheby's)$195

Chinoiserie wine glass with ogee bowl, on facet-cut stem, circa 1780, 6in. high. (Sotheby's)$245

French two-color gold and tortoiseshell powder box, Paris, 1789-92, 6.1cm. diam. (Sotheby's) $1,805

18kt. gold engine-turned snuff box by Daniel Hockly, London, 1819, 3in. long. (Christie's) $1,480

Victorian gold apple pomander with leaf ring lid, 1½in. high. (Woolley & Wallis) $595

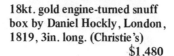

14kt. yellow gold mesh purse with engraved frame, cabochon garnet clasp and a pencil attached to side. (Robert W. Skinner Inc.) $800

Gold mounted whip, handle formed as a swan's head, 19th century, sold with another. (Christie's) $480

18kt. French Art Deco gold powder compact by Chaumet, 1923, 3¼in. long. (Christie's) $1,415

Louis XVI oval gold and enamel snuff box by Joseph Etienne Blerzy, Paris, 1776, 3¼in. wide. (Christie's) $20,790

Early 19th century French gold mounted glass scent bottle, 3.2cm. wide. (Sotheby's) $235

19th century Swiss diamond set rectangular gold snuff box, 3½in. long. (Christie's) $3,535

GOLD

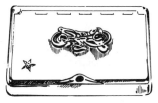

Gold buckle by Myer Myers, New York, circa 1765. (Sotheby's) $10,000

Gold and hardstone necessaire of rectangular form, circa 1760, 5cm. high, restored. (Sotheby's) $3,395

Gold cigarette case by Faberge, St. Petersburg, 1899-1908, 8.7cm. wide. (Sotheby's) $2,760

9kt. gold guard chain with four girdled links, 22cm. long overall. (Sotheby Beresford Adams) $280

Large gold mounted scent bottle, probably Portuguese, 5in. long, circa 1780. (Christie's) $660

9kt. gold vesta case, Birmingham, 1920, and an 18kt. gold and platinum guard chain, 44mm. diam. (Sotheby Beresford Adams) $205

Gold Art Nouveau brooch with rose-diamonds, in the style of Boucheron, circa 1900. (Locke & England)$1,455

18kt. gold mounted ornament with pink hardstone base, 21.5cm. long, 1979.(Sotheby's Belgravia) $825

Oblong gold Royal presentation cigarette case, London, 1886, 3¼in. long.(Christie's) $1,230

HARDSTONE

Silver gilt and hardstone snuff box, French, circa 1740, 7.7cm. wide. (Sotheby's) $610

Small English gold and hardstone vinaigrette, late 18th century, ¾in. wide. (Sotheby's) $295

A solid agate silver shaped sauceboat. (Christie's) $3,500

A striated fluorspar flattened baluster vase and cover with dragon finial, 14cm. high. (Christie's) $1,150

Guangxu hardstone flowering shrub in cloisonne jardiniere, 61cm. high. (Sotheby's Belgravia) $725

George III circular gold mounted gray agate toilet box and cover, circa 1800, 5in. high.(Christie's) $7,485

Solid agate pectin shell teapot and cover, 16cm. high. (Christie's) $1,250

Early 20th century Austrian or Hungarian agate bon bon dish with gem-set mounts, 9.1cm. diam. (Sotheby's Belgravia) $745

A malachite group of two ladies, one standing, one seated, 20cm. high. (Christie's) $2,400

18th century rhinoceros horn libation cup with handle, 15.5cm. wide. (Christie's) $575

Guangxu carved rhinoceros horn on rosewood stand, 55cm. wide. (Sotheby's Belgravia) $790

19th century Japanese rhinoceros horn cup in the shape of a lily pad, 5¾in. long. (Robert W. Skinner Inc.) $1,400

18th century rhinoceros horn bowl of honey color, 18cm. wide. (Christie's) $810

Good stagshorn sashi netsuke showing Ashinaga, signed Isshin. (Sotheby's)$605

19th century Japanese rhinoceros horn cup with flared rim, 4in. high. (Robert W. Skinner Inc.) $1,550

17th century rhinoceros horn libation cup carved with dragons, 17cm. wide. (Christie's) $470

19th century carved horn, pierced with immortals amongst trees, on rosewood stand, 74cm. wide.(Sotheby's Belgravia) $845

19th century Japanese rhinoceros horn cup with flaring top, 4in. high. (Robert W. Skinner Inc.) $800

Small 19th century inro
of two cases, carved in
low relief, unsigned,
slightly cracked.(Sotheby's)
$545

Single-case inro of natural
wood, decorated in col-
ored takamakie, signed
Toshie. (Sotheby's)$530

Small 18th century three-
case inro decorated with
butterflies among plants,
unsigned. (Sotheby's)
$560

Small 18th century five-
case inro decorated in
gold and silver takamakie,
chipped, unsigned.
(Sotheby's) $820

18th century four-case inro
decorated with travelers in
a boat, unsigned.(Sotheby's)
$705

Late 18th century small
four-case inro of cylin-
drical form, unsigned.
(Sotheby's) $370

Very good five-case inro
of tall shape, decorated
with gold takamakie,
signed Kajikawa Bunry-
usai. (Sotheby's)
$3,640

Small late 18th/early 19th
century two-case inro
decorated in pewter, unsigned. (Sotheby's)$315

19th century Hirado
porcelain inro of
four cases, unmarked.
(Sotheby's)$550

19th century three-case inro of wood, carved with two panels, unsigned, sold with a wood netsuke. (Sotheby's) $325

18th century single-case inro of wide oval shape, brown-ground decorated with shell-gatherers, unsigned.(Sotheby's) $590

Four-case inro of dark-brown-ground with falling cherry blossoms, signed Inagawa saku. (Sotheby's)$985

Late 18th century gold lacquer inro of five cases, decorated in gold takamakie, hiramakie and kirigane, unsigned. (Sotheby's) $745

Unusual 18th century three-case inro of gold and black lacquer, unsigned. (Sotheby's) $630

Four-case inro of roun-ded form, signed Shokosai, slight chips. (Sotheby's)$690

Early 18th century four-case inro decorated with three sages, unsig-ned. (Sotheby's) $325

Unusual two-case inro deco-rated with fish and waves, chipped, signed Kyukoku with kakihan. (Sotheby's) $985

Four-case inro, signed Kajikawa saku with red pot seal.(Sotheby's) $590

INSTRUMENTS

Captain George's R.N. patent double sextant by Elliott Bros., London, 12.5cm. diam. (Phillips) $810

19th century brass four-draw telescope with mahogany outer tube. (Phillips) $155

Late 19th century J. T. Letcher oxidised brass Henderson dial, magnetic compass 5½in. diam. (Sotheby Bearne) $430

Early brass microscope of Culpepper design, in tapering mahogany case, 32.5cm. high. (Phillips) $680

Late 19th century mechanical bellows in black painted cast iron and brass, 23½in. high. (Sotheby Beresford Adams) $170

Ebony and brass mounted octant by Cary of London, with ivory scale and nameplate. (Phillips)$625

19th century gilt metal pocket compass in the form of a watch by Webb, London, 5.5cm. diam. (Phillips) $90

Late 19th century English Sewell brass sextant with silvered scale and vernier, 8½in. radius. (Sotheby Beresford Adams)$160

19th century miniature terrestrial globe, 3cm. diam., in green painted cylindrical case and cover. (Phillips) $295

Mid 19th century post-mortem set, inscribed Place & Co., in fitted mahogany case. (Sotheby Beresford Adams) $230

19th century six-draw monocular telescope by I. Abraham, Bath, outer tube inlaid with mother-of-pearl. (Phillips) $155

Brass box sextant by Elliot Bros., in drum-shaped case, 7.5cm. high. (Phillips) $165

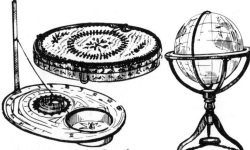

19th century Russian universal equinoctial dial by Mills of Petersberg, 9.5cm. (Phillips) $535

17th century universal pocket sundial by Pierre Norry, Gisors, 7cm. long, in original tooled leather case. (Phillips) $3,130

Mahogany terrestrial globe by E. Stanford, dated 1878, 23in. diam. (Sotheby's Belgravia) $1,655

Early 19th century brass theodolite of small size, by W. & S. Jones, London. (Phillips) $1,215

17th century ivory German diptych dial, dated 1650, with the trade mark of Leonhardt Mire of Nuremberg. (Phillips) $3,405

Mid 19th century English pocket sextant by W. & S. Jones, 3in. diam. (Sotheby Beresford Adams) $215

INSTRUMENTS

Early 20th century French brass sextant, inscribed A. J. Fortier, Havre, 9½in. radius. (Sotheby's) $355

Early 19th century brass plotting protractor, signed Troughton, London, 16cm. diam. (Phillips) $390

Early 19th century American scrimshaw jagging wheel in the form of a horse's head, 6in. long. (Robert W. Skinner Inc.) $550

17th/18th century surgeon's iron brace with turned head, 8½in. long. (Christie's S. Kensington) $1,080

Marconiphone television model 705, 1940's, 36¾in. wide, in walnut veneered cabinet with hinged lid. (Sotheby's Belgravia) $480

Right hand precision bench lathe by F. Lorche on cast iron frame. (Sotheby's) $320

Victorian brass monocular microscope. (Cooper Hirst) $290

Set of brass drawing instruments by Rowney & Co., with boxwood and ivory rules, 25.5cm. wide. (Phillips) $100

Rare 2¾in. 'Silex Multiplier' spinning reel, stamped D.W., with ebonite handle. (Sotheby's) $455

Late 18th century micro-
scope specimen slicer in
original mahogany box,
by A. Cumming, London,
(H. Spencer & Sons Ltd.)
$4,185

Unusual narrow-drum
'perfect' trout reel of
aluminium and brass,
marked Hardy Bros.
Alnwick. (Sotheby's)
$415

Electric fan heater, designed by Wells Coates,
1930's, 29.5cm. high.
(Sotheby's Belgravia)
$195

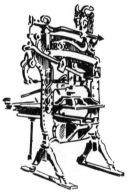

Late 19th century Adco
false tooth vulcanizer
with cast iron shell, 24¾in.
high. (Sotheby's)$145

Mid 19th century monocu-
lar microscope in fitted
mahogany case, 13in. high,
with two boxes of slides.
(Sotheby's) $185

Columbian printing press
with cast iron caduceus
frame, eagle and dolphin
counterweight, 1820,
91in. high. (Sotheby's
Belgravia)$5,150

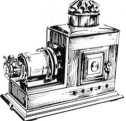

French drum microscope,
inscribed Nachet, Paris,
circa 1850, 9in. high.
(Sotheby's) $165

Late 19th century maho-
gany and brass magic lan-
tern with tinplate chim-
ney above. (Sotheby's)
$270

Late 19th century mech-
anical bellows of black
painted iron construction,
20in. high. (Sotheby's)
$250

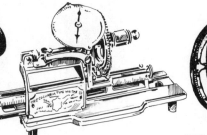

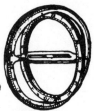

19th century six-draw monocular by Gilbert, London, with carved ivory decoration, 10cm. fully extended.(Phillips) $110

Columbia typewriter with circular dial and maker's plaque at front, circa 1895, 9¾in. wide. (Sotheby's Belgravia) $1,470

17th/18th century brass universal equin-octial ring dial, unsig-ned, 14.8cm. diam. (Phillips) $970

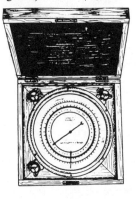

Pocket compass by Jeremias Koglet, Danzig, 1680, 7cm wide. (Phillips) $785

19th century brass com-pound pocket microscope, unsigned, 16.3cm. wide. (Phillips) $300

19th century brass Lords Patent calculator by W. Wilson, London, 32cm. square. (Phillips)$390

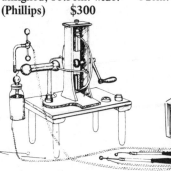

Mahogany framed plate electrical machine, unsigned, 36cm. wide. (Phillips) $505

Eight-day marine chrono-meter by Duncan McGre-gor & Co., Glasgow, 145mm. diam. (Sotheby's)$3,325

Late 19th century set of Avery scales and seven brass weights, 31in. high.(Sotheby's) $270

INSTRUMENTS

17th century brass ring dial by J. Stammer, Sacrow, 80mm. diam. (Sotheby's) **$1,560**

Early 19th century brass ellipsograph by Farey of London, in original case, 165mm. long.(Sotheby's) **$1,080**

Ferguson's terrestrial globe inscribed G. Wright, 17in. diam. (Woolley & Wallis) **$890**

Mid 19th century Smith & Beck brass monocular microscope, 12½in. high, in mahogany case. (Sotheby's Belgravia) **$295**

Columbia typewriter No. 2, circa 1885, in original wooden carrying case. (Sotheby's Belgravia) **$2,760**

Brass compound monocular microscope by Ross, London, 44.5cm. high.(Phillips) **$935**

18th/19th century brass Islamic celestial globe, 84mm. diam. (Sotheby's) **$2,080**

Two-day marine chronometer by Breguet & Cie, 16cm. square. (Phillips)   **$5,480**

Shaped ivory spy-glass with silver mounts and dust cap, 5.4cm. diam. (Phillips) **$120**

Mid 19th century Troughton & Simms brass level with 3in. diam. compass, 15in. long. (Sotheby's Belgravia) $290

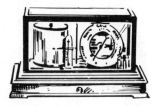

Early 20th century oak cased aneroid barometer with skeleton chapter ring, 14in. wide. (Sotheby's) $440

Early 19th century chart template signed James Wright, London, 13in. long. (Phillips) $1,345

19th century Roth's Adding Machine, marked Wertheimber Patentee, 39cm. long. (Phillips) $485

American typewriter by Merritt, No. 12095, 12¼in. wide, circa 1895, on oak base. (Sotheby's Belgravia) $1,015

John Browning brass spectroscope with refracting prism, telescope, 15in. long. (Sotheby's Belgravia) $575

Mid 19th century brass level by F. Day, London, 19in. long, in mahogany case. (Sotheby's Belgravia) $325

William's No. 2 typewriter with grass-hopper mechanism, circa 1894, 14½in. long. (Sotheby's Belgravia) $515

INSTRUMENTS

Steelyard letter scale with brass beam, circa 1840, 13in. high overall. (Sotheby's) $335

George III swan-necked beam scale with wooden overhead platform and a 19¾in. wooden yard. (Eldon E. Worrall & Co.) $330

Mahogany and brass spirit level by J. Pallant, London, 2ft. long. (Phillips) $255

Georgian brass camera Lucida by Watkins & Hill, London, with table screw and clamp. (Phillips) $205

Early 19th century 2½in. James Watson brass Gregorian reflecting telescope on stand, 11in. long. (Sotheby's Belgravia) $810

Unusual early 20th century set of four graduated brass beam scales. (Sotheby's Belgravia) $385

Early 20th century brass Post Office letter scale, 10in. long, with five weights. (Sotheby's) $250

Roberval type brass letter scale by S. Mordan & Co., circa 1871, 8½in. long. (Sotheby's) $110

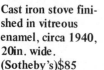

Cast iron stove finished in vitreous enamel, circa 1940, 20in. wide. (Sotheby's)$85

Iron group of two horses by P. J. Mene, signed, 21in. long. (Sotheby, King & Chasemore) $1,675

Late 19th century Komai iron box and cover, inlaid with gold and silver, 9cm. high. (Sotheby's Belgravia) $975

Rare 17th century German miniature iron sword pommel of Hercules and the Hydra, 5.5cm. high.(Christie's) $2,110

Komai inlaid iron incense chest with inlaid panels, circa 1900, 8cm. high. (Sotheby's Belgravia) $850

One of a pair of mid 19th century cast iron garden urns of campana form, 30in. high. (Sotheby's) $1,045

French cast iron stove finished in mid brown vitreous enamel, circa 1920, 20in. square. (Sotheby's) $85

Early 18th century American wrought iron pipe kiln, 13½in. long. (Robert W. Skinner Inc.) $350

17th century iron strong box, 30in. wide. (J. M. Welch & Son) $1,365

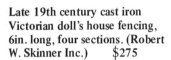

Early 19th century steel footman, pierced with scroll and star design, 14½in. high. (Lawrence Fine Art)$165

Late 19th century cast iron Victorian doll's house fencing, 6in. long, four sections. (Robert W. Skinner Inc.) $275

18th century pair of French steel and brass cresset spit dogs, 28in. high. (Robert W. Skinner Inc.) $200

Iron model of a pointer after Mene, 7½in. high. (Sotheby, King & Chasemore) $445

One of a pair of 15th/16th century wrought iron pricket candlesticks, 19in. high. (Christie's) $840

Iron group of a cow and suckling bullock, 8¾in. wide. (Sotheby King & Chasemore) $145

Salamandre cast iron stove finished in mid green vitreous enamel, circa 1900, 23½in. wide. (Sotheby's) $250

Late 17th century iron 'Armada' chest with key, 3ft.7in. wide. (J. M. Welch & Son) $875

Iron model of an ostrich, 3¼in. high. (Sotheby, King & Chasemore) $100

Mid 19th century French ivory group of two children, on gilt metal base, 9.5cm. high. (Sotheby's Belgravia) $455

Carved ivory bird catcher, Japanese, circa 1900, 10¾in. long, slightly cracked. (Robert W. Skinner Inc.) $625

Japanese carved ivory figure of a peasant, 12¼in. high, unsigned, circa 1900.(Sotheby's) $1,000

Mid 19th century French ivory figure of a tinker carrying a basket, 13.8cm. high. (Sotheby's Belgravia) $745

Large mid 19th century French ivory group of Bacchus and two nymphs and three children, 30cm. long. (Sotheby's Belgravia) $8,270

Mid/late 19th century German ivory standing cup and cover carved with hunting scenes, 49.5cm. high.(Sotheby's Belgravia) $4,135

Early 19th century teak and ivory crucifix, 28½in. long. (Robert W. Skinner Inc.) $350

Rare 19th century English chess set in red and natural, 4.5cm. to 10cm. high. (Sotheby's Belgravia) $745

Mid 17th century Flemish ivory group of a woman and two children. (Sotheby's) $26,880

470

One of a pair of 19th century Dieppe ivory candlesticks on circular bases, 9in. high. (Christie's)$890

French ivory group of Venus and Cupid, 1870's, 24.7cm. long. (Sotheby's Belgravia) $660

Japanese carved ivory figure of a peasant, circa 1900, 8¾in. high. (Sotheby's) $330

Dieppe ivory figure of a young girl feeding doves and farmyard animals, circa 1895, 14cm. high. (Sotheby's Belgravia) $1,200

Late 19th century French carved ivory figure of Cupid, 16cm. high. (Sotheby's Belgravia) $785

Late 19th century carved figure of a naked nymph, 18.5cm. high. (Sotheby's Belgravia) $455

Ivory tankard with silver gilt mounts, 17th century, 28.5cm. high. (Sotheby's Belgravia) $3,720

One of a pair of late 19th century figures of Courtiers, 9.5cm. high. (Sotheby's Belgravia) $660

Chinese stained ivory group of a fourteen-armed female Boddhisattva, late 19th century, 65.5cm. high. (Christie's) $2,880

Good ivory figure of a cook, signed Homin with kakihan. (Sotheby's) $335

Late 18th/early 19th century ivory study of a monkey seated on a large gunsen uchiwa, unsigned. (Sotheby's) $780

Ivory figure of a young child by F. Preiss, inscribed, 9cm. high. (Christie's) $615

19th century Japanese carved ivory flowering narcissus bulbs, signed, slightly damaged, 7¾in. high. (Robert W. Skinner Inc.) $260

Fine 19th century French ivory oliphant carved with portraits of kings, 69cm. long. (H. Spencer & Sons Ltd.) $630

Attractive ivory group of four boys, signed, circa 1880-90, 3in. high. (Sotheby, King & Chasemore) $575

17th century German ivory statuette of the infant Bacchus, 16cm. high. (Christie's) $1,585

19th century Japanese carved ivory basket vendor, with inlay decoration, 7¼in. high. (Robert W. Skinner Inc.) $1,000

17th century Goanese ivory statuette of the sleeping Christ Child on carved base, 38.5cm. high. (Christie's) $1,690

IVORY

Ivory model 'Thoughts', carved from a model by F. Preiss, on green and black onyx base, 15.8cm. high. (Christie's) $2,675

18th century Austrian rococo ivory half-length statuette on boxwood base, 15cm. high. (Christie's)$1,690

Good Komezawa ivory figure of Hotei, signed, 4in. high. (Sotheby, King & Chasemore) $670

18th century ivory figure of Gama Sennin, of the Kyoto school, unsigned. (Sotheby's) $355

One of a pair of late 19th century carved ivory figures of goddesses, 8¾in. high. (Sotheby Beresford Adams) $620

One of a pair of early 20th century Chinese carved ivory goddesses, 12¼in. high. (Robert W. Skinner Inc.) $575

Ivory group of Ebisu, holding a large carp, 5¼in. high, circa 1900. (Sotheby, King & Chasemore) $595

Early 18th century Dutch ivory handled carving knife and fork with steel blades. (Sotheby's) $570

18th century French or German ivory group of a satyr abducting a nymph, 16cm. high. (Christie's)$1,585

Ivory okimono of a rat and some nuts, circa 1900, 3in. high.(Sotheby's) $250

Anglo-Indian coromandel-wood workbox inlaid with ivory, circa 1830, 15in. wide. (Sotheby, King & Chasemore) $345

20th century ivory figure of a horse on a rectangular base, 36cm. wide.(Sotheby's Belgravia) $680

Early 18th century Northern French ivory snuff rasp carved in relief, 7½in. high. (Sotheby's) $455

Flemish ivory group of the Virgin and Child and St. John, circa 1650, 12½in. high. (Sotheby's) $29,105

17th century Flemish ivory crucifix figure, 16¼in. high. (Sotheby's) $2,600

Early 20th century ivory figure of an Immortal with a fishing rod, 34cm. high. (Sotheby's Belgravia) $300

Pair of 18th century North Italian fruitwood and ivory Commedia Dell'Arte figures, 11in. high. (Sotheby's) $2,910

One of a set of four 17th/18th century ivory carvings of bearded Daoist immortals, 28cm. high. (Christie's)$2,015

IVORY

Small ivory group of Kanzan and Jittoku with good detail, signed Yoshitomo. (Sotheby's) $345

German ivory snuff box of cartouche shape, circa 1730, with silver mounts, 7.8cm. wide. (Sotheby's) $1,320

Small early 19th century ivory netsuke of a dog with a large ball, unsigned. (Sotheby's) $345

Ivory figure of a nude young woman, inscribed F. Preiss, 23cm. high. (Christie's) $2,015

Early 18th century ivory head of one of the Three Fates, inspired by Michelangelo, mounted as a seal. (Sotheby's) $580

Unusual Guangxu ivory acrobatic group of four articulated figures, 12.5cm. high. (Sotheby's Belgravia) $320

19th century engraved scrimshaw whale's tooth, 7in. high.(Robert W. Skinner Inc.) $300

Indian ivory carving of a female divinity, circa 1900, 9in. high. (Sotheby's) $375

Early 18th century Franco-Flemish ivory river god, plinth of brass inlaid with bone. (Sotheby's) $3,430

JADE

18th century pale celadon jade bowl with dragon head handles, 22cm. wide. (Christie's) $15,760

18th century mottled white jade pebble carved as a deer, with wood stand, 9cm. wide. (Christie's) $3,990

Rare Shang/Western Zhou dynasty jade deer pendant of flattened form, 4.1cm. long. (Sotheby's)$4,320

Han dynasty jade carving of a pig of flattened cylindrical form, 11.2cm. long. (Sotheby's) $3,085

Mottled celadon and brown jade rectangular table screen, wood stand, 21.2cm. wide. (Christie's) $945

18th century pale jade cylindrical brush-holder, carved in cameo, 11.5cm. high. (Christie's) $10,085

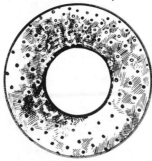

Zhou dynasty archaic celadon and brown jade disc carved on each side, 13.5cm. diam. (Christie's)$1,680

Late Ming dynasty grayish celadon jade mythical beast, wood stand, 10cm. long. (Christie's) $840

Small Ming dynasty mottled jade group of a horse and a monkey, 6cm. long. (Christie's) $5,885

Pale celadon jade bowl carved with dragons, with inverted rim, 1774, 15.5cm. diam. (Christie's)
$18,910

Western Zhou dynasty green jade fish pendant with incised eyes, 4.2cm. long. (Sotheby's) $660

Song dynasty pale celadon and mottled brown jade figure of a tiger, with wood stand, 6.9cm. long. (Christie's)
$3,360

Late 18th century celadon jade chrysanthemum pierced bowl and cover, 14.5cm. wide. (Christie's)
$2,100

Large 17th century grayish-celadon jade boulder carved and pierced in high relief, 31.3cm. high. (Christie's)
$14,705

19th century yellowish celadon jade group carved and pierced as three peaches, 9cm. wide. (Christie's)$840

Zhou dynasty pale celadon jade disc carved on both sides, 15.5cm. diam. (Christie's) $1,785

Oval ruby and diamond cluster ring in white gold setting. (Hy. Duke & Son) $715

Gold and diamond brooch/pendant of scroll form, set with six diamonds and a center pearl. (Robert W. Skinner Inc.) $325

Two row diamond set crescent brooch, in graduated sizes. (Geering & Colyer) $1,655

Victorian gold and enamel bangle bracelet, ½in. wide, 21gm. (Robert W. Skinner Inc.) $275

Diamond and platinum circle pin set with eighteen round and eighteen baguette diamonds. (Robert W. Skinner Inc.) $1,800

Arts and Crafts pendant possibly by Professor Joseph A. Hodel, 1.5cm. across. (Phillips) $145

Gold vari-colored enameled openwork pendant with pearl tassel fringe, by Carlo Giuliano. (Christie's S. Kensington) $1,955

Strand of sapphire beads with 14 karat white gold clasp, 18½in. long. (Robert W. Skinner Inc.) $525

Art Nouveau silver plique-a-jour pearl pendant, French, on silver chain. (Robert W. Skinner Inc.) $800

478

Square emerald set with diamond surrounds in 18 karat white gold. (Honiton Galleries) $5,550

Oval sapphire and diamond cluster ring in white gold setting. (Hy. Duke & Son) $655

Two-color gold set fire opal, diamond, sapphire, emerald and ruby crested kingfisher brooch by Cartier, signed. (Geering & Colyer) $1,610

Diamond and baguette diamond openwork plaque bracelet. (Christie's S. Kensington) $4,230

Diamond and platinum bracelet set with sixteen round diamonds. (Robert W. Skinner Inc.) $750

14 karat yellow gold chain, composed of alternating textured arrow and oval links, circa 1900, 22in. long. (Robert W. Skinner Inc.) $275

Art Nouveau pearl and enamel pendant, circa 1900, slightly damaged. (Robert W. Skinner Inc.) $90

Snake bracelet in green and white enamel on silver. (Robert W. Skinner Inc.) $300

Swiss gold and enamel brooch watch, 32mm. long. (Christie's) $5,235

479

Sapphire and diamond clip of mitre shape, circa 1930, pierced and pave-set.(Sotheby's) $1,870

Victorian pearl and peridot necklace on 15kt. gold chain. (Lawrence Fine Art) $520

Jade, diamond and emerald pendant within a gold and platinum frame with pearl drop. (Sotheby's) $1,385

Emerald and diamond bracelet designed as two tonneau-shaped panels. (Sotheby's) $20,790

Victorian diamond tiara of scrolling form, in fitted case from Carrington & Co. (Lawrence Fine Art) $4,055

Jade and diamond brooch of oblong shape. (Sotheby's) $2,175

Diamond brooch designed as a posy of ribbons and flowers, one stone missing. (Sotheby's)$2,090

15kt. gold, pearl and peridot pendant on fine gold neck chain. (Sotheby Beresford Adams) $405

Diamond brooch in the form of an inverted crescent, in gold and silver setting. (Sotheby's) $1,110

480

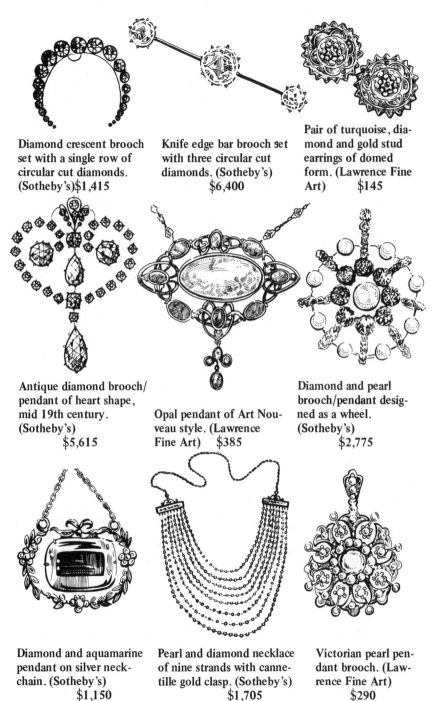

Diamond crescent brooch set with a single row of circular cut diamonds. (Sotheby's)$1,415

Knife edge bar brooch set with three circular cut diamonds. (Sotheby's) $6,400

Pair of turquoise, diamond and gold stud earrings of domed form. (Lawrence Fine Art) $145

Antique diamond brooch/ pendant of heart shape, mid 19th century. (Sotheby's) $5,615

Opal pendant of Art Nouveau style. (Lawrence Fine Art) $385

Diamond and pearl brooch/pendant designed as a wheel. (Sotheby's) $2,775

Diamond and aquamarine pendant on silver neckchain. (Sotheby's) $1,150

Pearl and diamond necklace of nine strands with cannetille gold clasp. (Sotheby's) $1,705

Victorian pearl pendant brooch. (Lawrence Fine Art) $290

LAMPS

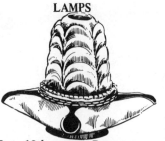

Handel reverse painted and patinated metal table lamp, Meriden, circa 1930, 20½in. high. (Robert W. Skinner Inc.) $400

Late 19th century Burmese fairy lamp by Mt. Washington Glass Co., 6in. high. (Robert W. Skinner Inc.) $150

Miniature American satin glass 'Gone with the Wind' lamp, circa 1880, 8½in. high. (Robert W. Skinner Inc.) $250

Galle cameo glass table lamp signed on shade and base, 52cm. high. (Phillips) $6,445

One of a pair of late 19th century bronze and Favrile glass candlesticks with shades, by Tiffany Studios, New York, 12in. high. (Robert W. Skinner Inc.) $1,550

Le Verre Francais cameo glass table lamp with conical shade, signed, 37.5cm. high. (Phillips) $1,255

Miniature American cranberry glass lamp with molded dot and panel shade and font, circa 1880, 9½in. high. (Robert W. Skinner Inc.) $325

Galle cameo glass circular hanging lampshade of shallow domed form, signed, 44cm. diam. (Phillips) $3,220

Miniature American porcelain lamp with globe-shaped opalescent white shade, circa 1880, 9¼in. high. (Robert W. Skinner Inc.) $125

482

Miniature American 'Gone with the Wind' lamp with cranberry coin spot shade and font, circa 1880, 8¼in. high. (Robert W. Skinner Inc.) $200

19th century Chinese champ-leve opaque enamel on bronze lamp base and shade, 20½in. high. (Robert W. Skinner Inc.) $400

Miniature mauve satin glass lamp with half shade, circa 1880, 7in. high. (Robert W. Skinner Inc.) $225

Galle cameo glass table lamp with domed shade, signed, 42cm. high. (Phillips)$6,445

One of a pair of parcel gilt candelabra, circa 1850, 30½in. high. (Sotheby's Belgravia) $790

Tiffany Studios 'Nautilus' gilt bronze table lamp in-set with mother-of-pearl studs, 33.5cm. high. (Phillips) $2,505

Pairpoint reverse painted glass and brass table lamp with signed shade, circa 1920, 23½in. high. (Robert W. Skinner Inc.) $1,500

Daum cameo glass hanging lampshade, acid etched with branches around rim, signed, 45cm. diam. (Phillips) $1,180

Early 20th century Pair-point bronze and reverse painted table lamp, 23in. high.(Robert W. Skinner Inc.) $1,150

LAMPS

Queen's Burmese fairy lamp by Thos. Webb & Sons, circa 1902, with domed shade, 5¼in. high. (Robert W. Skinner Inc.) $300

Fulper pottery lamp, Flemington, New Jersey, circa 1900-10. (Robert W. Skinner Inc.) $550

Mid 19th century Bulpitt & Sons brass lantern with cylindrical funnel and swing handle, 20in. high. (Sotheby's) $150

Miniature American opaque blue lamp, shade in overlapping leaf motif, circa 1880. (Robert W. Skinner Inc.) $75

Art Deco piano lamp, amber shade with floral motif supported by a bronze nude, on green marble base, circa 1925, 14½in. long. (Robert W. Skinner Inc.) $375

Miniature American cranberry thumbprint lamp with half shade, circa 1880, 7½in. high.(Robert W. Skinner Inc.) $160

Handel reverse painted and painted metal table lamp, no. 712, circa 1920, 23½in. high. (Robert W. Skinner Inc.) $2,400

Tall oil lamp with brass fluted column stem, 28in. high, with glass shade. (Dickinson, Davy & Markham) $160

Handel bronze and reverse painted table lamp, 24½in. high. (Robert W. Skinner Inc.) $1,900

LAMPS

Acorn leaded glass and bronze table lamp by Tiffany Studios, 47cm. high. (Christie's) $1,850

Austrian glass and gilt bronze lamp in the form of a peacock, circa 1920, 16in. long. (Sotheby's Belgravia) $1,050

One of a pair of late 19th/early 20th century brass carriage side lamps, 15in. high. (Sotheby's)$130

Tall oil lamp with embossed metal base, green glass reservoir, 24in. high.(Dickinson, Davy & Markham) $65

20th century American bronze table lamp in the form of a peacock, 16½in. high.(Robert W. Skinner Inc.) $100

Bronze and cameo glass table lamp by G. Raspellier, signed, 53cm. high.(Christie's) $4,115

American half shade table lamp by Bradley & Hubbard, circa 1870, 20in. high. (Robert W. Skinner Inc.) $180

Miniature American opalescent 'Gone with the Wind' lamp on square base, circa 1880, 8¼in. high. (Robert W. Skinner Inc.) $230

Handel reverse painted glass and bronze table lamp, signed and numbered 6819, circa 1920, 23½in. high. (Robert W. Skinner Inc.) $1,800

485

LAMPS

Old Sheffield plated lampstand with globe, marked Hinks/Duplex/Patent, circa 1860. (Sotheby, King & Chasemore)$510

Tiffany Studios poinsettia leaded glass shade, domed, circa 1900, 40cm. diam. (Sotheby's Belgravia) $3,025

Maltese library oil lamp in silver by Gaetano Offennaghel, circa 1800, 22½in. high, 52oz. (Christie's) $3,080

Modernist standard lamp, 1930's, 203cm. high, on spiral glass column. (Sotheby's Belgravia) $135

Tiffany Studios daffodil lamp, marked on base, circa 1900, 66cm. high. (Sotheby's Belgravia) $11,035

Late 19th century ornate brass and copper tripod telescopic standard lamp. (T. Bannister & Co.) $140

Art Deo electric table lamp in glass. (J. M. Welch & Son) $75

Lacemaker's lamp with loop handle and pad foot, 23.5cm. high. (Phillips) $205

Tiffany Studios gilt bronze reading lamp, 1920's, marked, 135cm. high.(Sotheby's Belgravia) $980

LAMPS

Early 19th century American painted tin and glass whale oil hand lamp, 10¼in. high. (Robert W. Skinner Inc.) $625

Desny chromed metal and glass table lamp with movable square of green tinted glass, 1920's, 12.5cm. (Sotheby's Belgravia) $675

Tiffany bronze and Favrile glass three-light lily table lamp, circa 1900, 16in. high. (Robert W. Skinner Inc.) $2,300

Art Deco bronze figural table lamp. (Capes, Dunn & Co.) $355

Daum etched glass lamp on wrought iron base, shade engraved, 1920's, 50.5cm. high. (Sotheby's Belgravia) $855

Red painted standard lamp with triangular stem and spiral geometric tripod base, 228.5cm. high. (Christie's) $165

Art Deco molded glass lamp base in the form of a nude female, 13in. high, circa 1930. (Robert W. Skinner Inc.) $300

Modernist lamp with spherical green glass shade on blue glass base, 1930's, 31cm. high. (Sotheby's Belgravia) $360

Tiffany leaded Favrile glass and Dore bronze bridge lamp, circa 1900, 57½in. high. (Robert W. Skinner Inc.) $3,200

487

MARBLE

17th century Italian marble head of a satyr, 27cm. high, with two bases. (Christie's) $1,265

19th century Indian marble seat, back of pointed arched form, 4ft. 3½in. wide. (Sotheby's) $2,755

19th century Italian marble bust of a lady, inscribed G. Gambacciani Firenze, 72cm. high.(Christie's) $1,195

Mid 19th century Belgian marble statue of the Repentant Magdalen, by Willem Geefs, 136.5cm. high, 1841. (Christie's) $4,060

Pair of English white marble busts of Queen Elizabeth I and Robert Dudley, circa 1600, 26in. high.(Sotheby's) $10,395

Marble figure of a medieval woman carrying a book, 6ft. high. (Woolley & Wallis)$535

18th century Italian marble bust of a matron, cracked, 66cm. high. (Christie's) $2,325

Late 19th century French marble, enamel and porcelain pedestal with octagonal column, 112cm. high. (H. Spencer & Sons Ltd.) $1,870

Roman marble portrait head of a lady, 2nd century A.D., 11¼in. high. (Christie's)$2,285

488

Roman marble pilaster capital, 2nd century A.D., 10½in. wide. (Christie's) $270

One of a pair of ormolu models of chimerae, on marble bases, 9in. wide. (Christie)$985

North Italian marble relief of Cherubim, circa 1690, 18in. wide. (Sotheby's)$4,160

White marble statue of Venus, circa 1880, 38in. high. (Sotheby, King & Chasemore) $985

16th century Italian white marble elephant, 9¾in. wide, base damaged and restored. (Sotheby's) $5,200

17th century Flemish marble figure of Venus, an urn at her side, 21in. high. (Sotheby's) $1,870

19th century Florentine marble group of three children, inscribed F. Andreini Firenze, 75cm. high. (Christie's) $1,450

Bronze and marble encrier on yellow marble base, circa 1840, 11in. wide. (Sotheby's Belgravia) $245

Late 19th century American marble bust of the Greek Slave, by H. Powers, 39.5cm. high.(Christie's)$6,186

Cut glass picture frame by Hawkes, Corning, New York, circa 1900, 7in. long. (Robert W. Skinner Inc.) $150

George III mahogany serpentine-fronted toilet mirror, circa 1790, 17½in. wide. (Sotheby, King & Chasemore) $625

Lalique circular easel mirror, signed, 39cm. diam., with glass molded frame. (Phillips) $895

20th century American Chippendale style mahogany mirror with painted glass plates, 48in. high. (Robert W. Skinner Inc.) $275

'George III' rococo giltwood wall mirror, circa 1840, with pagoda top, 78½in. high. (Sotheby's Belgravia) $1,440

20th century George III style giltwood wall mirror, 73in. high.(Sotheby Beresford Adams) $560

George II carved giltwood wall mirror with candle sconce, circa 1750, 60in. high. (Sotheby, King & Chasemore)$1,380

One of a pair of George III giltwood mirrors with later plates, 43in. high.(Christie's) $3,330

George III giltwood wall mirror, circa 1770, 61in. high.(Sotheby, King & Chasemore) $4,025

George II giltwood mirror with arched beveled plate, cresting centered by a pierced cartouche, 48½in. high. (Christie's) $1,850

Early 19th century Regency mahogany toilet mirror on a bow-fronted three-drawer base, 21in. wide. (Sotheby Beresford Adams) $150

Small George III oval giltwood mirror, re-gilded, circa 1760, 1ft.6½in. wide. (Sotheby's) $1,215

WMF silvered pewter mirror with Art Nouveau maiden reaching upwards to branches, 37cm. high.(Phillips) $825

Gilt rectangular wall mirror with ball, star and scroll fluted columns, 26in. high. (John Hogbin & Son) $90

Early 20th century George III style giltwood mirror in pierced frame, 55in. high. (Sotheby Beresford Adams) $295

Early 20th century George III style mahogany toilet mirror with oval swing plate, 18in. wide.(Sotheby Beresford Adams)$165

Late 19th century Dresden mirror of oval form, slightly damaged, 17¼in. high. (Sotheby Beresford Adams) $315

Reproduction, figured walnut toilet mirror in Queen Anne style, 14in. wide, on bracket feet. (Locke & England) $205

Carved giltwood 'Sun-burst' framed convex mirror. (Gilbert Baitson) $130

Early George III carved giltwood overmantel mirror, circa 1760, 4ft.3½in. wide. (Sotheby's) $3,205

Regency mahogany swing toilet mirror with brass urn-shaped finials. (Gilbert Baitson) $380

George II carved gilt-wood looking glass, circa 1750, 2ft.3in. wide. (Sotheby's) $1,570

Early 19th century Empire mahogany and gilt bronze cheval mirror, 41in. wide. (Sotheby Beresford Adams) $780

Dresden beveled oval mirror decorated with blue and white flower spray, 10½in. high. (Dee & Atkinson)$280

19th century Louis XV style kingwood occa-sional table, stamped Edwards & Roberts, 17½in. wide. (Hy. Duke & Son) $770

19th century painted wood-encased mirror, 18in. wide. (Robert W. Skinner Inc.) $250

George II looking glass in carved giltwood frame with two brass candle branches. (Christie's & Edmiston's) $3,110

Giltwood pier glass of Chippendale design, 31in. wide, with gadrooned border. (Lawrence Fine Art) $660

Regency gilt framed triple plate overmantel mirror, circa 1810, 4ft.7½in. wide. (Sotheby, King & Chasemore) $1,075

Georgian mahogany lyre frame swing toilet mirror with string inlay. (Gilbert Baitson) $140

Giltwood wall mirror with carved frame, 2ft. 7in. wide. (Sotheby's) $4,030

Late 19th/early 20th century Venetian giltwood mirror with shaped plate, 42in. high. (Sotheby's Belgravia) $740

Empire mahogany cheval mirror with arched cornice, on scrolled legs and paw feet, 78½in. high. (Christie's) $1,840

George II parcel gilt mahogany wall mirror, circa 1750, 1ft.6½in. wide. (Sotheby's) $1,595

Koening & Lengsfeld ceramic figure of a woman looking into a mirror, 70cm. high. (Christie's) $865

Early 18th century rare giltwood pier glass with divided beveled plate, 70½in. high. (Christie's) $3,865

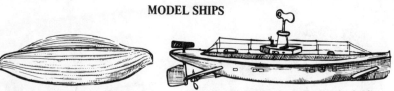

Small shipyard model of a ship's boat, with painted hull, 46cm. long. (Phillips) $275

Marklin tinplate submarine with clockwork mechanism, circa 1935, 22in. long. (Sotheby's Belgravia) $1,805

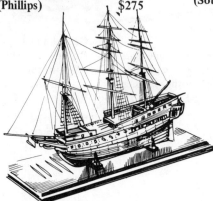

French prisoner-of-war bone model of a 48-gun frigate, 19½in. long. (Christie's) $2,455

Fully rigged bone and mahogany model of a 16-gun Admiralty cutter, 16in. wide. (Christie's) $1,135

Fully planked, framed and rigged wooden model of the frigate 'Endymion', by F. A. Chapman, Basildon, 53in. wide.(Christie's) $720

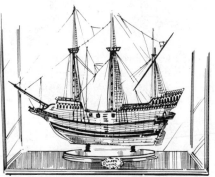

Well-presented fully planked model of the 'Golden Hind' of 1578, built by V. Rodriguez-Bento, Bath, 42in. long. (Christie's) $795

Nautical diorama of the Titanic and other vessels, circa 1915, 26½in. wide. (Sotheby's) $205

Bing tinplate gunboat with clockwork mechanism, circa 1910, 15in. long. (Sotheby's) $955

494

Tin Ocean liner, U.S. Zone Germany, circa 1947, 20in. long. (Robert W. Skinner Inc.) $410

Shipyard model of a ship's boat with patent specification, 95cm. long. (Phillips) $570

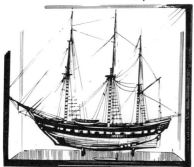

Early 19th century French bone model of a frigate, 13½in. wide, on wooden base. (Sotheby Beresford Adams) $205

Early 19th century Admiralty Board Room fully rigged model of the 120-gun 'Caledonia', 70in. long. (Christie's) $4,160

Contemporary bone, horn and boxwood fully rigged French prisoner-of-war model frigate, 13in. wide. (Christie's) $5,670

Exhibition standard scale fully planked model of H.M.S. Victory, by J. Bright, Gosport, 40in. long. (Christie's) $2,455

Fleischmann twin-funnelled tinplate liner with clockwork mechanism, 12in. long, circa 1950. (Sotheby's Belgravia) $235

Fleischmann tinplate liner, circa 1945, 9in. long, with clockwork mechanism. (Sotheby's Belgravia) $65

MODEL SHIPS

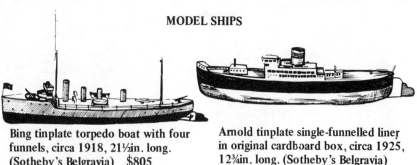

Bing tinplate torpedo boat with four funnels, circa 1918, 21½in. long. (Sotheby's Belgravia) $805

Arnold tinplate single-funnelled liner in original cardboard box, circa 1925, 12¾in. long. (Sotheby's Belgravia) $180

Contemporary French prisoner-of-war bone and horn model of a 112-gun man-of-war, 12in. long. (Christie's) $9,450

German tinplate carpet convoy by Hess, circa 1915, of four ships. (Sotheby's Belgravia) $360

Steam launch 'Chough', circa 1972, by Monachoram Plastics, Ltd., Plymouth, 16ft. long. (Christie's) $2,835

Shipbuilder's detailed model of a freighter built by Wm. Doxford, Sunderland, 1947, 4ft.8in. long. (Anderson & Garland) $4,485

Exhibition standard boxwood and pine model of a single screw steam yacht, circa 1900, by W. Morrison, Saltcoats, 43in. long. (Christie's) $7,560

Scale radio-controlled model of the salvage tug 'Lloydsman' of Hull, built by E. R. Warwick, Sevenoaks, 56in. wide. (Christie's) $1,040

Incomplete live steam model of a 3½in. gauge locomotive and tender, by Percival Marshal & Co., 3ft.10½in. long. (Phillips) $755

Exhibition standard 5in. gauge model of a 4-6-0 locomotive and tender 'King John', by J. Perrier, Ringwood, 73in. long. (Christie's) $14,175

Bassett-Lowke gauge 'O' electric 4-4-0 locomotive with matching tender. (Sotheby's Belgravia) $320

Hornby 'O' gauge clockwork train set in original cardboard box, circa 1924. (Sotheby's) $200

Hornby gauge 'O' clockwork train set in original cardboard box, dated 1924. (Sotheby's) $355

7mm. scale model of a London and North Eastern Railway 1st Class sleeping car, 19in. long. (Christie's) $415

Bassett-Lowke gauge 'O' electric 4-6-0 locomotive 'Royal Scot', with matching tender. (Sotheby's Belgravia) $850

497

Gauge 'one' carette live steam spirit-fired 2-2-0 locomotive with four wheeled tender, 14¾in. long. (Sotheby Beresford Adams)$205

7mm. scale electric model of a condensing side tank locomotive No. 10, by B. Miller, 8¾in. long. (Christie's) $1,605

3½in. gauge model of an Ivatt Atlantic 4-4-2 locomotive and tender by A. F. Farmer, Stechford, 1967, 44½in. long. (Christie's) $1,795

Hornby 4-4-2 gauge '0' clockwork engine 'Lord Nelson' and tender. (Allen & May) $140

Exhibition standard 7mm. fine scale model of a 2-6-0 goods locomotive and tender, by J. S. Beeson, Ringwood, 15½in. long. (Christie's) $2,270

Lionel tinplate gauge '0' clockwork Disney train, circa 1940, 30in. long. (Sotheby's Belgravia) $570

5in. gauge model of the Welsh quarry 0-4-0 tank locomotive No. 1, by S. F. Price, Sheppey, 31½in. long.(Christie's) $4,535

3½in. gauge display model of a Webb 2-4-0 side tank locomotive by H. A. Taylor, Bletchley, 22in. long. (Christie's) $1,700

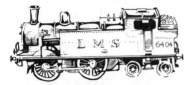

7mm. fine scale model of a Johnson class 2P 0-4-4 side tank locomotive, by J. S. Beeson, Ringwood, 9¾in. long. (Christie's) $1,230

7mm. fine scale electric model of a 'Jinty' class 0-6-0 side tank locomotive, by J. S. Beeson, Ringwood, 9in. long. (Christie's) $905

7mm. scale electric model of a 4-2-2 locomotive and tender 'Lorna Doone', by·P. G. Rose, 16in. long. (Christie's) $1,795

Gauge 'one' clockwork L. & N.W.R. tank locomotive by Bassett Lowke, 16¼in. long. (Sotheby's)$375

Bassett Lowke 4-6-0 railway engine 'Royal Scot', and tender. (Allen & May) $360

5in. gauge model of the Johnson 'Spinner' 4-2-2 locomotive and tender 'Princess of Wales', 64in. long. (Christie's) $4,915

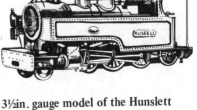

Exhibition standard 7mm. fine scale electric model of a Webb class 1P 2-4-2 side tank locomotive, by J. S. Beeson, Ringwood, 9½in. long. (Christie's) $1,890

3½in. gauge model of the Hunslett narrow gauge 2-6-2 side tank locomotive 'Russell', 34½in. long. (Christie's) $2,270

MODELS

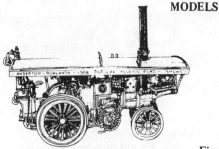

2in. scale model of a coal-fired Burrell showman's engine. (Lacy Scott) $2,785

Fine model of an 1830's stagecoach in hardwood with brass fittings, modern, 16in. wide. (Sotheby's) $250

Brass and copper 1/12 scale gas-fired model of a steam plant, 36in. wide. (Christie's) $380

Detailed 1/12 scale model of fishermen and equipment on Worthing beach, circa 1920, by S. Bunker, 29¼in. wide. (Christie's) $850

Contemporary 4-pillar table engine, circa 1845, 25in. high. (Christie's) $755

Modern replica of a 19th century fairground in fibre-glass, 10ft.10in. wide. (Sotheby Beresford Adams) $655

American carved and painted stagecoach model and four-horse team, circa 1900, 53in. long. (Robert W. Skinner Inc.) $550

Model of a Stuart single cylinder beam engine, 14in. wide. (Dickinson, Davy & Markham)$95

500

MODELS

1½in. scale live steam Allchin traction engine. (Phillips) $3,070

Model single horizontal cylinder bayonet frame mill engine by A. H. Allen, Keighley, 11¼in. wide. (Christie's) $340

Well-engineered coarse scale coal-fired live steam model of a traction engine, 54cm. long. (Sotheby, King & Chasemore) $890

3in. scale model of a single cylinder Burrell agricultural traction engine, by K. B. Thirsk, Driffield, 1973, 45in. long. (Christie's) $6,425

Finely engineered patent model of a twin cylinder vertical reversing steam plant, by W. Morrison, Saltcoats, circa 1900, 10½in. wide. (Christie's) $1,095

1½in. scale model of a road roller, living van and water cart, by J. McW. Morrison, Thatcham. (Christie's) $1,700

Detailed 1/8 scale wood and metal model of a gig of circa 1850, by A. Lee, Hendon, 17½in. long. (Christie's) $190

Scale model of a steam fire engine by Shands & Mason, 1863, London. (Edwards, Bigwood & Bewlay) $4,210

501

Late 19th century American cast-iron negro and shack money bank, 4¼in. long. (Sotheby's Belgravia) $300

American cast-iron Tammany money bank, circa 1880. (Sotheby's Belgravia) $200

19th century American cast-iron mechanical bank 'Eagle & Eaglets'. (Wm. Doyle Galleries Inc.) •$150

German Mickey Mouse tinplate mechanical bank, both sides having different scenes, circa 1930, 6¾in. high. (Sotheby's Belgravia) $345

Late 19th century American cast-iron mechanical bank, 'Paddy and the Pig', 8in. high. (Sotheby's Belgravia) $320

Late 19th century American Uncle Sam cast-iron mechanical bank by Shepard Hardware Co., 11½in. high. (Sotheby's Belgravia) $285

German tinplate monkey money bank with decorated base, 6½in. high. (Sotheby's Belgravia) $100

Cast iron 'Novelty Bank' money box with hinged front, 6½in. high, American, circa 1875. (Sotheby's) $215

One of a pair of German electroplated Britannia metal 'porker' money boxes, 13.7cm. long. (Sotheby's Belgravia) $415

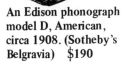

Kalliope disk music box with bells in inlaid fruit-wood case, 15¾in. wide. (Robert W. Skinner Inc.) $1,600

An Edison phonograph model D, American, circa 1908. (Sotheby's Belgravia) $190

Columbia AJ disk graphophone with 7in. turntable, circa 1902, complete with original case. (Sotheby's Belgravia) $510

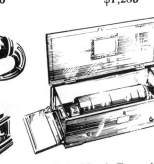

Rare Francois Nicole key-wound overture cylinder musical box, No. 101, circa 1830, 18in. wide. (Sotheby's Belgravia)$7,480

Nicole Freres Swiss musical box in rosewood veneer, 24in. wide. (Woolley & Wallis) $650

Alfred Junod Alexandra 'bells and drum in sight' cylinder musical box, 21in. wide, circa 1895. (Sotheby's Belgravia) $1,280

Nicole Freres key-wound cylinder musical box in fruitwood case, circa 1835. (Sotheby's Belgravia) $825

Edison opera phonograph, No. 2948, with self-supporting laminated horn, circa 1912. (Sotheby's) $3,740

Swiss Nicole Freres key-wound two-perturn cylinder musical box, circa 1858, 20in. wide. (Sotheby's Belgravia) $1,770

MUSICAL BOXES & POLYPHONES

Mira Orchestral Grand musical box, in mahogany case, 29½in. wide.(Robert W. Skinner Inc.)
$5,250

Swiss bells in sight cylinder musical box by Nicole Freres, in rosewood case, 26in. wide. (Sotheby Beresford Adams)
$2,245

Musical box with nine bells, in inlaid walnut case. (Hall Wateridge & Owen) $1,130 £600

Late 19th century walnut cased polyphon made for H. Peters & Co., London, sold with nineteen disks. (Locke & England)
$2,775

Swiss interchangeable bells in sight cylinder musical box, dated 1890, 15¼in. wide, with additional cylinders. (Sotheby Bearne)
$785

Late 19th century walnut cased floor standing symphonium with twenty-four disks. (Locke & England)
$3,235

Polyphon disk music box with serpentine front mahogany case, 11in. wide. (Robert W. Skinner Inc.)
$500

Sirion disk music box in inlaid fruitwood case, complete with ten disks, 25in. wide. (Robert W. Skinner Inc.)
$3,250

Symphonion disk musical box in maple case, with twenty-seven extra disks, 10¾in. wide. (Robert W. Skinner Inc.)
$750

Symphonion disk musical box in rosewood case, complete with twenty disks, 13¼in. long. (Robert W. Skinner Inc.) $650

Swiss cylinder music box with butterflies and bells, in grain painted case, 18¾in. wide. (Robert W. Skinner Inc.) $800

19th century Swiss musical box in rosewood with marquetry lid, 19in. wide. (Woolley & Wallis) $560

Late 19th century German symphonion disk musical box with thirty-four disks, 47½in. high, in walnut veneered case. (Sotheby Beresford Adams) $2,055

Edison fireside phonograph, circa 1909, with approximately one hundred cylinders. (Sotheby, Beresford Adams) $655

Regina disk music box in cherry case with two disks, 14½in. wide. (Robert W. Skinner Inc.) $900

Swiss bells and drum in sight cylinder musical box in rosewood veneered case, circa 1880. (Sotheby Beresford Adams) $935

Swiss cylinder music box with drum, bells and butterflies, 27¼in. wide, in rosewood case. (Robert W. Skinner Inc.) $2,200

Swiss bells in sight cylinder musical box in grained wood case with brass handles, 19in. wide. (Sotheby Beresford Adams) $935

MUSICAL BOXES & POLYPHONES

Amopette Atlas organette in black painted case, with twelve disks, 17in. wide. (Robert W. Skinner Inc.) $275

Late 19th century Swiss bells in sight cylinder musical box, 19in. wide. (Sotheby's) $1,975

Swiss cylinder music box, in inlaid rosewood case, 25in. wide, with ten tunes. (Robert W. Skinner Inc.) $1,400

Kalliope panorama automat disk music box in rosewood and walnut case, 25½in. wide. (Robert W. Skinner Inc.) $5,000

Late 19th century Swiss cylinder musical box playing eight airs, 25in. wide. (Sotheby's) $2,080

Criterion No. 5 disc music box in mahogany case, with matching stand, 26in. wide. (Robert W. Skinner Inc.) $2,600

Amoretto disk organ in ebonized wood case with twelve disks, 20½in. wide. (Robert W. Skinner Inc.) $500

Stella disk music box in walnut cabinet, carried on barley-twist supports, 28in. wide. (Locke & England) $1,685

Polyphon disk music box with serpentine front rosewood veneer case, 11in. wide. (Robert W. Skinner Inc.) $550

MUSICAL BOXES & POLYPHONES

Swiss cylinder musical box in walnut case with box-wood stringing, circa 1880's, 23in. wide. (Sotheby's)$1,350

Columbia disk phonograph with outside horn, 78 speed, 10¾in. wide. (Robert W. Skinner Inc.) $550

Regina accordion top disk music box in oak case, with thirteen disks, 34½in. wide. (Robert W. Skinner Inc.) $4,500

Regina music and gum machine in oak case with glass door, 16in. wide. (Robert W. Skinner Inc.) $2,600

Edison home phonograph with black japanned shaped octagonal horn, patent date 1906. (Sotheby Bearne) $205

Upright American symphonion in oak case, complete with ten disks, 28in. wide. (Robert W. Skinner Inc.) $3,500

German polyphon disk musical box and fifteen disks, retailer's label Edward Dale, Chester, circa 1900, 50½in. high. (Sotheby Beresford Adams) $1,775

Academy gramophone with bell-shaped tinplate horn, circa 1930, 13in. square. (Sotheby's) $455

Small carved music box showing three bears, 9in. high. (Robert W. Skinner Inc.) $180

507

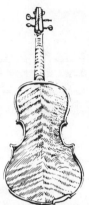

English violin by Arthur Richardson, Crediton, 1932, labeled, length of back 14in., sold with a silver mounted bow. (Sotheby's) $1,525

Early 19th century English serpent, possibly by Thos. Key, London, in leather on wood. (Phillips) $770

Fine French violin by Jean Baptiste Vuillaume, Paris, 1862, labeled, length of back 14in. (Sotheby's) $18,720

18th century French ivory treble recorder, 19½in. long. (Phillips) $3,845

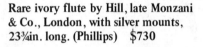

Rare ivory flute by Hill, late Monzani & Co., London, with silver mounts, 23¾in. long. (Phillips) $730

Italian violin attributed to Carlo Ferdinando Landolfi, Milan, length of back 14in., circa 1766. (Sotheby's) $10,175

Violin by Paul Bailly, signed and dated London, 1891, length of back 14in. (Phillips) $2,070

Italian violoncello by Giorgio Taningar, Rome, 1703, labelled, length of back 29¾in. long. (Sotheby's) $8,955

Unlabeled violin with two-piece back 14¼in. long, circa 1860, in shaped leather case. (Sotheby's) $775

Late 18th century cittern by Frederick Hintz, London. (Phillips) $950

French viola by Charles Louis Buthod, labeled, with one-piece back 15⅜in. long.(Sotheby's) $1,320

Early 19th century flute by Monzani & Co., London, with silver mounts, 23¼in. long. (Phillips) $1,005

18th century ivory treble recorder by I. B. Gahn, 20in. long. (Phillips) $8,785

Fine violin by Joseph Hill, London, length of two-piece back 14in. (Phillips)$7,020

Italian viola of the Amati School, circa 1700, reduced in size to 15in. (Phillips) $7,560

Violin by Paul Bailly, signed and dated Leeds, 1898, No. 1013, length of back 14in. (Phillips) $4,140

French hurdy-gurdy by Jean-Baptiste Pajot, 1795, 26¼in. long. (Christie's) $2,705

Violin labeled Francesco Ruggieri detto il per Gremona, 1676, length of back 14in., circa 1800. (Sotheby's) $2,035

Unlabeled Neapolitan mandoline of fluted maple ribs, neck inlaid with mother-of-pearl, 22¾in. long. (Christie's) $345

Tanzbar accordion roller organ in black case, closed width 11in. wide. (Robert W. Skinner Inc.) $600

Neapolitan mandoline by Antonio Vinaccia, 1763, 22½in. long. (Christie's)$1,450

Unsigned monochord, keyboard with beech naturals and stained beech accidentals, 47½in. long. (Christie's) $540

Italian violin ascribed to Gennaro Gagliano, 1773, with two-piece back, length of back 14in. (Christie's) $13,530

Late 18th century French pedal harp, unsigned, 36 strings, overall height 55in. (Christie's) $1,355

Italian violin, labeled Antonion Mariani/ Pesaro 16–, length of back 14in. (Christie's) $615

Good netsuke group of two pups playing, signed Ittan with kakihan. (Sotheby's) $590

Early 19th century ivory netsuke of a dog and a shell, unsigned, Osaka School. (Sotheby's) $355

Osaka School ivory netsuke of two biwa fruit on a branch, signed Koho.(Sotheby's) $1,085

Small ivory netsuke figure of a karako seated, playing with a turtle, signed Gyokuyosai. (Sotheby's) $395

Small wood netsuke of Shoki seated on a sack, signed Ryukei.(Sotheby's) $375

Wood netsuke of a baby boy, signed Shumin saku. (Sotheby's) $945

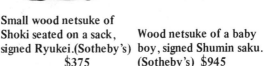

18th century ivory netsuke of a tiger, unsigned, eyes inlaid with horn. (Sotheby's) $630

Ivory netsuke of a monkey with young, signed Sadayoshi. (Sotheby's) $1,025

Late 18th century netsuke study of a Tengy No Tamago, signed Tametaka. (Sotheby's) $825

511

NETSUKE

Wooden netsuke model of a coiled mouse with inlaid eyes, signed Masakiyo. (Sotheby's) $1,155

18th century wood netsuke group of three chestnuts, one containing an ivory maggot, unsigned. (Sotheby's) $225

Ivory netsuke of a Shishi, signed Gyokuyosai, seated with a paw on a ball. (Sotheby's) $335

Early 19th century Kyoto School netsuke of a Kirin. (Sotheby's) $1,205

Late ivory netsuke figure of a Sambaso dancer, stained, signed Masakazu. (Sotheby's) $230

Large wooden netsuke figure of a Raiden, signed Hokyudo Itsuminto, seated beside a drum. (Sotheby's) $630

Mid 19th century wood netsuke of a kappa on a clam. (Christie's S. Kensington) $315

Ivory netsuke Okimono style figure of a young boy kneeling on the ground, inscribed Kaigyoku. (Sotheby's) $355

Large ivory netsuke study of a wolf with human skull, signed Tomonobu. (Sotheby's) $485

18th century ivory net-
suke model of a rat be-
side a large overturned
mushroom, unsigned.
(Sotheby's)$280

Wooden netsuke group of Juro-
jin with two Karako seated in a
boat, signed Ikkosai.(Sotheby's)
$445

Unusual wooden netsuke
study of a rat on a rice
bale, signed Ryukei.
(Sotheby's) $240

18th century ivory net-
suke of a Nio holding a
club, unsigned.
(Sotheby's)$390

Late ivory netsuke figure of
Saishi, signed Kounsai Kosen.
(Sotheby's) $385

Wood and ivory netsuke
of a young boy holding
some fruit, signed on red
lacquer Hideyuki.
(Sotheby's) $565

Small ivory netsuke model
of a skeleton beating a
mokugyo, signed Tomo-
chika. (Sotheby's)
                $160

Late 18th century ivory netsuke model of a dragon, unsigned. (Sotheby's)$835

Attractive early 19th
century ivory netsuke
of a snail on a mush-
room, signed Kogyoku.
(Sotheby's)$385

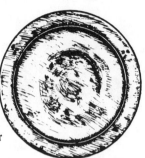

Commonwealth pewter tankard, circa 1650, 5¾in. high. (Sotheby's) $2,790

15th century pewter spoon with latten 'sceptre' knop, possibly unique, 5¾in. long. (Sotheby's) $650

Mid 17th century bossed pewter dish, 15¾in. diam. (Sotheby's) $975

Mid 18th century Bernese stegkanne with hexagonal spout, 34.5cm. high. (Sotheby's) $1,445

William and Mary pewter candlestick, 6in. high, circa 1690-96. (Sotheby's) $2,135

18th century German Peterskirchen stoneware handled jug with pewter lid, 18in. high.(Robert W. Skinner Inc.) $250

One of a pair of painted pewter mantel ornaments, circa 1790, 12¼in. high. (Robert W. Skinner Inc.) $750

Broad-rimmed 'Mount Edgecumbe' pewter plate by ND, circa 1660-80, 10in. diam. (Sotheby's) $530

19th century European pewter communion flagon with double domed hinged lid, 14in. high. (Robert W. Skinner Inc.) $200

German or Bohemian pewter passover plate, circa 1803, 34.3cm. diam. (Sotheby's) $1,755

'Diamond-point' pewter spoon with stem and terminal of pentagonal section, 6½in. long. (Sotheby's) $185

One of a pair of WMF silvered pewter and brass two-branch candelabra, 25cm. high. (Christie's) $2,250

Early 18th century North Country pewter baluster measure with flat cover, 6½in. high. (Sotheby's) $1,425

18th century German pewter mounted stoneware flagon with applied white decoration, 13½in. high. (Robert W. Skinner Inc.) $1,000

19th century South German hexagonal pewter cannister, 13in. high. (Sotheby's) $600

One of a pair of rare Georgian pewter candlesticks, circa 1720, 6¾in. and 6½in. high. (Sotheby's) $915

Early 18th century pewter wrigglework plate with single reeded border, 8½in. diam. (Sotheby's) $470

18th century Swiss pewter covered flagon with domed hinged cover, 12½in. high. (Robert W. Skinner Inc.) $1,200

515

PEWTER

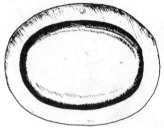

Dutch pewter beaker,
Amsterdam, circa 1760.
(Sotheby's) $290

One of a pair of late 18th century oval pewter dishes, 18in.
wide. (Woolley & Wallis)
$595

One of a pair of Scottish
pewter flagons, circa
1786, 13in. high.
(Sotheby's) $950

One of a fine pair of
Charles I pewter flagons,
circa 1635, 11in. high.
(Sotheby's)$6,615

WMF Art Nouveau wafer barrel
and lid. (Capes, Dunn & Co.)
$150

Charles I pewter flagon
with plain 'muffin'
cover, circa 1630-40,
11½in. high.(Sotheby's)
$1,220

Rare pewter Stuart lid-
less tavern pot by James
Donne, London, 6½in.
high, circa 1685-90.
(Sotheby's)$1,525

Decorated pewter Charles II
charger, circa 1670, 20½in.
diam. (Sotheby's)$1,015

Small 'York' acorn flagon
in pewter, circa 1725-50,
8¾in. high. (Sotheby's)
$1,525

18th century Swiss pewter covered glockencanne with fixed ring carrying handle, 12in. high. (Robert W. Skinner Inc.) $500

Bavarian pewter dish, rim embossed with flower petals, circa 1800, 41.7cm. diam. (Sotheby's) $435

Stuart pewter flat-lid tankard by W. W., circa 1690, 6½in. high. (Sotheby's) $2,135

Norwich Friendly Society flagon in pewter, by Gerardin & Watson, circa 1819, 13½in. high. (Sotheby's) $2,950

Large North German pewter flagon by CTN, Stade, circa 1823, 64.5cm. high.(Sotheby's) $1,075

Rare mid 17th century Saxon spouted flagon in pewter, with double-domed cover, 33cm. high. (Sotheby's) $1,965

Rare Stuart pewter flat-lid flagon or tall tankard, circa 1690, 8¾in. high. (Sotheby's)$1,015

Dutch wriggleworked Corporation dish in pewter, circa 1661. (Sotheby's) $1,640

18th century pewter flagon, inscribed on drum, 12½in. high, with spray thumbpiece. (Sotheby's) $775

517

18th century tapering cylindrical pewter flagon, by Graham & Wardrop, Glasgow, 14¼in. high. (Sotheby's) $420

Liberty & Co. pewter muffin dish and cover by Archibald Knox, circa 1905, 29cm. wide. (Sotheby's Belgravia) $300

WMF pewter mounted green glass decanter, circa 1900, 42cm. high. (Sotheby's Belgravia) $390

One of a pair of mid 19th century pewter table candlesticks with fixed nozzles, 11in. high.(Sotheby's) $145

Liberty & Co. 'Tudric' pewter tea service by Archibald Knox. (Christie's) $400

Late 16th century 'horse-hoof' knop spoon, 6½in. long. (Sotheby's) $650

18th century pewter tapered cylindrical flagon by Graham & Wardrop, 10½in. high. (Sotheby's) $460

Art Nouveau pewter framed mirror from a model by Charles Jonchery, 72cm. wide. (Christie's) $1,455

WMF green glass and pewter claret jug of trumpet form, 40.5cm. high. (Christie's)$475

PEWTER

Late 17th century German or Dutch pewter beaker engraved with wrigglework panels, 6¾in. high. (Christie's) $475

18th century pewter barber's bowl of oval outline, 11¾in. wide. (Christie's) $675

18th century German pewter wasserbehalter by Georg Ludwig Ruepprecht, Memmingen, 12½in. high. (Christie's) $1,465

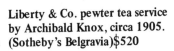

WMF pewter mounted green glass decanter with pierced and cast stopper, circa 1900, 38cm. high.(Sotheby's Belgravia) $500

Liberty & Co. pewter tea service by Archibald Knox, circa 1905. (Sotheby's Belgravia)$520

Pewter spouted flagon of spreading cylindrical shape, 15¼in. high, spout with hinged cover. (Lawrence Fine Art) $150

Urania pewter bucket and cover with fixed arched handle, stamped, 28.5cm. high, circa 1900. (Sotheby's Belgravia) $170

Early 18th century circular pewter charger with broad rim, 18in. diam. (Sotheby's) $210

Early 18th century lidded baluster measure of half-pint capacity, 4¾in. high.(Sotheby's) $260

Eavestaff 'minipiano pianette' with matching stool, 86cm. wide, 1930's. (Sotheby's Belgravia) $535

Baby grand piano by Carl Meverstein, in floral lacquered satinwood case. (John Hogbin & Son) $3,180

Broadwood square piano, crossbanded in rosewood and with ebony stringing, circa 1813. (Cooper Hirst) $605

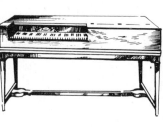

Late 19th century French 20-key barrel organ with pinned wooden cylinder, 27in. wide. (Sotheby's Belgravia) $2,165

Late 18th century George III clavichord by Schoene & Insen, London, 66in. long. (Robert W. Skinner Inc.) $125

Keith Prowse 'pennyano' cafe barrel piano in stained wood case, circa 1900, 40in. wide. (Sotheby's Belgravia) $1,475

Wurlitzer military band organ in oak case, 84in. wide, needs restored. (Robert W. Skinner Inc.) $9,500
520

Steinway & Sons ebonized wood upright piano, New York, circa 1903, 62in. wide. (Robert W. Skinner Inc.) $300

Boudoir grand piano in polished case, by C. Bechstein, Berlin, no. 74474. (John Hogbin & Son) $3,105

Hurdy-Gurdy monkey organ in mahogany case, 18½in. wide. (Robert W. Skinner Inc.) $2,300

Small organ grinder in grain painted case, 12½in. wide. (Robert W. Skinner Inc.) $170

Haines Bros. player piano with ampico action, complete with thirty-six rolls, 63in. wide. (Robert W. Skinner Inc.) $700

Satinwood grand piano by Bluthner, top with crossbanded border, 74in. wide. (Sotheby's Belgravia)$3,610

Coin operated barrel organ by Cannon A. O. Wintle. (Lacy Scott) $1,885

Broadwood marquetry oak boudoir grand piano with iron frame, circa 1880. (Sotheby's Belgravia) $1,850

Jazz band barrel organ in beech case, with automatic barrel, 32in. wide. (Robert W. Skinner Inc.) $550

Baillie Scott Manxman upright pianoforte by John Broadwood & Sons, London, in oak case, 144cm. wide. (H. Spencer & Sons Ltd.) $740

Street automatic piano in beech case, slightly damaged, 40in. wide. (Robert W. Skinner Inc.) $250

Late 19th/early 20th century Meerschaum cheroot holder, 11.3cm. long.
(Sotheby's Belgravia) $125

Late 19th century Austrian Meerschaum
pipe carved as the head of a negro boy,
17cm. long. (Sotheby's Belgravia)
                              $580

Mid 19th century blue glass pipe with long
curved stem, 70.5cm. long. (Sotheby's
Belgravia) $150

Well carved Meerschaum cigar
holder in the form of a head
of a Kaiser, 3¼in. (Burrows &
Day) $110

One of two late 19th century German
Meerschaum pipes, 9½in. long. (Robert
W. Skinner Inc.) $150

Austrian Meerschaum pipe, bowl carved
as a young woman carrying a parasol,
20.3cm. long, circa 1880. (Sotheby's
Belgravia) $660

Mid 19th century three-color glass pipe
with knopped stem, 48.2cm. long.
(Sotheby's Belgravia) $320

Meerschaum cigar holder in the form of
a young boy in a skittle alley, 4in. long.
(Burrows & Day) $90

Carved Meerschaum pipe with elderly Eastern gentleman's head, 6¼in. long, in case. (Dacre, Son & Hartley) $175

Austrian Meerschaum pipe with carved bowl, circa 1905, 16.4cm. long, with case. (Sotheby's Belgravia) $350

Large Meerschaum pipe with amber mouthpiece and heavily carved bowl, early 20th century, 28.5cm. long. (Sotheby's Belgravia) $2,070

Austrian silver mounted Meerschaum pipe with hinged cover, Vienna, 1824, 5in. long. (Sotheby's) $450

Austrian Meerschaum cheroot holder, elaborately carved, 28.5cm. long, 1880's. (Sotheby's Belgravia) $2,480

Large Viennese Meerschaum bowl with silver mount, circa 1870, 20.3cm. long, in case. (Sotheby's Belgravia) $4,550

Late 19th century Meerschaum pipe carved as a skull, with silver collar and amber mouthpiece, 6¼in. long. (Sotheby's) $155

Meerschaum pipe, bowl carved as woman with a fur collar, circa 1900, 15.5cm. long, probably Austrian. (Sotheby's Belgravia) $160

Silk patchwork bedcover lined with Paisley pattern cotton, circa 1830, 89in. square. (Lawrence Fine Art) $335

One of a pair of early 20th century cotton and lace bedcovers with filet-work panels, 82 x 90in. (Sotheby's Belgravia)$595

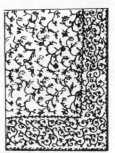

Mid 18th century embroidered cotton bedcover with white ground and green threads, 92 x 85in. (Sotheby's Belgravia) $850

Sino-Portuguese brocade bedcover, mid 18th century, with crimson ground, 115 x 120in. (Sotheby's Belgravia) $2,310

Embroidered silk bedcover with pheasant on a tree, circa 1900, 92 x 74½in. (Sotheby's Belgravia) $695

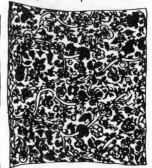

One of a pair of early 18th century crewel-work bedhangings or curtains, sold with a pelmet. (Sotheby's Belgravia) $3,220

20th century tapework bedcover with central flower, 113in. square. (Sotheby's Belgravia) $305

19th century American appliqued and patchwork quilt, 88 x 94in. (Robert W. Skinner Inc.) $400

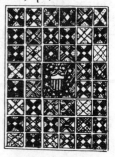

Civil War patriotic quilt, 68 x 88in., dated 1864.(Robert W. Skinner Inc.) $450

Striking patchwork quilt of tiny hexagons using late 18th/early 19th century chintzes. (Christie's S. Kensington)$660

Mid 18th century Indo-Portuguese silk embroidered quilted bedcover, 72 x 56in. (Sotheby's Belgravia) $390

Pennsylvania pieced quilt of 'Spider's Web' pattern in multi-colored cottons, 84in. square, 1860-70. (Sotheby's Belgravia) $730

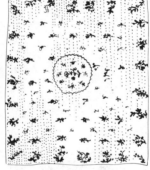

Early 19th century embroidered satin bedcover with central medallion, 91½ x 84in. (Sotheby's Belgravia)$1,540

Indian silk-embroidered bedcover with white satin ground, circa 1700, 91 x 85in. (Sotheby's Belgravia) $2,310

Brocade bedcover of gold thread on crimson ground, circa 1900, 102 x 71¾in. (Sotheby's) $3,150

19th century pieced and appliqued quilt, slightly faded, 84in. square. (Robert W. Skinner Inc.) $450

White American Marseilles-type quilt with cotton face, circa 1820, 80 x 66in. (Robert W. Skinner Inc.)$350

19th century American pieced appliqued quilt with white cotton field, 102 x 82in.(Robert W. Skinner Inc.)$600

Ispahan rug with all-over floral design on dark blue field, 6ft.9½in. x 4ft.5in. (Geering & Colyer) $1,755

Kuba rug with deep blue field within a main border of white, 3ft.5in. x 5ft.7in. (Robert W. Skinner Inc.) $2,900

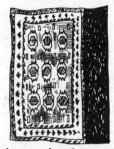

Turkoman chuval rug with liver red field, 3ft.3in. x 2ft.2in. (Robert W. Skinner Inc.) $450

Yoruk rug, large panels of blue, green and red filled with medallions, 3ft.6in. x 7ft.4in. (Robert W. Skinner Inc.) $800

Sarouk rug with mulberry red field and pendanted blue medallion, 4ft.4in. x 7ft. (Robert W. Skinner Inc.) $400

Kerman mat, ivory field with central medallion depicting a lady, circa 1930, in fair condition, 1ft.8in. x 1ft.2in. (Sotheby's) $250

Moghan runner with blue field and ivory border, 3ft.8in. x 7ft.3in. (Robert W. Skinner Inc.) $1,900

Interesting multi-bordered Oriental rug, 35 x 47in. (John Hogbin & Son) $75

Trans Caucasian rug with rich blue field and geometric motifs, 3ft.2in. x 5ft. (Robert W. Skinner Inc.) $900

Kuba rug, white field filled with rows of geometric motifs, 4ft. x 5ft.3in. (Robert W. Skinner Inc.) $2,500

20th century American Santa Claus hooked rug, 31¾ x 39in. (Robert W. Skinner Inc.)$450

Shiraz rug with triple lozenge pole medallion on magenta ground, 5ft.9in. x 4ft.2½in.(Geering & Colyer) $460

Kuba rug, field of greyblue with five medallions, dated 1347. (Robert W. Skinner Inc.) $2,300

20th century Persian/ Lillihan mat with magenta red field, 2ft.3in. x 3ft.7in. (Robert W. Skinner Inc.)$200

Persian/Lur rug with midnight blue field and five white medallions, 4ft.2in. x 9ft.6in. (Robert W. Skinner Inc.)$1,500

Bidjar mat with cherry red field and blue central medallion, 2ft.6in. x 4ft.3in. (Robert W. Skinner Inc.)$350

Caucasian/Sileh rug with four rows of four 'Z' motifs, 3ft. 4in. x 8ft.7in.(Robert W. Skinner Inc.) $3,700

20th century Shiraz area rug with blue field, 2ft. 9in. x 4ft.5in. (Robert W. Skinner Inc.) $200

Kayseri Anatolian rug with stylised cyprus trees and arches, 6ft. 6in. x 4ft. (Smith-Woolley & Perry) $590

Kirman pictorial mat depicting a seated royal figure, 2ft. 2in. x 2ft.10in. (Robert W. Skinner Inc.) $325

'Small Isphahan carpet with ivory field and two floral borders, 10ft.2in. x 7ft.1in. (Richard Baker & Thomson) $1,870

Kirman rug in good condition with deep blue field and red border, 6ft.9in. x 4ft.3½in. (Lawrence Fine Art) $1,120

Tibetan saddle cover with pastel blue field, 2ft.4in. x 3ft.7in. (Robert W. Skinner Inc.) $550

Turkish embroidered prayer rug with tree-of-life design, 72 x 48½in. (Lawrence Fine Art)$785

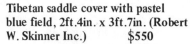

Kurdish rug with indigo field, 8ft. x 4ft. 5in. (Sotheby, King & Chasemore) $890

Bahktiari carpet with midnight blue field, 10ft. x 6ft.6in. (Robert W. Skinner Inc.) $2,000

Shirvan rug, indigo field with stepped medallions and two guls, 7ft.7in. x 3ft.11in. (Sotheby, King & Chasemore) $1,480

Kashan rug with all-over diapered tile pattern, 6ft.11in. x 4ft.5½in. (Lawrence Fine Art) $1,400

Soumak bagface, central panel containing one Lesghi star, 2ft.2in. x 1ft.10in. (Robert W. Skinner Inc.) $200

Kashan rug with blue field woven with a navette medallion, 6ft.7½in. x 4ft.3in. (Lawrence Fine Art) $2,055

Caucasian runner woven with six panels, 11ft.2in. x 3ft.7in. (Lawrence Fine Art) $485

North West Persian Kelim saddlebags of trellis design, 2ft. x 4ft.6in. (Robert W. Skinner Inc.) $850

One of a pair of good Kashan rugs with blue fields strewn with floral sprays, 6ft.11in. x 4ft.5in. (Lawrence Fine Art) $4,115

Persian tribal rug, possibly Lur of Kurd, with dark blue field, 3ft.11in. x 7ft.3in. (Robert W. Skinner Inc.)$350

Kazak rug with red field of medallion, leaf and bar design, 4ft. x 6ft.11in. (Robert W. Skinner Inc.) $900

Bokhara Susanni panel worked in colored silks, 98 x 57in. (Lawrence Fine Art)$1,010

529

Early 19th century sampler 'On Easter Day'. (Edwards, Bigwood & Bewlay) $200

Linen worked sampler with central inscription, 19½in. wide, sold with another. (Sotheby's) $165

William IV linen worked sampler by Fanney Wood, April, 1831, 17½in. square. (Sotheby's) $175

An early needlework sampler dated 1677. (Phillips) $675

Needlework sampler in circular reserve on linen ground, 1817, 20½ x 19½in. (Robert W. Skinner Inc.) $1,300

Early 17th century needlework sampler worked in cross stitch and running stitch, 86 x 16.5cm. (Phillips) $500

American needlework sampler with wide floral border, circa 1825, 18in. square. (Robert W. Skinner Inc.) $350

Silk worked picture of a map of England and Wales, by Elizabeth Foley, 1819, 21½in. wide. (Sotheby's) $315

Early 19th century sampler by Emma Toogood, framed, 16 x 12in. (Sotheby's Belgravia) $270

Early 19th century needlework sampler by Selina Doughty, 1835, framed and glazed, 38 x 32cm. (Phillips) $260

18th century needlework sampler 'A Trusty Servant', bearing arms and initials W.W. (Edwards, Bigwood & Bewlay) $345

Sampler by Sarah Ann Hunt, aged 12, 1839, in rosewood frame, 24½ x 20in. (Sotheby's Belgravia) $270

Spot-motif sampler with geometric panels outlined with silver thread, circa 1630, framed, 20 x 8in. (Sotheby's Belgravia) $1,635

Mid 19th century needlework sampler by Ann Rebecca Willingham, 1842, 63 x 56cm. (Phillips) $275

Embroidered border band sampler by Elizabeth Woodworth, 1758, 17¾ x 8½in. (Sotheby's Belgravia) $695

'Stone' family register by Anna Stone, 1810, 21½ x 15½in. (Robert W. Skinner Inc.) $400

Fine spot-motif sampler on ivory linen ground, 20 x 6½in., circa 1630, framed. (Sotheby's Belgravia) $1,840

Late 18th century needlework sampler, altered, framed and glazed, 31.5cm. square. (Phillips)$335

531

Regency three-sided engraved crystal swivel seal in gold serpent handle. (Woolley & Wallis) $450

Late 18th/early 19th century Italian lavastone desk seal with gold eyes, 11.5cm. high. (Sotheby's) $1,380

Regency gold seal, inset with a milky stone and chased gold ring. (Woolley & Wallis)$200

French gold mounted rock crystal desk seal, 5.4cm. high, circa 1910. (Sotheby's Belgravia) $825

Ivory seal carved with a squirrel on a grapevine, circa 1900, 7.5cm. high. (Sotheby's Belgravia) $75

Mid 19th century Italian gold and hardstone desk seal, 8.3cm. high. (Sotheby's)$1,205

SHIBAYAMA

One of a pair of Minko enameled silver shibayama vases, circa 1900, 17.5cm. high, on wood stands. (Sotheby's Belgravia) $2,125

Late 19th century Masahura shibayama elephant, inlaid with colored stones, 5cm. high. (Sotheby's Belgravia) $340

Shibayama and ivory basket and cover with loop handle, circa 1900, 20cm. high. (Sotheby's Belgravia) $805

Sunlight Soap, enamel sign of boy holding bars of Sunlight soap, 33½ x 32½in., circa 1905. (Sotheby's Belgravia) $320

American bicycle shop sign, circa 1900, with applied molding, 77in. wide. (Robert W. Skinner Inc.) $600

Hodges Inn sign with oval shield, Vermont, circa 1790, 31¾in. wide. (Robert W. Skinner Inc.) $5,000

Morse's Distemper, enamel sign by Hassall, 60 x 40in.(Sotheby's Belgravia) $695

18th century toacco figure of 'The Black Boy', on ebonized column, 42in. high. (Sotheby's) $3,445

'Selo Film' enamel sign in yellow, red and black, 14in. wide. (Sotheby's Belgravia) $355

A Barringer, Wallis & Manners Ltd. printed sign, 14in. high, circa 1910. (Sotheby's Belgravia) $40

Ogden's St. Julien Tobacco, enamel sign showing two blends of tobacco against green brick background, 18 x 60in., circa 1900. (Sotheby's Belgravia) $120

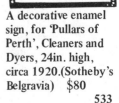

A decorative enamel sign, for 'Pullars of Perth', Cleaners and Dyers, 24in. high, circa 1920.(Sotheby's Belgravia) $80

SILVER

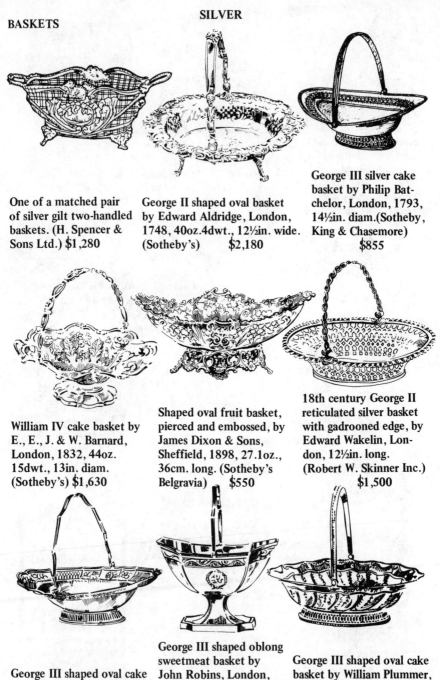

One of a matched pair of silver gilt two-handled baskets. (H. Spencer & Sons Ltd.) $1,280

George II shaped oval basket by Edward Aldridge, London, 1748, 40oz.4dwt., 12½in. wide. (Sotheby's) $2,180

George III silver cake basket by Philip Batchelor, London, 1793, 14½in. diam.(Sotheby, King & Chasemore) $855

William IV cake basket by E., E., J. & W. Barnard, London, 1832, 44oz. 15dwt., 13in. diam. (Sotheby's) $1,630

Shaped oval fruit basket, pierced and embossed, by James Dixon & Sons, Sheffield, 1898, 27.1oz., 36cm. long. (Sotheby's Belgravia) $550

18th century George II reticulated silver basket with gadrooned edge, by Edward Wakelin, London, 12½in. long. (Robert W. Skinner Inc.) $1,500

George III shaped oval cake basket by Michael Plummer, 1793, 15in. long, 26oz. (Christie's) $2,055

George III shaped oblong sweetmeat basket by John Robins, London, 1796, 10oz.7dwt., 6½in. wide. (Sotheby's) $1,255

George III shaped oval cake basket by William Plummer, London, 1775, 13¼in. long, 27oz.5dwt.   (Sotheby's) $2,195

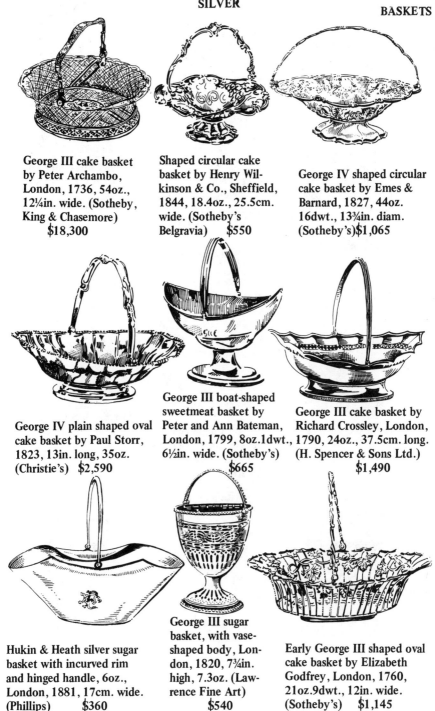

George III cake basket by Peter Archambo, London, 1736, 54oz., 12¼in. wide. (Sotheby, King & Chasemore) $18,300

Shaped circular cake basket by Henry Wilkinson & Co., Sheffield, 1844, 18.4oz., 25.5cm. wide. (Sotheby's Belgravia) $550

George IV shaped circular cake basket by Emes & Barnard, 1827, 44oz. 16dwt., 13¾in. diam. (Sotheby's) $1,065

George IV plain shaped oval cake basket by Paul Storr, 1823, 13in. long, 35oz. (Christie's) $2,590

George III boat-shaped sweetmeat basket by Peter and Ann Bateman, London, 1799, 8oz.1dwt., 6½in. wide. (Sotheby's) $665

George III cake basket by Richard Crossley, London, 1790, 24oz., 37.5cm. long. (H. Spencer & Sons Ltd.) $1,490

Hukin & Heath silver sugar basket with incurved rim and hinged handle, 6oz., London, 1881, 17cm. wide. (Phillips) $360

George III sugar basket, with vase-shaped body, London, 1820, 7¾in. high, 7.3oz. (Lawrence Fine Art) $540

Early George III shaped oval cake basket by Elizabeth Godfrey, London, 1760, 21oz.9dwt., 12in. wide. (Sotheby's) $1,145

SILVER

Tapering cylindrical beaker by Niels Svendsen, Copenhagen, 1689, 11cm. high, 7oz.2dwt. (Sotheby's)
$2,125

Parcel gilt and niello beaker with everted rim, Moscow, 1848, 7.7cm. high. (Sotheby's) $615

Russian silver gilt beaker by Grigory Lakomkin, Moscow, circa 1750, 3½in. high. (Christie's)
$460

Silver beaker of tapering form by V. Nikitin, Moscow, 1740, 14.3cm. high. (Sotheby's) $735

George III plain beaker by James McEwen, Glasgow, circa 1780, 4oz.16dwt. (Christie's) $345

Swedish tapering beaker by Johan Hamargren, Pitea, 1780, 6¼in. high, 8oz.11dwt. (Christie's)
$940

Mid 17th century Batavian silver beaker, 8oz.15dwt., 15.3cm. high. (Sotheby's)
$1,805

Cylindrical silver beaker by A.B. & F.G., Moscow, 1792, 8.4cm. high. (Sotheby's)
$450

Swedish parcel gilt beaker on fluted foot, by Nils Reetz, Umea, 1764, 6½in. high, 8oz. 14dwt. (Christie's)
$1,190

German parcel gilt beaker with strapwork band, Dresden, circa 1725, 5oz. 10dwt., 14.7cm. high. (Sotheby's) $1,700

Early 18th century silver beaker of flared cylindrical form, 6oz.8dwt., 2½in. high. (Sotheby's) $1,255

German silver beaker by Moritz Krelle, Augsburg, circa 1730, 3½in. high. (Christie's) $1,295

Cylindrical silver beaker by Savelev, Moscow, 1796, 8.7cm. high. (Sotheby's) $530

Finnish parcel gilt beaker by Anders Tidstrom, Vasa, 1772, 6½in. high, 9oz. 2dwt. (Christie's) $2,445

German silver beaker with spiral fluting, by Thomas Kuntze, Breslau, circa 1700, 3¼in. high. (Christie's) $1,015

Silver beaker of tapering cylindrical form, possibly by Gergori Serebryanikov, Moscow, 1758, 7.9cm. high. (Sotheby's) $490

Large Danish silver beaker by Johann Henrich Mundt, Copenhagen, 1706, 4¾in. high, 7oz.5dwt. (Christie's) $2,160

Early George II flared cylindrical beaker by William Darker, London, 1727, 3oz., 3¼in. high. (Sotheby's) $725

537

Early 20th century circular two-handled fruit bowl, 31cm. wide, 21.4oz. (Sotheby's Belgravia) $305

Circular sugar bowl with embossed edge, London, 1890, 3oz.(Dickinson, Davy & Markham) $85

Lobed circular fruit bowl by Manoah Rhodes & Sons Ltd., London, 1908, 64.1oz., 34.5cm. diam. (Sotheby's Belgravia) $995

Modern silver and gem-encrusted punch bowl with ladle, by Deirdre Peterson, Birmingham, 1970. (Alfred Mossop & Co.) $985

Large pierced rose bowl with engraved inscription, by James Deakin & Sons, Sheffield, 1904, 54.1oz., 20.1cm. diam. (Sotheby's Belgravia) $1,345

Silver gilt Cellini pattern rose bowl by Charles Boyton, London, 1891, 61.3oz., 27.5cm. diam. (Sotheby's Belgravia) $2,110

Pedestal rose bowl by R. & S. Garrard, London, 1878, 31.6cm. diam., 69.9oz. (Sotheby's Belgravia) $1,760

Boat-shaped bowl by Viners Ltd., Sheffield, 1934, 49cm. long, 81.3oz. (Sotheby's Belgravia) $1,585

Silver gilt shallow circular bowl by Edward Barnard & Sons Ltd., London, 1937, 35oz., 35cm. wide. (Sotheby's Belgravia) $350

Early 20th century boat-shaped fruit bowl with chased and pierced sides, 45.2oz., 39cm. long. (Sotheby's Belgravia) $950

Early George II punch bowl by Humphrey Payne, 1727, sold with a ladle, 61oz.11dwt., 11in. diam. (Sotheby's) $6,270

Mid 18th century French silver sucrier, 4¾in. high, 12 troy oz. (Robert W. Skinner Inc.) $150

George III hemispherical punch bowl, London, 1810, 9¾in. diam., 37oz.12dwt. (Sotheby's) $1,740

Late 19th century Indian presentation rose bowl, 108.8oz., 46cm. wide. (Sotheby's Belgravia) $1,265

Oval openwork fruit bowl by Elkington & Co. Ltd., London, 1900, 39.5oz., 31cm. long. (Sotheby's Belgravia) $1,445

George II circular bowl by Samuel Walker, Dublin, circa 1745, 7in. diam., 18oz.14dwt. (Sotheby's)$4,090

BOWLS

Dutch parcel gilt two-handled brandy bowl, Rotterdam, 1689, 6in. diam., 6oz. (Christie's)　$2,990

Late 19th century Dutch parcel gilt oval brandy bowl, 24.7cm. wide, 8.8oz. (Sotheby's Belgravia)　$240

George IV fruit bowl, Sheffield, 1827, 10¼oz. diam. (Sotheby, King & Chasemore)　$420

George IV silver punch bowl by Benjamin Smith, London, 1827-28, 5¾in. high, 40 troy oz. (Robert W. Skinner Inc.)　$1,000

Two-handled circular rose bowl by Sibray, Hall & Co., London, 1890, 88.1oz., 44.5cm. wide. (Sotheby's Belgravia)　$1,555

William IV small shaped circular silver bowl by John Tapley, 1836, 6½in. diam., 16oz. (Christie's)$2,220

Mid 18th century two-handled silver bowl, 4in. diam., 3oz.7dwt. (Christie's)　$875

Circular silver rose bowl by T. Wilkinson & Sons, Birmingham, 1905, 25.3cm. diam., 33.8oz. (Sotheby's Belgravia)　$550

Modern silver fruit bowl by Lee &
Wigfull, Sheffield, 1931, 24oz., 10¼in.
wide. (Lawrence Fine Art)$250

Dutch oval invalid feeding bowl and
cover, Rotterdam, 1671, 5in. long, 6oz.
1dwt. (Christie's) $3,555

Late 19th century Dutch chased oval
brandy bowl, 25.7cm. long, 6.6oz.
(Sotheby's Belgravia) $240

Circular flower bowl by C. S. Harris &
Sons Ltd., London, 1898, 25cm. diam.,
29.7oz. (Sotheby's Belgravia)
                                                    $935

George II plain circular bowl by Christopher Locks, 6in. diam., 10oz., Dublin,
1732. (Christie's) $1,090

Victorian silver footed compote with
scalloped rim, Sheffield, 1886-87,
6in. high. (Robert W. Skinner Inc.)
                                                    $275

One of a set of six rare George III fin-
ger bowls by Rebecca Emes and
Edward Barnard, London, 1815, 46oz.
(H. Spencer & Sons Ltd.)
                                        $4,465

Pair of boat-shaped fruit bowls, pierced
with slats, by the Goldsmiths & Silversmiths Co. Ltd., London, 1897, 52.1oz.
(Sotheby's Belgravia) $2,340

Oval brandy bowl by Obbe Ydema,
Sneek, 1770, 25cm. wide, 6oz.4dwt.
(Sotheby's) $955

Charles II plain circular bleeding bowl,
1682, 7oz.5dwt. (Christie's)
                    $2,900

Dutch oval brandy bowl by Jan Papinck,
Groningen, 1716, 9oz.10dwt., 23.3cm.
wide. (Sotheby's) $1,870

Silver compote by S. Kirk & Son, with
removable rim and embossed decoration, 42oz. (Wm. Doyle Galleries Inc.)
                    $1,100

Keswick School of Industrial Arts silver
bowl, Birmingham, 1899, 7cm. wide.
(Sotheby's Belgravia) $160

Liberty & Co. two-handled silver bowl,
Birmingham, 1913, 4¼oz., 14.6cm.
wide. (Christie's) $275

George III oval sugar basin by Heron,
Edinburgh, 1818, 8in. wide, 10oz.2dwt.
(Sotheby's) $290

George II circular bowl by William
Townsend, Dublin, circa 1747, 6in.
diam., 12oz.4dwt. (Sotheby's)
                    $2,215

20th century sterling silver handled bowl of oval form, 15¼in. long, 37.8 troy oz. (Robert W. Skinner Inc.) $325

Plain circular bowl by William Sutton, Dublin, 1729, 6¼in. diam., 13oz.5dwt. (Christie's) $3,215

Oval Russian silver sugar box by A. Afanasiev, Moscow, 1777, 6oz.15dwt., 12.2cm. wide. (Sotheby's) $1,445

Sterling silver fruit bowl, Connecticut, early 20th century, 4½in. high, 46 troy oz. (Robert W. Skinner Inc.) $450

Circular rose bowl in Burmese style by Carrington & Co., London, 1887, 23.7oz., 23.3cm. diam. (Sotheby's Belgravia) $535

Boat-shaped pedestal fruit bowl by Edward Barnard & Sons, London, 1894, 46cm. high, 114.4oz. (Sotheby's Belgravia) $4,135

18th century hemispherical punch bowl, circa 1750, 42oz.16dwt., 10½in. diam. (Sotheby's) $1,145

George I hemispherical bowl, London, 1718, by Samuel Lea, 5in. diam., 5oz. 18dwt. (Sotheby's) $3,590

Reeded oval biscuit box, cover inset with shell cameo, circa 1880, 14.7cm. long, London, 1921. (Sotheby's Belgravia) $580

Parcel gilt casket with cedar lining, by Leslie G. Durbin, London, 1961, 17cm. long. (Sotheby's Belgravia) $495

Oblong silver box by Alfred Taylor, Birmingham, 1861, 15oz., 15.2cm. long. (Sotheby's Belgravia)$805

One of a pair of rare and unusual George III silver gilt oval-shaped spice boxes by Thomas Heming, 28oz., 5½in. wide. (Sotheby, King & Chasemore) $9,515

Rectangular silver cigarette box by Walker & Hall, Sheffield, 1903, 18.4cm. long. (Sotheby's Belgravia) $760

19th century Viennese jewelry casket, urn containing a watch, 12¾in. high. (Christie's) $8,880

Freedom casket and cover by V. & S., Birmingham, 1912, 28.8cm. long. (Sotheby's Belgravia) $1,550

Engraved gilt metal jewel casket with corded borders, 21.2cm. long, circa 1860. (Sotheby's Belgravia)$660

Silver enameled box showing King Cole and his fiddlers, by Omar Ramsden. (Graves, Son & Pilcher) $1,335

Silver pill box with inset hinged cover, Birmingham, 1893, 1¾in. wide. (Dickinson, Davy & Markham)$85

Unusual George III freedom box, circa 1795, 3in. wide. (Sotheby's) $6,060

Circular silver gilt and enamel box, stamped 'Made for Tiffany & Co.', Moscow, 1887, 5cm. diam. (Sotheby's) $820

Electroplated beehive biscuit box on stand, by Martin, Hall & Co. Ltd., circa 1875, 23.5cm. high. (Sotheby's Belgravia) $620

Continental silver gilt oblong marriage casket, circa 1660, 5¾in. long, 10oz. 6dwt. (Christie's) $4,600

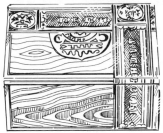

Late 19th century Austrian pill box by J. C. Klinkosch, Vienna, 4.2cm. long. (Sotheby's Belgravia) $455

Rectangular silver cigarette box, Moscow, 1892, 10.1cm. wide. (Sotheby's) $980

One of two octagonal
baluster toilet boxes,
London, circa 1685,
2½in. high, 6oz.19dwt.
(Sotheby's) $665

Omar Ramsden silver and enamel
cigar box, inscribed, 1936, 21cm.
wide. (Sotheby's Belgravia)
$675

George III taper box
by Hester Bateman,
London, 1783, 3in.
high, 4oz.13dwt.
(Sotheby's)$955

18th century German sha-
ped silver gilt pill box,
Augsburg, circa 1775,
2½in. wide. (Woolley &
Wallis) $815

Oblong spice box
by D. S., circa 1680,
1¾in. wide.
(Sotheby's)$590

Colonial circular bowl
and cover with bud
finial, 8¾in. diam.
(Sotheby's)
$1,005

BRANDY SAUCEPANS

George III brandy sauce-
pan and cover by Thos.
Death, London, 1818,
3½in. high, 5.9oz. (Law-
rence Fine Art)
$615

George II baluster brandy
saucepan by Paul de
Lamerie, London, 1741,
11oz.17dwt., 3¼in. high.
(Sotheby's)$5,015

George I baluster brandy
saucepan by Benjamin
Pemberton, Chester,
1724, 2oz.2dwt., 1¾in.
high. (Sotheby's)
$550

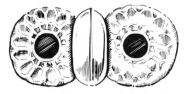

Liberty & Co. silver and enamel belt buckle in the form of two flowers, Birmingham, 1909, 8.25cm. wide. (Sotheby's Belgravia) $70

Liberty & Co. 'Cymric' silver and enamel belt buckle of butterfly shape, Birmingham, 1902, 9.25cm. wide. (Sotheby's Belgravia) $300

Liberty & Co. silver and enamel belt buckle, Birmingham, 1903, 8cm. wide. (Sotheby's Belgravia) $140

William Hutton & Son Ltd., silver and green hardstone waist clasp of open-work design, Birmingham, 1902. (Christie's) $165

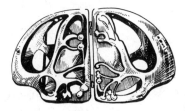

Theodor Fahrner silver and stone buckle, London, 1902, 6.75cm. wide.(Sotheby's Belgravia) $300

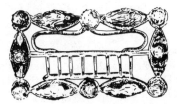

Late 19th century lava belt buckle in gold plate, set with carved round and navette-shaped heads. (Robert W. Skinner Inc.) $150

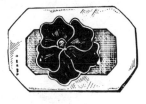

Unusual belt buckle by H. Hobson & Sons, Birmingham, 1910, 7cm. wide. (Phillips) $125

Art Nouveau silver buckle by William Comyns, London, 1898, 13cm. wide. (Phillips) $230

Victorian candelabrum centerpiece by E. & J. Barnard, 1855, 30¼in. high, 196oz. (Christie's) $4,440

One of a pair of 20th century Georg Jensen silver candelabra, Copenhagen, 8½in. high, 70 troy oz. (Robert W. Skinner Inc.) $3,700

One of a pair of George V four-branch table candelabra, London, 1917, 88oz., 45cm. high. (H. Spencer & Sons Ltd.) $2,205

One of a pair of George III four-light candelabra by Digby Scott and Benjamin Smith, 1804, 419oz. (Christie's) $68,640

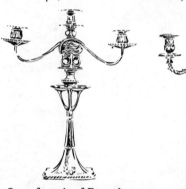

One of a pair of Ramsden & Carr three-light candelabra, 1905, 104oz., 22½in. high. (Christie's) $18,300

One of a pair of Victorian four-light candelabra, maker's mark AM, 1873, 198oz., 23¼in. high. (Christie's) $8,140

Five-light candelabrum by C. Boyton & Son, London, 1899, 62cm. high. (Sotheby's Belgravia) $1,280

Electroplated four-light candelabrum, stamped C. Kay, 1930's, 55cm. high. (Sotheby's Belgravia) $1,245

One of a pair of Regency candlesticks by J. Cradock and W. Reid, 1817, 18in. high, 101oz. (Christie's) $4,810

One of a pair of Victorian Corinthian column table candelabra by H. Wilkinson and J. Batt, 53cm. high. (H. Spencer & Sons Ltd.) $1,460

German five-light candelabra in silver colored metal, 1937, 15cm. high. (Sotheby's Belgravia) $300

One of a superb pair of silver gilt candlesticks in rococo style, London, 1967, 85oz., 30cm. high. (H. Spencer & Sons Ltd.) $1,590

Edward VII silver Corinthian column five-light candelabrum, Sheffield, 1903-04, 19in. high, 45oz.6dwt. (Geering & Colyer) $1,710

One of a pair of silver plated on copper three-light candelabra, 20in. high. (Sotheby, King & Chasemore) $360

Victorian five-light candelabrum centerpiece by Martin Hall & Co., 1862, 32¾in. high, 290oz. (Christie's) $6,105

One of a pair of five-light candelabra with shaped square bases, 21¼in. high. (Sotheby Beresford Adams) $480

One of a pair of George III three-light candelabra by John Parsons & Co., Sheffield, 1791, 17¾in. high. (Lawrence Fine Art) $4,055

Large six-light candelabrum in silver plate, by Elkington & Co., 1884, 29½in. high. (Sotheby's) $660

CANDLESTICKS

One of a pair of George III Ionic column candlesticks by John Carter, 1773, 13in. high. (Christie's)$1,955

One of a pair of George II table candlesticks by John Priest, 1748, 8in. high, 36oz. (Hy. Duke & Son) $2,590

One of a pair of silver table candlesticks by Hawkesworth, Eyre & Co. Ltd., Sheffield, 1916, 28.2cm. high. (Sotheby's Belgravia) $770

One of a pair of large George IV candlesticks by Robt. Garrard, 1829, 12½in. high, 99oz. (Christie's)$4,625

One of a pair of silver and enamel candlesticks of dwarf column form, late 18th century, 5¾in. high. (Christie's) $720

One of a pair of 18th century George III table candlesticks by D. Smith and R. Sharp, London, 1762-3, 10½in. high. (Robert W. Skinner Inc.)$3,300

One of a set of four table candlesticks by Goldsmiths & Silversmiths Co. Ltd., London, 1897, 27.5cm. high. (Sotheby's Belgravia)$1,935

George II taperstick by James Gould, London, 1733, 3oz.14dwt., 4½in. high. (Sotheby Beresford Adams) $610

One of a set of four silver candlesticks by Matthew Boulton & Co., circa 1830, 11¼in. high. (Sotheby Beresford Adams) $775

One of a pair of table candlesticks, Sheffield, 1900, 11½in. high. (Hy. Duke & Son)$490

One of a pair of George II table candlesticks by John Priest, London, 1752, 6in. high, 26oz.12dwt.(Sotheby's) $1,515

One of a pair of George III cluster columns candlesticks by Peter Werritzer, 1767, 11½in. high. (Christie's) $1,590

One of four George III candlesticks by George Hill, Dublin, 1770, 96oz., 11¼in. high. (Christie's) $5,430

One of a pair of George IV silver candlesticks by Wm. Burwash, 1820, 8in. high, 34oz. (Christie's) $1,755

One of a pair of Regency silver gilt tapersticks by R. Emes & E. Barnard, 1819, 5½in. high, 12oz. 12dwt. (Christie's) $2,035

One of a pair of early George II tapersticks, London, 1727, 7oz. 4dwt., 4¼in. high. (Sotheby Beresford Adams)$1,295

One of a pair of table candlesticks by J. Dixon & Sons, Sheffield, 1900, 34.5cm. high. (Sotheby's Belgravia) $815

George II taperstick by James Gould, London, 1730, 4oz., 4½in. high. (Sotheby Beresford Adams) $610

551

One of a set of four shaped-oval table candlesticks by Walker & Hall, Sheffield, 1920, 24cm. high.(Sotheby's Belgravia) $1,055

One of a pair of candlesticks by William Hutton & Sons Ltd., London, 1909, 30cm. high. (Sotheby's Belgravia) $590

One of a pair of table candlesticks by Martin, Hall & Co., Sheffield, 1891, 29.5cm. high. (Sotheby's Belgravia) $845

One of a pair of George II table candlesticks by William Cafe, London, 1757, 34oz.3dwt., 9½in. high. (Sotheby's) $2,180

One of a pair of George I candlesticks by Thomas Sutton, Dublin, 1717, 6¼in. high, 18oz.17dwt. (Christie's) $2,925

One of four George II table candlesticks by John Cafe, London, 1756, 82oz.16dwt., 10in. high. (Sotheby's) $4,600

One of a pair of George III table candlesticks by John Smith II, London, 1771, 12¾in. high. (Sotheby's) $3,030

One of a set of four George II candlesticks by John Cafe, 1746, 7¼in. high, 61oz. (Christie's) $6,280

One of a pair of George II bedroom candlesticks, London, 1759, 8¼in. high. (Lawrence Fine Art) $1,060

One of a pair of early George III table candlesticks by John Carter, London, 1768, 12¼in. high. (Lawrence Fine Art) $850

One of four George III candlesticks by John Younge & Sons, Sheffield, 1791, 12¼in. high. (Christie's) $5,435

One of a set of four George III table candlesticks by Edmund Vincent, London, 1769, 13in. high. (Sotheby's) $4,600

One of a set of four George III table candlesticks by John Carter, London, 1774, 10¾in. high, 92oz. (Sotheby's) $18,390

One of a pair of George II candlesticks, Dublin, circa 1745, 8¼in. high, 31oz.8dwt. (Christie's) $3,555

One of a set of four George III table candlesticks by David Bell, London, 1763, 94oz. 15dwt., 10in. high. (Sotheby's) $6,235

One of a pair of George III table candlesticks by Ebenezer Coker, London, 1763, 27oz.16dwt., 8¾in. high. (Sotheby's) $2,080

One of two matching George III table candlesticks, 8½in. high, 21oz.4dwt. (Sotheby's) $1,560

One of a pair of George II table candlesticks by John Cafe, London, 1749, 37oz.7dwt., 8½in. high. (Sotheby's) $2,715

Rectangular card case with a view of Newstead Abbey, by Taylor & Perry, Birmingham, 1836, 9.5cm. high. (Sotheby's Belgravia) $385

Rare shaped rectangular card case by A. & S., Birmingham, 1858, 10cm. long. (Sotheby's Belgravia) $285

Shaped rectangular card case by Nathaniel Mills, Birmingham, 1844, 10.1cm. high.(Sotheby's Belgravia) $345

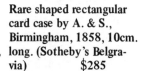

Silver card case by Gervase Wheeler, Birmingham, 1839, 3¾in. long. (Sotheby's) $415

Austrian silver and enamel rectangular cigarette and card case, stamped. (Christie's) $275

William IV silver gilt rectangular card case by Joseph Willmore, Birmingham, 1834, 3¾in. long. (Sotheby's) $280

Parcel gilt card case by Edward Smith, Birmingham, 1850. (Sotheby's Belgravia) $480

Shaped rectangular card case by Joseph Taylor, Birmingham, 1844, 10cm. high.(Sotheby's Belgravia) $455

Silver card case by Taylor & Perry, Birmingham, 1842, 9.2cm. high, stamped with views.(Sotheby's Belgravia) $265

Baluster-shaped silver caster with pierced cover, London, 1751, by John Berthelot, 9oz. (Lacy Scott) $750

George I vase-shaped caster by Samuel Welder, London, 1725, 5¾in. high, 6oz.1dwt. (Sotheby's) $835

Silver caster by Henricus de Potter, Brussels, 1778, 8oz.9dwt., 19.5cm. high. (Sotheby's)$1,020

George I plain caster of inverted baluster form, by Augustine Courtauld, 1719, 8¼in. high, 13oz. 9dwt. (Christie's) $4,935

One of a pair of Queen Anne lighthouse casters by Joseph Ward, London, 1702, 11oz. 13dwt., 6½in. high. (Sotheby's) $3,450

George II vase-shaped caster, London, 1734, 7¼in. high, 9oz.7dwt. (Sotheby's) $940

One of a set of three George II vase-shaped casters by Charles Martin. London, 1730, 21oz.1dwt., 7in. high. (Sotheby's) $1,665

Large silver sugar caster with pierced cover, Sheffield, 1899, 6½in. high, 5¼oz. (Dickinson, Davy & Markham) $150

George II silver muffineer by Simon Pantin, London, 1725-26, 6¼in. high, 11 troy oz. (Robert W. Skinner Inc.) $600

SILVER

Epergne by William Comyns
& Sons, London, 1898,
48cm. long, 114.8oz.
(Sotheby's Belgravia)
$2,585

Early 19th century Ital-
ian parcel gilt model of
the Virgin Immaculata,
22.9cm. high, 19oz.
(Sotheby's)$550

George II epergne pierced
scroll feet, by William
Cripps, circa 1755-56,
20½in. high, 193oz.
(Christie's)$11,285

Victorian table center-
piece by S. Smith and
W. Nicholson, 1853,
27in. high, 158oz.
(Christie's) $3,885

Set of three silver dessert
dish stands, German, circa
1870, 61.6oz. (Sotheby's
Belgravia) $1,370

'English electroplated
centerpiece with glass
nautilus shell, 1860's,
36.4cm. high.(Sothe-
by's Belgravia) $310

Epergne by Henry Wilkin-
son & Co., London, 1900,
17¼in. high, 70oz.18dwt.
(Sotheby Beresford Adams)
$1,480

Large silver plated table
candelabrum cum center-
piece by Padley, Parkin &
Co., circa 1860, 34in. high.
(Sotheby's) $1,920

Large electroplated des-
sert stand with ivory
stem, 1890's, 55.4cm.
high. (Sotheby's Bel-
gravia) $390

Electroplated table centerpiece by W. & G. Sissons, Sheffield, circa 1860, 60.5cm. high. (Sotheby's Belgravia) $730

Silver epergne with cut glass dishes, by Walker & Hall, Sheffield, 1900, 65.6oz., 53.5cm. wide. (Sotheby's Belgravia) $1,005

Electroplated table centerpiece by Elkington & Co., 30cm. high, 1898. (Sotheby's Belgravia)$370

Silver centerpiece by Edward Barnard & Sons, London, 1860, 38cm. high, 61oz. (Sotheby's Belgravia) $1,315

Elkington & Co. three-piece garniture, Birmingham, 1890, 115oz. (Sotheby, King & Chasemore) $1,520

Table ornament of a man holding a shell on his head, by Barnard & Co., 1910, 15¾in. high, 71oz. (Christie's) $1,260

Victorian centerpiece by S. Smith and W. Nicholson, 1862, 20¼in. high, 52oz. (Christie's)$1,295

Silver and glass epergne and condiment set by Christopher Haines, Dublin, 1786, 14½in. high. (Robert W. Skinner Inc.) $2,600

Victorian table centerpiece by S. Smith and W. Nicholson, London, 1862, 39oz., 16¼in. high. (Lawrence Fine Art) $850

557

French shaped circular chamber candle-stick, Paris, 1722-26, 5oz.4dwt.
(Christie's) $3,075

Maltese silver chamberstick with ribbed and fluted pan, circa 1760, 6oz.12dwt.
(Sotheby's) $1,380

George III chamber candlestick by William Stroud, London, 1815, 5in. diam., 8oz.5dwt. (Sotheby's) $665

French chamber candlestick on rim foot with reeded border, 1787, 7oz. 15dwt. (Christie's) $2,535

French plain circular chamber candle-stick, Marseilles, 1741, 5oz.13dwt.
(Christie's) $3,440

One of a pair of William IV chamber candlesticks by T. J. & N. Creswick, Sheffield, 1834, 19oz.1dwt., 6in. diam.
(Sotheby's) $1,565

One of a pair of George IV shaped cir-cular chamber candlesticks by Matthew Boulton, Birmingham, 1827, 23oz.
(Christie's) $2,220

Mid 18th century French plain chamber candlestick by Jean Vieuseux, Albi, 10oz.18dwt. (Christie's) $2,355

Mid 18th century French plain pear-shaped chocolate pot with wood handle, 7½in. high, 15oz. 14dwt. (Christie's) $2,995

Continental white metal chocolate pot with turned wood handle. (J. M. Welch & Son) $530

George II pear-shaped chocolate pot by Charles Kandler, circa 1745, 11in. high, 41oz. (Christie's) $17,160

CIGARETTE CASES

German enameled cigarette case on silver colored metal, circa 1910, 9.4cm. high. (Sotheby's Belgravia) $1,445

Rectangular cigar box by Horace Woodward & Co. Ltd., London, 1896, 25cm. long. (Sotheby's Belgravia) $785

Oval black lacquer cigarette box, stamped Charlton & Co., 1920's, 7cm. high. (Sotheby's Belgravia) $550

Plain oblong enamel cigarette case, Birmingham, 1905, 9.1cm. high. (Sotheby's Belgravia) $1,135

Austrian rounded rectangular silver cigarette case designed by Georg Anton Scheidt, 8.8cm. wide. (Christie's) $235

Engine-turned oblong cigarette case, with secret compartment, London, 1922, 3¾in. wide. (Sotheby's) $895

CLARET JUGS

SILVER

Plated metal and glass claret jug designed by Christopher Dresser, with hinged cover, 23.5cm. high. (Phillips) $145

Late 19th century decorative claret jug, 15in. high. (Sotheby's) $895

One of a pair of silver gilt mounted clear glass claret jugs by W. & G. Sissons, Sheffield, 1866, 24.5cm. high. (Sotheby's Belgravia) $1,555

Victorian silver and glass claret jug by George Fox, 1889, 12¼in. high. (Christie's) $1,755

Bulbous glass claret jug with ribbed body, silver mounted neck and lip, Sheffield, 1904, 8in. high. (Burrows & Day) $330

One of a pair of German gilt metal mounted cut glass claret jugs, circa 1890, 31cm. high. (Sotheby's Belgravia) $1,075

Victorian urn-shaped claret jug with plain glass body and silver fittings, Sheffield, 1883, 10in. high. (Burrows & Day) $335

Glass claret jug with bulbous body and silver mounts, London, 1896, 7¾in. high. (Burrows & Day) $330

One of a pair of silver gilt mounted Victorian claret jugs by J. W. Figg, London, 1865, 16¼in. high. (Sotheby's) $6,615

Fine late 19th century cameo glass claret jug with Continental silver mounts, 9½in. high. (Locke & England) $485

Silver mounted clear glass claret jug by C. E. Nixon, Sheffield, 1894, 30.5cm. high. (Sotheby's Belgravia) $990

Silver mounted clear glass claret jug by Charles Boyton, London, 1874, 26.4cm. high.(Sotheby's Belgravia) $660

German silver mounted etched glass claret jug, Bremen, circa 1879, 36.5cm. high.(Sotheby's Belgravia) $665

Plated metal and glass lemonade jug, engraved, 22cm. high, with ebonized wooden handle. (Phillips) $145

Victorian silver mounted glass claret jug, Birmingham, 1872, 10½in. high. (Sotheby's) $980

Late Victorian claret jug by Dixon & Sons, Sheffield, 1890, 33cm. high, 29oz. (H. Spencer & Sons Ltd.) $645

Silver mounted clear glass claret jug by J. Grinsell & Sons, Ltd., London, 1898, 27.5cm. high. (Sotheby's Belgravia) $650

Silver mounted cut glass claret jug by S. Drew & Sons, London, 1899, 28.7cm. high.(Sotheby's Belgravia) $730

SILVER

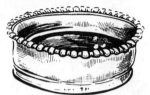

One of a set of four George III decanter coasters by R. & S. Hennell, London, 1808, 14cm. diam. (H. Spencer & Sons Ltd.) $2,695

One of a pair of George IV wine coasters, by John and James Settle, Sheffield, 1822, 6in. diam. (Sotheby's) $1,535

One of a pair of early Victorian wine coasters by Joseph and John Angell, London, 1838, 5¼in. diam. (Sotheby's) $915

One of a pair of George IV wine coasters by John Bridge, London, 1826, 5¾in. diam. (Sotheby's) $3,980

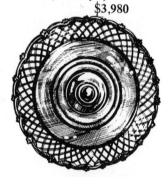

Set of four silver wine coasters by John and Thomas Settle, Sheffield, 1818. (Phillips) $1,810

One of a pair of Victorian plated shallow shaped circular coasters, circa 1860, 20cm. diam. (Phillips) $235

One of a set of four George III silver gilt wine coasters by Jonathan Alleine, London, 1771, 5in. diam.(Sotheby's) $6,695

One of a set of four George III circular coasters by Robert Hennell, London, 1776, 5in. diam. (Sotheby's) $3,970

George I tapered cylindrical coffee pot by Edward Vincent, London, 1725, 16oz.16dwt., 7¾in. high.(Sotheby's) $2,965

Early George II cylindrical coffee pot by John le Sage, London, 1728, 8½in. high, 23oz.16dwt. (Sotheby's) $5,320

George II tapered cylindrical coffee pot by Thos. Tearle, London, 1732, 23oz.9dwt., 9¼in. high. (Sotheby's)$4,025

George II baluster coffee pot by John Payne, London, 1757, 23oz.9dwt., 9½in. high. (Sotheby's) $2,715

Mid 18th century Irish provincial coffee pot, by Samuel Johns, Limerick, circa 1770, 34oz.15dwt., 10½in. high. (Sotheby's) $4,225

George II coffee pot by Thomas Whipham, London, 1744, 30oz., 35.5cm. high. (H. Spencer & Sons Ltd.) $2,850

Belgian pear-shaped coffee pot with domed cover, Brussels, 1759, 8¾in. high, 14oz.10dwt. (Christie's)$3,285

George II plain pear-shaped coffee pot on gadrooned foot, by D. Smith and R. Sharp, 1766, 9¾in. high, 25oz. (Christie's) $2,665

Plain tapering circular coffee pot by Mappin & Webb Ltd., London, 1965, 27.8oz.(Sotheby's Belgravia) $675

Silver coffee pot by Thos. Bradbury, Sheffield, 1903, 22oz., 10½in. high. (Lawrence Fine Art) **$540**

George III coffee pot on stand by Paul Storr, London, 1802, 12¾in. high, 55oz. (Lawrence Fine Art) **$3,860**

Victorian silver coffee pot by Hands & Son, London, 1858, 10in. high, 30oz. (Lawrence Fine Art) **$985**

George III pear-shaped coffee pot by Tudor & Leader, Sheffield, 1774, 12in. high, 23oz. (Christie's) **$2,055**

Early George III pear-shaped coffee pot, London, 1764, 27oz. (H. Spencer & Sons Ltd.) **$1,505**

George II coffee pot with ivory handle, London, 1747, 25oz. (H. Spencer & Sons Ltd.) **$1,090**

George II tapered cylindrical coffee pot by Edward Feline, London, 1743, 24oz.2dwt., 8¾in. high. (Sotheby's) **$2,910**

Victorian silver coffee pot by E. & J. Barnard, London, 1862, 31oz., 10in. high. (Lawrence Fine Art) **$1,060**

George III pear-shaped coffee pot by Benjamin Gignac, 1767, 11¼in. high, 32oz. (Christie's) **$2,355**

George III coffee pot by William Cripps, London, 1775, 10in. high. (Sotheby, King & Chasemore) $720

George III pear-shaped coffee pot by D. Whyte and W. Holmes, 1762, 12in. high, 32oz. (Christie's) $2,195

George II pear-shaped coffee pot by Robert Calderwood, Dublin, circa 1760, 9¼in. high, 27oz. (Christie's) $2,880

George II plain tapering pot by Samuel Wilmott, Plymouth, 9½in. high, 24oz.18dwt.(Christie's) $3,260

George III vase-shaped coffee jug by Fogelberg & Gilbert, London, 1784, 24oz.17dwt., 12¾in. high.(Sotheby's) $2,910

George II vase-shaped coffee pot by James Gould, 1743, 9in. high, 30oz. (Christie's) $2,510

Tapering circular coffee jug by Tessiers Ltd., London, 1928, 14.3oz., 19cm. high. (Sotheby's Belgravia) $590

George II pear-shaped coffee pot by Lothian & Robertson, Edinburgh, 1759, 12in. high, 36oz. (Christie's) $3,345

Tapering cylindrical coffee pot by Tessiers Ltd., London, 1927, 17.8oz., 21.5cm. high. (Sotheby's Belgravia) $530

Heavy silver octagonal-shaped coffee pot with domed lid and wooden handle. (Butler & Hatch Waterman) $235

Compressed circular coffee pot with reeded girdle, by J. & H. Lias, London, 1838, 26oz., 20cm. high.(Sotheby's Belgravia) $890

George II pear-shaped coffee pot by John Swift, 1756, 35oz., 10¾in. high. (Christie's)$3,860

George II tapered cylindrical coffee pot by Gabriel Sleath, London, 1744, 20oz., 8¼in. high. (Sotheby's)$2,615

George III baluster coffee jug, by John Edwards III, London, 1806, 27oz. 13dwt., 8in. high. (Sotheby's) $735

One of a pair of tapering circular jugs for coffee and hot milk by Tessiers Ltd., London, 1928, 51.2oz., 23cm. high. (Sotheby's Belgravia) $1,240

One of a pair of tapering circular pots by Collingwood & Co. Ltd., London, 1966, 49.6oz., 24.5cm. high. (Sotheby's Belgravia) $1,200

Victorian oval tapering coffee pot by J. Whipple & Co., Exeter, 1877, 27oz. 9¼in. high. (Christie's) $1,130

George II plain tapering cylindrical coffee pot by Humphrey Payne, 1736, 8¾in. high, 17oz.13dwt. (Christie's)$3,430

Small silver cream jug decorated in Art Nouveau style, by Walker & Hall, Sheffield, 2¾oz. (Butler & Hatch Waterman) $100

George IV compressed circular milk jug by William Eaton, London, 1822, 16oz. 1dwt., 4in. high. (Sotheby's) $565

George III milk jug, London, 1812, with reeded handle.(Lawrence Fine Art) $185

George III helmet-shaped milk jug by John Emes, London, 1805, 7oz.14dwt., 6¼in. high. (Sotheby's) $580

American silver footed cream jug with high pouring spout by John Allen, Boston, 3in. high, 3 troy oz. (Robert W. Skinner Inc.) $1,700

Silver gilt milk jug by R. & S. Garrard & Co., London, 1869, 13.5oz., 18.5cm. high.(Sotheby's Belgravia) $1,445

Silver cream jug by Stokes & Ireland, London, 1900, 4½in. high.(Lawrence Fine Art) $115

George II cream pail, maker's mark WM, London, 1751, 3oz.3dwt., 2¼in. high. (Sotheby's) $715

George III fluted helmet-shaped milk jug by H. Chawner, London, 1792, 7oz., 5½in. high. (Sotheby's) $580

567

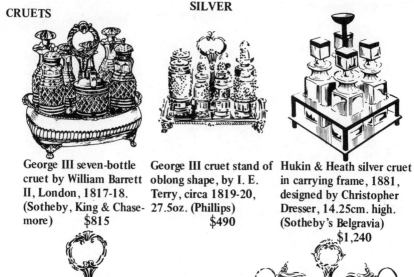

George III seven-bottle cruet by William Barrett II, London, 1817-18. (Sotheby, King & Chasemore) $815

George III cruet stand of oblong shape, by I. E. Terry, circa 1819-20, 27.5oz. (Phillips) $490

Hukin & Heath silver cruet in carrying frame, 1881, designed by Christopher Dresser, 14.25cm. high. (Sotheby's Belgravia) $1,240

Regency rectangular egg cruet by Rebecca Emes and Edward Barnard, London, 1814, 27.5oz. (Woolley & Wallis) $680

George IV four-bottle cruet frame by Philip Rundell, London, 1820, 43oz.15dwt., 11in. high. (Sotheby's) $3,220

Electroplated eight-bottle cruet frame, mounts by Elkington & Co., 1867, 32.7cm. long.(Sotheby's Belgravia) $435

One of a pair of Victorian cruet frames, by Robert Harper, London, 1875, 11oz.7dwt., 4¾in. high. (Sotheby's) $1,385

George II Warwick cruet frame, Edinburgh, 1736-7, 32oz.9dwt., 8½in. high. (Sotheby's)$2,080

George III Warwick frame, complete with casters and bottles, by Thomas Daniel, London, 1776, 37oz.7dwt., 9¾in. high. (Sotheby's) $2,380

Parcel gilt egg cruet of six, by R. Hennell & Sons, London, 1850, 27.9oz. (Sotheby's Belgravia) $1,135

George IV silver cruet stand with glass bottles. (May, Whetter & Grose) $400

George IV egg cruet by J. E. Terry & Co., London, 1829, 64oz. (H. Spencer & Sons Ltd.) $810

George III navette-shaped seven-bottle cruet frame by Henry Greenway, London, 1795, 38oz.11dwt., 16¾in. wide. (Sotheby's) $1,710

George III three-bottle decanter stand, London, 1818, 30oz. (H. Spencer & Sons Ltd.) $940

George III cruet frame with pierced gallery sides, by John Delmester, 1764, 16.25oz. (Phillips) $615

George II composite Warwick frame by Samuel Wood, circa 1755, London, 35oz.17dwt. (Sotheby's) $510

Beaten silver three-handled cup, Sheffield, 1910, 20oz. (J. M. Welch & Son) $380

William III two-handled cup and cover by Thomas Bolton, Dublin, 1696, 6in. high, 11oz.11dwt. (Christie's) $2,255

One of a pair of George III bell-shaped two-handled cups by Bergin & Macklin, Dublin, 1817, 7½in. high, 32oz. (Sotheby's) $845

Two-handled cup and cover by E. C. Purdee, London, 1896, 65.6oz., 40cm. high. (Sotheby's Belgravia) $1,035

Replica of a steeple cup by Goldsmiths & Silversmiths Co. Ltd., London, 1921-29, 24oz., 41.5cm. high. (Sotheby's Belgravia) $385

George III coconut cup and cover by Phipps & Robinson, London, 1794, 6¾in. high. (Sotheby's) $830

George III two-handled silver gilt cup and cover by W. Burwash and R. Sibley, 1810, 17in. high, 109oz. (Christie's) $3,695

George III vase-shaped two-handled cup and cover by John Scofield, 1796, 16½in. high, 78oz. (Christie's) $3,900

George III two-handled silver gilt cup and cover by W. Burwash and R. Sibley, 1808, 18in. high, 96oz. (Christie's) $2,870

Circular presentation cup
and cover, by Horace
Woodward & Co. Ltd.,
1890, 173.7oz., 68.5cm.
high. (Sotheby's Belgravia)
$2,480

Sterling silver and agate
three-handled loving cup,
circa 1900, 4½in. diam.
(Robert W. Skinner Inc.)
$200

Large two-handled bell-
shaped cup by Elkington
& Co., Birmingham, 1868,
81.9oz., 40cm. high.
(Sotheby's Belgravia)
$730

One of a pair of Dutch orna-
mental standing cups, London,
1911, 76oz., 34cm. high. (H.
Spencer & Sons Ltd.)
$2,945

One of a pair of George
III silver gilt mounted
ostrich cups and covers,
by Thos. Robins, 1808,
11¼in. high. (Christie's)
$5,800

German parcel gilt beaker-
shaped cup and cover,
circa 1880, 39.5cm. high,
60.3oz. (Sotheby's Bel-
gravia) $1,240

Victorian christening cup
by Richard Hennell,
1865, 4in. high. (Law-
rence Fine Art)$185

One of a pair of German
parcel gilt cups by B.
Neresheimer & Sohne,
Chester, 1902, 9oz.5dwt.,
7in. high. (Sotheby's)
$450

George II two-handled
cup by Joseph Jones,
Limerick, circa 1730,
8½in. high, 36oz.
(Christie's)
$3,080

One of a pair of George III oblong entree dishes and covers, London, 1809, 127oz. 2dwt., 11½in. wide. (Sotheby's) $3,970

One of a pair of George III silver entree dishes and covers by John Edwards III, London, 1795, 75oz., 14¼in. wide. (Lawrence Fine Art) $1,660

One of a pair of silver William IV octagonal meat dish covers, London, 1831-34, 15in. wide. (Sotheby's) $2,135

One of a pair of George III shaped oblong entree dishes and covers by W. Burwash and R. Sibley, 1808, 110oz., 11in. long. (Christie's) $3,260

Victorian oval revolving breakfast dish with plain hinged cover, by Fenton Bros., Sheffield, 54oz.8dwt. (Sotheby Beresford Adams) $1,110

William IV parcel gilt large shaped circular sideboard dish by Benjamin Preston, 1833, 25¾in. diam., 77oz. (Christie's) $2,590

One of four George III plain oblong entree dishes and covers by John Edwards III, 1808, 11¼in. long, 208oz.(Christie's) $9,460

George III Irish dish ring by Thomas Jones, Dublin, 1787, 9oz.15dwt., 7½in. diam. (Sotheby's) $2,345

One of a pair of Sheffield plated entree dishes, covers and stands, 15in. wide. (Lawrence Fine Art) $500

One of a pair of presentation shaped oval entree dishes, covers and handles, 103.4oz., 35cm. long. (Sotheby's Belgravia) $2,470

One of four plain George III octagonal entree dishes and covers by D. Scott and B. Smith, 1803, 234oz., 11¾in. long. (Christie's) $9,955

One of a pair of George III oblong entree dishes and covers by T. & J. Guest and J. Cradock, London, 1811, 120oz.9dwt. (Sotheby's) $3,450

One of a pair of George IV silver gilt shaped circular sideboard dishes by Edward Farrell, 1822, 18in. diam., 108oz. (Christie's) $8,325

Irish sterling silver dish ring, Dublin, 1796, 8in. diam., 13 troy oz. (Robert W. Skinner Inc.) $950

Victorian melon pattern silver dish cover by Robert Garrard, London, 1841, 30oz.18dwt., 11½in. wide. (Sotheby Beresford Adams) $760

One of a pair of George III plain oblong entree dishes and covers by Paul Storr, 1809, 155oz., 12½in. long. (Christie's) $11,765

DISHES

Circular silver dish with embossed rim, standing on four feet. (Biddle & Webb) $270

One of a set of four George III entree dishes and covers by P. & W. Bateman, 1807, 11in. long, 229oz. (Christie's) $8,150

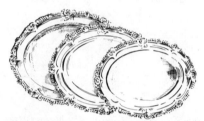

Set of three George III shaped oval meat dishes in sizes, by Paul Storr, London, 1811, 266oz. (Sotheby's) $15,960

George III silver gilt shaped circular dish by William Pitts, 1809, 15½in. diam., 51oz. (Christie's)$4,625

Early 20th century decorative hardstone dish with silver gilt mounts, 14.5cm. long. (Sotheby's Belgravia)$725

Plain oval breakfast dish and liner, Sheffield, 1926, 75oz., 34.4cm. wide. (Sotheby's Belgravia) $1,240

Deep silver dish with embossed rim, standing on three feet. (Biddle & Webb) $270

One of a pair of silver gilt oval sweetmeat dishes by Henry William Curry, London, 1887, 17.6oz. (Sotheby's Belgravia) $370

574

One of a set of four George III oblong entree dishes and covers by Benjamin Smith II, 12in. long, 285oz. (Christie's) $12,000

Novelty trinket dish in the form of a walnut and a rat, 11.4cm. long, 5.2oz. (Sotheby's Belgravia) $270

One of a pair of George IV butter shells by William Eley, London, 1825, 7oz. 12dwt., 4¾in. long. (Sotheby's) $1,165

Georgian oval silver gilt dish, by Richard Williams, Dublin, circa 1770, 16oz. 10dwt., 11¾in. wide. (Sotheby's) $775

Georg Jensen silver compote, Copenhagen, 20th century, 9½in. diam., 28 troy oz. (Robert W. Skinner Inc.) $1,000

One of a set of five pedestal dessert stands by H. & Co., London, 71.7oz., 1919. (Sotheby's Belgravia) $1,935

Circular vegetable dish and cover on Sheffield Plate base, 47.6oz., 26.5cm. diam., circa 1849. (Sotheby's Belgravia) $970

One of a pair of shaped circular open-work salt dishes by C. T. & G. Fox, London, 1841, 11.8cm. diam. (Sotheby's Belgravia) $370

EWERS

George III inverted pear-
shaped cream ewer by
Nathaniel Appleton and
Ann Smith, London, 1780.
(Woolley & Wallis)
$340

Helmet-shaped ewer by
Giuseppe Palmentiero,
Naples, circa 1720, 25oz.
10dwt., 23.5cm. high.
(Sotheby's)$7,430

20th century American
silver presentation ewer
of helmet shape, 14in.
high, 32 troy oz.
(Robert W. Skinner Inc.)
$300

Armada pattern ewer
richly chased, 59.3oz.,
46.5cm. high.
(Sotheby's Belgravia)
$2,275

Pompeian Ascos shaped wine
ewer by Paul Storr, London,
1838, 8¾in. high, 35oz.18dwt.
(Sotheby's) $7,525

George III inverted pear-
shaped ewer by Fred.
Vonham, London, 1767,
51oz.7dwt., 16¾in. high.
(Sotheby's)$4,630

One of a pair of late 19th
century Austro-Hungarian
decorative ewers, 18.4cm.
high. (Sotheby's Belgravia)
$530

American silver ewer by J.
& I. Cox, New York, circa
1835, 34oz.10dwt., 12¼in.
high. (Sotheby's)
$965

Lobed circular wine ewer
with rustic handle, by
Edward Barnard & Sons,
London, 1860, 30.6oz.,
33cm. high. (Sotheby's
Belgravia) $975

Austrian ewer with sterling silver overlay, by Loetz, circa 1900, 5¼in. high. (Robert W. Skinner Inc.) $1,050

William IV large ewer by Morris and Michael Emanuel, London, 1835, 218oz., 27½in. high. (Sotheby's)$5,705

19th century decorative gilt metal ewer with pentafoil foot, 13in. high.(Sotheby's) $1,080

FLASKS

Victorian brandy flask by James Dixon & Sons, Sheffield, 1875, 3oz.11dwt., 6¼in. high. (Sotheby's) $460

Oval spirit flask with detachable base, by Elkington & Co., London, 1872, 13.9oz., 18cm. high. (Sotheby's Belgravia) $540

17th century silver flask, circa 1675, 2oz.13dwt. (Sotheby's)$800

FRAMES

Victorian rectangular dressing glass with silver frame, by William Comyns, 1885, 15¾in. high. (Lawrence Fine Art) $655

WMF mirror frame cast with a young girl, circa 1900, 34cm. high. (Sotheby's Belgravia) $800

Art Nouveau silver photograph frame by W.N., Chester, 1903, 31cm. high.(Christie's) $765

FLATWARE

Part of a set of twelve George II three-pronged table forks, London, 1737, 26oz. (H. Spencer & Sons Ltd.) $1,210

Fine shagreen cased St. Cloud cutlery set, 19cm. wide, circa 1720. (Sotheby, King & Chasemore) $560

One of twelve silver tablespoons by Geo. Timberlake, circa 1756, 26oz. (Woolley & Wallis) $395

One of a set of six unusual silver and enameled coffee spoons with Mickey Mouse terminals, 11cm. high, Birmingham, 1929. (Phillips) $500

Victorian presentation trowel by Martin Hall & Co., Sheffield, 1879, 13¼in. long. (Sotheby's) $385

Sheffield plate pie server with turned wooden grip, 1777, 15in. long. (Robert W. Skinner Inc.) $70

One of twelve dessert spoons, maker R.R., London, 1770-74, 13oz. (Woolley & Wallis) $305

16th century seal top spoon probably by John Quycke, Barnstaple, circa 1590. (Sotheby's) $625

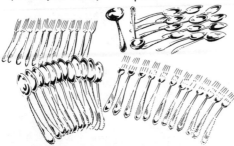

Old English and bead pattern cutlery canteen, London, 1884, fifty pieces in all. (Locke & England) $2,640

Cased set of cutlery by Vintner's of Sheffield, 1930, in bow-fronted mahogany case. (Phillips) $3,660

Part of a set of twelve fruit knives and forks by Atkin Brothers, Sheffield, 1937, in wood case. (Sotheby's Belgravia) $515

Twelve-setting canteen of cutlery in mahogany box, marked Jayes, Oxford Street, London. (Allen & May) $1,415

One of a set of twelve three-prong table forks, by Wm. Wooler, London, 1764, 28oz. (Woolley & Wallis) $595

Electroplated dessert spoon, designed by Charles Rennie Mackintosh, circa 1903, 15.5cm. long. (Sotheby's Belgravia) $1,515

Gibson patent-type caster-oil spoon by Henry Flavelle, Dublin, circa 1835, 5½in. long. (Sotheby's) $1,870

George III traveling apple corer by Joseph Willmore, Birmingham, 1814, 4in. long. (Sotheby's) $545

One of six Hanoverian pattern table-spoons, circa 1750, by Hugh Ross, Tain, 14oz.13dwt. (Sotheby's) $1,665

Charles I apostle spoon by Ralph Herman, Exeter, circa 1630. (Sotheby's) $1,880

Late 19th century fiddle and thread composite suite of ninety-three-pieces of cutlery, 158oz. (Lacy Scott) $4,070

Part of a set of twelve fruit knives and forks with green hardstone handles, by Atkin Brothers, Sheffield, 1900. (Sotheby's Belgravia) $310

Gibson-patent type castor oil spoon, circa 1800, 2oz., 5¼in. long. (Sotheby's) $325

One of a set of twelve Elkington & Co. silver teaspoons, designed by Charles Rennie Mackintosh, circa 1907, 13.5cm. long. (Sotheby's Belgravia) $710

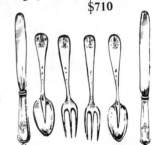

Part of a Georg Jensen table service of eighty-four pieces, 1939, 106oz. (Christie's) $5,305

Part of a George I Hanoverian table service, engraved with Prince of Wales' feathers, 92oz. (Christie's) $7,295

Composite canteen of fiddle pattern table cutlery, 130oz. in all. (Lacy Scott) $1,850

Part of a late 19th/early 20th century Austrian canteen of cutlery, by J. C. Klinkosch, Vienna, in fitted case. (Sotheby's Belgravia) $2,955

Electroplated spoon and two forks designed by Charles Rennie Mackintosh, circa 1903, 18.5cm. long. (Sotheby's Belgravia) $360

Large punch ladle by Wood & Hughes, New York, circa 1870, 15¾in. long, 8 troy oz. (Robert W. Skinner Inc.) $475

Silver soup ladle by Hester Bateman, 1782. (Christie's) $360

George III jockey cap caddy spoon by Joseph Taylor, Birmingham, 1798. (Woolley & Wallis) $295

Pair of William IV silver gilt grape scissors, by William Traies, London, 1833, 4oz.14dwt. (Sotheby's) $750

Part of a Hanoverian silver gilt dessert service by Lewis Mettayer, 1709, 72oz.(Christie's) $8,580

Part of a set of six Victorian silver gilt dessert knives, forks and spoons, London, 1857, 38oz. (H. Spencer & Sons Ltd.) $1,140

Part of a set of twelve fiddle pattern teaspoons and a pair of sugar tongs, 12.8oz. (Sotheby's Belgravia) $155

Arts & Crafts silver caddy spoon, Birmingham, 1919, 9.5cm. long, handle set in mother-of-pearl. (Phillips) $135

Part of a canteen of table silver by James Dixon & Sons, Sheffield, contained in brass bound oak box. (Sotheby's Belgravia) $4,330

Pair of French parcel gilt salad servers, Paris, circa 1880, 9oz. 15dwt.(Christie's) $260

Pair of late 19th century vine pattern grape scissors, 18cm. long, 3.8oz. (Sotheby's Belgravia) $175

Guild of Handicrafts Ltd. silver teaspoon by C. R. Ashbee, London, 1907. (Christie's) $440

GOBLETS & CHALICES

Victorian engraved silver goblet, 19½oz. (Phillips) $255

Gorham sterling silver chalice in Renaissance revival style, Rhode Island, circa 1864, 9½in. high, 14½ troy oz. (Robert W. Skinner Inc.) $275

George II vase-shaped goblet by Henry Chawner, London, 1792, 10oz.8dwt., 6¾in. high. (Sotheby's)$450

One of a pair of George III wine goblets by Walter Brind, London, 1774, 16oz.4dwt., 6½in. high. (Sotheby's) $1,290

One of six George IV silver gilt goblets by Joseph Angell, 1826, 6¾in. high, 55oz. (Christie's) $4,440

One of a pair of Victorian goblets by George Fox, 1869, 8in. high, 23oz. (Christie's) $1,200

One of a pair of George III wine goblets by Walter Brind, London, 1774, 13oz. 18dwt., 6in. high. (Sotheby's) $3,555

William IV chalice by Joseph and John Angell, London, 1835. (Sotheby's) $340

One of a pair of George III bell-shaped goblets by Robert and David Hennell, London, 1796, 14oz.4dwt., 6½in. high. (Sotheby's)$1,165

One of a rare set of eight George III silver goblets by Rebecca Emes and Edward Barnard, London, 1816, 32oz., 12.5cm. high. (H. Spencer & Sons Ltd.) $5,580

Silver gilt recusant chalice on spreading hexafoil foot, circa 1630, 8¼in. high, 14oz.7dwt. (Christie's) $10,725

One of a set of six goblets on pedestal feet, by Gladwin Ltd., Sheffield, 1946, 55.1oz., 16.9cm. high. (Sotheby's Belgravia) $550

Goblet formed as an oak tree on hexagonal base, 1902, 6¾in. high, 24oz. (Christie's)$1,385

One of a set of four William IV silver goblets by Charles Price, London, 1832-33, 27oz.9dwt., 6in. high. (Sotheby's)$3,760

19th century lacquered silver goblet decorated in enamel and gold hiramahie, 15cm. high. (Sotheby's Belgravia) $1,400

Silver goblet by Omar Ramsden, 4½in. high. (Graves, Son & Pilcher) $675

German silver gilt chalice with hexagonal stem, circa 1500, 8oz.3dwt., 15.8cm. high. (Sotheby's) $2,015

Fireman's coin silver chalice by John Curry, Philadelphia, 17½ troy oz., 9½in. high. (Robert W. Skinner Inc.)$400

INKSTANDS

William IV shaped oval inkstand by Thomas Wimbush and Henry Hyde, London, 1833, 86oz.13dwt. (Sotheby's) $3,740

American Kutani and sterling silver inkstand, circa 1900, 12¼in. long, by John Wanamaker. (Robert W. Skinner Inc.) $550

Shaped oblong double well inkstand by Pearce & Sons, London, 1912, 33oz., 31cm. long. (Sotheby's Belgravia) $650

Late 19th/early 20th century white metal novelty inkstand, 43cm. wide. (Sotheby's Belgravia) $660

Two-bottle inkstand with pierced gallery border, by R. & S. Garrard & Co., London, 1853, 46oz., 29.1cm. long. (Sotheby's Belgravia) $1,135

Silver shaped double well inkstand by Henry Wilkinson & Co., Sheffield, 1869, 9¾in. long, 26oz.8dwt. (Sotheby's) $625

Shaped oval double well inkstand by Edward Barnard & Sons, London, 1853, 28.4oz., 35.5cm. long. (Sotheby's Belgravia) $825

Shaped rectangular two-bottle inkstand by James Dixon & Sons, Sheffield, 1837, 39.8oz., 28cm. long. (Sotheby's Belgravia) $970

Continental silver colored metal inkstand in the shape of two shells. (H. Spencer & Sons Ltd.) $745

Shell-shaped single well inkstand by D. & C. Houle, London, 1875, 28.5cm. wide, 19.6oz. (Sotheby's Belgravia) $455

Shaped oval two-bottle inkstand by Henry Wilkinson & Co., Sheffield, 1853, 30.9oz., 35cm. long. (Sotheby's Belgravia) $850

Spanish shaped oval inkstand on claw and ball feet, Madrid, 1786, 11in. long, 62oz. (Christie's)$3,980

Victorian inkstand by Charles T. and George Fox, London, 1847, 10in. wide, 23oz. (Lawrence Fine Art) $850

Rectangular two-bottle inkstand by Charles Stuart Harris & Sons Ltd., London, 1903, 24oz.11dwt., 9¼in. long. (Sotheby's) $540

Oval two-bottle inkstand on four panel feet, by Edward Barnard & Sons, London, 1873, 14.6oz. (Sotheby's Belgravia) $850

George III oblong three-bottle inkstand by T. & G. Guest & Cradock, London, 1809, 19oz.8dwt., 8½in. wide. (Sotheby's) $1,075

INKSTANDS

19th century rosewood inkstand, inlaid with brass scrolls, and with brass handle, 14in. wide. (Edwards, Bigwood & Bewlay) $330

One of a pair of George III oblong inkstands by T. & J. Guest and J. Cradock, 1808, 66oz. (Christie's) $4,290

Victorian granite and antler mounted oblong silver inkstand and letter knife, mid 19th century, 14in. wide. (Sotheby's) $1,080

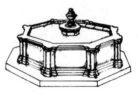

Silver gilt inkstand by Charles & Richard Comyns, 1920, 12½in. wide, 137oz. (Lawrence Fine Art)
                    $1,540

George III unusual silver gilt inkstand by Robert & Samuel Hennell, London, 1805, 16oz.1dwt., 5½in. high. (Sotheby's) $1,850

Rectangular two-bottle inkstand by Charles Stuart Harris & Sons Ltd., London, 1903, 24oz.11dwt., 9¼in. long. (Sotheby's) $540

George I oblong inkstand by Paul de Lamerie, London, 1721, 9¾in. wide, 30oz. (Sotheby's) $13,165
586

George II oblong silver gilt inkstand by Paul de Lamerie, 1731, 9in. long, 23oz. (Christie's) $11,600

Silver mounted cut-glass claret jug with leaf-capped scroll handle, Sheffield, 1895, 10in. high. (Sotheby, King & Chasemore) $435

Louis XVI pear-shaped hot milk jug, Paris, circa 1786-87, 6¾in. high, 10oz.12dwt. (Christie's) $2,000

Liberty & Co. 'Cymric' silver hot water jug designed by Archibald Knox, 1904, 10oz., 20cm. high. (Phillips) $550

George I baluster beer jug by Thomas Morse, London, 1721, 7½in. high, 29oz.3dwt. (Sotheby's) $6,300

George III silver gilt covered jug by Paul Storr, London, 1799, 47oz.6dwt., 13¼in. high. (Sotheby's) $41,350

Large early 19th century German pear-shaped wine jug, Luneburg, 15in. high, 47oz. (Christie's) $1,435

Jensen silver jug, designed by Johan Rohde, 1920, 22.75cm. high. (Sotheby's Belgravia) $1,045

Silver mounted glass jug of flattened circular body, by Heath & Middleton, Birmingham, 1907, 16.5cm. high. (Sotheby's Belgravia) $165

North Italian baluster covered jug, body fluted and ribbed, circa 1775, 15.5cm. high.(Sotheby's) $850

SILVER

George II pear-shaped hot water jug by John Hamilton, Dublin, circa 1740, 11in. high, 43oz. (Christie's)$1,465

George II plain pear-shaped beer jug by W. Shaw and W. Preist, 1759, 9¾in. high, 35oz. (Christie's) $5,575

George II pear-shaped hot water jug on reeded rim foot, by Peze Pilleau, 1730, 8½in. high, 29oz. (Christie's) $11,155

William IV vase-shaped jug by C. Reily and G. Storer, 1831, 11¼in. high, 38oz. (Christie's) $1,755

George II plain pear-shaped beer jug by Charles Leslie, Dublin, circa 1730, 7¾in. high, 33oz. (Christie's) $3,800

George II baluster covered jug by Erasmus Cope, Dublin, 1736, 33oz.9dwt., 11in. high. (Sotheby's) $5,435

Circular silver jug, chased round foot and shoulder, by C.T. & G. Fox, London, 1845, 37.5oz., 23cm. high. (Sotheby's Belgravia) $970

Mid 19th century silver water pitcher with shaped rim and pouring spout, 11in. high, 23 troy oz. (Robert W. Skinner Inc.) $250

George II pear-shaped jug and cover by John Hamilton, Dublin, circa 1745, 42oz., 9¾in. high. (Christie's)$1,900

Silver George II beer jug by R. A. Cox, London, 1759, 16oz., 7½in. high. (Sotheby, King & Chasemore) $1,599

Liberty & Co. 'Cymric' silver jug, Birmingham, 1901, 4½oz., 11cm. wide. (Christie's) $510

Regency style Victorian hot water jug, 1898, 25oz., 9in. high. (Hy. Duke & Son) $480

Gorham sterling silver pitcher in Renaissance revival style, Rhode Island, circa 1864, 15½in. high. (Robert W. Skinner Inc.) $500

German silver baluster jug, circa 1890, 20.4cm. high, 19.1oz. (Sotheby's Belgravia) $870

George III vase-shaped hot water jug with domed lid by Wakelin & Taylor, London, 1777, 12¼in. high. (Sotheby's) $1,880

Hungarian pear-shaped hot water jug by Johannes Georgius Puskailler, circa 1720, 14oz. (Christie's) $2,470

George II plain pear-shaped beer jug by Wm. Grundy, 1750, 7¾in. high, 28oz. (Christie's) $6,865

Silver hot water pot by Thomas Bradbury, Sheffield, 1903, 10½in. high, 21oz. (Lawrence Fine Art) $335

SILVER

One of a pair of silver plated plant troughs, 13½in. diam., with lion mask and ring handles. (Gilbert Baitson) $285

Guild of Handicrafts Ltd., mace head in silver colored metal, circa 1900, 17.5cm. high. (Sotheby's Belgravia) $240

Liberty & Co. silver stopper by Archibald Knox, Birmingham, 1906, 6.5cm. high. (Sotheby's Belgravia) $260

George I circular lemon strainer with pierced handles, by John Albright, 1724, 1oz. 18dwt. (Christie's) $965

George III vase-shaped argyle by John Scofield, 1786, 7in. high, 12oz. 8dwt. (Christie's) $2,260

George IV beehive honey pot by Rebecca Emes and Edward Barnard, London, 1828, 16oz., 14.5cm. high. (H. Spencer & Sons Ltd.) $4,370

Silver plated egg coddler on spirit stand with lid, on circular base. (Butler & Hatch Waterman) $35

Silver table lighter on black marble base, by E. H. Stockwell, London, 1879, 15.5cm. long. (Sotheby's Belgravia) $505

George III silver wax jack by J. Langford and J. Sebille, London, 1764, 5½in. high, 8¼oz. (Christie's S. Kensington) $1,080

590

Late 19th/early 20th century silver bell in the form of a lady, German, 4.4oz., 10.5cm. high. (Sotheby's Belgravia) $590

Pair of George III military spurs by J. Aldous, London, 1815, 5oz. (H. Spencer & Sons Ltd.) $560

One of two 19th century silver mounted snuff mulls, 3½in. long. (Sotheby's) $375

Silver plated wax jack with reeded base and nozzle, 6¾in. high. (Lawrence Fine Art) $230

George III vase-shaped argyle by Henry Green, London, 1793, 13oz., 7in. high. (Sotheby's) $920

Silver gilt and cloisonne enamel tea glass holder by Maria Semyonova, Moscow, 1908-17, 8cm. high. (Sotheby's)$1,225

Silver mounted shagreen triple spectacle case, early 19th century, 13cm. high, complete with spectacles. (Sotheby's) $855

Rare early 18th century solid gilt winepot, cover and cup, 14.6cm. and 8.6cm. high. (Sotheby's) $925

One of a pair of silver replicas of 17th century ginger jars and covers by Searle & Co., London, 1911, 40.8oz., 24.5cm. high. (Sotheby's Belgravia) $1,550

591

SILVER

George IV table bell by William Eaton, London, 1821, 3in. high, 4oz. 7dwt. (Sotheby's) $830

Unusual set of silver gilt letter scales, complete with a set of brass weights, London, 1903. (Sotheby, King & Chasemore) $435

George III table bell by Abraham Portal, London, 1764, 6oz.11dwt., 4¾in. high. (Sotheby's) $775

Oval vesta case in the form of a creel, by Thomas Johnson, London, 1883, 5.7cm. long. (Sotheby's Belgravia) $1,445

Table ornament in the form of an elephant, 28cm. long, by B. Neresheimer & Sohne, Hanau, 63.6oz. (Sotheby's Belgravia) $1,280

Late 19th/early 20th century electroplated copper wall sconce, one of a pair, 38.4cm. high. (Sotheby's Belgravia) $550

Small Puiforcat beaker with gently flared body, 1920's, 7.75cm. high. (Sotheby's Belgravia) $220

Silver plated Victorian triple shell biscuit warmer. (Christie's S. Kensington) $310

One of two silver Race Tickets, for Doncaster racecourse, 1777. (H. Spencer & Sons Ltd.) $4,460

19th century Continental silver model of a fox with detachable head, 12½in. long, 18oz. (Geering & Colyer) $670

German model of a stag, circa 1770, 10oz.17dwt., 28.3cm. high. (Sotheby's)
$2,125

Cast model of a running fox by F. B. Thomas & Co., London, 1930, 50oz., 42cm. long. (Sotheby's Belgravia) $1,415

Early 20th century gilt metal figure of an equestrian knight, 32.5cm. high. (Sotheby's Belgravia) $930

German decorative model of an ostrich with damaged body, circa 1880, 50.5cm. high. (Sotheby's Belgravia)
$1,450

Continental cast silver model of a stag, 78oz. (Christie's S. Kensington) $2,560

Cast silver model of a racehorse by Roberts & Belk, Sheffield, 1967, 55oz. (H. Spencer & Sons Ltd.)
$805

Pair of late 19th century German silver hand raised pheasants with articulated wings, 12½ and 15½in. long. (Robert W. Skinner Inc.)$725

Full-sized silver model of a hare by Asprey & Co., London, 1963, 184oz., 14½in. high. (Sotheby, King & Chasemore)
$4,915

SILVER

Cylindrical mug by Atkin Brothers, Sheffield, 1887, 5.3oz., 9.8cm. high. (Sotheby's Belgravia) $125

Queen Anne mug on reeded foot, by John Elston, Exeter, 1712, 3½in. high, 5oz.10dwt. (Christie's) $1,115

George I baluster mug by Nathaniel Gulliver, London, 1725, 4½in. high, 14oz.6dwt. (Sotheby's) $1,390

Octagonal spool-shaped christening can by John Evans, London, 1846, 5.2oz., 10.3cm. high. (Sotheby's Belgravia) $280

George III tapered cylindrical mug by Charles Wright, London, 1778, 16oz.12dwt., 5in. high. (Sotheby's) $925

Fluted baluster mug by W., London, 1837, 4.4oz., 9.8cm. high. (Sotheby's Belgravia) $205

American silver cann with molded lip and pedestal foot, 5½in. high, 14 troy oz. (Robert W. Skinner Inc.) $2,750

Victorian child's christening mug by Martin Hall & Co., London, 1880, 3oz.13dwt., 3¼in. high. (Sotheby's) $255

George II baluster-shaped mug with scroll handle, by Richard Zouch, 1737, 4¾in. high, 12oz.16dwt. (Christie's)$1,640

Victorian silver pint mug
of barrel form, London,
1863, 10oz., 4½in. high.
(Sotheby's) $335

Rare dated silver moun-
ted saltglaze mug, 1721,
9¼in. high, chipped.
(Sotheby's)$1,000

Early George I quart
mug by Gabriel Sleath,
London, 1727, 25oz.,
6¼in. high. (Lawrence
Fine Art) $870

Faceted mug of waisted
form by Henry Wilkin-
son & Co., Sheffield,
1854, 4.6oz., 9.5cm.
high. (Sotheby's Belgra-
via) $205

Queen Anne tapering cy-
lindrical mug by Alice
Sheene, 1708, 4¾in. high,
11oz.14dwt. (Christie's)
$1,640

Campana-shaped mug by
E., E., J. & W. Barnard,
London, 1836, 5.7oz.,
10cm. high. (Sotheby's
Belgravia) $310

George III baluster mug
by Thomas Evans, Lon-
don, 1774, 4¾in. high,
9oz. (Sotheby, King &
Chasemore) $370

Victorian silver octagonal
mug on bracket feet,
1847, 4in. high, 7oz.
15dwt. (Christie's)
$1,110

Tapering cylindrical mug
engraved and flat-chased,
by Alfred Ivory, London,
1880, 5.7oz., 10.4cm.
high. (Sotheby's Belgra-
via) $225

MUSTARDS & PEPPERS

Silver mustard pot by J.F., Edinburgh, 1806. (Phillips) $130

Victorian mustard pot in George III style, Birmingham, 1889. (Hy. Duke & Son) $55

William IV cylindrical mustard pot by J. McKay, Edinburgh, 1834, 2¾in. high, 4oz.17dwt. (Sotheby's)$250

Kangaroo pepperette by GB & Co., London, 1908, 3.6oz., 10cm. high. (Sotheby's Belgravia) $370

One of a pair of silver mounted tooth owlet pepperettes, 7.8cm. high, in novelty box. (Sotheby's Belgravia) $705

William IV bell-shaped pepperette by Charles Fox, London, 1832, 2oz.8dwt., 3in. high. (Sotheby's)$295

Silver gilt mustard pot and spoon, London and Birmingham, 1838, 5.2oz. (Sotheby's Belgravia) $890

Dutch pepper caster in the form of a quail, Chester, 1917, 3¾in. high.(Lawrence Fine Art) $290

Unusual early Victorian mustard pot by Richard Sibley, London, 1841, 4¾in. diam., 12oz. (Sotheby's) $915

Large three-masted silver nef by B. Neresheimer & Sohne, Hanau, 81.5cm. high, 200oz. (Sotheby's Belgravia)$9,720

Early 20th century silver model of a two-masted sailboat, 15in. high, 40 troy oz. (Robert W. Skinner Inc.) $1,300

Silver nef by Neresheimer & Sohne, Hanau, 1925, 22.3oz., 32.5cm. high. (Sotheby's Belgravia) $895

NUTMEGS

George III oval nutmeg grater by Samuel Pemberton, Birmingham, 1798, 2½in. wide. (Dickinson, Davy & Markham) $140

William IV tube nutmeg grater by Rawlings & Sumner, London, 1835, 2½in. long. (Sotheby's) $635

George III oval nutmeg grater by Roger Biggs, London, 1795, 2in. wide. (Sotheby's) $495

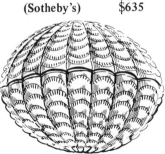

Vase-shaped nutmeg grater, unmarked, circa 1800, 3½in. high. (Sotheby's) $575

Unusual clam-shaped nutmeg grater by Hilliard & Thomason, Birmingham, 1853, 4.7cm. wide. (Sotheby's Belgravia) $745

George III oblong hanging nutmeg grater by J. Reily, London, 1818, 4in. long.(Sotheby's) $655

PORRINGERS

Charles II porringer, maker's mark TC, London, 1681, 3¼in. high, 7oz.3dwt. (Sotheby's) $885

Charles II porringer, London, 1674, 9oz. 4dwt., 4in. high. (Sotheby's) $2,610

William III porringer by Robert Peake, London, 1699, 10oz., 4in. high. (Sotheby's) $1,790

James I bleeding bowl or porringer, London, 1686, 8oz.10dwt., 20cm. long. (H. Spencer & Sons Ltd.) $1,840

William and Mary porringer with everted rim, London, 1691, 6oz., 8.5cm. high. (H. Spencer & Sons Ltd.) $1,065

Charles II porringer by DG, London, 1679, 3in. high, 5oz.9dwt.,(Sotheby's) $1,205

QUAICH

Large two-handled circular quaich, unmarked, circa 1680, 7in. diam., 10oz. (Christie's) $3,860

Two-handled silver quaich of ornate design by JD/WD, Chester, 1894, 7in. wide, 2½oz. (Dickinson, Davy & Markham) $60

One of a set of four compressed circular salt cellars by Charles Stuart Harris, London, 1894, 33oz., sold with spoons. (Sotheby's Belgravia) $885

One of two salt cellars by Robert and Samuel Hennell, 1803-04, sold with two spoons, London, 7oz. 4dwt. (Sotheby's)
$495

One of a set of four salt cellars by Robert Hennell, London, 1783, 10oz.2dwt., 3¼in. wide. (Sotheby's)
$1,195

One of a pair of William and Mary capstan form trencher salts, London, 1698, 2oz.15dwt., 2¼in. high. (Sotheby's)
$1,720

One of a pair of pedestal salt cellars with coiled dolphin stems, by Smith Nicholson & Co., London, 1852. (Sotheby's Belgravia)
$790

One of a set of four circular salt cellars by Paul de Lamerie, 1730, 23oz. (Christie's)
$19,855

One of two George III oval salt cellar stands by Wm. Abdy, London, 1802, 4oz. 17dwt., 4¾in. wide. (Sotheby's) $275

One of a pair of oval boat-shaped salt cellars by H. Chawner, London, 1791, 6oz.10dwt., 5¾in. wide. (Sotheby's) $440

Charles II octagonal trencher salt, London, 1680, 1oz.14dwt., 3in. diam. (Sotheby's) $625

SALTS

One of a set of four
George III oval salt
cellars by D. & R.
Hennell, 1765, 8oz.
16dwt. (Christie's)
$600

One of a pair of George
III compressed salt cellars
and spoons, Glasgow &
London, 8oz., 3in. diam.
(Sotheby's) $460

One of a set of four George
III circular fluted two-
handled salt cellars, by D.
Pontifex, 1806, 21oz.
(Christie's) $1,610

One of a set of six circular
salt cellars by Joseph and
John Angell, London, 1838,
39.6oz., 8.6cm. diam.
(Sotheby's Belgravia)
$2,070

One of a pair of salt cellars in 16th century
taste, by S. Garrard,
1902, 10½in. high.
(Christie's)
$2,960

One of a pair of circular
salt cellars by Joseph and
John Angell, London,
1844, 13.3oz., 8.6cm.
diam. (Sotheby's Bel-
gravia) $455

One of a set of four George
II salt cellars by Edward
Wood, London, 1731, 11oz.
14dwt., 3in. diam. (Sotheby's)
$3,345

George III cauldron
salt by Chas. Hougham,
London, 1783, 2½in.
diam., with blue glass
liner. (Dickinson, Davy
& Markham) $75

One of a set of six George
III salt cellars, by John
Emes, London, 1801,
(Sotheby, King & Chase-
more) $945

One of a pair of George III oval salts by J. Weldring, London, 1771, 3in. wide., 4oz. (Dickinson, Davy & Markham) $175

One of a set of four George III salts by I.G., 1801, 12oz. (Hy. Duke & Son) $575

One of a pair of George III oval salts by Robt. Hennell, 1782, 3in. high, 3.6oz. (Hy. Duke & Son) $180

One of a set of three George III oval salt cellars by Robt. Hennell, London, 1777, 5¼in. wide, 13oz.10dwt. (Sotheby's)$960

One of a pair of silver table salts by R. & S. Garrard & Co., London, 1857, 57.2oz., 14.5cm. high. (Sotheby's Belgravia) $8,270

One of a matching set of four shell-shaped salt cellars, by Robt. Gainsford, Sheffield, 1814-19, 21oz.3dwt., 5¼in. long. (Sotheby's)$1,065

One of a pair of George I octagonal trencher salts by Edward Wood, London, 1722, 3oz.1dwt., 3in. wide. (Sotheby's) $625

One of a set of six oval salt cellars by Peter Desvignes, London, 1777, 7oz.15dwt., 3½in. long. (Sotheby's)$1,045

One of three Regency oval salt cellars with gadrooned borders, by Paul Storr, 1817, 19oz. 10dwt. (Christie's) $1,825

One of a pair of George II oval sauceboats by George Hodder, Cork, circa
1745, 7¾in. wide, 19oz.9dwt.
(Sotheby's) $3,745

One of a pair of George II oval sauceboats by Peze Pilleau, London, 1732,
28oz.19dwt., 8¼in. wide. (Sotheby's)
                              $6,480

Tiffany silver sauceboat, New York,
circa 1860, with scrolled handle, 9
troy oz., 6in. high. (Robert W.
Skinner Inc.) $200

One of a pair of oval sauceboats by
Fordham & Faulkner, Sheffield, 1900,
29.2oz., 21.5cm. long. (Sotheby's Belgravia) $870

George III oval sauceboat by Matthew
West, Dublin, 1790, 10oz., 8in. wide.
         (Sotheby's) $645

One of a pair of shell-shaped sauceboats
by C. S. Harris & Sons Ltd., London,
1900, 34.7oz., 19cm. long. (Sotheby's
Belgravia) $1,135

One of a pair of George II oval sauceboats by John Kincaid, London, 1745,
27oz.14dwt., 8in. wide. (Sotheby's)
                              $2,090

One of a pair of rare early George II
circular sauceboats by Isaac Cookson,
Newcastle, 1728, 15oz.11dwt., 6½in.
wide. (Sotheby's) $3,240

One of a pair of George IV shell-shaped sauceboats, 1828, 31oz. (Christie's) $2,405

One of a pair of George II cast silver sauceboats, London, 1747, 7¾in. wide, 36oz. (Wm. Doyle Galleries Inc.) $5,500

George II shaped oval creamboat by Isaac Cookson, Newcastle, 1745, 4oz. 12dwt. (Christie's) $1,025

George II oval sauceboat by Peze Pilleau, London, 1758, 18oz.10dwt., 9in. wide. (Sotheby's) $1,595

George III oval sauceboat by Thomas Daniell, London, 1783, 8oz.1dwt., 7in. wide. (Sotheby's) $665

George II sauceboat by Richard Kersill, London, 1743, 7oz.10dwt., 14.5cm. long. (H. Spencer & Sons Ltd.) $625

Oval creamboat by Melchior Faust, Goteborg, 1768, 18.8cm. wide, 8oz. 17dwt. (Sotheby's) $4,245

One of a pair of silver sauceboats, London, 1911, 24oz. (J. M. Welch & Son) $545

SCENT BOTTLES

SILVER

English gold and hardstone scent bottle with agate stopper, 8.7cm. high, circa 1765. (Sotheby's) $2,550

Early 19th century gold mounted glass scent bottle, 2¼in. high. (Christie's) $665

Silver gilt mounted double overlay scent bottle, interior stamped S. Mordan & Co., London, 1850's, 9.2cm. high. (Sotheby's Belgravia) $190

Unusual silver gilt mounted enamel scent flask in the form of an egg, 8.6cm. high, London, 1882. (Sotheby's Belgravia) $1,035

Late 18th century gold and glass scent bottle and stopper, 12.5cm. long. (Sotheby's) $190

Mid 19th century Palais Royale gilt metal mounted engraved glass scent stand, 29.5cm. high. (Sotheby's Belgravia) $445

Wiener Werkstatte cut glass globular bottle with electroplated bottle top, circa 1910. (Sotheby's Belgravia) $1,780

French parcel gilt silver mounted clear glass scent flask, circa 1844, 11.4cm. high. (Sotheby's Belgravia) $660

Silver mounted and tortoiseshell veneered scent bottle case complete with silver mounted scent bottle, London, 1910. (Sotheby's Belgravia) $445

604

William IV oblong snuff box by Reily & Storer, London, 1834, 3¼in. wide. (Sotheby's) $350

Rectangular silver snuff box, lid inset with an unusual medal, by Norbert Roettier. (Woolley & Wallis) $465

George III Irish oval snuff box by Alexander Ticknell, Dublin, 1795, 3¼in. long. (Sotheby's) $735

Silver and tortoiseshell pique snuff box, lid decorated with a figure, circa 1710, 8.5cm. long. (Sotheby's) $730

Late 17th/early 18th century French silver and tortoiseshell pique snuff box, 7.2cm. wide. (Sotheby's) $490

Circular silver snuff box, hinged lid set with tortoiseshell portrait of Charles I, 2½in. diam. (Woolley & Wallis) $505

Silver and Neapolitan pique snuff box of oval form, 7cm. wide, circa 1730. (Sotheby's) $320

Oval silver gilt snuff box by Lawrence Oliphant, Edinburgh, circa 1740, 2½in. long. (Sotheby's) $270

Shaped silver snuff box, inset with tortoiseshell, lid with bust of George II, 3½in. wide.(Woolley & Wallis) $545

Presentation snuff box, London, 1812, 7.4cm. wide, in red leather case. (Sotheby's) $1,380

Carved coquilla nut snuff box of boat shape, circa 1800, 2¾in. long. (Christie's) $370

Early 19th century silver gilt snuff box with gold rims, 3½in. long.(Christie's) $555

Rectangular silver gilt and shaded cloisonne enamel snuff box, Moscow, 1899-1908, 6.3cm. wide. (Sotheby's) $735

German oval silver and tortoiseshell snuff box, 1750, 7.7cm. wide. (Sotheby's) $325

Rectangular silver and elephant's tooth snuff box by Joseph Willmore, Birmingham, 1834, 9cm. wide.(Sotheby's) $405

Silver and niello snuff box by I.K., Moscow, 1829, 7.5cm. wide.(Sotheby's) $940

Russian silver snuff box, Moscow, 1838, 3in. long, 2.5 troy oz. (Robert W. Skinner Inc.) $300

Silver gilt mounted horn snuff box with hinged lid, London, 1880. (Sotheby's Belgravia) $265

Oval silver and tortoiseshell pique snuff box, circa 1720, 8.3cm. wide. (Sotheby's) $550

Silver gilt and mother-of-pearl snuff box of kidney form, circa 1835, 7cm. wide. (Sotheby's) $385

Early 19th century coquilla nut snuff box of boat form and with silver gilt thumbpiece, 3½in. long. (Christie's) $295

Silver gilt and hardstone snuff box by Nathaniel Mills, Birmingham, 1828, 6.8cm. wide. (Sotheby's)$305

Nathaniel Mills rectangular silver snuff box with a castle view, Birmingham, 1837, 2½in. long. (Christie's)$460

Rectangular silver and niello snuff box, Moscow, 1880, 7.5cm. wide. (Sotheby's) $570

Parcel gilt and niello snuff box, by O.B., Moscow, 1842, 7.5cm. wide.(Sotheby's) $775

SILVER

Early George I oval wine bottle stand by Anthony Nelme, London, 1715. (Sotheby's)$8,230

One of a pair of shaped circular fruit stands by Reily & Storer, London, 1837, 50.1oz. (Sotheby's Belgravia) $825

One of a pair of circular tazzas by C. T. & G. Fox, London, 1853, 43.8oz., 25.5cm. diam. (Sotheby's Belgravia) $1,550

One of a set of three George III oval dessert stands, by Pitts & Preedy, London, 1795, 4¾in. wide, 25oz.3dwt. (Sotheby's)$1,455

Art Deco silver plated tazza with lobed dish. (J. M. Welch & Son) $225

One of a set of four George III silver gilt oval sweetmeat stands, by Pitts & Preedy, 1792, 31oz,10dwt. (Sotheby's) $1,695

Circular fruit stand by R. H. Halford & Sons, London, 1900, 22.8cm. high, 28.5oz.(Sotheby's Belgravia) $510

George III oval teapot stand by Peter and Ann Bateman, London, 1792, 4oz.18dwt., 8in. wide. (Sotheby's) $310

One of a pair of Tiffany & Co. enamelled silver comports, 14cm. high, 22oz. (Phillips) $610

Charles II plain cylindrical tankard by E. G., 1684, 8in. high, 36oz. (Christie's)
$4,805

Cylindrical tankard by Claus Sulsen Hamburgensis, Hamburg, circa 1645, 29oz.11dwt., 20.2cm. high.(Sotheby's)
$8,915

George I plain cylindrical tankard by Thomas Mason, 1722, 7in. high, 24oz. (Christie's)
$2,925

Silver tankard by David King, Dublin, 1704-06, 8in. high, 30oz. (Christie's)$2,895

Reeded tapering cylindrical mug by William Knight, London, 1837, 11.3oz., 10.7cm. high. (Sotheby's Belgravia) $495

George I plain cylindrical tankard by Augustine Courtauld, 1719, 8in. high, 51oz. (Christie's)
$4,105

George I tapering cylindrical tankard on molded foot, by Richard Bayley, 1723, 7¼in. high, 27oz. (Christie's) $1,845

George I plain tapering cylindrical tankard on rim foot, by Edmund Pearce, 1715, 8in. high, 36oz. (Christie's) $3,860

George I tapering cylindrical tankard by Thos. Bolton, Dublin, 1718, 9in. high, 35oz. (Christie's)
$4,290

George I plain tapering
cylindrical tankard,
Exeter, 1718, 7¾in.
high, 29oz. (Christie's)
$3,135

Mid 17th century silver gilt
mounted serpentine tankard,
4¾in. high. (Christie's)
$2,715

Large Continental silver
tankard, hinged cover
inset with lapis lazuli,
38oz., 7½in. high.
(Dickinson, Davy & Mark-
ham) $665

George III plain cylindrical tankard by John
Langlands, Newcastle,
1795, 8in. high, 28oz.
(Christie's)$1,720

George III tapering cylindrical tankard by Hester
Bateman, London, 1785,
26oz.5dwt., 6¾in. high.
(Sotheby's)$1,620

Early George II baluster
tankard by James Man-
ners, London, 1735,
7¾in. high, 29oz.4dwt.
(Sotheby's)$3,135

Mid 18th century Danish
plain cylindrical peg tankard
by Knud Rasmussen Brandt,
7¼in. high, 22oz.(Christie's)
$3,800

Charles II cylindrical tankard, London, 1675, with
later engraving, 6¾in. high,
24oz.15dwt. (Sotheby's)
$3,680

George I tapering cylin-
drical tankard by James
Smith I, London, 1720,
7¼in. high, 24oz.16dwt.
(Sotheby's)
$2,455

Queen Anne tapering cyl-
indrical tankard by Augu-
stine Courtauld, 1707,
6¾in. high, 28oz. (Chri-
stie's) $4,180

Lidded silver tankard by
William Shaw, London,
1765, now converted to
a jug. (H. Spencer & Sons
Ltd.) $1,250

George I plain cylindrical
tankard by George
Boothby, 1718, 8in. high,
34oz. (Christie's)
    $3,345

George I tapering cylindrical tankard by Michael
Boult, London, 1723, 7¼in.
high, 30oz.11dwt.
(Sotheby's) $4,390

Presentation silver tankard
by Smith, Nicholson & Co.,
London, 1858, 35.7oz.,
27.5cm. high. (Sotheby's
Belgravia) $750

George III baluster tan-
kard by Thomas Wallis,
London, 1781, 23oz.
12dwt., 8in. high.
(Sotheby's)
         $1,880

William III cylindrical
tankard by Anthony
Nelme, London, 1699,
39oz.9dwt., 8½in. high.
(Sotheby's)
    $4,705

George III baluster tankard
by Jacob Marsh or John
Moore, London, 1766, 24oz.
4dwt., 7¾in. high.(Sotheby's)
    $1,920

William III tapered cylindrical tankard by Robert
Peake, London, 23oz.
3dwt., 6¾in. high.
(Sotheby's)
    $6,690

James II cylindrical tankard, 1686, 8¾in. high, 43oz. (Christie's) $6,005

Charles II cylindrical tankard by E.G., 1679, 7¼in. high, 29oz. (Christie's) $6,280

One of a pair of George III cylindrical tankards by Robert Gaze, 1796, 7¼in. high, 58oz. (Christie's) $3,675

Continental parcel gilt tankard with mermaid thumbpiece, circa 1600, 8¼in. high, 26oz. (Christie's) $4,795

George II tapered cylindrical quart tankard by Benjamin Godfrey, London, 1737, 44oz.5dwt., 9¾in. high. (Sotheby's) $3,945

George III cylindrical tankard with reeded girdle and skirt foot, by Langlands & Robertson, Newcastle, 25oz.17dwt. (Sotheby's)$1,930

George III tapered cylindrical tankard with flat cover, by E. Fernell, London, 1787, 35oz. 15dwt., 8in. high. (Sotheby's)$1,415

Large silver tankard by J. H. Rawlings, London, 1893, 30cm. high, 95.1oz. (Sotheby's Belgravia) $2,380

Early George II quart tankard by Wm. Darker, London, 1733, 7½in. high, 26oz.10dwt.(Woolley & Wallis) $1,710

Four-piece tea and coffee service of squat melon form, Sheffield, 1966, 86oz. (Sotheby, King & Chasemore) $1,275

Gorham sterling silver teaset, Rhode Island, 1960, 60 troy oz. (Robert W. Skinner Inc.) $1,250

Four-piece tea and coffee set by Hayne & Cater, London, 1840, 73.1oz. (Sotheby's Belgravia) $2,365

Five-piece tea and coffee set by Goldsmiths & Silversmiths Co. Ltd., London, 1909/10, 56oz. (Sotheby's Belgravia) $1,280

Continental silver tea and coffee service and tray. (Sotheby, King & Chasemore) $1,640

613

Silver three-piece tea service designed by Kate Harris, 1901, teapot 11cm. high.
(Sotheby's Belgravia) $800

Late 18th century New York silver three-piece teaset by Joel Sayre, 45oz. (Wm.
Doyle Galleries Inc.) $2,500

German silver four-piece teaset, marked '950·Wilh. Giese', 67oz. (Sotheby,
King & Chasemore) $1,235

Victorian three-piece inverted pear-shaped teaset, by Mackay & Chisholm,
Edinburgh, 1842, 44oz.1dwt. (Sotheby's) $1,120

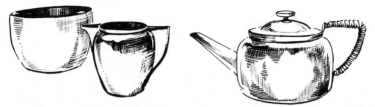

Hukin & Heath silver traveling teaset, London, 1880, designed by Christopher Dresser. (Sotheby's Belgravia) $855

Regency oblong tea service in three pieces, by George Fenwick, Edinburgh, 1811, 73oz. (Christie's) $2,510

George III silver tea service by John Robins, 1806, 71oz. (Christie's)
$5,335

Victorian circular three-piece teaset by J. McKay, Edinburgh, 1844-45, 47oz. 18dwt. (Sotheby's) $1,245

TEA & COFFEE SETS

Four-piece teaset and tea tray by Elkington & Co. Ltd., Birmingham, 1947, 190.6oz., 67.7cm. wide. (Sotheby's Belgravia) $2,480

Three-piece teaset with fluted circular bodies by A. B. Savory & Sons, London, 1858. (Sotheby's Belgravia) $1,050

William IV three-piece teaset by Charles Fox, London, 1836, 56oz.8dwt. (Sotheby's) $1,840

Silver plated four-piece teaset with vase-shaped bodies, circa 1900, by WMF. (Sotheby's) $310

Matching six-piece tea and coffee set, 1907-30, 147.4oz. (Sotheby's Belgravia) $2,070

Three-piece teaset with vase-shaped bodies, by Martin, Hall & Co. Ltd., London, 1879, 48.4oz. (Sotheby's Belgravia) $990

Teapot and milk jug by William Hunter, London, 1851, 31.8oz. (Sotheby's Belgravia) $935

Five-piece tea and coffee set by Edward Barnard & Sons, London, 1896-97, 141.7oz. (Sotheby's Belgravia)　　　　$2,895

Four-piece tea and coffee set and two-handled tray, circa 1910, 178.1oz. (Sotheby's Belgravia) $2,935

Four-piece tea and coffee set by Martin, Hall & Co. and M. Rhodes & Sons Ltd., 73.5oz. (Sotheby's Belgravia)　　　$1,550

William IV three-piece compressed circular teaset by Hawksworth, Eyre &
Co., Sheffield, 1836, 42oz.8dwt. (Sotheby's) $1,210

William IV four-piece tea and coffee set by Richard Smith, Dublin, 1836, sold
with sugar tongs, 96oz.8dwt. (Sotheby's) $4,295

Three-piece teaset by Reily & Storer, London, 1841, 47.5oz. (Sotheby's
Belgravia) $970

Victorian four-piece tea service by E. & J. Barnard, London, 1863, 62oz.16dwt.
(Sotheby's) $1,750

618

Silver tea service by P. Ovchinnikov, Moscow, 1887-1893. (Sotheby's)
$4,090

Three-piece silver and enamel coffee set by P. Ovchinnikov, Moscow, 1887.
(Sotheby's) $1,840

Victorian three-piece teaset by Barnard Bros., London, 1868, 40oz.4dwt.
(Sotheby's) $1,150

Four-piece teaset by C. S. Harris, London, 1912-15, 81oz.10dwt.(Sotheby's)
$1,410

Silver tea caddy, Bergen, 1713, 12.5cm. high, 5oz. 11dwt. (Sotheby's) $2,865

Guild of Handicrafts Ltd. silver tea caddy, London, 1906, 7cm. high, on four ball feet. (Sotheby's Belgravia) $220

George II oval bombe tea caddy, by Samuel Taylor, London, 1745, 12oz.6dwt., 5in. high. (Sotheby's) $1,535

George III rectangular tea caddy by J. E. Terrey, London, 1818, 4½in. high, 12oz.6dwt. (Sotheby's) $970

George III tea caddy and sugar basin by Wm. Plummer, 1773, in silver mounted wood case, 12oz. 16dwt. (Christie's) $1,810

George III oblong tea caddy by Elizabeth Godfrey, London, 1765, 6in. high, 12oz.1dwt. (Sotheby's) $1,140

One of a pair of early George III bombe tea caddies by J. Langford II and J. Sebille, London, 1763, 24oz.9dwt. (Sotheby's) $2,610

George III oval tea caddy by A. Lestourgeon, London, 1777, 4½in. high, 11oz.6dwt. (Sotheby's) $2,820

One of a set of two George II oblong tea caddies and a sugar box by D. Smith and R. Sharp, 1761, 25oz. (Christie's) $5,605

George III oval tea caddy
by Fogelberg & Gilbert,
London, 1783, 4½in.
high, 12oz.6dwt.
(Sotheby's) $2,180

George III shaped oval
tea caddy by Aldridge &
Green, London, 1783,
4¾in. high, 12oz.13dwt.
(Sotheby's)$3,310

George III oval tea caddy
and cover by H. Chaw-
ner, London, 1786,
12oz. (H. Spencer & Sons
Ltd.) $765

George II octagonal tea
caddy by Simon Pantin,
London, 1738, 7oz.
5dwt., 4in. high.
(Sotheby's)$1,620

Pair of George III rectangular
tea caddies and covers of
bombe form, by Wm. Vincent,
21oz. (Neales) $1,570

One of a pair of sterling
silver tea caddies, Lon-
don, 1732, 15 troy oz.,
5in. high. (Robert W.
Skinner Inc.)
          $1,600

One of two George II
bombe tea caddies in
sizes, by Emick Romer,
London, 1762, 5¼in. high,
19oz.5dwt. (Sotheby's)
          $1,750

George III cylindrical tea
caddy by Parker & Wake-
lin, London, 1763, 14oz.
1dwt., 4¼in. high.
(Sotheby's)$3,275

One of a set of three
George II oval caddies
by John Newton, circa
1730, 31oz. (Christie's)
$2,445

TEA KETTLES

SILVER

George III plain oval tea kettle, stand and lamp, by William Fountain, 1799, 75oz.(Christie's) $2,175

Electroplated teapot, designed by Christopher Dresser, on triangular stand with burner, 19.5cm. high. (Phillips) $215

Victorian circular plated tea kettle on stand with hardwood handle, 12in. high.(Dickinson, Davy & Markham) $85

Late William IV silver water kettle on stand by J. & J. Aldous, London, 1837, 14in. high, 78oz. (Wm. Doyle Galleries Inc.) $1,800

Large pear-shaped tea kettle, stand and lamp by R. Smith, Dublin, 1843, 15¼in. high, 119oz. (Christie's) $2,900

George II inverted pear-shaped tea kettle and stand by P. Archambo, 1742, 68oz.(Christie's) $3,085

George II melon-shaped tea kettle, lamp and stand, by Paul de Lamerie, 1734, 61oz. (Christie's) $4,475

Silver tea kettle on lampstand, with detachable burner, by Robert Stocker, London, 1907, 33cm. high, 57.5oz. (Sotheby's Belgravia) $695

George II inverted pear-shaped tea kettle and lampstand by Charles Woodward, London, 1747, 55oz.12dwt., 15in. high.(Sotheby's) $2,515

Late 19th century baluster hexagonal tea kettle on stand, Dutch, 70.6oz., 32cm. high. (Sotheby's Belgravia) $1,435

Victorian plated tea kettle on lampstand with turned wood handle, 12in. high. (Dickinson, Davy & Markham) $95

George III tea kettle with stand and burner by R. Crossley, London, 1799, 42oz. (H. Spencer & Sons Ltd.) $820

Oblong tea kettle, stand and burner by William Hutton & Sons Ltd., London, 1894, 51oz., 12¾in. high.(Sotheby's) $475

Swiss spherical tea kettle and stand with burner, circa 1800, 38.3cm. high, 1,970gm. (Sotheby's) $4,605

Early George III tea kettle on lampstand by T. Whipham and C. Wright, London, 1760, 47oz.19dwt., 14¼in. high. (Sotheby's) $1,985

George II circular tea kettle, stand and lamp by Richard Bayley, 1738, 56oz. (Christie's) $4,165

George V tea kettle, stand and lamp by Goldsmiths & Silversmiths Co. Ltd., 48oz. (H. Spencer & Sons Ltd.) $590

Large Russian tea kettle on stand with lobed body, 1887, 15¼in. high, 107oz. (Lawrence Fine Art) $1,450

623

TEAPOTS

Circular teapot by J. & G. Angell, London, 1847, 22.5oz. (Sotheby's Belgravia) $490

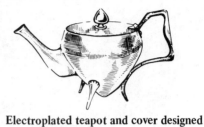

Electroplated teapot and cover designed by Christopher Dresser, 1880, 18cm. wide. (Christie's) $925

Victorian teapot by Joseph and Albert Savory, London, 1839, 20oz. (Lawrence Fine Art) $385

Circular teapot by Edward Barnard & Sons, London, 1852, 18.1oz., 13cm. high. (Sotheby's Belgravia) $400

George I plain bullet-shaped teapot by Anthony Nelme, 1718, 14oz.10dwt. (Christie's) $3,495

Plain circular teapot, hinged cover with strawberry button, by J. J. Keith, London, 1841, 22oz. (Sotheby's Belgravia) $425

Dutch pear-shaped teapot Groningen, 1740, 10oz.15dwt. (Christie's) $1,685

Tapering circular teapot by Martin, Hall & Co. Ltd., Sheffield, 1879, 26.2oz. (Sotheby's Belgravia) $505

Late George III silver teapot by Wm. Bruce, London, 1819. (Sotheby, King & Chasemore) $380

Oval silver teapot with engraved decoration, London, 1804, 16½oz. (Lacy Scott) $480

William IV teapot by E. & J. Barnard, London, 1830, 25.5oz., 5¾in. high. (Lawrence Fine Art) $520

George III oval teapot by William Plummer, London, 1787, 16oz.11dwt., 5in. high. (Sotheby's) $830

George III shaped oval teapot by Hester Bateman, 1785, 13oz.4dwt. (Christie's) $1,450

Walker & Hall silver tea kettle, London, 1886, 13cm. high, 17oz. (Phillips) $270

George III shaped oval teapot and stand by Henry Chawner, 1788, 18oz.3dwt. (Christie's) $1,085

Georgian teapot and stand with domed lid and wood handle, London, 1786. (Hall Wateridge & Owen) $660

Compressed silver teapot with silver handle, by William Moulson, London, 1841, 26.6oz., 13.7cm. high. (Sotheby's Belgravia) $455

Rare 18th century Scottish provincial bullet teapot, by IS., Banff, circa 1740, 14oz.8dwt., 4½in. high. (Sotheby's) $13,515

Pear-shaped teapot on molded foot, The Hague, 1739, 9oz.5dwt., 10.6cm. high. (Sotheby's) $1,380

George III compressed circular teapot by William Burwash, London, 1817, 26oz.13dwt., 5¼in. high. (Sotheby's) $725

George II bullet-shaped teapot by John Main, Edinburgh, 1742, 19oz., 5¾in. high. (Sotheby's) $1,215

Shaped oblong teapot by Frederick Brasted, London, 1883, 19oz., 13.2cm. high. (Sotheby's Belgravia) $620

George III pear-shaped teapot by W. & J. Priest, London, 1770, 6¾in. high, 16oz.2dwt. (Sotheby's) $1,025

George III inverted pear-shaped teapot by Ebenezer Oliphant, Edinburgh, 21oz., 6½in. high. (Sotheby's) $905

George III teapot and stand by Wm. Plummer, London, 1786, 15oz.5dwt., 5¾in. high. (Sotheby's) $770

Compressed circular teapot with silver handle and button, by Richard Wm. Elliott, London, 1842, 20.4oz. (Sotheby's Belgravia) $390

George II bullet-shaped teapot by I.F., London, 1734, 15½oz., with shaped fruitwood handle. (D. M. Nesbit & Co.) $2,685

George III octagonal teapot and stand by Henry Chawner, London, 1790, 19oz. (Sotheby's) $1,535

Pear-shaped teapot by Tessiers Ltd., London, 1927, 30.1oz. (Sotheby's Belgravia) $660

Victorian silver teapot by Squire & Brother Co., New York, circa 1850, 19.5 troy oz., 7in. high. (Robert W. Skinner Inc.) $275

Victorian teapot in 'aesthetic' movement taste, by Francis Elkington, 1880, 21oz. (Lawrence Fine Art) $470

Pear-shaped teapot with floral decoration, by Francis Crump, London, 1769, 16oz. (Woolley & Wallis) $790

627

TOAST RACKS

SILVER

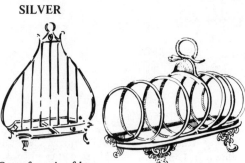

Hukin & Heath electroplated toast rack designed by Christopher Dresser, 1881, 12.5cm. high. (Phillips) $360

One of a pair of lyre-shaped toast racks by A., F. & A., Pairpoint, London, 1929, 15.1oz., 20.5cm. high. (Sotheby's Belgravia) $420

One of a pair of seven-bar toasters by Samuel Whitford, London, 1874, 17.7cm. long, 17.6oz. (Sotheby's Belgravia) $870

TOILET REQUISITES

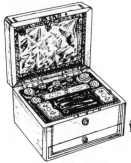

Fitted rosewood vanity case with cut glass bottles, London, 1849. (Sotheby, King & Chasemore) $665

Early 20th century seven-piece 14 karat gold dresser set, Massachusetts. (Robert W. Skinner Inc.) $2,000

Silver gilt and tortoise-shell manicure box and fittings, by C. H. Dumenile Ltd., London, 1919, 21.7cm. wide.(Sotheby's Belgravia) $325

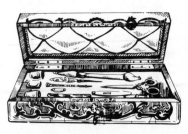

French lacquered etui of tapering form, circa 1760, 9.6cm. high. (Sotheby's) $265

Rectangular necessaire, wood body veneered in mother-of-pearl, 1854, fully fitted. (Sotheby's Belgravia) $490

English gilt metal necessaire in the manner of James Cox, 14.5cm. high, circa 1770. (Sotheby's)$850

SILVER

TOILET REQUISITES

Rectangular papier-mache necessaire with hinged lid inlaid with mother-of-pearl, circa 1850, 14.4cm. long. (Sotheby's Belgravia) $315

Gilt metal beehive necessaire applied with honey bees, circa 1875, 18.5cm. high.(Sotheby's Belgravia) $425

Fitted coromandelwood traveling toilet case, London, 1850, with silver-topped glass bottles. (Sotheby, King & Chasemore) $510

Mid 18th century etui, oval tapered body, fully fitted. (Sotheby's) $525

Reproduction Queen Anne eighteen-piece dressing table set of gilt Britannia silver, London, 1915-16. (Sotheby, King & Chasemore) $17,290

English silver mounted shagreen lancet case, circa 1800, 7.7cm. high. (Sotheby's) $405

Gentleman's traveling dressing case of brass bound hardwood, by Francis Diller, London, 1845. (Sotheby's Belgravia) $610

George III silver and tortoiseshell folding comb by George Hall, London, 1804, 6in. long.(Sotheby's) $585

George IV dressing case by John and Archibald Douglas, London, 1822. (Sotheby's) $875

629

SILVER

George III snuffers tray by Joseph
Creswell, London, 1774, 9oz.8dwt.,
7¾in. long. (Sotheby's) $605

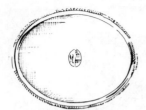

One of a pair of George III oval salvers
by John Scofield, London, 1777, 25oz.
15dwt., 9in. long. (Sotheby's)
$3,450

George III oval salver by Solomon
Hougham, London, 1806, 10in. wide,
16oz.8dwt. (Sotheby's) $665

Shaped rectangular two-handled tray
by William Aitken, Birmingham, 1903,
141.9oz., 74cm. long. (Sotheby's Belgravia) $1,660

Oval two-handled tea tray by Edward
Barnard & Sons, London, 1865,
80.2cm. wide, 153.7oz. (Sotheby's
Belgravia) $3,205

Large electroplated tea tray by Elkington & Co., 1871, 69cm. long.
(Sotheby's Belgravia) $350

George III shaped oblong snuffers tray
by Cradock & Reid, London, 1818,
8oz.12dwt., 9¾in. wide. (Sotheby's)
$470

Two-handled shaped circular fruit
stand with pierced body, 41.5cm. wide,
43.5oz. (Sotheby's Belgravia)
$785

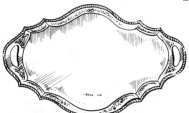

Shaped oval gallery tray by Walker & Hall, Sheffield, 1920, 101oz., 60.7cm. wide. (Sotheby's Belgravia) $2,070

One of a pair of crested shaped circular dishes by Hunt & Roskell, London, 1845, 43cm. long, 108.6oz.(Sotheby's Belgravia) $1,965

Large rectangular tea tray with lobed border by Cooper Brothers, Sheffield, 1896, 116.5oz., 69.5cm. wide. (Sotheby's Belgravia) $1,550

One of eleven shaped circular dinner plates, late 19th/early 20th century, 217oz., 25.7cm. diam. (Sotheby's Belgravia) $3,100

William and Mary circular salver on foot by Jonah Kirk, London, 1691, 16oz.19dwt., 10¾in. diam.(Sotheby's) $3,220

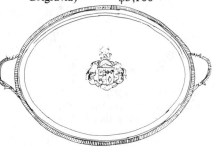

George III oval tea tray by Hannam & Crouch, London, 1803, 104oz.14dwt., 26½in. wide. (Sotheby's) $4,830

Large presentation two-handled tea tray by Henry Wilkinson & Co., Sheffield, 1845, 167oz., 76.5cm. wide. (Sotheby's Belgravia)$3,720

George III small circular salver by Hester Bateman, 1783, 6in. diam. (Lawrence Fine Art) $540

Silver diamond-shaped pin tray with embossed center, London, 1884, 4½in. wide. (Dickinson, Davy & Markham) $35

Set of three George III plain oval salvers by J. Wakelin and W. Taylor, 1786, 100oz., 18¾in. and 9in. long. (Christie's) $5,790

George II plain circular salver by William Williamson, Dublin, 1727, 12¼in. diam., 30oz. (Christie's) $3,600

George II circular waiter with pie crust and shell edge, J. Morrison, London, 1750, 5¾oz., 6¼in. diam. (Dickinson, Davy & Markham) $310

Sheffield sterling silver tray by J. E. Caldwell & Co., Sheffield, circa 1930, 171 troy oz., 31in. long. (Robert W. Skinner Inc.) $2,000

Large shaped circular salver by West & Son, Dublin, 138.9oz., 60.5cm. diam. (Sotheby's Belgravia) $1,610

Victorian silver gilt shaped circular salver, 11in. diam., 27oz. (Christie's) $1,075

One of a set of four Regency shaped oval meat dishes by William Stroud, 1814, 17in. long, 210oz. (Christie's) $6,660

George III salver by John Mewburn, London, 1812, 78oz., 18½in. diam. (Sotheby, King & Chasemore) $1,440

Large and heavy two-handled silver tray by Walker & Hall, Sheffield, 1920, 132oz., 2ft.5½in. wide. (Dickinson, Davy & Markham) $1,455

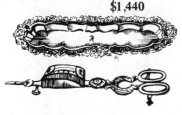

Good pair of George IV candle snuffers and tray by Rebecca Emes and Edward Barnard, London, 1825, 14oz. (H. Spencer & Sons Ltd.)$910

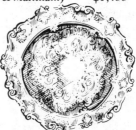

Shaped circular salver by Edward Barnard & Sons, London, 1888, 25.5cm. diam., 16.2oz. (Sotheby's Belgravia) $255

One of a pair of George III stands by Thomas Wallis, London, 1787. (Sotheby, King & Chasemore) $815

Shaped rectangular two-handled tray by Joseph Rodgers & Sons Ltd., Sheffield, 1901, 157oz., 72cm. wide. (Sotheby's Belgravia) $1,575

Fine George IV silver two-handled rectangular tray by S. C. Younge & Co., Sheffield, 1820, 142oz. (Geering & Colyer) $2,775

One of a pair of George IV shaped circular entree dishes by J. C. Edington, 1829, 9½in. diam., 50oz. (Christie's) $2,260

Large silver tea tray by James Deakin & Sons, Sheffield, 1902, 26in. wide, 147oz. (Lawrence Fine Art) $1,485

Novelty ash tray cast as a frog, by R. Hennell & Sons, London, 1884, 10.1cm. diam., 2.2oz. (Sotheby's Belgravia) $475

19th century Kate Greenaway silver plated tray of pentagonal shape, 6in. high. (Robert W. Skinner Inc.) $125

Victorian silver plated oval tea tray with beaded scroll handles, 28½in. wide. (Lawrence Fine Art) $200

Chinese silver tea tray and teapot, stamped mark Guangxu, 1,538gm. (Sotheby's Belgravia) $545

George II silver gilt shaped circular salver by Wm. Cripps, 1754, 14¼in. diam., 53oz. (Christie's) $3,430

George III oval coffee tray by Smith & Hayter, London, 1794, 22¾in. wide, 78oz.18dwt. (Sotheby's)$3,240

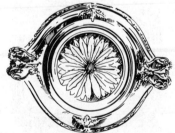

One of a pair of George III stands by Thomas Heming, London, 1776, 17½in. wide, 105oz.17dwt. (Sotheby's) $2,760

One of a set of four George III faceted
navette-shaped sauce tureens and
covers by Henry Chawner, London,
65oz.6dwt. (Sotheby's) $4,430

One of a pair of Regency rectangular
Sheffield plate sauce tureens, with
gadrooned edges, 7½in. wide. (Woolley
& Wallis) $650

Sheffield plate lobed oval soup tureen
and cover, 41cm. wide, circa 1840.
(Sotheby's Belgravia) $1,760

One of a pair of two-handled boat-shaped sauce tureens and covers, 23.5cm.
wide, 24.3oz. (Sotheby's Belgravia)
                                $735

One of a set of four George III two-
handled oval sauce tureens and covers,
by J. Wakelin and W. Taylor, 1776,
66oz. (Christie's) $2,445

One of a set of four oval sauce tureens
and covers by Charles Wright, London,
1778, 77oz.10dwt., 9½in. wide.
(Sotheby's) $8,780

One of a pair of George III boat-shaped
sauce tureens and covers, by Charles
Hougham, London, 1791, 28oz.11dwt.,
9½in. wide. (Sotheby's) $2,455

George III oblong sauce tureen and
cover by J. Angell, London, 1816, 8in.
wide, 25oz.7dwt. (Sotheby's)
                                $820

TUREENS

One of a pair of George III plain oval sauce tureens and covers by John Robins, 1798, 33oz. (Christie's) $3,700

Peruvian oval two-handled soup tureen and cover, mid 20th century, 44cm. long, 54.6oz. (Sotheby's Belgravia) $695

Victorian octagonal two-handled soup tureen, cover and stand by Robert Garrard, 1843, 20¼in. long, 201oz. (Christie's) $8,325

One of a pair of George III sauce tureens by Samuel Whitford, London, 1814, 8½in. long, 65oz. (Phillips & Jolly's) $2,930

One of four George III two-handled oval sauce tureens and covers by D. Smith and R. Sharp, 1780, 80oz. (Christie's) $3,980

Two-handled fluted boat-shaped soup tureen and cover, London, 1897, 39cm. wide, 51.8oz. (Sotheby's Belgravia) $1,795

Georgian sauce tureen in Adam style, London, 1782. (Hall Wateridge & Owen) $525

One of a pair of George IV compressed oblong sauce tureens and covers, 37oz. 6dwt., 8½in. wide. (Sotheby's) $1,495

George III sauce tureen by Robert Hennell, II, London, 1810. (Sotheby, King & Chasemore) $930

Lobed oval two-handled soup tureen and cover by Gorham Manufacturing Co., America, 36.7oz., circa 1910, 32cm. wide. (Sotheby's Belgravia) $620

George III oval sauce tureen and cover by William Burwash, 1818, 28oz.3dwt., 8¼in. wide. (Sotheby's) $1,415

Silver plated on copper tureen and cover, on stand, 13in. high. (Sotheby, King & Chasemore) $475

Hukin & Heath electroplated soup tureen supported on three spike feet, 20.5cm. high. (Phillips) $1,165

One of four George III two-handled oval sauce tureens by John Gibson Leadbetter, 55oz. (Christie's) $2,535

Lobed oblong two-handled sauce tureen and cover by Walker & Hall, Sheffield, 1894, 42.2oz., 24cm. wide. (Sotheby's Belgravia) $1,100

George IV shaped oval two-handled soup tureen and cover by William Eaton, 1824, 12¾in. long, 181oz. (Christie's) $9,250

TUREENS

One of a pair of George III oval sauce tureens by W. Holmes and N. Dumee, 1774, 26oz. (Christie's) $1,930

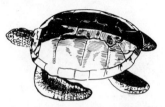

Silver plated soup tureen in the form of a turtle, circa 1860, 21in. long. (J. M. Welch & Son) $1,820

One of a pair of George III sauce tureens and covers by Robert & Samuel Hennell, London, 1804, 13oz.10dwt., 5in. high. (Sotheby's) $1,965

Large shaped oval soup tureen and cover by Reily & Storer, London, 1838, 176.2oz., 44cm. wide. (Sotheby's Belgravia) $6,620

George III oval soup tureen and cover by Thomas Holland II, London, 1809, 14¾in. wide, 94oz.15dwt. (Sotheby's) $4,295

Electroplated tureen and cover in the form of a broody hen, by G. R. Collins & Co., 1850's, 22cm. wide. (Sotheby's Belgravia) $705

One of a pair of George III oval sauce tureens, covers and stands by Thomas Heming, London, 1769, 9in. wide. (Sotheby's) $5,320

Hukin & Heath sauce tureen, designed by Christopher Dresser, 1880, 13.5cm. high. (Phillips) $930

George II tea urn by Wm. Holmes, 1776, 94oz. (Louis Taylor & Sons) $1,805

Large Victorian Sheffield plate tea urn with curving handles, 14in. high. (Dickinson, Davy & Markham) $225

George III tea urn by Francis Crump, London, 1768, 71oz.17dwt., 19in. high. (Sotheby's) $1,380

Silver tea urn of neo-classical design with vase-shaped body on square base, dated 1771. (W. H. Lane & Son) $1,910

Regency two-handled circular vase-shaped tea urn by B. & J. Smith, 1810, 15½in. high, 157oz. (Christie's) $5,350

George III two-handled vase-shaped tea urn by Henry Chawner and John Emes, 1796, 17½in. high, 133oz. (Christie's) $3,060

George III vase-shaped tea urn by John Robins, London, 1786, 100oz. 3dwt., 20½in. high. (Sotheby's)$1,680

George III tea urn by Daniel Smith and Robert Sharp, London, 1770, 102oz., 19½in. high. (Sotheby's)$2,560

George III partly fluted tea urn by Richard Cooke, 1804, 19¾in. high, 198oz.(Christie's) $4,525

Liberty & Co. 'Cymric' silver and lapis lazuli vase, Birmingham, 1910, 2½oz., 7cm. high. (Christie's) $330

Art Nouveau Russian silver flared vase with clear glass liner, 20.5cm. wide. (Christie's) $535

Georg Jensen trumpet-shaped silver vase, 1929, 15.5cm. high, 6¾oz. (Christie's) $510

One of a pair of late 19th/early 20th century German amphora-shaped vases, 28cm. high, 34.4oz. (Sotheby's Belgravia) $565

Set of three George III two-handled sugar vases and covers by John Scofield, 1787, 46oz. (Christie's) $2,790

Late 19th century Japanese silver and shibayama vase decorated in mother-of-pearl, 29cm. high. (Geering & Colyer) $660

Liberty & Co. 'Cymric' silver bullet-shaped vase, Birmingham, 1903, 2¾oz., 11.2cm. high. (Christie's) $345

Late 19th century cloisonne enameled silver vase, with urn-shaped body, 9¼in. high. (Robert W. Skinner Inc.) $1,600

Guild of Handicrafts Ltd. silver vase, London, 1905, 8½oz., 13cm. high. (Christie's) $310

Victorian silver vase with two side handles, 15in. diam., 80oz., London, 1852. (Sotheby, King & Chasemore) $1,420

Late 19th century Faberge silver vase in Art Nouveau style, 6in. high. (Christie's) $3,330

One of a set of three German die-stamped slipper vases, late 19th/early 20th century, 20oz., 21cm. long. (Sotheby's Belgravia)$1,345

Omar Ramsden silver vase on short knopped stem, London, 1936, 10½oz., 15.6cm. high. (Christie's) $655

Set of three Charles II oviform vases and covers of different sizes, 1669, 107oz. (Christie's) $14,500

Victorian posy holder by E. H. Stockwell, London, 1877, 3oz.12dwt., 5in. high. (Sotheby's) $750

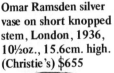

Sterling silver vase by Arthur Stone, Gardner, Massachusetts, circa 1920's, 10 troy oz., 6¾in. high. (Robert W. Skinner Inc.) $120

Victorian silver gilt replica of the Warwick vase, by Barnard & Co., 1901, 11½in. high, 243oz. (Christie's)$6,475

Large Art Deco electroplated vase, urn-shaped on pedestal foot, 1920's, 47cm. high. (Sotheby's Belgravia) $285

VINAIGRETTES

SILVER

Small shaped oblong vinaigrette with engraved initials, Birmingham, 1855, 3.7cm. long. (Sotheby's Belgravia) $150

19th century silver mounted horn vinaigrette, 2in. wide, lid set with agates. (Sotheby's)$290

Silver vinaigrette in the form of a seated cow, by Henry Wilkinson, Sheffield, circa 1838, 2½in. long. (Christie's) $555

George III oval shaped silver vinaigrette, circa 1810. (Sotheby's) $390

Mid Victorian hallmarked vinaigrette with pierced floral grille, by Joseph Turner. (Locke & England) $380

George IV silver gilt vinaigrette, by W.S., Birmingham, 1825, 1½in. wide. (Lawrence Fine Art) $230

Large rectangular vinaigrette by Francis Clark, Birmingham, 1845, 5.1cm. long. (Sotheby's Belgravia) $1,075

Early 19th century Scottish silver gilt mounted hardstone vinaigrette, 2in. high. (Christie's)$760

Rectangular silver gilt vinaigrette with view, by Taylor & Perry, Birmingham, 1836, 5cm. long.(Sotheby's Belgravia) $870

George IV oblong vinaigrette by T. & W.S., Birmingham, 1824, 1¾in. wide. (Sotheby's) $330

George III oblong vinaigrette by Joseph Willmore, Birmingham, 1815. (Sotheby's) $360

Large rectangular silver gilt vinaigrette by Nathaniel Mills, Birmingham, 1838, 2½in. long. (Christie's) $1,295

William IV silver gilt vinaigrette of oblong form, by Nathaniel Mills, Birmingham, 1835, 2in. long. (Sotheby's) $345

19th century Scottish gold mounted citrine vinaigrette with faceted sides, 1¾in. high. (Christie's) $600

George III oblong vinaigrette decorated with lobes, Birmingham, 1806, 1½in. wide.(Sotheby's) $165

George IV silver gilt vinaigrette by Nathaniel Mills, Birmingham, 1827, 1½in. long. (Sotheby's) $285

Purse-shaped vinaigrette by L. & C., Birmingham, 1817. (Sotheby's) $485

Shaped rectangular vinaigrette with detached grille, by Frederick Marson, Birmingham, 1857, 4.4cm. long. (Sotheby's Belgravia) $170

George IV vinaigrette in the form of a flower-filled basket, by John Shaw, Birmingham, 1820, 1in. long. (Sotheby's) $770

Silver gilt vinaigrette in the form of a lamp, by H. W. & L. Dee, London, 1870, 3.4cm. high. (Sotheby's Belgravia) $870

Early Victorian vinaigrette in the form of a book, by Joseph Willmore, Birmingham, 1838, 1¼in. long. (Sotheby's) $325

Rectangular silver gilt vinaigrette by Nathaniel Mills, Birmingham, 1837, 1¾in. long. (Christie's) $705

Victorian shaped rectangular vinaigrette by Yapp & Woodward, Birmingham, 1845, 1¾in. wide.(Lawrence Fine Art) $155

Shaped rectangular vinaigrette by Nathaniel Mills, Birmingham, 1842, 4.4cm. long. (Sotheby's Belgravia) $305

643

WINE COOLERS

SILVER

One of a pair of Sheffield plated campana-shaped wine coolers. (J. M. Welch & Son) $820

One of a pair of Sheffield plate wine coolers of campana shape, 10¾in. high. (Lawrence Fine Art) $1,400

One of a pair of campana-shaped wine coolers, circa 1825, 10¼in. high, in silver plate. (Sotheby's) $2,300

One of a pair of campana-shaped wine coolers, in silver plate, circa 1810, 10in. high. (Sotheby's) $1,470

Silver two-handled wine cooler on square base, Sheffield, 1906, 10½in. high. (Gilbert Baitson) $1,585

One of a pair of silver plated wine coolers, circa 1835, 10¼in. high. (Sotheby's)$1,880

One of a pair of mid 19th century twin-handled plate mounted wine coolers, 11in. high. (Christie's) $2,035

One of a pair of plate mounted bell-shaped glass wine coolers, 12in. circa 1820. (Sotheby's) $1,560

One of a pair of mid 19th century two-handled plate mounted wine coolers and liners, 11in. high. (Christie's)$1,940

Large wine funnel with applied reeding to stem, 6in. high, London, 1838, 3¼oz. (Dickinson, Davy & Markham) $160

George III wine funnel of plain design, by John Emes, London, 1801, 2½oz., 5½in. long. (Dickinson, Davy & Markham) $130

Silver wine funnel, London, 1785, 3oz. (Phillips) $145

WINE LABELS

George III wine label for Port, by John Whittingham, London, 1792. (Lawrence Fine Art) $65

Pair of Victorian vine leaf wine labels by George Unite, Birmingham, 1859. (Lawrence Fine Art) $105

George III wine label of navette form, by W. S., circa 1790. (Lawrence Fine Art) $75

George III embossed decanter label, Sherry, Sheffield, 1808. (Dickinson, Davy & Markham) $75

Pair of George III plain crescent shape wine labels, circa 1790. (Lawrence Fine Art) $195

George III wine label for Brandy, by Wm. Snooke Hall, 1817. (Lawrence Fine Art) $105

Agate snuff bottle and stopper with raised panels, 2¼in. high. (Sotheby's) $20

Chinese green jade snuff bottle, circa 1900, with jade stopper, 2¼in. high. (Robert W. Skinner Inc.) $50

Double overlay glass snuff bottle of flattened globular form, carved with hawks, 2¼in. high. (Sotheby's) $40

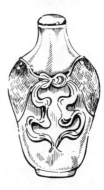

Rare 18th century Imperial yellow glass snuff bottle with stopper, in rich tone. (Sotheby's) $1,205

Mid 19th century ivory snuff bottle and cover carved with the Eight Immortals, 10cm. high. (Sotheby's Belgravia) $255

Reticulated porcelain snuff bottle carved in relief and decorated in famille rose, 2½in. high. (Sotheby's) $60

Pekin glass snuff bottle of faceted hexagonal shape in rich ruby tone, 1800/1860, with stopper. (Sotheby's) $165

Rare double overlay glass snuff bottle of disc shape, white ground overlaid in red and black. (Sotheby's) $1,040

Chinese moss agate snuff bottle, circa 1900, with carnelian top, 2¼in. high. (Robert W. Skinner Inc.) $50

STONE

14th century Belgian sandstone relief of Two Apostles, one with missing head, 36cm. wide. (Christie's)$3,170

One of a pair of early 19th century stone Talbot hounds on sandstone plinths, 50in. wide.(Sotheby's)$1,255

One of a pair of late 17th century Italian limestone statues of the Annunciation, 75cm. high. (Christie's)$6,970

Khmer sandstone head of Buddha, on wood stand, circa 12th century, 7¾in. high.(Sotheby's) $790

Tall stone sculpture of a figure in a cloak, 72cm. high. (Phillips) $395

Khmer sandstone head of Buddha, carved in low relief, circa 12th century, 6¾in. high. (Sotheby's) $435

One of a pair of Ilminster stone garden urn ornaments on pedestals. (David Symonds) $395

10th/12th century buff sandstone male head with pointed beard, 12½in. long.(Sotheby's) $885

10th/12th century Central Indian buff sandstone female figure with jewelled girdle, 22¼in. high. (Sotheby's) $4,725

647

TAPESTRIES

Early 18th century Dutch armorial tapestry cushion cover, 22 x 26in. (Sotheby, King & Chasemore) $1,115

One of two early 17th century Flemish tapestry border fragments, 62 x 12in. (Sotheby's Belgravia) $625

Brussels tapestry woven with a scene from Roman history, 9ft.4in. x 7ft. 11in. (Christie's) $1,920

Aubusson verdure tapestry depicting a landscape, 4ft.4in. x 9ft.10in. (Robert W. Skinner Inc.) $700

19th century Brussels 'Art of War' tapestry by Gaspar van der Borcht, 86 x 94in. (Sotheby, King & Chasemore) $1,490

One of a pair of Aubusson tapestry portiers, 43in. wide, circa 1840. (Sotheby's Belgravia) $1,140

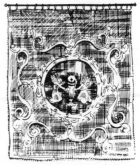

Arts & Crafts style carpet, designed by C. F. A. Voysey. (Sotheby's Belgravia) $3,020

Early 20th century Persian wall-hanging, 167 x 104in. (Sotheby's Belgravia) $205

Early 17th century Florentine red velvet altar hanging embroidered in silks, 75 x 63in. (Sotheby, King & Chasemore) $1,115

TAPESTRIES

17th century Brussels armorial tapestry with arms of the Contreras family, 13ft.3in. x 9ft. (Christie's)$6,530

Early 18th century Gobelins tapestry in muted colors, 15ft.2in. x 11ft.3in. (Christie's) $9,600

Late 19th century Indo-portuguese embroidered wall-hanging from Goa, 129 x 105in.(Sotheby's Belgravia) $4,575

19th century Japanese wall-hanging worked in ivory silk and gray and blue thread, 2.32 x 1.07m. (Phillips) $1,200

19th century wall-hanging in gold and gray thread, 2.20 x 1.52m. (Phillips) $1,145

Early 19th century American embroidered picture on a silk ground, 15 x 18½in. (Robert W. Skinner Inc.) $400

17th century silk work picture, mainly in tent stitch, framed and glazed, 22 x 23cm. (Phillips)$350

Balkan-Middle Eastern embroidery panel in pink, red and blue, 3ft. 9in. x 6ft.6in. (Robert W. Skinner Inc.)$100

Flemish biblical tapestry from the story of Esther, circa 1600, 10ft.10in. wide. (Sotheby's) $4,990

German tinplate ambulance, probably
by Fischer, 10½in. long, circa 1918.
(Sotheby's Belgravia) $1,165

19th century papier-mache games box
by Jennens & Bettridge's, 11¼in. wide.
(W. H. Lane & Son) $450

Unusual Bing tinplate horse-drawn fire
engine, hand-enameled, circa 1903,
12in. long. (Sotheby's Belgravia)
$6,040

French tinplate child's cooking stove
complete with utensils, circa 1900,
17½in. wide. (Sotheby's Belgravia)
$300

German mechanical boxers 'Pit and Fox',
early 1930's, by Gebruder Einfalt, 6½in.
long. (Robert W. Skinner Inc.)
$300

Ham and Sam 'The Minstrel Team', by
Ferdinand Strauss Corporation, New
York, 1921, 7½in. high. (Robert W.
Skinner Inc.) $230

French 'walking griffon' automaton,
circa 1920, 14in. long. (Sotheby's
Belgravia) $325

Late 19th century English carved wood
rocking horse with horsehair mane and
leather saddlery, 54in. long. (Sotheby's
Belgravia) $525

Dinky toy, A.E.C. double-decker bus with Dunlop Tyres slogan, circa 1938. (Sotheby's) $90

English horse-drawn road cleaners cart, circa 1880, 32in. long. (Sotheby's Belgravia) $565

Spic and Span 'The Hams What Am', by Louis Marx & Co., New York, circa 1925, 10in. high. (Robert W. Skinner Inc.) $575

Cast iron 'Old Dutch' pull toy, America, circa 1925, 9in. long. (Robert W. Skinner Inc.) $725

German wind-up beetle by Lehmann, 1895, in excellent condition, 3¾in. long. (Robert W. Skinner Inc.) $100

Early 20th century English fairground galloper with flowing mane and glass eyes, 64in. long. (Sotheby's Belgravia) $765

French child's 'galloper' tricycle with applied mane, tail and saddlery, circa 1880, 29in. long. (Sotheby's Belgravia) $965

Early 20th century horse-drawn pantechnicon removal van, 28½in. wide overall. (Sotheby's) $25

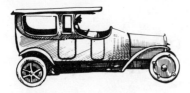

German tin auto by Whitan Co., circa 1925, 13½in. long. (Robert W. Skinner Inc.) $175

'Buddy L Model T' pickup truck, East Moline Illinois, circa 1925, 12in. long. (Robert W. Skinner Inc.) $525

One of six tin wind-up toys, circa 1925-50, 3¾in. to 8¾in. high. (Robert W. Skinner Inc.) $190

Six T.T. Bury fantascope disks in original folder, circa 1833, 9½in. diam. (Sotheby's Belgravia) $480

Bing tinplate tram with clockwork mechanism, circa 1920, 7in. long, slightly rusted. (Sotheby's Belgravia) $530

French tinplate peacock with clockwork mechanism, circa 1905, 10in. long. (Sotheby's Belgravia) $255

Late 19th century American tin kitchen with stove, cupboard and pump, 19in. wide. (Robert W. Skinner Inc.) $320

Hubley two-seated brake drawn by a pair of horses, 16½in. long. (Robert W. Skinner Inc.) $4,000

Schoenhut 'Barney Goggle' and 'Spark Plug', Pennsylvania, circa 1924, 6in. and 7in. high. (Robert W. Skinner Inc.) $675

German EPL I tinplate Zeppelin, by Lehmann, circa 1910, 7½in. long. (Sotheby's Belgravia) $340

Early 20th century Steiff ride-on donkey and two-wheel cart, 47in. long. (Robert W. Skinner Inc.) $575

American child's pedal car, circa 1925, by Steelcraft, 36in. long. (Robert W. Skinner Inc.) $350

Late 19th century American rocking horse with horsehair mane and tail, 47in. long. (Robert W. Skinner Inc.) $400

Wolverine 'Sunny Andy Kiddie Kampers', Pittsburgh, 1928, 14in. long. (Robert W. Skinner Inc.) $190

French chamois-covered pig automaton, probably by Decamps, circa 1910, 10¼in. long. (Sotheby's Belgravia) $160

Early 20th century toy vehicles in excellent condition, 18¾in. and 23½in. wide. (Robert W. Skinner Inc.) $80

French P2 Alpha Romeo, probably by CIJ, circa 1925-30, 21in. long. (Sotheby Beresford Adams) $245

French tinplate 'collision' racing car in yellow and gold, circa 1910, 8in. long. (Sotheby Beresford Adams) $205

Large hand-enameled tinplate limousine, probably by Carette, circa 1911, 16½in. long. (Sotheby's Belgravia) $1,295

French 'walking pussy cat' toy with white fur covering, circa 1930, 30cm. long. (Sotheby, King & Chasemore) $240

German hand-enameled tinplate duck in original cardboard box, circa 1905, 7in. long. (Sotheby's Belgravia) $85

Bing tinplate limousine with clockwork mechanism, circa 1910, 7½in. long. (Sotheby's Belgravia) $480

Tinplate limousine by Carette, circa 1912, 14in. long, with clockwork mechanism. (Sotheby's Belgravia) $700

Bing gauge 'one' electric tram, circa 1909, finished in red and cream, 9in. long. (Sotheby Beresford Adams) $505

Britain's civilian model of a motorcycle and sidecar, circa 1939. (Phillips) $1,685

Lineol tinplate Krupp Prime Mover truck. (Christie's S. Kensington) $705

German tinplate steam-fired automobile, probably by Doll & Cie, circa 1910, 18in. long. (Sotheby's Belgravia) $700

Late 19th century pull-along carved wooden horse and cart in poor condition, 23in. long. (Sotheby Beresford Adams) $85

Lehmann Li-La tinplate carriage, no. 520, circa 1915, 5½in. long. (Sotheby's Belgravia) $405

Victorian dark polished and gilt painted softwood miniature gypsy van, circa 1900, 21in. wide. (Sotheby Beresford Adams) $85

German tinplate novelty toy of a man and a trolley with two geese, circa 1935, 7½in. long. (Sotheby Beresford Adams) $300

Philip Vielmetter tinplate drawing clown, 5in. wide, circa 1905, with six metal cams. (Sotheby's Belgravia) $645

Printed tinplate dancing couple with clockwork motor, probably French, circa 1905, 8in. high. (Christie's S. Kensington) $370

Bing tinplate monoplane, 1930's. (Christie's S, Kensington) $180

Trooper of the Camel-Mounted Detachments, 1910. (Phillips) $475

Early American hand-enameled tinplate horse and carriage, circa 1880, 15½in. long.(Sotheby's Belgravia) $1,105

Chad Valley tinplate van with opening rear door, circa 1935, 10¼in. long. (Sotheby's Belgravia) $340

Large plush-covered cartoon figure 'Felix the Cat', English, circa 1830, 28½in. high.(Sotheby's Belgravia) $1,060

Lane's telescopic view of the Great Exhibition within printed cardboard envelope, circa 1851. (Sotheby's Belgravia) $370

German 'Oh-My' tin-, plate dancer by Lehmann, 10in. high, circa 1925, in original box. (Sotheby's Belgravia)$425

French Cinematograph-Toy viewer with eight paper bands, circa 1900. (Sotheby's Belgravia) $515

Special mounted commission of Henry V, signed R. Courtney, and accompanied by an historical note. (Phillips)$240

Two Fun-e-Flex painted wooden toys, Mickey & Minnie Mouse, circa 1931, American, 6¾in. high. (Sotheby's Belgravia) $205

Rare Lehmann 'zig-zag' rocking vehicle with two figures, circa 1910, 5in. wide. (Sotheby's Belgravia) $850

Early 20th century set of Britain's Spanish dragoons. (Phillips) $1,375

Unusual painted lead and papier-mache tea-drinking toy, probably French, circa 1880, 12in. high. (Sotheby's Belgravia) $710

Czechoslovakian Gaiety Cinema viewer, 1920, 8¼in. high. (Sotheby's Belgravia)$200

Stuffed toy 'Minnie Mouse' by Dean's Rag Book Ltd., circa 1930, 7in. high. (Sotheby's Belgravia) $135

TOYS

Meccano Dinky toy with metal wheels, circa 1935, rear doors repaired. (Sotheby's) $310

Modern cast plaster figure of a negro entertainer, 70in. high. (Sotheby's Belgravia) $300

Scale model of a timbered Tudor house with oak beams and red brickwork, 21in. wide. (Boardman's) $445

Marx lithographed tin wind-up 'Donald Duck Duet', New York, 1946, in good condition, 9in. high. (Robert W. Skinner Inc.) $325

Marx tin wind-up 'Tidy Tim', New York, 1933, in excellent condition, 9in. long. (Robert W. Skinner Inc.) $160

Early German hand-enameled tinplate carousel, 15¼in. high, circa 1895. (Sotheby's Belgravia) $905

Marx lithographed tin wind-up 'Popeye Express', New York, 1935, in original box, 9in. diam. (Robert W. Skinner Inc.) $250

Papier-mache figure of 'Nipper', the R.C.A. trademark dog, 17½in. high. (Robert W. Skinner Inc.) $300

Stevens & Brown tin mechanical Champion velocipede, patented 1870, 9¼in. high. (Robert W. Skinner Inc.) $1,000

TRANSPORT

Early 20th century French child's hippo tricycle with black painted chassis. (Sotheby's) $165

1926 Jewett two-door sedan, 6 cylinder, blue and white body, restored. (Robert W. Skinner Inc.) $3,500

Mid 18th century Italian giltwood and black leather sedan chair with brass studded canopy, 32in. wide. (Christie's) $1,655

20th century English stagecoach designed to harness ponies, 7ft. wide, damaged. (Sotheby's) $935

1960 Mercedes 220 S.E. convertible with dark green exterior, mileage 73,563. (Robert W. Skinner Inc.) $20,000

Early 20th century American wicker baby carriage with parasol, 56½in. high. (Robert W. Skinner Inc.) $225

Mid Victorian velocipede with cast iron frame and iron rimmed wooden wheels. (Samuel Rains & Son) $1,180

Cadillac, 1979, blue Biarritz coupe with many extras. (Robert W. Skinner Inc.) $10,300

Early 20th century Edwardian mahogany tray with boxwood and mahogany gallery, 24in. wide. (Sotheby's) $140

Papier-mache desk folder, front inlaid with mother-of-pearl, circa 1860, 12in. high. (Sotheby's Belgravia) $115

Early 19th century toleware tray, probably Connecticut, 12½in. long. (Robert W. Skinner Inc.) $150

Emile Galle marquetry octagonal tray inlaid with a landscape, 49.3cm. wide. (Christie's) $885

Mid 19th century Williams' Burton papier-mache King Gothic tea tray, 32in. wide. (Sotheby's) $210

Tole bread tray, probably New York, early 19th century, 13in. long. (Robert W. Skinner Inc.)$370

Small rectangular tray with incurved sides, decorated with colored takamakie, 19.5cm. long. (Sotheby's) $2,360

Papier-mache tray with molded serpentine border, painted in gilt, circa 1850, 30½in. long. (Sotheby's Belgravia) $450

Sukashi tsuba of oval form, details in gold nunome and copper, 7.9cm. high, unsigned. (Sotheby's) $205

Kinai school tsuba of mokko form, pierced with a rain dragon, eye in gold, 8.1cm. high, signed Echizen ju Kinai saku. (Sotheby's) $120

Soten school tsuba of circular form, pierced within the rim, unsigned, 8.3cm. high. (Sotheby's) $240

Higo school tsuba of circular form, 7.3cm. high, unsigned. (Sotheby's) $110

Oval tsuba applied in silver, gold and colored enamels, unsigned, 7.9cm. long. (Sotheby's) $670

Circular tsuba, pierced and applied in relief, 8.2cm. long, signed Tetsugendo. (Sotheby's) $570

One of three 19th century Japanese cut-out iron tsubas of round shape, signed. (Robert W. Skinner Inc.) $175

Tsuba of mokko form applied with two spiders, details in silver and gold nunome, 7.9cm. high, signed Chikatoshi. (Sotheby's) $345

One of three 19th century Japanese cut-out iron tsubas, signed. (Robert W. Skinner Inc.) $170

INDEX